DANCING ON MY GRAVE

DANCING ON MY GRAVE

AN AUTOBIOGRAPHY BY
Gelsey Kirkland

WITH
Greg Lawrence

DOUBLEDAY & COMPANY, INC.
GARDEN CITY, NEW YORK
1986

Library of Congress Cataloging-in-Publication Data
Kirkland, Gelsey.
Dancing on my grave.
1. Kirkland, Gelsey.   2. Ballet Dancers—United States.
3. American Ballet Theatre.   I. Lawrence, Greg.
II. Title.
GV1785.K49A33   1986   792.8'2'0924 [B]   86–8857
ISBN 0-385-19964-3

Copyright notices from publishers granting
permission to reprint material are listed on
pages 287 and 288.

In memory of Joseph Duell, 1956–1986,
that the cry for help might yet be heard.

NOTE: A few of the names have been changed for the usual literary or legal reasons and are introduced with quotation marks on first appearance. My efforts to render foreign accents are not intended to ridicule any person or national group, but to lend authenticity to the voices as I heard them. Some of the individuals recalled in this book have in fact won acclaim on the stage or in films, for those readers who might wish to hear the real voices for themselves.

CONTENTS

Hence it is from the representation of things spoken
by means of posture and gesture that the whole of the art
of dance has been elaborated.

—PLATO

All the dancer's gestures are signs of things, and the
dance is called rational, because it aptly signifies and
displays something over and above the pleasure of the senses.

—ST. AUGUSTINE

Genuine art . . . does not have as its object a mere
transitory game. Its serious purpose is not merely
to translate the human being into a momentary dream
of freedom, but actually to MAKE him free.

—FRIEDRICH SCHILLER

ACKNOWLEDGMENTS

At the risk of omitting a few and in no particular order, my thanks to the following people, without whom this book would not exist, at least not in its present form.

My husband and co-writer, Greg Lawrence. My mother, Nancy Salisbury, and stepfather, Robert Salisbury. My brother, Marshall Kirkland, and sister, Johnna Kirkland. Greg's mother, Marilyn Lawrence, and sister, Paula Stricklin.

Richard Malina and his good offices at Doubleday. My editor, Jacqueline Onassis, who believed in the project from the beginning and—in spite of the authors' occasional resistance—did make it possible. For her ability to weather the storms, Shaye Areheart. Alex Gotfryd, Glenn Rounds. Heather Kilpatrick. Ellen Mastromonaco. Marianne Velmans.

For his perspicacity and attention to detail, my creative consultant, Barry Laine, a friend and worthy critic. Dina Makarova, whose constant and loving contribution goes beyond reckoning. Christopher Kirkland, who did the picture research and provided a wealth of enthusiasm and insights. For affection and wise counsel, Lisa Filloramo. For services and wit rendered along the way, Bonnie Egan. For years of familial encouragement, Don Bevan, Pat Kirkland Bevan, Robin Kirkland MacDonald, and Delta Mitchell Hoadley.

For their time, advice, and support: Antony Tudor, Natalia Makarova, Peter Schaufuss, Arthur Mitchell, Edward Villella, Anthony Dowell, Joan Moynagh, David Howard, Pilar Garcia, Georgina Parkinson, Barna Ostertag, Haila Stoddard, Carl Michel, Patrik Moreton, Peter Stelzer, Laura Stevenson, Stephen Greco, Brooke Adams, Lynne Adams, Angela Vullo and Patrick McCormick, Meg Gordon, Deane Rink, Marvin Frankel, Joseph Stricklin, Dr. Robert Cancro, Dr. Steven Ajl, Victor Sendax, Patricia Bromley and Charles Grant, Carlo Levi Minzi, Peter and Judith Wyer, Lisa Drew, Brooke Cadwallader, Christopher White, Jonathan Lash, Marcia Merry, and all those who had courage enough to speak in confidence.

DANCING ON MY GRAVE

Chapter One

SEEN BUT NOT HEARD

I was not born a ballerina. I did not emerge from the womb on pointe, nor did I wear a tutu instead of diapers. I was a baby pudgeball, with a head like a tulip bulb and a belly to match. I came into the world December 29, 1952, in Bethlehem, Pennsylvania. My crib soon became the center of attention in my family's homestead in Bucks County. I played the game of being seen but not heard to the hilt, giving everyone the silent treatment. My parents worried that I might be mute, or that I was deliberately refusing to speak.

I remained speechless for months after my second birthday. When a friend of the family prepared to leave after a visit, she heard a little voice cry out, "Please don't go." The startled visitor, who still delights in telling the story, exclaimed, "Why, you little fraud. You can talk!" Little did anyone suspect that someday I would speak with silence—that I would make a career out of being seen but not heard.

When I was still young enough to catch fireflies and collect them in a jar, I already possessed my own inner world of dancing lights and fantastic creatures, an imaginary world where dreams were kindled. Like the character of Clara whom I would later portray in the ballet *The Nutcracker,* I fell for the beauties of night. I experienced dreams as if they were real, unable to distinguish them from the world outside my mind.

I was frequently carried away. A flying horse once saved me from the monster in the lake on our land. I traveled through water and air in my sleep. During my waking hours, I roamed and played from room to room in our enormous house. One summer day in my third year, I crawled out from under the dining room table and told my father that I saw Mommy in the water. He laughed and lifted me into the air.

I had seen my mother at the edge of the lake. I remember her braided hair and sparkling eyes. The image was only a reflection shimmering on the surface, but I insisted that Mommy was in the water.

In crossing the border between the real and imaginary, I discovered a secret place where some measure of tenderness might prevail. I was fiercely protective of my private world. Though somewhat sheltered, I was as daring as I was delicate. I was not reluctant to display my feelings. If I tied a bow within my breast, it was sure to unravel at the slightest touch. I had an endless ribbon of laughter and tears.

My parents, both artists themselves, bestowed certain intangible gifts. One was their love. Another was an active sense of wonder. It might be said that as an inquisitive and oversensitive child, I was predisposed to develop an artistic sensibility. But there was a darker side to this inclination, as there was a darker side to my dreams, a tragic undercurrent which almost prevented me from realizing the value of my inheritance. The transition from dreamer to artist involved years of intensive study and passionate struggle, difficult lessons which had to be learned before I could accept my legacy.

In recollecting that vanished time during the fifties when we lived on the family farm, I hold a picture framed by a little girl's innocent hands. Those years left their mark, like a smudged fingerprint on the heart. Each fragmentary image is a clue to the mysterious continuity of love. The line of devotion can be traced back in our family to the romance that brought my father and mother together.

During the violent decade before I was born, they met in a theatrical production of *Tobacco Road*. My father, Jack Kirkland, had adapted the story by Erskine Caldwell for the Broadway stage; my mother, Nancy Hoadley, was an actress who played one of the leads in the touring company. They lived outside of New York entirely, where my father, like many successful writers at the time, had acquired property. He liked the idea of raising a family in the country, a setting that he used to advantage in his writing and a refuge where his privacy would not be invaded.

My older sister, Johnna, my younger brother, Marshall, and I took our places in the family portrait, along with our half brother, Christopher, and two half sisters, Robin and Patricia, who was almost my mother's age and had children of her own. I hated having my picture taken—I wanted to be invisible.

Our extended family made for a busy household. The children from my father's previous marriages were often with us, as were a couple of his former wives. The women in my father's life remained devoted to him. The friendships survived even after the marriages broke apart. The farm was a gathering place for the social set to which my parents belonged. My mother had friends from her college days and, like my father, friends from the theatre.

The actor, Yul Brynner, boarded with us for a while. He was down and out in those days. During an ice storm, he almost burned down our house. It was an accident. According to family legend, he tried to make a fire in the nursery where he was keeping one of his children. The flames leaped from the fireplace. The room filled with smoke. Buckets of water were carried from one side of the house to the other. After the actor moved out and became famous, my father called him cheap and ungrateful. They were no longer friends.

Adults made me wary. I tested any prospective lap before sitting upon it. At the urging of my parents, I imitated a snowflake and performed bits of mimicry. I was the only one who took my act seriously, much to the glee of my grown-up audience. Vulnerable to ridicule and confused by those who towered over me, I went through a phase of withdrawal quite early in the game.

It must have been my father who first taught me about the holiness of life, and the adversities. He was something of a gentleman farmer. As a thinker, he expressed his ideas in his writing and sought to apply them in the world. As a sportsman, he hunted the lands and fished the waters. Involving himself in the business of agriculture, he ran a dairy farm. He was the provider, though my mother recalls having to milk the cows.

My father had his eccentricities and expectations, in which we children figured prominently, though sometimes imperfectly. When my sister had reached the age of six, my father decided that she was old enough to see a chicken beheaded. Johnna was about three years older than I was. Marshall was a year my junior. My sister confided to me how Daddy had to drag her out of the house to witness the bloody ritual. She had been in tears, bewildered at seeing the headless chicken perform its dance of death, leaving its tracks in the yard. The trauma obscured whatever lesson or rite of passage had been intended.

There is no question of my father's affection, the pride he took in raising his children. He wrote in a letter to us, while he was in Hollywood working on a screenplay, "Won't it be wonderful to think back someday to when you three were ittsy-wittsies too small to paddle in the pool." And so it is. Elsewhere he advised us, "Take this to heart, that things are not what they seem." And so I did. Distrusting appearances, I would learn to look and listen for a deeper truth.

Father taught us to sound out the syllables of our words in order to spell them. One of those words was "perfection," which became a guiding principle for me. He praised us, but always qualified his approval, as if deliberately preparing us for a world that would make impossible demands for excellence. With my father, communication was difficult, especially when he attempted to communicate his love.

I had no understanding of adult communication problems. When I was three, a friend of the family took me for a walk on Halloween, alternately humoring me with talk of ghosts and goblins and muttering about the pageantry of autumn. Holding me by the hand, he led me through the woods near our house, and I waddled beside him, the tiniest of ugly ducklings. He repeated himself, and I lost my patience. With my childhood lisp, I scolded him, "You thet it, and you thet it, and you thet it . . . and don't thay it again."

The anecdote has been repeated by my family for years as evidence of how cute I was. I recoil now when adults talk down to children, or when dancers use baby talk to speak to each other. I have always been touchy that way.

I was more interested in my horse than in the superstitions of the harvest season. I had a blind horse by the name of Sugar, to me a winged Pegasus. With a child's infinite compassion for animals, I worried over his useless eyes. I was sorry that I could not grant him vision, that he would spend his entire life bumping into things.

I was not old enough to see why my horse had to be left behind when we sold the farm. Who would lead him on his dark and lonely trail? Who would fill his pail with oats when we were gone? In this time of crisis, Mother was the one who broke the bad news to us and did her best to answer our impossible questions, questions which my father could not bear from his children. The move depleted his spirit. In planning his autobiography, my father intended to use this disruption of our lives as the end of his story. Giving up the farm meant giving up his life, a fact which the notes he left behind make clear enough:

Indeed, even when that loved farm, that tie with my heritage, went on the block and a dream of aging squirehood exploded—even that shattering occasion, with which I plan appropriately to end my story for it likely was the end of me, can be said to carry the woof of ironic comment: the man who bought it, swept along by the mesmerizing threnody of the auctioneer's chant, bid more than $100,000 for the place and didn't even want it.

My mother shielded us from the truth. She did not tell us that a combination of my father's extravagant generosity and waning literary fortunes had driven us from our country home. She made vague promises about the paradise we were about to enter. Her gentle assurances prevailed over our pouts and tantrums. In the end we were forced to trade our pastoral horizons for the urban skyline of Manhattan. Fortunately for children, the uncertainties of the present always give way to the enchanted possibilities of the future.

When I was almost four, my family trooped into New York City to take up residence on Central Park West. That was the middle of the decade, around the time that Elvis Presley sang, "You ain't nothin' but a hound dog . . ." My brother and sister and I were small enough for our father to catch us in his arms, like a midget acrobatic team, jumping from the top of the bunkbed we two sisters shared. On one occasion, Daddy was so tipsy that we managed to throw him off balance and tumble with him onto the floor.

As suddenly as a dream can turn into a nightmare, he split his forehead open. He bridled when my mother suggested that he see a doctor, as if seeking help would be a sign of weakness. His refusal to accept treatment left a nasty wound to remind us all of the episode. He said it was nothing, but made us feel it was our fault.

My father's attitude toward the world took a turn for the worse shortly after we settled into our first of three Upper West Side apartments. He had had five marriages and five heart attacks. Twenty years older than my mother, he was getting on and looking his age, a visible fact which made me feel ashamed for him.

My father and I had a game we played in the street, a running joke in which he would give me a surprise kick in the rear, hooking his leg around behind me while walking at my side, then feigning ignorance. I remember turning around during one of these playful interludes to see him leaning against the side of a building, favoring his bum leg and struggling to catch his breath. I was startled and disturbed to realize that he could no longer keep up with me. Our generation gap was, in reality, an abyss: he was pushing sixty, and I was pushing six.

My father remained the most formidable authority figure of my tender youth. Neither his children nor his wife cared to risk the consequences of his anger. He had accumulated the fury of a lifetime, as well as his share of wisdom, which I was able to appreciate only belatedly and by hindsight. In spite of frequent lapses in grace, he had his grander moments of gentleness and humor.

I can still see him playing the ukulele and singing to my mother, our family gathered in a spirited tableau around the hearth. When he belted out with all his heart, "Has anybody seen my gal?" I felt that I was his little girl. I also sensed, in an almost palpable way thanks to the music and merriment, the ardor of my father's passion for my mother, and the fervor of her love for him. When he taught me how to pluck music from that ukulele, I became the secret sharer in their wedded harmony. But there were other times when I would catch sight of my parents framed in the doorway of their bedroom, their hearts passing beyond the vanishing point of a child's comprehension.

Of course we children were the three little piglets, secure in the knowledge that our daddy would protect us from whatever wolf might appear at our door. One night, while I lay in my bed, I actually saw the wolf. He was wearing plaid overalls. I fled to my brother and sister for help, only to be turned away. I flew down the hallway and bolted into the bedroom of my sleeping parents. Though I begged my father to save me at once, he grumbled and growled his annoyance. Mother escorted me back to my room, but she was no match for the wolf. When I saw the demonic creature again prancing toward me, I went lickety-split straight back to the arms of my father. Cursing the devil and his hangover, he carried me to safety and tucked me into bed. His annoyance undermined his attempt to reassure me.

Thereafter, I slept with the light on, doubtful that I could ever again depend on my father to come to my rescue.

Undoubtedly my father sensed that he was running out of words and time. After he adapted Nelson Algren's novel *The Man with the Golden Arm* for the stage, he tried writing again for Hollywood, but gave his most passionate effort to his autobiography.

For years I watched him fill reams of yellow paper with longhand, scribbling away like a madman, leaving behind mountains of crumpled pages. Perhaps his life held too many contradictions for him to finally resolve with his command of language. But he did manage to express his feelings in a letter. During one of his West Coast junkets in 1958, he wrote to us from Los Angeles:

My darlings—

    I do miss all of you so much. But I have a game I play with myself to keep me happy. I close my eyes and see Johnna jumping into the deep water—and Gelsey paddling away like crazy—and Marshall running his cute little run in the park, banking on turns like an airplane. Of course, I sometimes see him throwing things out the window, but then I open my eyes and stop that nonsense.

    I manage to sit in the sun at the pool here almost every day, but very seldom go into the water. Of course, that is easily explained: I'm made of sugar and I might melt and then what would you do for a pop, who loves you and loves you and loves you!

                               Father

Trying to find a balance between the good and bad memories of my father, I am touched repeatedly by his words, so tender and disarming. The tragedy of our later misunderstandings and hostilities is offset by the sincerity of his paternal sentiment.

My father's bitterness over his decline was intensified by alcohol to the point where he became a tyrant in the eyes of his children. Each of us responded by acting out a uniquely personal rebellion. Marshall threw ashtrays out the window and smeared crayons on the walls. Johnna was more sophisticated, putting on the airs of a mature young lady while making mischief whenever she could get away with it.

I dared not raise my voice against our father, but defied him in a battle of wits. His drunken attempts to teach me table manners featured lectures delivered with slurred tongue, how to arrange one's fingers while holding the spoon and what route the fork should take on its journey to the mouth. I glared and carried out his instructions with exaggerated precision, giving him the evil eye. Quietly burning with rage, I said nothing. If his demands were excessive and arbitrary, my compliance was a calculated provocation.

When conflicts broke out across the table, Mother stepped in as the peace-maker, maintaining the appearance of domestic order.

In covering for my father's dissipation and financial difficulties, my mother put on a good front, especially during the holiday season. She fibbed to us every Christmas, preparing us to be disappointed. She warned her children in a solemn ceremony that Santa would not be carrying as much in his bag as he had last year. This was her way of telling us that hard times had come and that we should lower our expectations. But each year, in spite of her dire prediction, Christmas morning greeted us with a miracle. After the blizzards of ribbon and wrapping paper had been swept away, our eyes dazzled: not only had we received more gifts than the year before, but this year's presents were more lavish.

Mother made her sacrifices on our behalf. She did everything in her power to protect us from what she saw as a dangerous world, placing herself between us and whatever we might wish to attain. If I were to venture from behind her skirts to reach for a pearl, I could expect to have my hand slapped even as she placed a string of them around my neck. Growing up during the Depression steeled her to adversity and set her mind to prepare for the worst. She gave up her acting career to devote herself completely to her children, but her maternal devotion was not always appreciated.

When I was seven, she took me each morning to the skating rink in Central Park. I was fearless on ice, cutting quite a figure in my black velvet skating suit. Once I took a spill into a puddle of water and ruined the suit, making me very cross with myself. I was more determined than ever to prove my mettle as a skater. Shortly after my mishap, I went on a family skating party. The festivities were dampened when Mother insisted that I wear skates with double blades to guard against my falling down. She was sure I would destroy my good wool coat if left to my own devices. What a stink I raised. I preferred to lean against the guard rail for the entire after-noon rather than subject myself to the humiliation of wearing those skates that had been rigged for my safety.

I became livid with my mother whenever she interceded to deny me an experience because of fear that I might come to some harm. If she had had her way, I might never have been permitted to ride a horse. As it happened, I learned to ride while away from home one summer, establishing my eques-trian skills before my mother even knew that I had been in the saddle.

It is an old story that every girl falls in love with horses; I fell in love with the sport of riding. This was my introduction to both competition and show-manship, to which I committed myself with all the dedication that a little girl could muster.

Visiting the Connecticut home of family friends, I ingratiated myself with the local country club crowd by winning blue ribbons in series of horse shows. My serious attitude and ability to control my steed endeared me to the judges. Perhaps part of my success was due to the unlikely picture I made mounted on the back of a horse: I was too fragile and too tiny to be holding the reins of such a prodigious animal. Winning ribbons did not alleviate my feelings of inadequacy, but did allow me, for the first time, to prove myself in the eyes of both peers and adults, safely outside my mother's protective grasp.

My horseback riding days ended prematurely and without warning at a summer camp in New Hampshire. An overly serious nature made me the prime target of the pranks of my fellow campers. I was teased about my silly name and my peculiar eyes, which had a dark circle around the iris. The cry went out that Gelsey had rings around her eyes, and I felt stigmatized for life.

With sing-song rhymes, the other children taunted me about the disproportions of my body. I never let them know how much I was stung by their disparagements, but tried to compensate in other ways. My success with horses seemed to make up for my awkward size and shape. I turned my abdominal bulge to advantage by performing a belly dance to amuse those in my cabin. My bumps and grinds attracted such attention that I was goaded into dancing for my riding teacher, an event which took place on the night before the most important horse show of the season.

My riding teacher, a counselor named "Marty," was something of a ruffian, a young woman who had never given up the ways of a country tomboy. She wore her blond hair pulled straight back and strutted around with her riding crop, giving it a thwack on her thigh now and then for our benefit. On the night of my belly dance, while the other girls howled with mirth, she stood watching with her hands on her hips. It was impossible to read her reaction.

Afterward, she thanked me and wished me luck in the upcoming horse show. When she left, the cabin buzzed with whispers and giggles. They said something was queer about her, that I was her favorite.

On the following day, I rode a gigantic gelding named Tarzan. Before the show, Marty coached me in a practice ring. Filled with anxiety, I kept my distance from her. My horse was as skittish as I was and threw me face first into the mud. I was shaken, but not hurt.

Marty urged me to get back in the saddle before fear took over. But it was too late. Without confidence, I failed to place in the show. I went home so demoralized that I never wanted to see another horse for as long as I might live. I never told my mother about the incidents at camp. I told no one. The mysteries of womanhood were revealed over the years only by whispers in the dark and those secret rites of initiation shared by children.

At the end of the summer of my seventh year, I confirmed my mother's worst fears for my safety by falling off a slide in Central Park. With my head cracked slightly open, she held me in her arms and waited on line at a drinking fountain to wash my wound. She was paralyzed from the shock of seeing her daughter's blood and had to be encouraged to take me to a doctor. Behind my tears, I was as distraught about her hesitation to get me help as I was about my battered head. It never dawned on me that she was so afraid for my life, she was unable to move or know what to do.

My mother thought she was released from her fears for me when I became a ballerina. She assumed the world of ballet was safe.

As my family moved from apartment to apartment, my sister and I shared a bedroom. At first a curtain was hung to settle territorial disputes and give us some privacy. The curtain did not keep us from overhearing each other say our prayers at night. Mother often knelt with me beside my bed to recite the "Lord's Prayer." I thought the first line went, "Our Father, heart in heaven, Halloween be thy name . . ." A postscript was always attached to the effect, "God bless Mommy and Daddy, and Johnna and Marshall, and Granny and Dodo," and so on, but our family was so large that I had to be reminded about names I forgot to include.

When I was alone, I worried over my omissions, genuinely concerned that I might be responsible for the fates of persons whom I failed to name. If I were mad at my sister, I might not mention her one night, but double my petition on her behalf the next, certain that she would hear even if the Lord were deaf.

In saying my prayers, I discovered the voice of an innermost self, the raw nerve of my identity. I was no angel, but I was on intimate terms with my conscience. I learned that each action taken in this world has its echo in the heart. When we children would sneak in and steal my father's change from his bureau at night, I could not easily shake off pangs of guilt. The difference between right and wrong was clearest just before I fell asleep.

According to our unspoken code of honor, it was assumed that there was no lying in our family. I sensed hypocrisy and pinned the rap on my father. On birthdays, his painful love pats were usually followed by his demand for a kiss, as if he possessed the right to my unconditional affection. Surely he must have known my kiss was a lie even though I tried to conceal my revulsion at the foul smell of alcohol on his breath. I hated him for making me feel that I was supposed to please him, but at the same time, I desperately wanted to please him and win his respect.

My growing resentment made it impossible for me to accept my father's assurances that I was going to be beautiful enough someday to become an actress. He said I resembled Gina Lollobrigida and told me that my voice was the only thing that stood between me and stardom. In truth, I had no voice when I faced my father. I did not believe his optimistic estimation of my potential. I knew that Johnna was the real beauty; if either of us were blessed with looks, it was she.

I recall hiding under a piano to escape a party. Peering out from the safety of my niche, I watched my sister playing social butterfly. I was amazed by her. Johnna was able to flirt and flit about, while I refused to cultivate such graces. In the shadow of her natural beauty and poise, my jealousy drove me to find competitive areas of self-expression. Eventually, ballet would become the center ring in the arena of our sisterly warfare.

I sometimes wonder how sibling rivalry would have affected us if we had entered the medical profession. Johnna and I were close during an early bout with chicken pox. Misery loved company, even the sisterly variety. The disease heralded a crisis of faith for me at the age of eight.

Our parents had been sending us to Christian Science Sunday School, a choice based on the geographical convenience of the church rather than on any religious conviction. Johnna, Marshall, and I marched a block down Central Park West each Sunday to attend services, while my parents stayed home. We were introduced to the teachings of Mary Baker Eddy, whose doctrine rejected modern medicine in favor of the alleged healing power of God.

In spite of my doubts, I was intrigued by the idea that our minds participated in something larger than ourselves. Though I refused to sing the hymns, I did appreciate the choral harmony and the mysterious voices that emanated from the organ. But from what I can gather in retrospect, I was already exhibiting the turn of mind that resists leaps of faith. When the church authorities insisted that my sister and I were not ill, I suspected an outrageous trick.

Somehow Johnna and I survived our ordeal, eventually turning our shared quarantine into an excuse for playtime. I recall that we took a bath together in the last stage of convalescence. Splashing in the tub, we squealed with delight and wept tears of laughter. We hugged across the water.

These moments of sisterly affection lasted no longer than our illness. Some time after our recovery, my mother informed me that I would follow Johnna into ballet school. I was underwhelmed.

My mother's decision was not an attempt to choose a career for me. She thought of ballet school the same way she thought of camp and church, as a healthy activity for her daughters. One afternoon she took me to audition at the School of American Ballet, then located on Upper Broadway, not far from where we lived.

There was nothing elegant about the architecture or the decor. The place was drab, the classrooms smelled of perspiration and perfume. Paint peeled from the ceilings like dead skin. An elderly Russian teacher, Madame Antonina Tumkovsky, directed me to a wall covered with mirrors.

I was only eight years old, outfitted with red tights and saddle shoes. I saw my reflection distorted by smudges on the glass. The effect was like that of a fun house mirror—my head was blown up like a balloon that seemed large enough to float my body into the air. Standing on line at a barre with other children my age, I waited nervously for my turn. Each of us had to be examined individually.

As the teacher moved toward me, I was awestruck by her extraordinary blue eyes and delicate hands. She spoke with the heavy accent of her native land, gesturing with exuberance as she mispronounced my name, "Helsey!" To test the height and flexibility of my extension, she pulled one of my legs up. I dangled for a moment from the barre. My eyes blurred as I held back tears of humiliation, certain that I would fail to be accepted by the school.

When I was told that I had been placed in the first division of the School of American Ballet, I was furious. I figured the only reason the school would have me was because of my sister's good standing. It was like that old Groucho Marx joke in which you would not want to belong to any club that would have you for a member. I was forced to join. The anger that I felt after that first audition became one of the guiding emotions for my entire career.

Chapter Two

CAT'S CRADLE

During those early days, when my sister and I shared a bedroom and attended ballet school together, we sometimes amused ourselves with a game called "cat's cradle." By tying the ends of a string, we constructed a circular loop, and by manipulating the loop between the fingers of both hands, we fashioned a cradle that could be passed back and forth between us. With each pass, the complexity of design increased, as did the challenge of manual dexterity. After witnessing this birth of form many times, we discovered, almost without knowing it, the principles that determined the pattern of the string.

Playing by myself, I contrived cradles of amazing intricacy. Lying on my bed with my legs in the air, I could transfer the twisted string from my hands to my feet. I heard somewhere that Houdini was able to tie knots with his toes; I did him one better, sprawled on my back, stringing a web from toe to toe. Placing the elaborate mesh between my hands, I tested its design by holding it up between my face and the mirror. Crossing my eyes, I was startled to see that the left side of my face did not match the right side. The symmetry of the string accentuated my facial lines, reminding me that I was not beautiful.

My fascination with the string became an obsession. I spent hours playing the game, long after my sister lost interest. One evening, waiting for Johnna to come to bed, I fell asleep. When she finally arrived to turn in, she found me, still asleep, trespassing on her side of the curtain. Having already ransacked the room, I was rifling the trash can. Johnna woke me as I was saying, "I gotta find the string." I repeated the phrase over and over. When my sister finally forced me to admit that I had been sleepwalking, I accepted responsibility for the rampage. But I could not remember why I was looking for the string. After returning to bed, I found it under my pillow; I must have fallen asleep with the cradle in my hands.

I can now imagine a cat's cradle large enough to cover the entire floor of the stage upon which I dance. By extending the imaginary grid into three dimensions, I create a mental image of the space within which the dancer performs. Within the holy circle of the stage, geometrical principles are used to organize physical energy so that the beauty of the human form reveals a web of drama and truth—that is the essence of dance as I have come to know it.

I entered ballet school the same year that my mother embarked on a new professional career with *Sports Illustrated.* That was 1960, the beginning of a decade that I would experience, for the most part, from the inside of a ballet studio. As my father's royalties had dwindled, my mother sought employment to help support the family. The expenses included, until we received scholarships, the considerable cost of sending two daughters to the School of American Ballet. To contribute to the cause, I acquiesced to a brief stint as a child model.

I recall the day that my father collected me early from Professional Children's School to attend a photographic session. I was outraged that I would have to miss my ballet class. I refused to smile for the photographer and finally burst into tears to end the session. The photographs were used by a painter for a children's wear advertisement. There was no false modesty in my dismay at seeing myself immortalized on a page of the New York *Times Magazine.* I recognized the painted smile for the lie that it was. Altering the facial lines had falsified what I had experienced.

When my father said the picture was beautiful, I exploded. How could he call me beautiful when he was aware of the fraud that had been committed? Perhaps, with the fantastic simplicity of a child's logic, I knew that beauty somehow depended on truth. My denials were vehement, but I could not look my father in the eye.

Our domestic life degenerated over the years of his addiction. His dependence on alcohol was never acknowledged by spoken word. Consequently, I had no explanation for either his behavior or my animosity. There were many times I hated him. He seemed to be drunk more than he was sober. I was so intimidated by his presence that I tiptoed through the house trying to avoid him.

When I returned home between classes in the late morning, I would find him stumbling out of bed, hung over. His first act of the day was to throw up in the bathroom that he shared with Mother. Then he proceeded to his coffee, cigarettes, newspaper, and soap operas. When he was absorbed by the TV set in the kitchen, I would try to sneak around him, creeping through the rooms. The apartment was too cramped to elude him. Hearing me, he would holler, "What's the matter? You're not going to give your father a kiss?" My submission to this ritual was a violation of the heart. After the kiss, I always wanted to wipe my lips.

The high point of my father's day was his afternoon visit to Sardi's. Dressed without fail in a stylish suit and tie, he made a regular appearance at the bar with his drinking buddies, mostly theatre types. Seeing him leave and return hours later, I knew his mood had changed. He usually came home in time to listen to my mother's stories about her day in the office. While she prepared the evening meal and poured out her heart to him, he sat nearby with his drink.

After dinner, he drank himself into a stupor. I frequently heard him snore when he fell asleep on the couch. Following a brief nap, he arose to read paperbacks until the early hours of the morning, when more alcohol and a sleeping pill would put him temporarily out of his misery. His condition shamed me so much that I almost never brought friends to our home.

I sometimes witnessed him break down my mother. Their lives together seemed to be over except for the dinner hour, the quiet times when my mother would say he was a good listener. There were other times, more and more frequent, when he used his cynical wit to browbeat her. I dared intervene only once. At the age of twelve, I came to my mother's defense.

They had come to a standoff in the living room. His shouting made my hair stand on end. I could see that my mother was trembling and trying to hide her tears. I scrambled between them and faced my father. Thrusting my chin forward, I spit out my words. "I know who pays for the groceries around here!"

I had touched his masculine pride. There was a terrible silence as my mother disappeared out the door. I watched my father go into the kitchen and open a drawer. He pulled out a knife and turned toward me, saying, "You little . . ."

The expression on his face was as terrifying as the knife. As he came at me, I rushed behind the dining room table. He hesitated. Maybe he had second thoughts. I didn't wait to find out. I was quick enough to beat him out the door of the apartment.

After my escape, I raced to catch up with my mother. She reacted with mute anguish as I told her of my father's attack. She took me under her arm and led me to the local market. We returned to the scene of the crime with the very groceries that began the dispute. My mother told me that my father had paid for them.

We ate our dinner at the same table around which he had chased me only hours before. While she tried to make believe that nothing had happened, he and I exchanged wounded looks and kept our distance. The incident was never mentioned again, nor was it forgotten.

Ballet provided a convenient way to avoid my father and escape from home. It also gave me a creative arena in which to vent my rage. Over the years, my anger was transformed into a more complicated response to ballet itself, but the passion of my commitment can be traced to the turmoil of my childhood. If I was not able to control my social world, I could at least begin to coordinate the movements of my own body. By devoting myself to the discipline of dance, I was able to establish a measure of control that was otherwise lacking in my life, or so it seemed.

I was hurt when my father made wisecracks that told me he thought ballet was a frivolous pastime. During my first couple of years of ballet school, I enjoyed telling my mother how much I admired my teachers, Madame Tumkovsky, who had auditioned me, and Helene Dudin, another Russian woman. Their classes were an absorbing challenge, the most complicated game of monkey-see-monkey-do that I had ever played. I loved wrestling with myself, grappling with problems. The exercises demanded an investment of energy and produced results that I could see. The reward was not so much the feeling of outward accomplishment, but the inner sense that something had clicked, that a light had been turned on in my little brain. This was serious stuff as far as I was concerned.

I felt more secure as I began to understand the structure of the school, the ladder of annual progress that started with First Division, proceeded by numbers for the first five years, then changed to letters. I was climbing toward an unknowable future, but each rung was a new class that promised more exciting challenges where the rules seemed more complex. I knew that was so because I snuck in to watch my sister's advanced classes. She was already wearing pointe shoes.

Though I was capable of diligence and blessed with curiosity, academic studies were a distraction. Professional Children's School was convenient and offered a flexible schedule, allowing aspiring dancers, actors, and musicians to satisfy the legal requirements for public education. I learned how to cheat quite early, as did most of my peers. As we were bound for careers in the arts, what need did we have for books or scholarship?

I had no time for homework with the increasing number of hours devoted to ballet. What began as a few hours a week when I was eight years old became a couple hours a day several years later. Soon thereafter, dance began to consume all my days and nights. As my commitment to ballet became more passionate and fanatical, the rest of the world and my studies tended to be disregarded.

Yet passing grades were a necessity, if for no other reason than to stay out of trouble. I did want to impress my father, but he was an impenetrable mass of contradictions. No matter how well I did on my report card, he would not be satisfied. He seemed to be critical of the educational system. He had gone to Columbia University and considered his experience a waste of time and money. He was still looking forward to my acting career.

Not long after I started ballet, my sister decided to lecture me on proper attire, about which I had my own ideas. I had just finished a class when Johnna cornered me in the hallway. I was wearing the standard uniform: black leotard, pink tights, pink ballet slippers, and pink satin ribbons. The ribbons were supposed to be worn around the ankles, but I wore them around my knees. I suppose I was trying to hide my legs, which to my mind resembled a mosquito's. Johnna taunted me, "Gelsey, are you expecting a flood? Why don't you tie your ribbons a little higher?"

Devastated, I fled. Over the next month, I lowered my ribbons on the sly, little by little, until they went down to my ankles, making sure the descent was so gradual that my sister would fail to notice. I refused to give her the satisfaction of setting my style even on a matter of such trivial detail.

About this time Johnna hit upon the idea of swinging me upside down as a test of gymnastic ability. It was a trick called "skinning the cat," which our father had done for us on the farm. Standing behind me in our bedroom one evening, my sister told me to bend over and reach through my legs with my hands. Then she grabbed my wrists and tried to pull me under and up. In theory, I was supposed to flip and land on my feet. Instead, she let go, or lost her grip, and dropped me on my face.

From that moment on, it was war. Johnna had drawn the first blood. As she seemed to have all the natural advantages, I had no choice but to fight on the only front I had a chance to win—I would learn to dance rings around her.

The rivalry with my sister applied to boys as well as to ballet. At first I conceded defeat to Johnna's beauty. Her physical charms were exaggerated by the distorting lens of my insecurity. I tried to withdraw from the competition before I reached the age of ten. A handwritten note from this period survives. It records a telling wager between us: "I bet Johnna Kirkland ten dollars that a boy will never kiss or dance with me in my life. And I do mean never!" To the best of my recollection, my sister never tried to collect, and I never volunteered to pay. In ballet school, it was as if the rivalry had been multiplied by the number of girls in my class.

As a ten-year-old, the opportunity to play Clara in a holiday production of *The Nutcracker* was a special honor, a chance to appear on the stage with the company. I was thrilled with the prospect, but not enough to dance with a partner I considered unworthy. I was secretly infatuated with another boy. With the conceited airs of a little princess, I stubbornly refused to hold the hand of my partner during a rehearsal. As a consequence, a ballet mistress interrupted and drove me from the theatre in tears. I was not allowed to perform Clara that year, but I was given another small role. Someone was watching over me.

The girl who replaced me in the part of Clara was an adorable redhead by the name of Katherine Voinoff. According to my standards, she was a raving beauty. While wonderfully gifted, she had an "attitude problem." Kathy had been pushed into ballet and was never able to adjust to the pressure that had been placed on her to succeed. She was George Balanchine's goddaughter, an association that proved to be a curse rather than a blessing.

Mr. Balanchine, or "Mr. B," as we called him, was the founder and director of both the New York City Ballet and the School of American Ballet. Those positions gave him a status that, to me, was close to divine. He was

almost sixty, my father's age. As the head of the leading dance company and
school in America, Balanchine impressed my mother. His name was prestigious.

His goddaughter, Kathy, was one of a few friends my age with whom I
shared the secrets of growing up. Like every other student in our class, she
and I idolized George Balanchine from a distance. As he was a legend and
the authority figure within our world, we were naturally in awe of him.
Though seldom at the school, he was the stern master of our daily lives, the
patriarch of our extended family. His presence was felt by everyone. He
oversaw every detail of each of his productions at the New York City Ballet.
He was the one who had choreographed *The Nutcracker.*

Scheming to make a favorable impression, Kathy and I decided to send
Mr. B a card. It was a fan letter in the form of a watercolor and poem. As if
on a secret mission, we set out one night to deliver our handiwork to his
apartment, which was in the same building as my family's, the Apthorp on
Upper Broadway. At the time Balanchine lived there with his wife, Tanaquil
LeClercq, a former ballerina who had been tragically stricken with polio.

Kathy and I, like a pair of tiny thieves, pushed our card under Mr. B's
door and tiptoed away. Our reverence and terror were so great that we
dared not disturb his privacy. Nor were we bold enough to sign our names
to the card. Our act seemed nothing less than an attempt to communicate
with God.

I had been chosen to play the leader of an army of angels in *The Nutcracker,* one of my earliest appearances on the stage. Stricken with stage
fright and tormented by demons, I had a recurrent nightmare in which I
forgot the steps during a performance.

On the day that I was called for a costume fitting, I met Balanchine's
favorite designer, a Russian who used only one name, Karinska. She was an
elderly woman of distinguished appearance who had a peculiar habit of
dressing only in blue. Not only did she limit her wardrobe to a selection of
blue suits, but she dyed her hair with a blue tint. I was in her dressing room
preparing to try on my angel costume when Mr. B entered with a group of
theatre patrons, businessmen wearing dark suits and dour expressions. The
visitors looked so serious I thought I would be told to leave.

Instead, Mr. B asked me to change into the costume and model it for
them. Overcome with modesty, I was appalled that he expected me to
change in front of members of the opposite sex. There was something not
altogether right about the way those grown men giggled. Politely excusing
myself behind a screen, I blushed scarlet as Mr. B snickered along with the
others.

My confusion did not prevent me from going on stage to rehearse that
afternoon. The incident in the dressing room was almost forgotten. I was
flattered that Mr. B delegated me the responsibility of leading the crisscross-
ing rows of little angels, each carrying a miniature Christmas tree in the

opening scene of the second act. He could not be guilty of any impropriety; I trusted him implicitly. Without knowing it, I had caught the eye of George Balanchine, an event that would have a profound impact on my coming of age within the world of ballet.

I was no more than eleven when my mother found me sleepwalking in the middle of the night with my ballet bag in hand. She caught me as I was on the way out the door. Indignant at her questions, I insisted that I was late for my ballet class. Recognizing in my vacant look the sure sign of a sleepwalker, my mother woke me gently and led me back to bed.

The nature of my compulsion was such that I danced in my sleep. The entire household was sometimes awakened by loud thumping sounds coming from my room. The source of the disturbance was discovered to be the rhythmic blow of my foot against the wall next to my bed as I performed grand battements, a step that might be misconstrued as the classical version of a chorus line kick. Even in my sleep, I was struggling to perfect the technical execution of the step.

Driven as I was in my early quest for perfection, I did not yet have an ultimate goal in mind beyond the physical image that had to be fulfilled. My motivation had nothing to do with aspirations for stardom or becoming a prima ballerina. I did not even think about getting into the company. I was spurred on by the more immediate concerns that confronted me in the studio.

The technique I was exposed to at the School of American Ballet was an eclectic potpourri that had been assembled by Balanchine to meet the demands of his choreography. The school was intended to provide trained dancers for his New York City Ballet. The training and repertory reflected a tradition of ballet which had evolved over the past century, passed down through educational techniques that resembled behavioral conditioning. The methods of Pavlov seem to have found a way into the world of Pavlova.

Balanchine was schooled at the Imperial School of Theatre and Ballet in St. Petersburg before the Russian Revolution. He later described the program of study offered at his School of American Ballet as an accelerated version of his own training. He claimed to have simplified and speeded up the training process by stripping it of unnecessary elements. In much the same way, his abstract ballets sought to eliminate what he saw as superfluous elements of plot and character.

Early in my training, the names of the various steps, what is known as the classical lexicon of ballet, were written in French on a blackboard, never to be translated: Plié . . . Tendu . . . Frappé . . . Échappé . . . Fouetté . . . Ronds de jambe . . . Arabesque . . . Attitude . . . Développé . . . Glissade. The words were as foreign to my tongue as the movements implicit in each command were to my body. We were supposed to become as familiar with these basics as we were with the letters of the alphabet. Nobody ever really told us why.

Physical memorization was encouraged through countless sessions of drill and grill. We learned how to imitate the teacher, not how to create the step. That point would prove crucial. The teacher's version of the step was an interpretation that reflected his or her background and Mr. B's taste. The result was a seductive blend of tradition, angularity, and jazzy acrobatics. Neither he nor any of his carefully chosen teachers, with only one exception, possessed a generalized theory of movement that could be applied to each particular step. None of them knew how to verbalize what they were doing.

Mr. B was famous for his short cuts. With the snap of his fingers, he improvised adjustments that were designed to fit the idiosyncratic needs of his dancers. If you believed the myth as I did, he knew his dancers better than they knew themselves. In fact, he relieved them of the mental burden of having to create the steps for themselves. A ballerina proved herself only for him. He shaped each to fit his choreographic design. In a certain sense, by strict conformity to his demands, it was possible to dance for Balanchine without knowing how to dance.

Learning to dance was similar to learning geometry, my best subject. Each piece of physical movement could be thought of as a theorem that had to be proved. There were two ways to proceed with the proof, other than outright cheating. With a minimal expenditure of mental energy, the steps of the proof could be memorized for a test. Through this sleight of mind, I could make an impressive display of knowledge I did not possess. The second approach required the actual acquisition of knowledge through mastery of the creative principles expressed at each step of the proof. I was determined in this way to own the knowledge with which I would dance.

The teachers at the School of American Ballet were handpicked by Mr. B. Many of the women were former ballerinas who had danced for him in the old days. For some, he had acted as a personal Svengali, guiding their careers and their lives. One way or another, each of them continued to carry the torch for him. He was a reminder of the glory that had once been their own on the stage. They had responded to his personal call to pass on their gifts. In moving from the theatre to the classroom, the progress of a lifetime had been reversed. We students, who probably reminded them of their own lost youth, were the last audience they would ever face.

The rules of classroom decorum implied an aristocratic tradition that went back to the court dances of the Renaissance. At the end of class, we always observed the quaint ritual known as the reverence. Each dancer bowed or curtsied for the teacher. Balanchine, insisting on proper etiquette at all times, wrote as a commandment, "The children should respect the teacher." He did not admit the possibility that a teacher might not deserve respect. In my headstrong fashion, I refused to accept any lesson as an article of faith.

When I felt abused by a teacher—for example, when I was unfavorably compared with my sister—I used the reverence to reveal my true feelings. After all, I had practiced the art of the evil eye on my father.

My attitude did not endear me with the teaching staff. One of my early teachers, Madame Felia Doubrovska, recalled in a published interview, "Gelsey Kirkland was a difficult student, and she hate me because I ask her to leave class if she doesn't listen. She stops in the middle of a step and refuse to continue. But I admire her now."

Madame Doubrovska was one of the school's old guard, a former prima ballerina who had received the same Russian training as Balanchine. In his early ballets, she stole the hearts of European audiences during the twenties and thirties. After retiring from the stage, she taught at Balanchine's school for thirty years. I can still hear her shriek at me with her high-pitched voice and Russian accent, correcting my performance of a step. "Make nicer. Try little nicer!" Her range of adjectives was so limited that her criticism was virtually impossible to decipher. We had what might be called a communication problem.

Like many in her position, Madame Doubrovska seemed to be a creature of thwarted dreams. To me, her face told of her regret that she had neither married Balanchine nor engaged in a romantic affair with him, either of which might have been enough to ensure immortality. I knew she was married to Pierre Vladimiroff, a former premier danseur, another of my teachers. Yet whenever Mr. B looked at her, she seemed to be rejuvenated, like a woman splashed by the waters of a magical fountain. It was the fate of more than one generation of his ballerinas to glow only in his presence.

I shall never forget one afternoon when Mr. B made an unannounced appearance in her classroom. His surprise visits were always an event. Clad in a cowboy shirt, he would appear out of nowhere, as if he had just wandered off the set of a musical comedy version of the Lone Ranger. On that particular day, Madame Doubrovska had been demonstrating a series of steps for our class. With a nimbleness that was admirable for her years, she pranced in front of the mirror, showing off her latest color-coordinated ensemble—skirt, tights, leotard, and slippers—all very chichi and precious.

Sensing that he had entered, she picked up the chiffon scarf that matched her outfit and continued her impromptu performance. The flourish of her scarf attracted the attention of her little Yorkshire terrier, who watched from beneath a bench at her back. It so happened that Balanchine's entrance had coincided with the needs of nature in the dog. Yet when Madame Doubrovska caught wind of the misfortune that had been deposited on the floor by her pet, she carried on like a trooper. With barely a pause and before Mr. B could notice, she improvised a sweeping gesture and covered the unsightly spot with her scarf. However, the scent became increasingly unbearable as he sat on the bench and remained there for the rest of the class, much to our amusement.

Pleasure and pain were inextricably connected and integral to the study of dance. When I think of how much pain and how little pleasure were involved in the next few years of ballet school, I marvel at my perseverance and clarity of purpose. What distinguished me from other students was my early refusal to allow ideas to be imposed upon me without question. In my effort to fashion myself as a dancer, I adopted an instinctual strategy of passive resistance.

My early demands for autonomy came into conflict with one of the operative metaphors of the classroom. I was told to imagine a string that extended from my head to the ceiling, as if I were a puppet. This was intended to correct the line of the upper body. However, pulling myself up along this axis only prevented me from coordinating my entire body along the vertical line through my spinal cord, neck, and head. The primary impulse for movement was placed outside my "physical instrument" and, therefore, outside the sphere of my control.

I frequently received verbal corrections addressed to each part of my body in isolation, figuratively dismembering me and dispelling any semblance of grace. It was as if separate strings were arbitrarily attached to my head, arms, and legs; the teacher seemed to pull each without regard to the others, usually ignoring the torso entirely. Nevertheless, I forced my body to absorb the spastic effect of each correction.

My swayback and narrow hips might have been assets if I had been allowed to pursue my passion for riding horses. Instead, I found myself saddled with a set of physical impediments that had to be overcome. I was longlegged, but not pretty or sleek enough to fit the image of a "Balanchine ballerina." So I set about to alter my natural shape.

During a session of locker-room gossip, one of my classmates, Sasha, told me about an operation that was performed on a dancer to change the line of her foot. By surgically breaking the arch, the bones could be realigned to enhance the dancer's pointe. At the time, I thought the idea ghastly, but I understood the impulse to bring about a cosmetic miracle, to improve upon the imperfections of nature.

In order to circumvent the limitations of my own anatomy, I became a contortionist. With the help of my best friend, Meg Gordon, I undertook a regimen of torture worthy of the Marquis de Sade. By turning a bed into a makeshift rack, I stretched myself out like a victim of medieval abuse. Assuming various positions that forced my extension beyond its natural limit, I told Meg to hold me down no matter how much I might beg for release. She sat on me, disregarding my groans, allowing her body weight to restrain me until the pain became so excruciating that I collapsed into tears. This scene was repeated many times. Its effect would prove ultimately disastrous.

At this awkward stage of my development, I was especially challenged by the technical imperative known as "turn-out," one of the fundamentals of ballet. With the heels together and feet splayed at an angle approaching 180 degrees, the dancer rotates the thighs so as to effect a pose that is turned out to the audience.

The eighteenth-century choreographer Jean-Georges Noverre was one of the first to note the expressive advantages offered by dancing from a turned-out position: "In order to dance well, nothing is so important as the turning out of the thigh . . . A dancer with his limbs turned inward is awkward and disagreeable. The contrary attitude gives ease and brilliancy, it invests steps, position, and attitude with grace." According to modern medical science, early training to achieve turn-out is critical because the femur bone must be taught slowly to adjust within its socket. If this does not occur, aided by a sustained program of physical therapy, the dancer will compensate by twisting the ankles and feet into a dangerous parody of the desired effect.

Nobody told me any of this at the time. Years later I read Balanchine's views on the importance of proper training. In his 1945 essay, "Notes on Choreography," he certainly recognized the physical vulnerability of the child:

> Even with eight- or nine-year-old children, we must always keep in mind the fact that their bones are still soft and their muscles (particularly the ones around the knee) are still unformed. For this reason one should never force the feet of children to attain perfect ballet positions, nor insist on their making an effort to turn out their legs.

However, in actual practice, Balanchine and his teachers unwittingly encouraged young dancers to self-destruct, rationalized as part of the sacrifice that must be made to the art. The speed and shortcuts that he built into the training process called for physical cheating in which the dancer distorted the body to deliver the position or step that Balanchine demanded. The risk of injury was ignored. I watched many of my friends become casualties and fall by the wayside. I thought they were either unlucky or unsuited.

As turn-out was compulsory, I had no choice but to subject myself to chronic strain. They would bend my body but not my will. I have a vivid memory of one of the teachers stopping me in the middle of class to demand that I turn out my feet. There was no regard for the knees or hips, which in my case were distorted to the breaking point. The teacher refused to continue the class until I complied with her wishes.

After giving her a look that I hoped would maim if not kill, I cranked myself into an impossibly exaggerated position, with my feet literally pointing backward. Pretending innocence, I asked, "You mean like this?" I got off with a warning, but the physical problems which had begun to plague me could not be evaded so easily.

During my third year of training, I was introduced to toe shoes, the standard footwear for all ballerinas since the mid-nineteenth century. With its tapered toe, the shoe is designed to complete the line that runs along the top of the instep and through the ankle, knee, and hip. In going up on pointe, some constriction of the foot is unavoidable, creating yet another stress that works against proper placement and coordination.

Before I began pointe class, I borrowed an oversized pair of toe shoes that belonged to my sister and staged an informal exhibition in our living room. Encouraged by Johnna and her friends, I hopped about on one foot, amazing them with my ability to hold my balance. Yet there was something about their appreciative laughter that made me uncomfortable. Thereafter, withdrawing to my bedroom, I spent hours alone, practicing spins and turns, adjusting my visual focus to avoid getting dizzy. Perhaps I was already anticipating the great feat of the evil swan, Odile, who performs thirty-two consecutive fouettés, those one-legged spins that have been the downfall of so many ballerinas, in the third act of *Swan Lake*.

Misguided and caught between excessive demands for turn-out and pointe, my feet had already begun to deform. At the age of eleven, I came down with a severe case of bunions. Many of the teachers had the same malady, caused from years of strain placed on the foot. It was said that Balanchine cherished the aberration of line induced by bunions, that they contributed to the impression of winged feet.

I was initially pleased with the swollen bulge just below the joint of the big toe, but the discomfort soon became so crippling that I was forced to see a doctor. By the time I visited Dr. William Liebler, an orthopedic surgeon at Lenox Hill Hospital, my feet had turned purple from inflammation. A specialist in sports medicine, he was quite familiar with the problem and recommended the only reliable form of treatment. He advised me to quit ballet.

Ignoring his advice and keeping my distress secret from my mother, I danced through the pain and compensated as well as I could. At age twelve, the tendons in my ankles became acutely inflamed. I tried to inure myself to the aches and twinges. This became the standard operating procedure for all injuries throughout my early career. At the School of American Ballet, no viable alternative existed.

For whatever reasons, Mr. B seemed to favor me, and I was determined to prove myself worthy of his affection. During the fourth year of my training, he assembled a number of the teachers in the school for a review of my class. Accompanied by piano, he demonstrated a combination of steps across the floor of the studio and asked the students to follow his example in a line. His special instructions called for us to perform the steps with "energy," one of his pet concepts. When my turn arrived, I took off with such speed and exuberance, so anxious was I to please, that I took a nasty spill. With the resounding tumble of my body on the wood, the music stopped and all eyes glared at me, as if I had interrupted a church service with some blasphemous utterance. The exception was Balanchine.

In the midst of my terrible embarrassment, he alone applauded, saying, "You see, everybody, this girl is the only one who understood. I ask for energy, and all of you others were lazy, lazy, lazy. But Gelsey, she has it—energy!"

With his characteristic nasal inflection, he ordered me to repeat the exercise. I was astonished, uncertain whether or not he had just mocked me with his praise. I dutifully repeated the steps, this time without falling down. Shortly after that eventful class, I was informed that I would skip a year to the next level of instruction.

Ten years later, observing a ballet class in Russia, I experienced an episode of déjà vu in which I was reminded of that afternoon with Mr. B. At the Kirov School in Leningrad, an elderly Russian ballet teacher had arranged her students according to her estimation of their abilities, with the most talented at the front of the line. At the end of the class, she approached the little girl whose talents were deemed most promising. The teacher hugged and praised her in front of the others. I recognized the expressions of the other girls as those I had seen on the faces of my former classmates when Balanchine lauded my own potential. My heart went out to all those who had been overlooked.

Chapter Three

GOD INDISPOSED

There is an oft-repeated story about how Mr. B responded to a mother's question concerning the prospects of her daughter becoming a ballerina. He offered only an evasive quip, "La danse, Madame, c'est une question morale." He was nothing if not a showman, always somewhat aloof, with an air of dignity about him. How could we not adore such a man? Yet, for me and my fellow students, under the spell of his considerable charm and the force of his personality, dance was a technical question, exclusively.

My recalcitrance in the classroom and the fact that I had won Balanchine's favor created resentment in certain quarters of the teaching staff. I had progressed rapidly as a student but refused to acknowledge the authority of my teachers or credit them with my technical breakthroughs. Intermittently crippled with pain, I did not feel grateful. I found it difficult to know whom to blame other than myself.

At the age of twelve, when I was in "B Division," Madame Doubrovska tried to clip my wings. At the end of class, she dressed me down in front of the other students, "You know, girls, there is someone in this class who think she is ballerina. Well, she is in for surprise. She not pass to 'C' class when she think!"

She taunted me by saying one of my rivals, Colleen Neary, would advance to the next level ahead of me. Reduced to tears, I took heart as the other girls gathered around me and pleaded with Madame Doubrovska on my behalf, testifying to the sincerity of my commitment. Such a display of solidarity was unusual at the school, where the vicious pressure of competition invariably turned dancer against dancer.

Afterward, I was called in for a meeting with the head of the teaching staff, Diana Adams, a former Balanchine dancer who had recently retired from the stage with an untimely pregnancy. In her office, she put it to me point-blank: "Gelsey, if you don't change your attitude, we're going to have to do something about it." Without hearing my side of the story, she dismissed me. I retreated to the locker room, too stunned to speak. Unable to contain my indignation, I found the sympathetic ears of my girlfriends, who were eager to hear about this latest travesty of justice.

As I ranted about my confrontation with "that bitch," who should enter but Adams herself. We didn't see her, in our huddle between the rows of metal lockers. Recognizing her footsteps, we panicked. Certain she had over-heard me talking behind her back, my girlfriends hurried me out of her way, stuffing me into a large bin in the Lost and Found at the far end of the locker room. In the darkness of my hiding place, cramped among toe shoes and leg-warmers, I realized my terror was absurd; the only opinion that mattered was Balanchine's.

The emergency passed. Adams never did discover how I had managed to elude her. My experiences on stage, memories still fresh in mind, reassured me that I remained in Mr. B's good graces. I knew I was one of his favorites even if I seemed to others something of a juvenile delinquent in toe shoes. After all, I had already appeared in several of Balanchine's celebrated pro-ductions, including *A Midsummer Night's Dream.*

That was the ballet adapted by Balanchine from Shakespeare's play and set to music by Felix Mendelssohn. Its performance on April 24, 1963, marked the company's opening at the New York State Theater, a massive stage in Lincoln Center designed according to Balanchine's specifications for dance on the grand scale. I played a fairy in golden diapers, performing grand jetés and arabesques with all the polish I could manage at that age.

Once again, I allowed myself to be hurt by unintended ridicule. Running through a stage rehearsal, I heard laughter from the dancer who played Puck, a celebrated performer who later became the founder-director of the Dance Theatre of Harlem, Arthur Mitchell. He was joined by Hippolyta, a Balanchine creation named Gloria Govrin. Both these dancers were stars, which meant that they had somehow figured out how to progress within Balanchine's system. I assumed they knew what Balanchine wanted. Their laughter seemed to mock all my efforts. Apparently they had never seen anyone dance with such blind determination. This was not a compliment to a person with skin as thin as mine.

In the same production the part of Oberon was danced by Edward Villella, an extraordinary virtuoso who influenced me as much as any of the ballerinas of his generation. He was one of my earliest secret infatuations. A former boxer and college graduate, Eddie brought his streetwise personality into a theatre dominated by Balanchine's obsession with female dancers. Eddie's emphatic masculinity made it acceptable for American boys to enter ballet. Even when his success on a tour of Russia in 1962 aroused Balanchine's jealousy, Eddie remained unruffled by company politics. He felt no need to tiptoe in Balanchine's presence. Eddie's intelligence with regard to dancing confounded me, as did his ability to project his personality on the stage. He combined athletic skill and theatricality in such a powerful way that his pres-ence compelled as much interest as the dance itself.

I thought I had reached the high point of my career when I was cast in Balanchine's *Harlequinade* as one of two tiny harlequinettes, privileged at one point to mount the shoulders of Harlequin himself, played by Villella. In that production, loosely based on stock characters of the commedia dell'arte, my mirror image on the stage was my rival from class, Colleen Neary.

During one performance, when Colleen and I missed our entrance, Eddie dashed into the hallway of the theatre, yelling for us, "Where are those two little monsters?" Like bats out of hell, the two of us skittered onto the stage. In my haste to find the position in which my twin and I were to twirl a miniature fountain between us, I knocked my head against the prop so hard I saw stars.

After falling over backward and nearly blacking out, I recovered my balance and continued the performance. Later, Mr. B ordered a new prop designed to secure the fountain against future calamities. I took this as a sign of his concern. Little did I realize that his regard did not extend to therapeutic matters, or that his system of training could place a time limit on the careers of his dancers. I did not yet suspect that there might be a connection between my increasingly painful physical ailments and his technical approach to dance. After all, the artist was supposed to suffer.

My solitude in the ballet world was its own predicament. I had no criteria for judgment even in matters of art. My mother taught me how to cross my hands on the piano, part of a sporadic attempt at musical education. But I preferred to listen by myself to Prokofiev's score from *Romeo and Juliet,* music in which I found romance, fantasy, and escape.

While the social experiment of the sixties raged, I caught only occasional glimpses on television. My awareness of the outside world was a montage of televised images that equated the American invasion of Vietnam with the British invasion of the Beatles. Never living more than a ride away from a sideshow of urban blight and pornographic splendor, I did not need to be told about social problems. I had my own problems.

I was hooked on *Cosmopolitan* and *Seventeen.* The turmoil of puberty turned my preoccupation with my looks into a nightmarish obsession. In my fanatical pursuit of beauty, I was at war with myself, driven by vanity and mortified by my appearance. In my bedroom, I had a makeshift vanity table and one of those circular mirrors surrounded by a ring of light bulbs. The magnifying glass was capable of enlarging every pore.

I gazed at my reflection with self-contempt. I conducted an endless series of experiments with cosmetics. Each variation of makeup and hair dye was designed to transform my image, to create appeal where none existed. When Balanchine pushed the exotic curves of his favorite dancer, Suzanne Farrell, as a standard of beauty for the entire company, I tried to imitate the almond shape of her eyes by cutting the lashes off my lower lids and applying eyeliner with the meticulous strokes of a portrait painter.

When I contracted a severe case of acne, the plague of my early teenage years, I hit desolation row. I began taking antibiotics at the same time I started on Butazolidin, a dangerous anti-inflammatory drug used on race-horses and dancers with chronic tendonitis. I tried savage diets and birth control pills, both said to be cures for troublesome skin. My acne infection was so persistent that my mother bathed me daily with cotton swabs and alcohol.

My father tried to humor me with stories of his own teenage acne afflic-tions; the time when his face broke out so badly that he put his head in an oven. I was inconsolable. How could he expect me to live through this scourge? How could he presume to understand my problem? I found a dermatologist, who periodically lanced my infected boils with a needle. I experienced the same painful sensation in the ballet studio whenever a boy touched my skin. I felt like a leper.

As an early bloomer, I was swept into the tide of the menstrual moon, carried along by the havoc of my hormones. Upon learning that I had sprouted pubic hair, my mother burst into tears, a response not likely to inspire confidence in the flower of my sex. After a routine visit to the doc-tor's office, I found myself traumatized by her reaction, as if she had been told that her daughter was incurable. Nobody bothered to tell me the exact nature of my malady, but I was stricken for life.

My new condition was a source of enormous satisfaction for my sister, who delighted in my misery. I went into hiding. Whenever changing my clothes after class, I made sure never to remove my leotard lest the other girls see this darkest of all secrets. Faced with the prospect of exposure in a public shower, I shaved myself. When my breasts failed to develop, I wondered why it was that I had not been born a boy. Meanwhile, I watched my sister turn on the charm and begin the rituals of dating. I did enjoy a laugh when I saw her put on her first pair of stockings and high heels. With the sensual arrogance of a teenager, she dolled herself up, went marching toward the door, and fell on the floor of our apartment. She was not yet as secure in heels as she was in toe shoes.

When Johnna was fourteen and started going out at night under the pre-text of practice for a ballet workshop, I discovered her ruse. So did my mother. She called the school and was told that Johnna had not been spend-ing her evenings in the dance studio at all. Temporarily grounded, my sister continued her nocturnal adventures by climbing out a window of our apart-ment. Like my mother, I assumed that Johnna was already sexually active, which I later found was not the case.

I was consumed with envy as Johnna proceeded to flaunt her male con-quests, including one of the premier stars of the New York City Ballet. My sister's behavior seemed revolutionary by the conservative standards of the school and company. Motivated more by jealousy than concern, Balanchine encouraged an atmosphere that was a mixture of convent and harem.

Unlike Johnna and me, many of our fellow students had come to New York through Ford Foundation grants, recruited from regional schools. Balanchine urged his students and the members of his company to live in the same neighborhood as the school and theatre, the Upper West Side. Anyone who lived below Sixtieth Street was branded a "hippy." To have a boyfriend jeopardized the possibility of dancing for Balanchine. Marriage was thought to be the kiss of death.

I doubted that I would ever find romantic fulfillment. Soap operas inspired several playful episodes with my girlfriends that only increased my frustration. I found that I was equally dismayed by the groping advances of teenage boys. Accompanied by my pals, Meg and Sasha, I attended a "kissing party" in the basement of a Long Island summer home. Rather than take part, I withdrew to a stairwell seat, inwardly desolate and convinced that I was somehow deficient. Ballet seemed infinitely preferable to the kind of romantic exchange valued by my peers.

Students at the School of American Ballet shared a constant sexual conflict. The permissive attitude of our generation was at odds with the discipline of dance and its spartan work ethic. The temptation to rebel was thwarted by the necessity to pursue a career. However, under the strictures imposed by Balanchine, sex was about the only weapon his dancers possessed. Defying the sexual taboo made it seem possible to escape his domination. But to embark on any romance was professionally perilous, as was any lapse in image or lifestyle.

The proliferation of drugs that accompanied the counterculture found its way into the company in the middle of the decade. Balanchine squelched the news when the first of his dancers was caught with marijuana, firing a few individuals as an object lesson, reinstating them almost immediately. I was far too serious about dance to risk any misadventure of that sort.

My sister was wrongly accused of promiscuity and drug use by Mr. B. After her dismissal, one of Balanchine's secretaries informed her that she would only be taken back into the company if she admitted to these false accusations. Johnna was too intimidated to defend herself. This happened twice. Some years later, it would happen again, but then the charge of drug use would be true. I learned of these events only recently, long after my sister had reformed and recovered her life. I wish we had compared notes earlier.

Nobody ever really answered my questions, especially questions that began with "why." In order to satisfy my curiosity, I became a sneak. By this time, I was under the impression that knowledge had to be stolen. Anything precious enough to be loved had to be hidden. I snuck into the New York State Theater to watch Eddie Villella and his partner, Patricia McBride, in Balanchine's pas de deux *Tarantella*. I stole my way in to a number of productions by entering the theatre through a back fire escape. My obsession justified every risk.

Without asking permission, I continued to observe my sister's classes. One of her teachers, the British-born and Danish-educated Stanley Williams, would later become my first real mentor. I liked him already; he looked like Jack Lemmon. My sister's class included a number of major talents who dwarfed me in terms of natural gifts. From time to time, the class featured guest artists from the company, such as Allegra Kent and Violette Verdy. Each of them, in her own way, displayed an unusual degree of dedication and innovative intelligence. Each cultivated a theatrical persona adapted to Balanchine's stage. In my mind, at least for a while, they were beyond compare.

Allegra Kent achieved remarkable flexibility and strength. She coordinated the lines of her body with exquisite fluidity, as if calibrating the impact of her shape. Allegra was one of the first to stray outside the company to utilize the Pilates Method as taught by Carola Trier. This conditioning method involved elaborate machines capable of developing specific muscles. While Allegra connected technique and image with a somewhat mysterious logic, Violette adapted technique to character in a more straightforward fashion.

Attacking the problems implicit in Balanchine's more abstract choreography, Violette sometimes created an imaginary story to invest her steps with a reason for existence. Her idiosyncratic approach to phrasing the movement to the music was both dramatically expressive and technically precise. She refused to sacrifice the training that she had received in France before coming under the influence of Balanchine. Almost all the dancers in the company had started and, in many cases, completed their training outside the School of American Ballet. That was not encouraging.

During the two years of "C Division," when I was fourteen and fifteen years old, I took part in workshop performances at the school and occasionally appeared with a Long Island ballet company directed by André Eglevsky, another of my early teachers. He held a high-enough opinion of my technical prowess to have me demonstrate steps with him for the other students in his partnering class. Through these workshops and guest performances, I acquired a range of experience in solo roles and exposure to a varied repertory, which initially included ballets outside the realm of Balanchine. I stepped into other worlds.

In 1967, I was cast in the Precious Stones pas de trois from *The Sleeping Beauty*, a ballet choreographed during the late nineteenth century by Marius Petipa to music by Tchaikovsky. The workshop was directed by Alexandra Danilova, the Russian grande dame of the teaching staff. She was a former prima ballerina and one of Balanchine's lovers during the twenties.

At the beginning of a class, Madame Danilova approached me as I was putting on my toe shoes. My complexion had finally cleared, at least temporarily, and I was decked out in a chiffon skirt and leg-warmers I had knitted myself. I had devised a new hairstyle and adorned myself with pearl earrings, hoping for some dazzling effect. I was trying to keep my legs warm to ease the familiar pain of my tendons. When Danilova tried to compliment me, saying that I looked like Grace Kelly, I wrinkled up my nose to show my distaste. Without even knowing who Grace Kelly was, I was sure I did not want to be compared with her. She was not a member of the New York City Ballet.

I have no recollection of the performance, but I do recall my sense that the movement was supposed to tell a story, my earliest inkling that ballet had not been contrived as merely a clever accompaniment for the music. In the class taught by Stanley Williams, this concept tentatively came to fruition. He introduced me to the tradition of the Danish school, epitomized by the ballets of the Romantic choreographer Auguste Bournonville.

I learned for the first time that the object of style was not to reconstruct the past, but to recreate its method. One of the keys was musical phrasing. Through Stanley's methodical extrapolation of movement from music, I discovered that the meaning of dance is not contained in the individual steps, any more than the meaning of a phrase of music is contained in the individual notes. It was not enough to simply count music or to move on the beat. As in the case of musical counterpoint, the meaning of ballet was to be found in the development of a theme, in the relation of the compositional parts to the whole. The voice of the body had to harmonize in a dramatic way with the music. This was a breakthrough realization, a leap of understanding that took place not all at once, but over countless hours in Stanley's classroom. I would one day "sing" with the silence of my movement.

In retrospect, I can see that Stanley Williams rationalized and altered his own teaching within Balanchine's system. Stanley apparently saw no contradiction between means and ends; but, more and more, he stayed in the classroom, rarely attending the ballet over the next decade. Did he secretly lament the modern state of the art as he saw it on Balanchine's stage? In deference to Balanchine, he never made waves. Stanley's diplomacy in the theatre was usually matched by his courtesy in the classroom.

As a teacher, he provided the invaluable service of maintaining a connection to the heritage of ballet. His attention to detail set him apart from all other instructors. For him, the body was an integrated unit, the parts of which had to act in concert with each other and with the music. Where Balanchine demanded that movement should be executed, Stanley taught how movement should be composed.

I was challenged to translate Stanley's verbal cues into a language of physical movement. Although like all teachers he worked with a pianist and demonstrated or indicated steps for the class, his program of study was not confined to imitation. He expected more from a dancer than he could show or explain. I knew his frustration.

When at a loss for words once in class, he actually wrenched my leg, pulling and tearing the muscles, trying to mold me into a position he was unable to communicate. He was the only teacher at the School of American Ballet whom I would have forgiven for such an offense. I trusted his manner was not a pretense to cover for knowledge he did not possess. I even accepted his goading me with comments like "Maybe you should ask your sister how to do that step." Only with Stanley's wisdom was I able to take the first steps in beating Balanchine's system.

For my workshop production during the spring of 1968, I was fortunate to be cast with a member of the company, Robert Weiss, in the pas de deux from *Flower Festival in Genzano,* a Bournonville piece staged by Stanley Williams. In the same workshop, I danced in the famous pas de trois from *Paquita,* another of Petipa's ballets staged by Madame Danilova. These performances at the New York State Theater held a special significance for me: my father was in the audience.

This was the first time he was to see me perform. In the past, some pretext had always kept him away from the theatre. With my sister already in the company and with me following on her heels, my father had to acknowledge that his daughters were becoming ballerinas. For me to realize that he was there induced emotional terror that went beyond stage fright. I knew I would be judged by the only person other than myself whom it was impossible to please.

Only by actually being on the stage was I able to overcome the nerves and agony that preceded my entrance. My temples throbbed; my ankles were rigid with pain. Focusing my mind, I danced with frozen intensity, as if gazing upon a world within myself. I did not smile.

After the performance, my mother tried to congratulate me in the dressing room. I was more relieved than ecstatic, too self-conscious to appreciate her glow of maternal pride. She told me that my father had left the auditorium abruptly, before the house lights came up. He had been in tears. Later, I cried quietly by myself, shaken to think I had touched the paternal monster and that he had feelings.

When I returned home, I found my father alone in the dining room. Neither of us said a word. After an awkward silence, I blurted out my burning question: "Well, was that good enough for you?" Without waiting for his reply, I rushed from the room. Not only was our love blind, it was mute. A paralysis of the heart rendered us incapable of an exchange as gracious and as simple as a compliment.

On the following day, New York *Times* critic Clive Barnes wrote about my performance in *Flower Festival:* ". . . the young and fresh Gelsey Kirkland excelled . . ." When I arrived at ballet school, I was accosted in the hallway by my old nemesis, Madame Doubrovska. With a twitter of syllables and a Russian twang, she damned me with faint praise. "Oh, Gelsey, you were marvelous yesterday, technically wonderful; but, you know something, dear, you didn't make me cry."

Shortly thereafter, without fanfare, I was told that Balanchine had invited me to join the company. I was fifteen years old. I decided to quit public school and change my name. I hated the sound of it. My father stepped in, and a stern voice forbade me to adopt a stage name. I would be allowed to withdraw from my academic schooling, but only with the proviso that I continue to read. He opposed my leaving school, but consoled himself with the faith that I would complete my education through books. Literacy would save me. The years have turned my father's words into a prophecy.

In the movie *Sleeper*, Woody Allen plays a lovable schlemiel who awakens to find himself transported into the future where every home has a robot. Meeting one of these automatons, Woody remarks, "These robots are uncanny! They're alert and they respond . . . I've gone out with girls who had less movement." Could his dates have been members of the New York City Ballet?

Balanchine's conception of the human form was essentially mechanical. The body was a machine to be "assembled"—the same word that he used to describe the process by which he created his ballets. There were critics who complained that his dancers tended toward uniformity. A robotic quality was supposed to have derived in part from his attempt to forge a neutral vessel as the carrier of his choreographic ideas. The vessel itself, the human body, did seem to be one of his most important ideas.

But a dancer was never neutral. Flesh and blood and spirit could never really be turned into a robot, not completely. When we moved without life or energy, he sometimes called us "Zombies!" Stage presence and the ability to project were valued as well as shape and precision. Mr. B hated those critics who accused his dancers of being robots. He seemed to think that our physical exuberance in attacking his steps, our being alert and responding on the stage, were enough to answer his detractors. Yet was there more than a grain of truth in their criticism?

Motivation and psychological depth, emotion and dramatic intensity— these were qualities Balanchine attempted to repress in his dancers and in his ballets. He sought to replace personality with his abstract ideal of physical movement. Even in his choreography that retained plot and character, the drama was distilled and the passion of the dancers quelled. Those were his instructions. There were not supposed to be any stars in his theatre who might detract or steal thunder from his choreography.

The interpretive stamp of a dancer threatened to mar the choreographic design of the master. Mr. B's disciples still speak of his ballets as being "dancer-proof," as if technical proficiency guaranteed success. But his ballets succeeded or failed in part because of the personal touch bestowed by individual dancers, whose passion and personality manifested itself in spite of

Balanchine's best efforts to the contrary. To his credit, he knew how to take advantage of a personality when he saw one. In designing a role, he made use of whatever characteristic traits might be suggested by a dancer's physical appearance. His emphasis on form, chance, and spontaneity included the imagination of a dancer only as an unavoidable and often inadvertent contribution to his picture. As much as he tried, he could not do away with or do without the unique aspects of individual virtuosity.

In a sense, his dancers were the living content of his ballets. There was a compelling sort of drama implicit in meeting the technical challenge, in mastering the steps. The meaning of that kind of drama was limited for me, like a gymnastic exhibition set to music. The contradictions between Mr. B's words and actions kept me guessing about his intentions. What were his steps supposed to mean? I always figured he wanted something more than he was able to say. That "something" had to be character and dramatic motivation—even though he said just the opposite.

I knew that I was no robot, but I often fretted about having no real character, especially when I compared myself to the older generations. Those exceptional dancers who managed to move beyond the mechanical reproduction of style lent a special interest and coherency to his otherwise decorative choreographic statement. Knowing many had experience with drama and mime and having seen them distinguish themselves in his early, more dramatic ballets, I had trouble accepting Mr. B's verbal direction, "Just dance!"

Balanchine's aesthetic creed—technique for the sake of technique, dance for the sake of dance—found a receptive audience. When he arrived in New York in 1933, it was almost virgin territory as far as ballet was concerned; foreign companies toured, led by the Russians; the subjective calisthenics of modern dance enjoyed some popularity, but American ballet companies were virtually nonexistent. He stepped into a vacuum, filling a role that had been created for him by default and by design.

Balanchine's introduction to high society gave him access to the purse strings of the Eastern Establishment. His patron and spiritual twin was Lincoln Kirstein, the Harvard-educated scion of a Boston merchant family. Acting as impresario and oligarch, Kirstein recruited Balanchine for a special mission: they would bring ballet to the New World.

The timing was perfect. Balanchine's idol, composer Igor Stravinsky, had already blazed a path into America, bringing the music and aesthetic theories of the Paris school into the classical concert halls. The musical taste of the British Round Table found its way into the New York Metropolitan Opera by way of its director, Otto Kahn, impresario and banker. What Kahn had done for Gershwin and Stravinsky in the music world, Kirstein would accomplish for Balanchine in the world of dance. It would take thirty years of struggle to win universal popularity. The only serious competition was provided by ballerina Lucia Chase, whose American Ballet Theatre (founded in 1939 as Ballet Theatre) was backed by her own zeal and family fortune.

The new ballet company rose from what Kirstein described as the dust of the old Met. After securing initial funding through the Warburg, Rockefeller, and Vanderbilt families, the Balanchine-Kirstein enterprise eventually consolidated control of American ballet with the millions of dollars of Ford Foundation grants that began to pour in during the early sixties. By that time, most critical resistance had collapsed, and Balanchine had become an institution.

It was as if there were a conspiracy to displace the legacy of European classical ballet by developing a plotless facsimile in America. In 1939, New York *Times* critic John Martin, initially hostile to Balanchine, produced a document remarkable for it prescience, "The Ideal of Ballet Aesthetics." The piece concluded with a call to arms and want-ad for a new choreographer, a pop messiah to gear classical ballet to the modern age:

> Perhaps we must look for new values . . . In some new field (perhaps America, though there are no signs of it yet) a free choreographer may be able to sense the classic basis of the art in its modern application, skipping over the whole long development toward romanticism.
>
> Certainly, whoever he may be, he will have to be a courageous rebel, for the mere mention of such an idea is likely to produce foamings at the mouth in orthodox circles. He will have to be strong enough to face accusations of destroying progress and of trying to turn back the tide.

Enter George Balanchine, whose profile made him the perfect choice for such an endeavor. All of this raises the kind of political question that ballerinas are not supposed to ask: if Balanchine had not been born, would history have created him?

What Balanchine had discovered by the time I entered the School of American Ballet was that he did not need classical dancers to perform his ballets. All that he needed were dancers who could approximate some of the formal elements of classical technique. Mr. B altered and sometimes twisted classical line and proportion to such an extent that it was possible for him to create a ballet that not only exploited, but concealed the limitations of his dancers. His style was known as "neoclassical."

The word "classical" in dance can describe a broad range of styles, much as the word "table" describes many examples of the same basic piece of furniture. A classical dancer, in the modern sense, might be thought of as a kind of two-legged table. Similarities of form seem to justify that kind of general description. Historically, classical ballet usually refers to the style that flourished in Russia during the second half of the nineteenth century, with such works as *Swan Lake* and *The Sleeping Beauty*. I now include an older tradition when I use the term, reaching back another hundred years to find a different sort of connection between content and form. That link is the focus of my aspirations.

The eighteenth-century choreographer Noverre had a dream of classical dance, an idea that has seldom been fully realized. His words, defending himself to the audience of his age, might be offered to my own audience:

> But the dancing of our time is beautiful, it will be said, able to captivate and please, even when it does not possess the feeling and wit with which [I] wish it to be embellished. I will admit that the mechanical execution of that art has been brought to a degree of perfection that leaves nothing to be desired; I will even add that it often has grace and nobility; but these represent only a portion of the qualities which it should possess.

There are those who maintain that Balanchine's ballets set the standard of beauty for all time. To those who still deify him, he rescued the classic ballet and extended its expressive range. But what place did feeling and wit, love and reason, have in Mr. B's theatre? In his obsession with the mechanical execution of dance, what other qualities did his ballets possess or lack? What was the effect on his dancers when form overshadowed content?

The men were still cavaliers; the women were slender "pinheads," either ethereal or sensual. Mr. B was famous for describing ballet as "Woman." She, the ballerina, was apparently his inspiration, the love of his life. Yet, for us, an inspired approach to dancing was almost unthinkable. He often said, "There is no such thing as inspiration." Our devotion made us dependent on him for ideas and psychological motivation.

Likewise, we were spared any consideration of history. It was as if ballet were born with Balanchine. His official version of what was supposed to be the orthodox style of ballet made him the living repository of all practical knowledge pertinent to the art. We thought he had all the answers. In fact, he did not have to worry about the answers as long as he kept both the dancers and the audience asking the wrong questions. His explanations were rare. He did not intend to mislead anyone when he said, "It's very difficult to explain why I do what I do . . . I can teach and explain to pupils what to do better, but not because there's a reason."

With his own ballets as the testing ground, he was the only judge of talent. He set the style. His monopoly on taste and creative control was absolute. If anyone dared mention the unusual fashion of the emperor's new clothes, the hapless soul was banished from Mr. B's little empire. As if the faculty of reason were a dangerous threat, he encouraged his dancers not to think: "You have to be vairy careful when you use your mind . . . or you will get into trouble."

Mr. B reminded us whenever any dancer left the company that we could be replaced, that dancers were expendable. His ballets were another story.

He seemed to think they would die with him. He predicted his choreography would be performed after he was gone but would never be the same without him. Who would train the dancers, cast the productions, design and think them through? He must have known that he made himself indispensable.

The mechanism by which the style of dance is passed from generation to generation is fragile, even haphazard. The ballets of the past have no literal script; the only clues to form and content are vague descriptive notations and an equally unreliable oral tradition. The choreographic imprint, like a magnificent sand castle, is washed away by time, leaving behind only the footprints of the architect and the musical score.

Without a script, the style of a ballet provides the only instrument with which to penetrate its reality and reconstruct its inner meaning. The past acts as a constant provocation and guide to those principles of creative discovery that seem to speak to each age. The enduring subject of ballet was never to be found in the literal symbols of fairy tale or myth, nor was significance stored in the steps by themselves. Classical dance in the deepest sense, like classical drama and music, sought to inspire judgment, to enlighten and ennoble the human spirit. By its very nature, the method of classical ballet held the promise of a revelation that opposed escapism.

By removing the classical vocabulary—the academic steps and positions of ballet—from the traditional repertory, Balanchine divorced the steps from the historical environment and dramatic context in which they had once acquired meaning. He adapted a version of the Russian lexicon that had been established by choreographer Marius Petipa during the last century. Over the years, Mr. B derived a formula to fit what he saw as the essential speed of American life. This was his Evelyn Wood approach to classical dance.

What had come to life in former times as a revelation of divine harmony—a composition of movement, music, and dramatic action, as geometrically sublime as the secret coiled in the spiral of a seashell—was interpreted by Mr. B. in a new way. He performed an autopsy on what he saw as the corpse of classical ballet. Extracting a code of movement, he thought he had isolated its soul.

Even when he described ballet as an omelette and we dancers as the ingredients he would use to "cook something up," we thought his choice of culinary metaphor combined eccentric charm and metaphysical profundity. It seemed the height of modesty for him to refer to himself variously as chef, gardener, tailor, carpenter, and cabinetmaker. In his mind, ballet was not an art; it was a craft and should aspire to nothing more. Like all those who worshipped him, I was blind to the subtle reduction of values that took place in his classroom and on his stage.

Balanchine assembled steps that were supposed to have been predetermined by God and humbly described himself as an instrument of divine will. His word was holy. To have a private audience with such an exalted being was inconceivable; we settled for brief encounters, moments of confession and supplication outside the elevator that led to his office, catching him on his way, terrified to invade the inner sanctum of his thoughts.

In spite of my temperamental resistance, I internalized Balanchine's system with the fury of a fanatic, if not the devotion of a true believer. His place in the hierarchy was beyond question. I always hoped what I was doing would please him. I had to please him. I loved him more than my own father.

I had already become a member of the company by the time I realized that Mr. B was mortal after all. It happened on the day I saw him enter a men's room at the New York State Theater. I literally tiptoed down the hallway to avoid him, hurrying away in order to miss seeing him make his exit. The idea that Mr. B might have biological needs sent a shock wave through me. I was utterly aghast. From that moment, he was transformed in my eyes, a god shaken from his hold on heaven.

His descent in my esteem was gradual, hastened by the rumors about his sexual impotence and the scandalous details of his most recent divorce, all of which I was at a loss to understand. No longer quite so awed by him, I developed the habit of mentally undressing him, without any attraction, simply fascinated to know if he possessed all the attributes of the male anatomy. In an effort to rationalize the idle speculation about his sexual inadequacy, I told myself that when God gave out genius, the other areas might be slighted, like a blessing withheld. I never considered the possibility that both Balanchine's genius and sexuality might be aberrations.

The secret knowledge of his weakness caused games to be played with his affections, games in which he set the rules. A certain dancer might receive a refrigerator or a more practical gift if she allowed his fondling touch in private. I knew he had his way with a number of fellow dancers. The question of the week with my girlfriends was whether Mr. B preferred blondes or redheads.

On a higher level, a dancer's dream was that he might fall in love with her, that he might "choreograph a ballet on her," the expression used to describe what happened when Mr. B placed a ballerina on the pedestal of his stage, using her as his muse. Such a dancer became a fetish, whether he touched her or not.

When I became a member of the company, I automatically began to take Balanchine's class. He delighted in taunting me about what he considered to be the disproportions of my body. Flaring his nostrils and sniffling, he would ask me on occasion, "Dear, when are you going to grow into your head?"

He nicknamed me "Speedy-foot Gelso," encouraging the image of his dancers as racehorses. He gave us red horse blankets, each embroidered with a sobriquet. Speed was the name of the game as I played it. He demonstrated various combinations of steps in the studio, then asked us to accelerate the pace. He usually arrived late to class and did not take the time to warm up and stretch the muscles of his dancers, an omission that was professionally fatal for those with chronic injuries.

I felt like a test pilot trying to break the land speed record with my body, which was riddled with breaking parts, unable to withstand the strain. His distorted emphasis and shortcuts on pointe work, including his restriction that toe shoes should be worn at all times in class, delivered another blow to my Achilles tendons. I was lame, an unwitting victim of planned obsolescence. His technique targeted various parts of the body. Depending on physical type and the quality of previous training, each dancer was more or less vulnerable to premature breakdown at any time. I continued to dance through the pain as if I were set loose on a floor covered with broken glass.

I still placed enough trust in Mr. B to turn to him for advice about my physical agony. I caught him at the elevator after class and pleaded for his help. He sighed with infinite patience and lectured me: "Dear, you're young. Young people don't have injuries. Go home and read fairy tales. Try little red wine." Tears began to stream from my eyes as he continued: "You need nothing but this place. You don't need anybody else; you don't go anywhere else. You have a beautiful theatre here. You come in the morning. When you don't work, you go into studio by yourself; you do relevés. You just stay here all day; you go home, drink little red wine. That's all you need." He disappeared as the elevator door closed.

My own medical problems were suddenly overshadowed by my father's declining health. His heart and lungs were on the skids. When I visited him at Manhattan's Roosevelt Hospital, a nurse told me how he bragged about his daughters, how proud he was of us. But no bedside reconciliation was to take place. On February 26, 1969, I answered the phone at five in the morning to be told of his death. I later learned that he had fallen asleep for the last time while reading a book. I called my mother to the phone, saying only that the hospital was on the line. While she absorbed the tragic news, I forced myself to cry for her benefit. I was numb.

After the funeral in New York and after we disposed of his ashes at our old farm in Pennsylvania, I was finally hit by his passing. I was alone in our apartment one afternoon and happened upon my father's old coat hanging in a closet. Pulling that blistered jacket around my shoulders required an extreme act of will. I had to overcome my morbid fear. As if I possessed the touch of the blind, I was able to see with my fingers as I slowly pushed my hands through the sleeves. Turning up the collar, I felt the weather my father had endured, as well as the season that might have been. My eyes burned with the bitter anguish of regret. And I wished that my tears might roll backward beneath my closed eyelids. I wanted to call back my sorrow on his behalf. I loved and hated him with the passion of a heartbreak that would haunt me for years.

His mind and spirit had been killed through events which were due, in part, to his own failure of moral courage and, in part, to his victimization by forces seemingly beyond his control. I saw him become an accomplice in his own murder. Relentlessly, even if unknowingly, I have been tracking down his assassins throughout my career. It should come as no surprise that they would find me before I would find them.

Chapter Four

BREAKING THE MIRROR

After the death of my father, I turned with grim determination to the face that seemed to hold my fortune, the lines of age and guarded eyes, the gray luster that belonged to George Balanchine. I accepted the sentiment that was awakened in my benefactor, recognizing that surrogate paternity was preferable to the kind of inclination he displayed toward other dancers that he favored. I was relatively safe from the possibility of overt advances. Mr. B treated me like a wayward daughter, always trying to curb those wild tendencies and persistent questions that drove me to wonder about my place in the world, as well as my purpose in ballet.

My mother was put to the test, confronted with a hopeless task of mediating the rivalry between me and my sister, while my brother Marshall went away to boarding school. The home front, like the ballet studio, was the scene of a ludicrous beauty contest, with all of my wits and wiles pitted against my dear sister, who seemed to dance in my way. Yet Johnna and I both measured ourselves against a more alluring and more formidable adversary, Suzanne Farrell, the absolute standard of beauty, the one who had been chosen by Mr. B to be the goddess of our age.

Like the rest of our fair company at the New York City Ballet, my sister and I were constantly engaged in imitation. We young dancers were envious of Suzanne's appearance and style. Her long neck and legs, her exotic line and delicate features, made her Balanchine's perfect instrument. She conveyed a sense of movement, without the slightest pretense of thought or personality. She was a natural. There was complete empathy between Suzanne and Mr. B, which made for a kind of hypnotic witchcraft and an instantaneous stage sensation.

Her success and his fixation led to a company formula. Balanchine attempted to pass on those sensual attributes that had worked for Suzanne through further distortion of our training process and his own choreography. He tried to give Suzanne's endowments and facility to everyone, to replicate her everywhere, to reproduce even the shade and texture of her alabaster skin. In passing on those fine points, Mr. B magnified the demoralization of each female dancer; her despair that she did not look like somebody else. But how we tried, and to a certain extent, even succeeded.

In the spring of 1969, Suzanne had a famous falling-out with Mr. B, leaving with her husband for Europe to join the ballet company run by French choreographer Maurice Béjart. The impact of the Farrell formula and my own efforts at imitation were noted subsequently by critic Arlene Croce, writing in *Harper's:*

> In any decently written history of the New York City Ballet, the years 1963–1969 would consume several chapters. The Farrell Years saw the company remade in a new, younger, and more romantic image. For Farrell personally they began in glory and ended in estrangement . . . She was the prototypical Balanchine ballerina for her generation—today we can see her even in little Gelsey Kirkland . . .

Years later, the same critic would welcome Farrell's return to the company, but with a recognition that Balanchine's dancers had become "caricatures of a caricature."

In Suzanne's absence, my progress on the stage accelerated, even though I was not suited for most of the roles she vacated. I was never really her type. Mr. B had encouraged me to gather more experience in the corps and the school workshop. At the age of sixteen, the frustrations of virginity, my repertory ambitions, and the rivalry with my sister collided during a guest appearance at the Long Island Ballet.

I was cast with a friend, Ricky (Robert) Weiss, in a ballet called *À la Françaix,* the story of a flirt who got what she deserved, losing the male object of her affection. To play a coquette, with my acne, tendonitis, and insecurities, I turned to the ultimate model of flirtation, Suzanne Farrell, a wild thing caught in female skin. Her trademark was a gesture known as the "ginch," a seductive glance over the shoulder that seemed to epitomize the phrase "animal magnetism." My inability to master this Farrell quality was diagnosed by my partner, Ricky, who loved to play amateur psychologist. He and his future wife, Cathy Haigney, pinned me down in a studio of the New York State Theater and coaxed me into saying the words "I am as pretty as my sister."

Their good intentions instigated a fiasco. I was less than cooperative, exhibiting my characteristic resistance to those who presume to know me and try to pluck out the very heart of that which spurs me to dance, my fierce desire. My forced admissions and tears only clinched my feelings of inferiority.

In spite of my difficulties with the role, my performance provided a subtle contrast to the climax of the ballet, a burlesque in which my romantic competition, a sylph character, stripped down to a bikini and stole the man of my dreams. My effort was appreciated by the audience and critics. One of the reviews noted, "Kirkland is one of the youngest members of the company—petite and a real charmer." Whatever impish innocence I had at that age must have compensated for my failure to play the fickle femme. But I was not pleased by applause I felt had been gratuitous.

I soon tried playing the flirt off stage as well. A mad and prolonged infatuation drove me to distraction. I fell for a promising dancer at the school, a dreamboat named Fernando Bujones, who initially returned my feelings in kind. Our amorous encounters in my dressing room were as brief and tentative as they were daring. Unfortunately, the members of Fernando's Roman Catholic family felt that I was corrupting a teenage boy and jeopardizing his future, stealing him from the cradle. He was two years younger than I. His mother especially resented me, and was probably right on all counts except for my motives. I felt more than physical attraction. My romantic aspirations were always tied to my artistic curiosity.

Fernando's background intrigued me almost as much as his classical proportions. He was an American of Cuban descent. As a product of the tradition of Alicia Alonso, mixing Latin, Russian, and British influences, he posed a formal contrast to Balanchine's gospel. But in his conscientious approach to ballet, Fernando proved to be as puritanical as he was about his youthful sexuality. Here was a perfect example of classical line paralyzed through overemphasis placed on rules of technique. Bewitched as I was by the charm of looks, my awareness of such problems came slowly. Dancing a pas de deux with Fernando, I once saw myself in his dark eyes. He later kidded me, saying that Cuban girls had better figures than Americans.

There were moments of levity, even though I missed most of the leisure pastimes of my generation. I recall a merry afternoon at the Upper West Side apartment of a fellow dancer, when friends bet on my ability to consume an entire watermelon. On my side was my longtime girlfriend Patsy Bromley, whose fidelity has spanned the years. Through my stumbles and triumphs, this woman has always wagered on my life, even when the odds were against my ever drawing another breath.

The stakes were not as high here as later friendship would require. After I had devoured the last piece of melon and passed out from exhaustion, Patsy placed several slices of liverwurst over my lips. I awakened to peals of laughter. The bonds linking us were compulsory starvation, the dreams of food, and the drastic measures required to maintain our diets. We later induced vomiting by downing an emetic intended for babies. The forbidden fruit of the modern ballerina was thus disgorged.

Not long after the watermelon feast, I had an encounter with Mr. B in class which underscored his demand for starvation, a memory that is etched in my mind with all the pain of a fingernail being scraped across a blackboard. He halted class and approached me for a kind of physical inspection.

With his knuckles, he thumped on my sternum and down my rib cage, clucking his tongue and remarking, "Must see the bones."

I was less than a hundred pounds even then. Mr. B did not seem to consider beauty a quality that must develop from within the artist; rather, he was concerned with outward signs such as body weight. His emphasis was responsible in part for setting the style that has led to some of the current extremes of American ballet. I allowed him to use me to that end by trusting his advice. He did not merely say, "Eat less." He said repeatedly, "Eat nothing."

The physical line of a ballerina seemed to have been ordained. A thin body carried the most definition. A slender figure was supposed to be the prerequisite for movement. We were not taught how movement can generate the illusion of both line and shape, how a ballerina's facility can create the impression of weight. Only on my own and years later would I learn that by moving in a clever way, a dancer can appear heavy or light, adding or losing pounds by changing placement and dynamic.

Mr. B's ideal proportions called for an almost skeletal frame, accentuating the collarbones and length of the neck. Defeminization was the overall result, with the frequent cessation of the menstrual cycle due to malnutrition and physical abuse. A fulsome pair of breasts seemed the only attribute with which a ballerina could assert her sexuality.

Over the years, Mr. B's methods and taste have been adopted by virtually every ballet company and school in America—through faithful imitation, and by the encouragement of those ballet masters trained by Balanchine, and those teachers who champion "thin-is-in" as a requirement for admission into the schools. For those who refuse to go along with the crowd, professional employment is unlikely.

A "concentration camp" aesthetic leads to abuse of diet pills, quack weight-reducing formulas, and, ultimately, anorexia. The health problems have become epidemic. Without proper nourishment, the chances for recovery from dance-related injuries drop to nil, with a corresponding increase in susceptibility to disease and chronic disabilities.

Many of the excesses of American ballet seem to be a result of the slimness trend, turning the ideal of beauty into mere fashion. Mr. B pushed us in that direction, but he also popularized ballet. This offers the hope that the public may press for reform—as an increasing number of ballet parents become concerned for the welfare of their children.

Mr. B had a penchant for experimenting with stage partnerships, for putting together the magic combination of dancers who could promote the fame and popularity of the New York City Ballet. Johnna and I were briefly cast as a sister act. A production was conceived by an apprentice choreographer, John Clifford, a young man who would later become the head of the now defunct Los Angeles Ballet. His version of the plotless ballet *Reveries* was set to four movements of Tchaikovsky's Suite No. 1, with Johnna carrying out a romantic adagio while I delivered the fancy footwork of a sprite. The review which appeared in the New York *Daily News* on December 5, 1969, glossed over the obvious:

> The Kirkland Sisters are not a sister act, just two of this matchless company's younger dancers. Johnna, who must be all of 18, is petite and lovely and moves like a spring breeze. Gelsey, who is "16 going on 17," as the Rodgers-Hammerstein song goes, is even more petite and seems to spring right out of the ground with every step she takes. They're bubbly and expert.

Other reviews drove a wedge between Johnna and me by crediting me with the superior performance, explicitly suggesting that "Gelsey Kirkland . . . swept all before her, including her sibling."

The real story had taken place behind the scenes. I was too absorbed with myself to keep up with Johnna. She had only been about fifteen when she moved away from home. With her living in the West Village, I saw her only at the studio or the theatre. A not-so-blind-date of mine had made the mistake of paying her compliments whenever he made a pass at me. With that kind of incident in mind, I did not suspect that she might share my turmoil. How could she be jealous of me? Our estrangement from each other was incomprehensible, an emotional distance appropriate for the style of choreography.

Working on the ballet, I suffered the wit of the choreographer, who lacked the sensitivity to do more than maintain a precarious balance between two rival sisters. In a taxicab ride from the theatre, John leaned over to whisper in my ear, "Oh, Gelsey, you simply must do something about your mustache!" I wanted to crawl under the seat. After the ride, I went straight to the drugstore for some depilatory cream, which caused my upper lip to break out the next morning. The rash looked like a bright red mustache. I was not likely to be kissed.

At about the same time, one of my future partners conducted a disturbing truth session. Walking outside the theatre, he cooed, "Gelsey, dear, have you ever had an orgasm?" As I stammered about my lack of experience, he cut in, "Well, then you have something to live for. As for me, I simply want to die! I've had as many orgasms as I want. There's nothing left!" I was again at the mercy of uncontrollable blushing and internal havoc. I wanted to hide my face or trade it for a new one.

I went to absurd extremes in my vain effort to lure my reluctant sweetheart, Fernando Bujones, into promiscuity. Trusting the mirror, I was deceived into believing that some magical abracadabra might exist to enhance my femininity. To change my image, I embarked on a risky course of plastic surgery and silicone injections, major dental realignments and gruesome medical procedures. I pray that young dancers, those who imitate me at their peril, will avoid this blind alley. It is more than a dead end; it is a dead beginning.

I placed myself in the hands of surgeons whose commitment to providing health care was sometimes compromised by mercenary interests. They seemed to smile and repeat a single line: "Does that hurt?" I played their game, and they played on my naïveté, providing minor adjustments to my face and figure, which then required more surgery to reverse the damage, remove scar tissue, and satisfy my change of mind. I was never satisfied.

These distinguished physicians had a convenient set of rationalizations for their work, their "artistry." Each presumed that in my obsession to create the perfect ballet image, I would turn to some disreputable butcher, a contingency, which they were quick to inform me, would be disastrous. After all, I was a rising starlet and deserved the best care that money could buy.

The operations found me laid out on a table, yielding to the touch of their probing fingers. I watched my life through the eye of their needle, penetrating my heart as well as the outer layers of my skin. I would become hooked on the pain, addicted to the voluptuous misery that bound my sexual identity to ballet, to an ever-increasing threshold of anguish. I was on my way to stardom, to the Balanchine look, to every look that currently passes as fashion, and, in spite of it all, to a realization of my own inner beauty—and the wisdom of the classical arts. But first, the mirror had to be broken.

After Fernando Bujones rejected an ultimatum to partner me between the sheets, I took to pining with my mother, playing together at the piano in the evening, finally laughing our way through duets of that old song "Who's Sorry Now?" My mother soon remarried, and I remained on the prowl, a solo silhouette behind the drawn shade of melancholy. The strains of loneliness put me on edge, sent my nerves roaming and eyes wandering, though never beyond the familiar haunts of the ballet world.

Still a virgin, I set about the first phase of my desperate plan, undergoing the knife for breast implants. I was still a teenager and needed my mother's permission. Appealing to her sympathy, I convinced her of the absolute necessity of the procedure. In the middle of the operation, I sat up and demanded a mirror to check on the placement of the silicone, only to discover that the doctor had nothing portable enough to suit my need. In total panic, I turned to a nurse and told her that I would trust her judgment, perceiving the fear of my madness in her eyes.

Considering the remote chance of actually pleasing me, the operation turned out to be a moderate success, at least temporarily. The snag was the lie, the utter fraudulence of knowing that I was somehow a fake, that I had fabricated a shell in which to hide myself.

Almost straight from the table, I decked myself out in a miniskirt and green suede boots, allowing my nipples to peak through my tight sweater, in the sex-kitten tradition of Brigitte Bardot. Without further ado, I stole the husband of one of my best friends, sending my conscience on a vacation to the Riviera. At last the mystery of the rose had been cracked, and I was anxious to spread the news, informing my fellow dancers how sore my body was from wrestling with such ecstasy.

The man who despoiled me, "Jules," was a rock and roll performer, complete with electric guitar, motorcycle, and leather jacket—tall, dark, and, as I would discover, loathsome. His marriage broke up, and we lived together for a couple of years, during which time I managed to support him and keep him out of Balanchine's sight.

Jules considered himself an artist of the first degree, in the vanguard of the avant-garde. He played for the rock band at the Joffrey Ballet, filling in the background sound, providing accompaniment for some forgettable moments that passed as music and dance. Rather than narcotics, Jules introduced me to a kind of "narcolepsy," that practice of mental droning that goes by the brand name "Transcendental Meditation." Like many of my later boyfriends, he took a great interest in my career and mental health.

By repeating the idiot syllables of an Indian mantra, I was supposed to relax on a daily basis, emptying my mind to restore the life energy of my exhausted body. I might even have seen the godhead, but my own head always got in the way.

I was a slow learner when it came to Eastern religions, though I was fascinated at how my brain cells could be turned into breakfast cereal each morning, that I could hear them go "snap," "crackle," "pop." Such was the level of stimulation and exchange between Jules and me. Nevertheless, I felt I might be stepping onto another planet, that I was privy to secrets my parents had been denied, that I had snatched my life from the clutches of ballet. I even believed this nonsense.

Like my father and, later, like so many of my fans, Jules thought I had potential as an actress. He was the first to introduce me to the system of Konstantin Stanislavski. This was the Russian director and acting teacher who had devised a "method" for taking possession of the unconscious, for exerting conscious control over the artistic resources that were supposed to have been blocked or repressed by social conditioning. I would later find the technique of Stanislavski and his followers inadequate to the method of composition required for the classical arts.

Jules goaded me into playing the heroine's famous death scene from *Romeo and Juliet*. With my pillow as an outward focus of attention, I sought to create what Stanislavski called a "private moment." Calling up images of my father, his knife, and his coat, I worked myself into a fit of tears, a torrent of passion that had nothing to do with Shakespeare's play. My infantile regression did not provide the reason for Juliet's inward rage and suicide. I did not understand her entrapment or the quality of her mind at the moment she discovers Romeo's death.

In living with Jules, neither tragedy nor comedy ever led to enlightenment. I did not yet know what Shakespeare knew—that callous disregard and political circumstance can destroy the possibility of both love and art, as surely as the civil strife between the Capulets and Montagues thwarted Romeo and Juliet. I would learn this powerful truth in just a few years, after I had performed the ballet version of Shakespeare's play and been caught between those modern families whose feud divides the globe into East and West.

With the change of seasons and decades from 1969 to 1970, I had established myself at the New York City Ballet as the baby ballerina who had captured the imagination of the media. I was, it seems, too sweet at sixteen, and too tiny at five feet four inches and ninety-seven pounds, not to be adored for my extreme efforts in the limelight. My change in status was to be meteoric, but I was not prepared for the roles in which I would be cast, both on the stage and off.

After dancing with the corps in such ballets as Balanchine's *Stars and Stripes, Western Symphony,* and his version of *Swan Lake,* I made an impression in the "Rubies" section of his production of *Jewels.* As a last-minute replacement for another member of the corps, I had the chance to squeeze years of sustained concentration into a few frenzied hours before curtain.

On the day after my performance, Mr. B paid me an unusual compliment in class, remarking with raised finger, "You see, everybody, this girl learn in one day, whole ballet in one rehearsal. And you know, does better than anyone! Can do anything! Quick!" Pointing his finger to his temple, he continued with emphasis, "No mistakes. Maybe better no rehearsal. Like cold water—just jump in!"

This comment stressed his bias against any sort of premeditated preparation, against the thought process itself, which he saw as an impediment that could drown spontaneity. Putting his steps on a dancer was supposed to be a creative stop sign. Do not tamper with his perfect body, his perfect ballet. In his affection for me and in his estimation of my talent, Mr. B did not seem to notice that I had already chosen my own way of working. I suppose he did not imagine that any dancer might be capable of thinking while under his choreographic thumb. Indeed, how could any dancer think as fast as Mr. B?

I quickly garnered a solo role, playing the Butterfly in *A Midsummer Night's Dream,* and moved on to a coveted principal role, the Sugar Plum Fairy in *The Nutcracker.* By the time I appeared as the lead in *Monumentum pro Gesualdo,* partnered by the veteran Conrad Ludlow, I had been discovered and adopted by the public as something of a prodigy. Clive Barnes, then writing for the New York *Times,* identified me as the new darling of the dance world, capping his review with some generous advice that I am sure I took quite seriously:

. . . But you know the young Gelsey Kirkland—she's around 17 I think—in "Monumentum" is something quite unusual. She has grace, heart and spirit. What might happen to her is—dance is a fragile discipline—anyone's guess. She is, however, one of the rarest and most wonderful kids ever to emerge in American dance. She might be remarkable. If she takes it easy, gets conceited and blows it, she could be nothing. But this, I believe, is a special talent.

The *Times* followed up with an interview and article entitled "High School Dropout and, at 17, a Ballet Star." I was quoted as saying, "Dancing doesn't come easy for me. I have to work against everything." Everything included my body, my routine, my teachers, and, sometimes, my choreographer. I was often troubled by the media. On one hand, the reviews were a source of reward or punishment, which I characterized as a "report card." On the other hand, there was usually little correspondence between the reactions of the critics and my perceptions. Acclaim and popularity were dwarfed by my single-minded commitment to realizing the image demanded for each dance, by my seething dissatisfaction with my own accomplishments.

Writing again for the *Times,* on January 3, 1970, Clive Barnes noted my development in two of my roles in *The Nutcracker:*

And then there was Gelsey Kirkland leading the Marzipan Shepherdesses. It is a special pleasure to see Miss Kirkland right now in the springtime of her talents. Here is a girl destined for great things, but her present dancing is tinged with a very special joy, a very special awareness of her own developing accomplishment.

This was even more evident . . . when, partnered by a more than dashing and gallant Edward Villella, she danced the leading role of the Sugar Plum Fairy. There was no difference here—she took the ballet by right, as a young princess. There is already such authority and breeding that you can hardly wait to see the dancer she must surely develop into in a few more years.

Such adulation would go to anyone's head, but I could not bring the opinions of others into accord with my heart, which seemed always on the verge of breaking, with either joy or sorrow. I was a teenager in a tailspin, unable to accept love in any form except that which I gave to the lonely pursuit of myself, the vicious circle that led back to ballet, to the promise of fulfillment.

On my first tour with the company, I caused quite a commotion by ransacking my hotel room in my sleep. My habits, such as somnambulism, were accepted within a community that thrived on neuroses, slow starvation, and high anxiety.

At the invitation of Prince Rainier and Princess Grace, the company played Monaco during the summer of 1969. For Balanchine, this trip was a return to his roots as a choreographer, where he had served the Ballets

Russes of Serge Diaghilev, the iconoclastic impresario who ruled ballet during the twenties. I was dismayed by our royal reception in Monte Carlo, the sort of formal affair that generally puts me into a cold sweat, with the pins and needles that go with the atmosphere of aristocratic pretense, however hospitable.

Returning to Saratoga, the company's traditional summer camping ground, I became the target of an upstart dancer. During a break from rehearsal, the fellow used his homosexuality as a license to feel the breasts of various women. Catching me by surprise, he shocked me out of my daydreaming and announced to all within earshot, "Oh, Gelsey, why, they're freezing! Cold as a witch's tit!"

Even in my embarrassment, I found time to wonder at the motivation of such cruelty, how such insensitive creatures managed to rationalize themselves to the world as artists. Could talent exist without conscience? Was I unable to take a joke? Faced with such behavior, I would become more and more an offending spirit—cold as a bitch's wit.

My position within the company seemed to be consolidated when I was chosen for the title role of Mr. B's new version of Stravinsky's pre–World War I ballet *Firebird,* first choreographed by the rebellious Russian, Michel Fokine. With this memorable dance, the world was suddenly at my feet, beneath a tightrope stretched by the media.

Shortly after the production opened at the New York State Theater, May 28, 1970, I was startled to see myself spread out across six pages of *Life* magazine, yielding the honors of the cover to Nixon's old pal, Bebe Rebozo. Featured coverage followed with *Dance Magazine, Forbes, Seventeen, Saturday Review, Women's Wear Daily,* and so on, snippets of human interest and dance news, fashion and feminism. Everyone seemed to have an angle on me except me. The *Life* article was fraught with romantic illusions:

Gelsey Kirkland has huge, luminous blue eyes, clear pale skin and a body so frail-looking that the great choreographer George Balanchine could visualize her in the role of "a little golden bird"—the demanding Firebird of Stravinsky's ballet. At 17, scarcely more than a little girl herself, she is already the embodiment of every little girl's secret dream of glory . . . the youngest member in the company ever to have a principal role choreographed for her . . . Almost as if she feared pressing fortune, Gelsey speaks of learning and improving, not of applause . . . Her whole world is the world of ballet—difficult and unforgiving, flowing with loveliness.

My side of the story was lost somehow. I would have had no way to tell my version back then. I had never actually learned to speak or write. I did not think my opinions were worth repeating.

I was first informed that I had been cast as the Firebird by a stage manager. I assumed he had to be mistaken until I read my name on the posted schedule. That meant it had to be true. The very idea that Mr. B wanted to choreograph a ballet on me was enough to make me dizzy with excitement.

Though never my favorite ballet, the part of the Firebird offered an extraordinary challenge, for which I did not feel prepared. I had grown up seeing both Melissa Hayden and Violette Verdy dance in an older, more dramatic version of the same ballet. They had been favorably compared to Maria Tallchief, who had established the character in Balanchine's 1949 renovation after Fokine. The original Firebird, by default, had been Tamara Karsavina, who had received the historical opportunity when Anna Pavlova rejected the role. Pavlova apparently hated the music. I would soon discover how wise she had been, how well she knew the score.

The 1970 choreography was a remake undertaken by Balanchine with some help from Jerome Robbins, whose Broadway background and even broader outlook on ballet made him a match for Mr. B. Their egos always seemed to mesh, thanks to the contrast of their concerns and preferences, minimizing personal competition, helped along with the deference paid by the younger Robbins to the acknowledged master. Robbins, who had had his own company and served as associate artistic director at the New York City Ballet, brought the sensibility of *West Side Story* and *Fiddler on the Roof* into the popular arena that Balanchine had already constructed for ballet. Mr. B had done his stint on Broadway in the thirties.

In this new production of *Firebird*, elaborate sets and costumes, using original designs by Marc Chagall, almost took precedence over the dancers. For Mr. B, emphasizing the design and the score must have seemed consistent with the dictum formulated by his early mentor, Diaghilev, the first producer of the ballet, who stated, "The perfect ballet can only be created by the closest fusion of the three elements of dancing, painting, and music." Perfection for the dancer and the audience would depend on the kind of fusion that took place.

In *Firebird*, I found myself working for, and often against, three men ranked among the brightest artistic lights of the century: Balanchine the choreographer, Stravinsky the composer, and Chagall the painter. Their individual visions and common Russian heritage fused within the production, though Balanchine was the only one on the scene, constantly overseeing the synthesis. The role of the American, Robbins, was limited to secondary contributions, notably the comic monsters who appeared in the Danse Infernale.

Three Russian men against one American girl was not exactly a fair fight, and I consider myself lucky to have won a draw, or perhaps drawn a lesson from my defeat. I was fighting as always to give Mr. B what I thought he wanted. I limped through rehearsals, still suffering with tendonitis. My legs were often bandaged to the knee and covered with leg-warmers. I usually went home at night hoping to crawl inside one of my toe shoes and fall asleep forever.

A conflict emerged during the rehearsals. It was never put into words. Mr. B wanted me to play a bird, and I wanted to play a creature who would be something more. I was determined to endow the bird with character, with human compassion and strength. The story, as I remembered it, seemed to call for those qualities.

For the most part unspoken and unconscious, our antagonism became a clash of interpretations and personalities. According to the conventional code, the dancer had no right to challenge choreographic authority. My headstrong and instinctual defiance first took the outward form of supreme cooperation. On the conscious level, I was quite sincere in my commitment to deliver whatever he asked. But what he asked for ran against my grain to the point of constant frustration and intense pain. How could this wonderful man, with his two kindred spirits in the wings, have been asking ne to relinquish those qualities within the dance that I had come to identify as being most human?

In an interview with *Dance Magazine,* Balanchine reflected on the process through which he supposedly created the character and the dancer:

> For this ballet, I wanted a small dancer, a child, but with good elevation, so I took Gelsey. She is not yet grown but she is well-trained, out of our School. There are many fine dancers in the company but I chose this one. Gelsey will grow to a woman and who knows what she will be then? But for now she is my Firebird.

As for my training, one of my early teachers at the School, Elise Reiman, in a published interview, came closer to the truth:

> Gelsey Kirkland was eight years old when she started in my class. I don't think we can take credit for Gelsey. She is self-taught. She was a very difficult child who resisted . . .

Through the rehearsal process, I was only dimly aware that my resistance was a struggle to retain my as yet undefined dignity. Because I was unable to say why I disagreed with him, my convictions had to be denied. I tried to keep my anger bottled up inside me. I tried not to ask dumb questions. How could I defy his genius? There had to be something wrong with me. I began to identify my best impulses as the symptoms of a disease. I was somehow sick or wicked for thinking and working as I did.

As the opening drew near, I continued to be mystified by what Balanchine envisioned for my character. He was annoyed when I stopped in the middle of a solo variation to ask for his help: "Mr. B, what am I supposed to do with my arms?"

After flapping his own for a moment, he spluttered, "You know, dear, normal. Like canary."

His attitude intimidated me. He saw me only as a tiny bird who could move fast, with high elevation. From his point of view, it was not necessary to build any specific quality into my arms or my body as a whole, as long as I delivered the illusion of flight, speed, grace, soaring, and so forth. To have followed his instructions to the letter would have required little on my part in the way of character. He had to want something more; he was just not saying so.

Balanchine's image of me as a bird became a crisis by the time I tried on the costume. Karinska, the lady in blue, had executed Chagall's design, rendering what I saw as a flaming gold and red abomination. It was like something that an overgrown canary might wear, not something that a ballerina should ever have to put on, or dance in. The plumage was crippling. There was a gold bodice and red Miss America banner, no panties, and a long chiffon tail. Stepping into this contraption, I was a little ball of rage, not a Firebird. As the fitting session was prolonged for photographers, I spent the time glaring over my shoulder at Mr. B, giving him the old evil eye.

He took me aside, informing me with nasally muted tones, "You know, dear, I think you wear black page boy wig, like in original Chagall. Is way it should be." Unable to control my sobbing, begging him to reconsider, I was silenced suddenly when he grabbed me by the ears. He then did his best to console me on the wig. "Don't worry, dear. You'll see. Will be good." I took scant pleasure in his final decision to leave out the hairpiece.

Just before opening night, a costume parade was staged in the Promenade of the New York State Theater, attended by the paparazzi, who are always present for such events at Lincoln Center. This was part of the company's publicity campaign, in which I was to be introduced as the new Firebird. After marching in and about, I gravitated with the cast to one of the tables that had been laid out with hors d'oeuvre, to look if not to eat. With photographers and celebrities elbowing each other for my attention, Mr. B rushed into my immediate circle, grabbed me by my shoulders with some force, and lunged with his face toward mine, as if to plant a kiss on my lips.

I was too fast. To his considerable embarrassment, I turned my head away in time to avoid him. Looking over his shoulder, I saw my two friends, Ricky Weiss and Cathy Haigney, stunned by my behavior. How could anyone, any dancer, do such a thing, even think of doing such a thing, to George Balanchine?

My deliberate faux pas could be smoothed over, but my performance in *Firebird* could not. My trouble with the dance derived initially from Balanchine's neglect to tell any of the dancers what the ballet was about. In his pan of the opening performance for the *Times,* Clive Barnes noted, "Not even the story is fully told." It was apparently not meant to be told.

As is well known in the ballet world, *Firebird* originated with an old Russian fairy tale which appeared in countless variations. The story concerned a magical bird who rescued a Prince and his beloved Princess from the enchanted forest of an evil magician. The plot went as follows:

The hero, Prince Ivan, first captured the Firebird. Out of pity, he released her and, in return for his kindness, received one of the bird's feathers as a gift. This magical feather was to bring the Firebird to his rescue if the need should ever arise. The Prince then fell in love with a beautiful Princess, captive of an evil magician. In fighting the magician and his legion of monsters, the Prince pulled out the feather to call for the Firebird, who arrived, as promised, to save the day. The Prince and Princess married and presumably lived happily ever after, and the bird of fire flew away. Mr. B actually identified the hero with Stalin, at the same time ruling out any hidden meaning. So much for fairy tales.

Unlike his 1949 treatment, Balanchine had decided to abstract the story to bring the elements of the dance into harmony with the symbols of the music and the painting. I did attempt to give him the kind of bird he requested for the first performance. At the same time, I continued to work out my own version of the character and the drama, as indicated by Byron Belt's subsequent review, among others:

> In the handsome new "Firebird," Gelsey Kirkland's third performance was warmer and more effective, particularly in the "Dying Swan" use of her lovely arms.

After the production premiered, I performed the part throughout the year. I added touches to the character, as in the Firebird's final solo, endowing the dance more and more with her personal struggle to know her own nature, her own power and integrity. Through the deliberate placement of her steps, my character resisted the possibilities of defeat within the music. I found a way to allow my soul to soar above the hostile environment that enclosed me.

I did not change the steps that Mr. B had choreographed, but filled them with my own fire. I instilled her jetés, when she arrived to save the day, with the speed and strength necessary to distinguish the forces at work in the clash between the monsters and the human characters. To establish the trust between the Prince and the Firebird, I invested those subtle qualities in the movement that would allow him to depend on her to return, to have faith that she would answer his summons.

This last touch was especially important because Balanchine had removed the plot device of the feather that the Prince initially used to call for her help. The revision was noted by Clive Barnes:

I did not notice that Ivan, when threatened by the evil magician, Kotschei [sic], pulled out the magic feather to summon the Firebird, and without that incident the purpose of the narrative loses its continuity.

I continued to build the character through a long run of performances, playing off the qualities of the three leading men, Peter Martins, Jacques d'Amboise, and Jean-Pierre Bonnefous, who alternately danced the role of the hero, Prince Ivan. My favorite teacher at the school, Stanley Williams, privately complimented my performance to Mr. B. Stanley told him that I had made a unique contribution to the role. I learned that Mr. B reacted with furious silence. In the end, he would take the part away from me.

Our ways of looking at the world must have been irreconcilable almost from the beginning. I never knew what to do with my love for him. Peter the Great was famous for his "windows on the West." As a Westerner, I wanted to peer from my side through those windows; I was especially curious about the Russian ballet. In pursuing my approach to art, I would turn eventually to an older and broader classical tradition. Mr. B had already rejected that tradition, including most of the Russian repertory. It should have come as no surprise that I would find myself in deep trouble. Perhaps neither of us could see that we were moving in opposite directions.

Our cultural contention was complicated by our artistic temperaments. Without a shared vision, the making of art can be an explosive affair. The working relationships are volatile in a theatrical production. Each artist invests images and ideas with passion. Egos shatter with each disagreement. Contrary opinions threaten the integrity of the company. Balanchine solved these problems by forbidding dissent. That was his prerogative. But he abused that privilege to the point of discouraging even the most innocent question. He often invited those who did not approve of the way he ran his theatre to leave. The problem was, there seemed to be no place else to go.

In fairness to the many admirers of Balanchine, as critical as I may sound at times, I believe just as strongly in their right to challenge me, to make their own judgments, to allow our ideas to develop through passionate interplay and free discussion. I love to argue, to match wits, to test whatever wisdom I have managed to gather in life. The problem I have experienced in the world of ballet is that free discussion has been inhibited by idol worship and prejudice, by the pressures for success, by the fears of failure within the profession of dance.

I am sorry that Mr. B is gone. I have the feeling that we might be able to talk now. His disciples can defend him, but they cannot answer my questions with his inimitable voice. With time, my curiosity has sharpened. The difficulty with Balanchine, as with many of the Russian men I have known, was that he did not think women were capable of engaging him with ideas, or that Americans were capable of understanding his Russian homeland. We hurt each other in so many ways.

Within the context of the ballet, my efforts toward dramatic continuity were doomed to fail. As the heroine, I simply could not overcome a ballet that was not meant to be interpreted but experienced. I was caught, like my character, in the torrent of savage rhythm, in the flood of Chagall's floating images.

My first impression of Stravinsky's music caused me literally to place cotton in my ears. Mr. B revered the beauty of the music as tantamount to the ritual of an Orthodox service. He looked up to Stravinsky as a father figure, an ultimate intellectual authority. For the scores of his ballets, Balanchine turned to Stravinsky more than to any other composer. They shared faith in Russian Orthodoxy and a fierce allegiance to their Russian homeland. Regarding Mr. B's version of *Firebird,* Stravinsky raved, "I prefer Balanchine's choreography . . . to the whole Fokine ballet."

Stravinsky transformed the method of classical composition in music in much the same way that Balanchine had transformed the classical ballet. They were birds of a modern feather. Though I tried, I simply could not adopt their approach. Their paradigm for the mind of the artist was a technical formula that I sensed limited the scope of my creativity. According to their aesthetic code, the human condition was reflected primarily through animal and mechanical imagery, to be realized through the senses by way of instinct and imitation. As Stravinsky put it, "An artist is simply a kind of pig snouting truffles."

His music was intended to arouse primeval instincts. His career changed the course of musical history in our century and, by way of rhythmic invasion, altered the sensibility and dynamic of ballet. My instincts filled me with doubt. I dreaded most the final wedding ceremony of the Prince and Princess, when no dancer was allowed to move or distract from the music, as it rolled over the audience with wave after wave of Stravinsky magic.

As a dancer I rebelled against rhythm. I did not care for its effects. Rather than an expression of freedom or release, I felt rhythm obscured meaning and constrained my movement. In longing to tell a story through my dance, I was frustrated by music that appealed only to my sense of time and tempo. I needed more than the propulsion of a beat.

Stravinsky replaced the thematic development of classical music with a range of sensations that alternately jolted or lulled the mind. According to Roman Vlad's critical account, "Some of Stravinsky's works are designed as an opiate or a means of escape from reality." Such was the design of *Firebird,* though its effect on me was perhaps opposite from that intended by the composer. My desire for clarity caused me to impose my own musical concept on the dance. It was as if I provided my own accompaniment, interpreting the score with a set of physical accents which allowed me to move and maintain conscious control. I danced with a passion to spite the music.

What was the special quality that I brought to the stage that seemed inappropriate for Balanchine and Stravinsky? Why was I out of place? Why was I confounded by their steps and notes? The answers are all one: without knowing it, I was trying to be a classical artist on a modern stage.

I had already begun to address the problem of thematic development that is the key to my art. In each ballet, I would seize upon a theme, an idea that could be translated into a physical image. In the deepest sense, for a classical dancer, each note or step in context becomes a moment in the transformation of the theme, a continuous process toward the realization of an ideal voice. I was trying to speak through the dance.

The stage design was ultimately as insurmountable as the stumbling blocks in the music. I had vertigo when I looked at the set. Chagall's alteration of perspective caused an almost surreal sense of disorientation. I found an obstacle course rigged to trip the dancer at every turn. With each step, I could never be sure that my foot would meet a solid floor. I thought at any moment I might plunge through the stage, that a trapdoor might drop beneath me. The danger of a fall was more real than the dreams that filled the theatre.

To prevail against such a backdrop seemed to require that I dance on air. The field of vision, the projection of our three-dimensional world onto a two-dimensional surface, was obscured through the violent juxtaposition of colors—what Chagall called his "Fourth Dimension." He invited the spectators to surrender to his haunting nightmare images, to his symbols of hallucinatory sexuality. Yet for me, as overwhelmed as I was, there was something missing in his painting, an omission that threw me off balance. My secure frame of reference vanished.

As a dancer I find my way and keep my balance by means of light and gravity. Chagall chose not to conceive of light as a unifying principle of perspective; along the same lines, he painted in defiance of gravity. He was drawn to illusion, celebrating its triumph over reality. I kept losing my bearings.

I learned quickly how to recover my balance in a hazardous environment, how to make an accident look intentional. I owe that in part to Chagall. Thanks to him, as well as Stravinsky and Balanchine, I became expert in the art of getting out of a jam. But there were serious drawbacks in distinguishing myself from such authorities. I was learning who I might be on the stage only by learning who I was not. Without developing a positive sense of identity, without support for my ideas and aspirations, I was never really sure who I was from one moment to the next.

The beginning of the decade was especially significant because of my exposure to the Russian defectors Rudolf Nureyev and Natalia Makarova. Nureyev having defected almost a decade earlier, visited New York with London's Royal Ballet, partnering Margot Fonteyn. Makarova had only recently defected and was attempting to put her feet on the ground in the

West. These defectors from his homeland seemed to threaten Balanchine's monopoly on American ballet. He was human enough to be jealous.

Late in 1970, I was stunned to see Makarova in *Giselle,* the Romantic ballet originally choreographed by Jules Perrot and Jean Coralli in 1841. As far as many ballet fans are concerned, it is the "classic of classics," with the madness of the protagonist making her as complicated and challenging a character for the ballerina as Hamlet is for the actor. Makarova's performance was extraordinary and poignant in its dramatic impact, the most powerful dance I had ever seen. I was shocked when Mr. B said in class, "The only reason she's good Giselle is because she has time to change shoes between variations in first act. Soft to hard."

His comment indicated that her light touch and silent leaps could be explained by a technical trick, while I was enthralled by Makarova's daring mode of expression, the range of her voice as a dancer. He contended that the only dancer who was ever a great Giselle was the famous Russian ballerina Olga Spessivtseva, explaining that she had been able to excel because she was actually insane. For the life of me, I could not understand why Mr. B seemed to dislike the ballet and why he chose to mock Makarova, especially when he subsequently agreed to coach her in his ballet *Theme and Variations.*

In 1971, my mischievous friend Patsy and I, disguised as mod British dancers, stole our way into the Metropolitan Opera to see Nureyev and Fonteyn in *Romeo and Juliet,* a version of the ballet by Kenneth MacMillan, set to the Prokofiev score. The style of the Royal Ballet made the dancers look more like real human beings. I was instantly in love with "Rudi and Margot," overwhelmed by the sheer romantic spectacle, by the eloquent virtuosity of their partnership. His explosive dynamic seemed the perfect complement for her flair as an actress. Their ability to dance the drama comprised a moment that might be said to have changed my sensibility, providing a direction and model that left the New York City Ballet in the dust.

On the following day, I held back my tears when Mr. B dismissed the performances and slighted the dancers. He described Nureyev as a passable dancer whose problem was "always tries to be prince." Then he asserted that Fonteyn could not dance at all, that she had "hands like spoons." At those words, I rose from my place on the floor and hobbled out of Balanchine's class forever. I remember seeing the intent faces of the other dancers as I passed, hearing Mr. B's voice fading away behind me.

I remained with the company and continued with my performances of *Firebird.* I had already begun to attend classes given by Maggie Black, a former dancer who had studied with British choreographer Antony Tudor. I had realized that if I did not change my training, I would have to quit dancing, a victim of tendonitis. Under Maggie's guidance, I began concentrated work on placement and the linearity of movement, gradually undoing some of the damage that had been done to my body.

Regardless of my improvement, Mr. B would never forgive me for not returning to his class, for allowing someone else to have a hand in my career and my education. Perhaps he resented the source of my progress. As an indication of his hostility toward Maggie, he nicknamed her "Black Magic." She was the one who really guided me through *Firebird*.

A combination of factors—including my absence from his class and my success with the ballet—caused Balanchine to reduce my repertory and deny me new roles. I was probably allowed to continue with *Firebird* because the schedule for the season had already been announced. I was still too hot an item to bury completely. Mr. B gave me the silent treatment, snubbing me for more than a year, refusing to acknowledge my existence, even face to face in the elevator of the theatre. He attempted to coerce me back into the fold by punishing me, assuming that I would never hold out. He underestimated my stubborn will.

With Maggie, I knew that I had begun to therapeutically reverse the mistraining that I had received during those early years. The condition of my tendons was alleviated slowly, while the clarity and strength of my movement was enhanced. Mr. B offered no compliments, instead taunting me on occasion, "You know, dear, you look constipated."

Everyone seemed to be on his side, including my family. My mother received a letter from a successful actress who had been my father's fourth wife, Haila Stoddard. A gracious lady, Haila had remained a close friend of our family throughout my childhood, even after my father had passed away. The letter offered the following advice:

Dear Nancy,

. . . This is none of my business, but I think I should pass it on. Tamara Geva called last week. She's Balanchine's first wife and knows him well. She had a great interest in Gelsey and believes she has it to be a Prima, so she watches her career. She was puzzled—feeling Gelsey hadn't been given the parts she should have been given lately. She [Geva] was visiting Danilova's class and asked about Gelsey. Danilova told her Balanchine was angry because Gelsey was studying on the outside with a Maggie Black. Danilova also said she's talked to Gelsey, telling her about Balanchine's anger and his deep capacity for vengeance. He swore Gelsey wouldn't be given anything important until she stopped the outside studying. Apparently Gelsey feels she's being helped, but as Geva pointed out, nothing is worth stunting her career at this point. If you'd like to talk to Geva or have Geva talk to Gelsey, she'd be glad to. If not, just forget it. After a good deal of thought, it seemed to me that I should tell you about it, and you can use your knowledge and judgement about the matter . . .

Love,

    Haila

In spite of the efforts of those around me, I refused to change my mind. My progress continued in Maggie's class. She coached me in strict secrecy and worked with me as much as five hours a day, refusing to accept payment for her services. We were inseparable for two years. Our social lives were entirely given to ballet. Maggie was married to an actor. I was hurt and embarrassed when I heard absurd rumors about the two of us, the sort of gossip that sometimes occurs when two women spend an unusual amount of time together. The time was well spent.

Unfortunately, Maggie became overly possessive, too certain that she possessed complete knowledge with regard to ballet and my career. She warned that I would never achieve success without her, comparing me to one of the legendary Russian ballerinas: "Gelsey, you could be as great as Ulanova, but not without me."

This is a common problem with ballet teachers, who seem to become paranoid about losing their reputations and their students. The wise teacher recognizes that knowledge of the art grows only by allowing the student exposure to various disciplines and styles of teaching—only by encouraging the student's questions to multiply, to the point that the answers of each teacher are exhausted by each student.

The gift of the teacher is to let go before the aspiring artist becomes locked within a closed system of instruction. Maggie provided me with a special gift that in the end made my break with her inevitable. She was the first to teach me how to resist the habit of the mirror, how to dance without the constant partnership of my reflection. A process had begun that I would have to repeat every time I fell back into dependency, every time I had to look at my image for some form of reassurance. For the first time, I took over my destiny within the studio, even if my confidence did not yet extend into the outside world. I had chosen my own path.

Throughout the early phases of my career, the mirror was my nemesis, seductive to the point of addiction. Stepping through the looking glass meant confronting a double who exposed all of my flaws and pointed out all of my physical imperfections. Over a period of time, the image in my mind clashed with the image in the glass. Until the opposition between the images was resolved, I saw myself as a walking apology, unable to attain or maintain my constantly refined ideal of physical beauty.

With all of my insecurities intensified, I became my own worst critic, embarking on an aesthetic quest for perfection that in the end would heal the wounds I had inflicted upon myself. Trying to perfect both my appearance and the quality of my movement, I was unaware of a contradiction. As I continued to educate myself, my love and anger wed within my personality. I remained a child. I worked and lived in isolation, an almost absolute solitude that I now see was unnecessary. I was misled, sometimes deliberately. And I was not alone.

The endless repetition of barre exercises in front of a mirror reflects a distorted image many people have of ballet, an image shared by many dancers. The physical side of the discipline does involve a certain degree of tedium, to say nothing of the pain. But the hours of practice are minor compared to the emotional terror that can sometimes haunt a ballerina when she studies her reflection in the mirror. This anxiety is not due to simple vanity or fear of professional rejection.

As in the myth of Narcissus, the beautiful youth who falls in love with his own reflection, the relationship between the dancer and her mirror image is an intimacy of extraordinary power and potentially perilous consequence. Most dancers ultimately seem to drown themselves in their own images, pushed by forces unseen. The dimensions of the tragedy are revealed only when lives and personalities are destroyed. Until then the damage remains invisible.

I suspect that every dancer experiences the mirror in a uniquely personal way, although many are perhaps oblivious to the power it exerts over their lives and how that state of artistic servitude has come into being. Certainly few dancers have taken the relationship to the extremes of my early career, and fewer still have managed to reverse the hold of the mirror.

As a primary teaching tool for dance, the mirror fosters the delusion that beauty is only skin-deep, that truth is found only in the plasticity of movement. It seems preferable to imitate rather than create. Imitation can be varied to create the impression of originality. There are endless possibilities for breaking the human mold into novel patterns. To be daring in dance no longer involves risk, virtuosity, and strength of conviction. The dancer can win approval for steps that require no real decision in creative or compositional terms.

The dancer is trained to watch, to enter the world of the mirror until it is no longer necessary to even look. To the extent that a dancer becomes a complacent reflection, he or she does not learn how to test beauty, how to discover its inner life. In this way, the mirror can trap a dancer's soul, ultimately breaking creative spirit. Such a dancer is created, but does not know how to create. With success and popularity, the situation becomes more precarious. At any moment, with the capricious changes of fashion, a glance to check the mirror may reveal tragedy—that he or she has been created for nothing.

Lack of originality is nothing new. More than two centuries ago, Noverre expressed his concern over "this mad passion to imitate what is inimitable." He was appalled by the state of the art:

Must one be a dancer to perceive what little wit prevails in a pas de deux, the nonsense usually to be encountered in ballets, the lack of expression of the executants and the mediocrity of the talents of the composers?

Such deficiencies have become institutionalized through a system of formal education that seems more devoted to the mirror than to the art of dance. Noverre offered a diagnosis and prescribed a remedy:

> In order that our art may arrive at that degree of the sublime which I demand and hope for it, it is imperative for dancers to divide their time and studies between the mind and body, and that both become the object of their application; but, unfortunately, all is given to the latter and nothing to the former.

Ballet is a riddle of means and ends. Speaking from experience, that riddle cannot be solved solely through formal rules applied in the mirror. Classical virtuosity is more than technique, line, proportion, and balance. It is as if the performer and spectator come together to hold in their hands a bird with a broken wing. The creature can be felt to stir, to struggle for freedom. Its life responds to human warmth; its wing might brush your cheek as it flies away.

The classical performer invites the audience to eavesdrop on the most sublime conversation. To achieve such empathy through movement requires of the dancer the most demanding kind of inspiration: the mind must reckon with love, as if to bind and heal a broken heart. For the audience, this is best understood during those moments of enthusiasm when the clapping of hands signifies a kind of reverence, when thoughts are able to comprehend the feelings that have been inspired by the artist.

Such a performance has become rare indeed. Perhaps both audience and artist fail to notice what is often missing behind the steps of the dance and the notes of music. I confronted the problem for years. I asked questions endlessly. If I had a tickle for every time I was told to shut up during training and rehearsal, I might have died laughing. I suppose I was a real pain. Did I lack wisdom that I continued to ask, or did those who avoided my questions lack sufficient answers and courage to face cross examination from a child? I am still asking.

Chapter Five

FROM HOT BATH
TO COLD WAR

During the period that I studied with Maggie and lived with Jules, I passed through the first phase of my disentanglement from Balanchine. The physical and mental knots were not easy to untie, especially while I remained with the New York City Ballet. Between the time that I became a soloist in 1970 and a principal dancer in 1972, I came to the realization that the sun did not rise and fall with George Balanchine, even in the world of ballet.

Temporarily shut out of new roles in Balanchine's repertory, I did manage to gather experience with roles in ballets by the company's crew of resident choreographers, those who lived in Balanchine's shadow. I thought of them at the time as the American group who gave the critics something to compare with the work of the Russian master. But, from my point of view, the differences in style were minimal, arising merely from a choice of different scores and sets. Their techniques and formulas were spin-offs from Balanchine; their ideas were usually derivative.

The New York City Ballet fostered a kind of choreographic contest to determine who would become Balanchine's favorite disciple. The choreographers in 1971 included John Clifford, John Taras, Jacques d'Amboise, and Richard Tanner, as well as the more established figure of Jerome Robbins. Their personalities were as varied as the roles that I played in their ballets. I was cast as every kind of existential creature—from birds to bugs, from abstract symbols of the modern condition to more realistic and romantic characters—all related through the technique and aesthetic that had been spawned by Balanchine.

The vision of each of the choreographers was technically realized through Mr. B's system of expediency. Under the regime of his training, the dancers received facile classroom corrections along the lines of cupping a ball in the palm of the hand or extending the foot as if to balance a champagne glass on the heel. The cumulative effect was to turn hands and feet into claws and talons; such exaggerated images actually fit the design of a wide range of modern choreography. Twisted extremities provided interest and the illusion of depth to dancers who had been taught not to think.

In my Cook's tour of contemporary choreography, I turned each ballet into a problem of logistics. Within the limits of each role, I absorbed a massive vocabulary of steps and combinations. The trick was to make the individual steps invisible, to make them disappear completely through the musical and dramatic transitions that I constructed within the dance. Without actually changing choreography, I tried to compose each of the steps and variations according to my own ideas of phrasing and focus. With Maggie Black's guidance, I provided each ballet with a theme, an interpretative key that allowed me to place modernism in perspective.

My approach was motivated by both artistic preference and the physical need to survive. By composing each step rather than simply executing it, I was not only learning how to judge the choreography, I was saving my body through education. My knowledge in these areas would expand rapidly over the next few years.

One of my early lessons involved coming to terms with my sexuality on the stage. In a Jerome Robbins ballet, *The Cage,* set to an eerie Stravinsky score, I played a kind of femme fatale. For this dance, I had to alter the way that I was accustomed to carrying myself in order to change both sexual and human identity. The ballet told the story of female insects who ravish and then kill their mates. My character, the "novice," was not only an insect, but a born killer.

During a coaching session, Maggie and I hunted cockroaches in the studio, looking for an angle on the movement quality of my character. We were delighted to discover a number of healthy specimens. Observation confirmed hypothesis: bugs do not rely on eyes and ears, but antennae. They do not see where they are going, they seem to feel their way, wiggling, squirming, creeping, and darting. These were the qualities of movement that I would master. I continued my "entomological" studies, graduating from the cockroach to the praying mantis. The problem remained, how to translate such absurdity into the steps without looking like a complete fool.

In one of the rehearsals, Robbins offered advice on how to interpret my role: "Gelsey, in the very beginning, when you are born, the other bugs will remove a scarf from your face, and you should think of . . . well . . . have you ever seen *The Bride of Frankenstein?* It's just like when the monster's bandages are removed. That is what you should think of at that moment." I was now a cross between a cockroach and Frankenstein's bride, quite a predicament for a ballerina. Merely thinking of such images did not create the qualities that would animate the dance. The scarf was intended to suggest the larval membrane that initially enveloped the character. What was I supposed to do with my eyes when it was removed? How would I relate to the other bugs on the stage? How would I lure my prospective mate into the trap? How could my movement appear both seductive and deadly?

With Maggie I discovered a way of moving that corresponded to the birth or awakening of a monstrous insect. We worked to extend grotesque angularity through the rest of the moments in the dance. I took what I learned during these coaching sessions into the rehearsal hall. My insect had to mesh with the choreographical web that Robbins had in mind. Behind his back, we dancers joked that the ballet was the autobiography of Jerome Robbins. It seems that he was actually thinking of the ancient myth of the Amazons.

My perplexity with the part was complicated by my sense of propriety. The physical shape through which I expressed my sexuality had to be severely altered if I were to make a credible entry into the insect world. At a certain point in the ballet, my bug pointed its feelers down between her legs as a provocation for her approaching mate. I had to overcome my reticence about that part of my anatomy. I also had to fight against my technical reluctance to turn in on myself, once again resisting modernism.

The classical dancer turns out the entire body, opening from the heart as an expression of grace and strength. It is not so much a turn as a constant spiral, a circular dynamic that involves the torso, arms, and legs. There is a modern tendency in ballet training to shift the focus to the lower body, to dance only with the legs. Turning out solely from the hips and thighs places emphasis on the genital area. In *Dance-Movement Therapy,* psychoanalyst Elaine V. Siegel pinpoints turning out as an aspect of body image with a number of possible sexual connotations:

> The open crotch in all ballet positions not only allows for the "line" most pleasing to the balletomane but also reassures the audience that the dancer's physical prowess is not a sexual attack . . . Actually, turnout could also be seen as an expression of supreme sexual self-confidence. It depends on who is turning out how.

It is really a matter of how the impulse for turning out is translated into the body, whether that impulse originates above or below the hips. If the impulse is generated with a pelvic thrust, the ballerina may take her place beside the striptease artist.

In executing a sexual attack in the Robbins ballet, I was forced to assume a turned-in position, a placement closer to modern dance than classical ballet. Maggie did her best to bolster my confidence. Without going up on pointe, I had to stomp around and deliver vicious blows to the male who had intruded into my nest. I tried to think of boys who had betrayed me. I composed the movement to look like a creature that strikes by instinct. As directed, I caught the head of my mate between my thighs and broke his neck.

What looked to be a primitive act of savagery was actually the outcome of applied technique. The timing of the kill, prescribed by Robbins, required

premeditated choices. In order to be able to cause something to happen on
the stage, I had to be able to calculate how and why.

Before the opening of *The Cage*, I received a telegram from Jerry Robbins,
who was not able to attend:

DEAR NOVICE

SORRY YOUR PAPA COULDN'T COACH YOU ALL THE WAY BUT YOU
KNOW I AM WITH YOU TONIGHT WITH ALL BEST WISHES

BIG BUG JERRY

It was Maggie Black who usually coached me all the way during this period.
Our activities had to be carried out in strict secrecy. The New York City
Ballet would never have accepted the idea of outside coaching on any pro-
duction.

A contrast is often observed between the Robbins approach and that of
Balanchine. Robbins liked to mark or set a ballet at a speed somewhere
between a walk-through and a run-through, while Balanchine demanded a
total energy commitment at all times. Yet, they both encouraged spontaneity. Robbins accepted Balanchine's dictum: "Don't ask why it must be like
this. Don't analyze. Just do it." I found myself facing the same dilemma with
either choreographer: any ballerina who worried about means and ends
would soon find herself on her end without any means.

I worked with Robbins on a number of other ballets, always feeling that I
was groping in the dark. Rehearsing *Scherzo Fantastique*, I was challenged
with performing a slow, supported arabesque in the middle of a flurry of fast
steps. In the past, I might have resorted to the familiar Balanchine lift of the
leg, a cheat to achieve extraordinary extension by raising the hip. By this
time, I was determined to deliver the step keeping my hips level. Concentrating on placement and trying not to injure myself, I was interrupted by the
voice of Jerome Robbins blaring over the theatre microphone: "Miss Kirkland, will you take that goddamn tiara off your head!" I had nothing on my
head. What he was complaining about was the overly proper way I was
carrying myself. I was too stiff, too much of a "princess." My running off the
stage in tears brought Robbins to my side. He hugged me and offered words
of consolation: "Gelsey, I'm hard on you because I know how good you
could be if you would just relax." But I was not about to relax.

The ballet was a plotless marathon that required all the concentration and
stamina that I had at my command. The choreography—technique without
drama—defied my ability to supply a reason for the steps. I had to make a
constant effort to look like I was enjoying myself. The music was another
Stravinsky score. A year later, after Stravinsky had died, I performed *Scherzo*

at the Stravinsky Festival, a commemorative event organized by Balanchine.
It elicited the following comments from critic Clive Barnes:

> It is really interesting music, and Mr. Robbins has set a brilliant skim-
> ming dance to it. Led by Gelsey Kirkland and Bart Cook, the dancers
> have fun and make music.
> Mr. Robbins is adept at seeking the skeleton beneath the skin of
> Stravinsky's music . . .

My relationship with Jerome Robbins had begun as early as 1969 when
Eddie Villella recommended me for a part in the work that is generally
considered the choreographer's masterpiece, *Dances at a Gathering*. Robbins
took me in as if I were a stray puppy. His affection for me was never really in
doubt, though I had some difficulty in figuring out what he was attempting to
communicate. He must have been as frustrated as I was that our best intentions could not initially be realized in my performance. I simply had not yet
had the education to deliver the kind of theatricality and attention to detail
demanded by *Dances at a Gathering*—and Jerry did not know how to teach
those qualities of movement that would have been necessary to give him
what he wanted. I performed various roles in this ballet over the years and,
in a certain sense, it traces my progress inside the New York City Ballet. To
actually learn to dance the parts, I would ultimately have to go outside the
company for instruction.

Dances at a Gathering was quite exceptional in that Robbins provided the
bare skeleton of a classical dance, set to Chopin, resisting the trend of modern fashion. The choreographer shared his view of the ballet with Clive
Barnes:

> I'm doing a fairly classical ballet to very old-fashioned and romantic
> music. In a way it is a revolt against the faddism of today . . . I have
> been looking around at dance—seeing a lot of the stuff at Judson
> Church and the rest of the avant-garde. And I find myself feeling just
> what is the matter with connecting, what's the matter with love, what's
> the matter with celebrating positive things? Why, I asked myself, does
> everything have to be separated and alienated so that there is this almost
> constant push to disconnect? The strange thing is that young people are
> for love. Is that bad?

Such words are rare in the world of dance. I wish that Jerry had repeated
them to me at the time.

Dances at a Gathering was constructed around eighteen piano pieces—
waltzes, mazurkas, études, a scherzo, and a nocturne. Ten dancers—five men
and five women—appeared in various partnerships and combinations. Fleeting relationships materialized and disappeared during a fanciful outdoor
gathering. There was more mood than substance. Themes were intimated

rather than fully developed. The challenge was for the dancers to bring the relationships to life. The steps acquired meaning only through depth of articulation, through the silent dialogue of the dancers, requiring both technical facility and expressive range. It was a ballet composed almost entirely of hints.

When first faced with such a vague blueprint, I felt as if I were in limbo. The emphasis on the upper body and the idea that the arms followed the impulse of the torso posed further questions that were rarely asked at the New York City Ballet. Robbins himself did not have the answers—he had only an image of what he wanted the dance to look like. He was not in a position to train me for his ballet. Instead, he tried to slow my pace. But slowing down threatened to expose the deficiencies of my training. A character dance drew attention to the characteristically awkward positions of the arms in Balanchine's port de bras. When I first tried to dance a mazurka, I looked like an epileptic chicken. Even a simple step such as a plié, when performed in slow motion, demonstrated that I had not learned how to master gravity; I was still dancing on air.

Working more by intuition than conscious design, the choreographer insisted that I mark the ballet, which was not enough to tell me how to endow movement with ease, fluidity, and dramatic coherency. He described generalities, but I needed specifics. As if to underscore his desire for a casual approach, he always wore sneakers.

At the beginning of rehearsals, Robbins invited members of the company staff to watch. He elbowed those around him as I approached a crucial point of my little performance. He knew that I could not make it through a particular spin without falling. To deride my efforts may have been one of the ways Robbins chose to encourage me, or to teach me a lesson. But the laughter of the spectators only succeeded in making me feel humiliated.

My ability to accomplish the steps required something that I did not yet possess. I would learn how to build coordination just as I would learn how to build character, but not from Robbins. His reaction to my frustration at that time was to advise me to imitate other dancers, such as Patricia McBride and Kay Mazzo. The mirror told me that would be an exercise in futility.

It would take several years to make a distinct mark in *Dances at a Gathering*. Another Robbins ballet, *Goldberg Variations,* posed a similar set of problems. Before the premiere at the New York State Theater on May 27, 1971, I was pushed to the edge of physical and mental exhaustion. What was I supposed to look like on the stage? That was the concern that haunted my dreams each night, at one point actually causing me to sit up in bed and slug my boyfriend while we slept. For those around me, I was never easy to live with because I never had an easy time living with myself, whether asleep or awake. I had already been convinced that my intensity was a sickness. Each of my questions seemed to be another symptom.

I subsequently put my individuality and womanhood on the line with

Jacques d'Amboise, a premier danseur and choreographer. He had partnered me in *Firebird* and later cast me in two of his ballets, *Tchaikovsky Suite No. 2* and *Irish Fantasy*. He was a consummate entertainer, always providing enough spice to ensure the audience a pleasant time. Spice consisted of atmosphere and lighthearted antics. In attempting to prepare the dish that Jacques seemed to want to serve with each ballet, I created a world for myself on the stage. I did not speak his language and had some difficulty translating his recipe.

Acting as both partner and choreographer, Jacques flashed his smile and flew around the stage to illustrate his points. He had developed his own technique for lifting a ballerina, usually grabbing the costume and a fold of skin for a handle, making sure his grip closed tight as a vise. He taught his steps to me as if I were a female wrestler, clamping his arm around my shoulder and offering a ringside pep talk. I caught the steps, if not his enthusiasm.

In the *Tchaikovsky Suite,* I played a peasant girl who seemed to skip to the lilting cadence of the music. There was a joy in her dance that told me she was a girl in love with the idea of love. I tried to turn her charm in the direction of each of my partners, alternately Jacques and John Clifford. Such a literal interpretation lacked depth, limiting the personality of the character, making her a frivolous stock figure.

To expand the role, at Maggie's suggestion, I added another dimension. I focused all of the movement by imagining a shaft of light coming into the bare stage. It gave me a specific direction with which to orient myself, illuminating each of the steps along the way. A world came to life under an imaginary sun. I could almost feel the warmth of its rays on my skin. The pattern of my breath fell into line with the actions of the character. I had won the freedom to add a touch of flirtation simply by shifting the focus. I would not play to my partners or to the audience, but to a source of dramatic inspiration. The image of the sun, as a distant point of reference, became a concept that would guide me through the dance. I would use the same concept in the future, providing each ballet with a unifying framework upon which to build the qualities demanded by each role. This was a major breakthrough.

After transforming the character in this way, I showed my work to Jacques. We began a rehearsal of the first movement and finished without a stop, quite unusual for a process that is most often punctuated with fits and starts. After complimenting my effort, he said, "Just a few things to clean up." Escorting me to the place where I made my entrance, he gave me a demonstration, describing each step like a barker in a carnival: "Now, on this first step, over-cross front leg . . . and . . . make hands into fists . . . and . . . pound like so. Watch me. And one, and two, and over-cross and look there, and twist and back and look this way, and three and move and energy . . ."

After the walls stopped vibrating from the shock of his exhibition, I told him what was on my mind. "Jacques, when I first come out, I am moving toward a sun shining from that direction. I dance toward the light. I'm happy dancing your steps in the sunshine. I have thought this through very carefully, and I don't intend to explain more than that. I won't change my mind, so, please, get someone else if you don't like what I've done." I started to walk out of the rehearsal, but he stopped me at the door.

We came to a mutual understanding: I would do it my way. I had won his respect by standing up to him. This change in our relationship off the stage seemed appropriate to the interpretation I was hoping to bring to the ballet.

In light of his newfound admiration for me, Jacques tried to play matchmaker, suggesting that I wait for his young son Chris to grow up. The boy, about ten years my junior, had just started ballet classes and had a crush on me. I recall that I was so desperate for love, I gave the idea a moment of consideration. I thought perhaps a child could see through me and still find it in his heart to cherish what he saw.

At the time that I performed Jacques d'Amboise's *Irish Fantasy,* a critic writing for the New York *Times,* Don McDonagh, defined this transitional phase of my career:

> She dances like a girl enthralled with the humorous velocity of romantic entanglements. As a developing artist she has yet to make the full transition from sheer technical proficiency to smooth her characterizations into a long continuous line but she is well on the way.

Who was going to teach me how to act? I thought of myself mainly as a soubrette or allegro dancer, known for speed and precision. In my struggle to become a lyrical or adagio dancer, I was trying to take on those qualities of character that I associated with the drama of classical dance. I knew that I had to work against my training, but I did not realize the extent to which the limitations of that training were built into the roles and steps themselves. As the steps became disconnected from drama, the roles became disconnected from character. My physical type and technical proficiency decreed a specific place for me in the Balanchine repertory. My figure sealed my fate.

This was more than a problem of being typecast. The roles that I wanted to play represented what might be called the dramatic side of Balanchine's aesthetic. This was the side that he was attempting to diminish through his technical emphasis on training the dancer not to interpret the role, not to bring character into the dance. Closing the distance between studio and stage, Balanchine attempted to cure himself of the hangover of the classical tradition within his company. I must have seemed like a headache that would not go away.

I remained under Balanchine's power precisely to the degree that I measured success and failure in terms of his repertory. A number of his early ballets continued to attract me because I saw them through the eyes of the previous generation of dancers, those stars who had established the roles by bringing a personal and dramatic sensibility to his choreography. Ballets such as *Apollo* captured more than my imagination. Their beauty became an ironic source of anguish. In preparing an article for *CO-ED* magazine during 1971, Arlene Petroff interviewed me at the theatre:

> . . . I met Gelsey backstage. There she was, a shy, sensitive girl with tears in her eyes. She was trying to recover from watching Jacques d'Amboise and Allegra Kent . . . perform "Apollo." "They were so beautiful, it was so beautiful," Gelsey kept repeating. She could hardly stop weeping.

What Allegra Kent had done on the stage in *Apollo* was exactly what my generation of dancers was being taught not to do. She brought her personal style to the choreography, creating a sense of drama. Another dancer of that golden age, Violette Verdy, indirectly addressed this question in a published interview, speaking of her early career: "You forget that at that time, in the late fifties, the company had dancers with personalities." Over the years, character had been replaced by technique. In my effort to find myself as an artist and develop the resources of my own personality, I made the mistake of thinking that Balanchine's ballets might provide a means to that end.

My reaction to *Serenade* brought about another spectacle of tears. Created in 1934, this was the first work that Balanchine choreographed in America. While insisting that the ballet contained no story or concealed meaning, Mr. B stated that he had adapted the dance from the classroom. *Serenade* has been described as the story of how a young woman becomes a ballerina. It might be described more accurately as how a young woman becomes a Balanchine dancer. That aspect of the ballet had a powerful effect on me.

The choreographer related an incident about the making of *Serenade* that epitomized his approach to ballet and his attitude toward his dancers: "One day, when all the girls rushed off the floor area we were using as a stage, one of the girls fell and began to cry. I told the pianist to keep on playing and kept this bit in the dance." The beauty on the stage may seem a compensation for the plight of that anonymous girl. Although never asked to perform *Serenade,* I cried like that girl many times over the years.

When I returned to roles in Balanchine's repertory, I collapsed into tears after almost every performance. When my mother found me in the dressing room after a show, I was usually in hysterics, in spite of applause and accolades. The reason was simple: success had become impossible on my terms. The dramatic ideal that I had seen in another generation of dancers, that sense of dance that had inspired me, had been replaced by an ideal of shape and speed. Every time I attempted to bring drama into my performance, Mr. B tried to thwart me. I interpreted this as a personal attack.

He did not change his attitude toward me. Recognizing that I had become a popular dancer, he took advantage of my technical abilities to fill holes in casting his ballets. During the last half of 1971 and the beginning of 1972, I passed through his repertory like a speeding bullet. The impact was summarized in *Dance and Dancers* by Patricia Barnes:

Still only 18, but already in the company for three years, Gelsey Kirkland has been taking on a whole repertory of new roles, making the season into something of a personal festival. In all of them she has left a distinctly favourable impression . . . Her biggest challenge, perhaps, was the role of Columbine in *Harlequinade* . . .

In addition to *Harlequinade*, the Balanchine ballets in which I appeared during this period included *Concerto Barocco, Tarantella, Symphony in C* (second and third movements), the "Rubies" section of *Jewels*, the *Brahms-Schoenberg Quartet*, and the pas de deux mauresque from *Don Quixote*.

I intermittently danced *Theme and Variations*, which became a characteristic battle of interpretation. Mr. B had originally choreographed this work for Alicia Alonso and Igor Youskevitch at Ballet Theatre in 1947. They reportedly devised "an emotional logic all their own" to bring the steps to life. In approaching Tchaikovsky's music and Balanchine's abstract design, I struggled to find my own logic. This meant composing my entire body to make the steps flow from inner necessity.

The choreographer gave me only two pieces of advice during rehearsals. He said, "Dear, just . . . you know . . . be yourself. Don't try, just dance." Not pleased with the position of my arms, he corrected me. "Dear, it's . . . well, you see . . . like Fred Astaire. Jazzy. Cha . . . cha-cha. He was a great dancer."

In following Maggie's coaching advice, I moved my body in one piece. My arms were forward and low, a far cry from Fred and Ginger. That was the way I performed the role on the stage.

In *Concerto Barocco*, set to Bach's Concerto in D Minor for Two Violins, I caught on to Balanchine's game. He applied a simple method to squelch my effort to compose the movement according to the classical form I had in mind. Every time I succeeded in bringing a measure of grace into the picture, he speeded up the music. The faster the steps the more difficult it was to maintain lyrical coordination. When I tried to extend a step in a phrase, lingering on a particular quality through the notes, Balanchine accelerated the tempo, throwing me off. This way of working conformed to his mechanical interpretation of the score. It was as if he were constructing a clock on the stage, each of us keeping time like a cog in the mechanism.

The muscular action of each gesture was similar to the slow release of a coiled spring. A theme emerged from my refusal to synchronize with the metronomic interpretation of the music. I placed physical accents in the movement that corresponded to a distinction between human being and machine. By dancing between the notes, I found a way to introduce an element of personal drama into the pure motion of the ballet. I was not counting beats, but shifting the focus of the steps, ultimately illuminated in romantic terms through the support of my partner. There was a consistency of emotional texture to my performances even when the partnership changed from Conrad Ludlow to Peter Martins. My ability to beat the clock, in a certain poetic sense, was confirmed for me when I read Anna Kisselgoff's review in the New York *Times*. She described me as "a dancer who inclines toward lyricism rather than attack."

Critical response often provided subtle hints about my performances. I had to read between the lines just as I had to find the meaning of the steps between the notes of music. More than any other critic, Clive Barnes offered me encouragement through his reviews to become the kind of ballerina who might break out of the Balanchine mold. This push on his part was undoubtedly inadvertent. In a New York *Times* article on January 27, 1972, the critic typed me and told my future:

There are some great dancers who dance as if they are hardly aware they are dancing—they throw themselves to the winds. There are other great dancers—acute, aware and even wary—who dance out with a special consciousness. Fonteyn was of the latter category, and very soon in there will be Miss Kirkland.

The critic did not say that I had to leave the company in order to fulfill this destiny. I asked myself the following question: would a young Margot Fonteyn have been able to survive with the New York City Ballet? I was almost ready to throw caution to the winds.

I recall a night early in 1972 when I returned to my Upper West Side apartment after a rehearsal of *Harlequinade*. As usual, I plunged straight into a hot bath, churned by a portable Jacuzzi. I spent hours each day soaking in the tub, a necessary therapeutic treatment for both physical and mental knots. I was soothing my snarled muscles and temporarily escaping the snag of my life.

I spent the rest of the evening on the living room floor, hammering out toe shoes. This was a painstaking process that I used to soften the pointes in order to ensure silence on the stage. Hours were devoted to hammering the toes, tapering the shanks with a razor blade, and applying Fabulon floor wax to strengthen each shoe. The technique for fitting my shoes took years to perfect. Most dancers choose to avoid the extra labor. I hate the sound of toes tapping on the stage.

While I hammered away on shoes, my boyfriend, Jules, banged away on the piano. At the time, he was attempting to fashion himself into a classical composer. What I could hear told me that he was making no progress. Motivated somewhat by guilt, I felt that it was my duty to encourage him to develop his talent. The fact that we spent little time together seemed to be my fault. My days and nights were consumed with class, coaching, and physical therapy sessions, rehearsals and performances. When I saw him, he was usually in bed, either meditating or sleeping. What he did with his time in my absence was, according to him, none of my business. I stifled my growing resentment in exchange for the stability of the relationship. I did what I could to offer romantic inspiration and reassurance. Sometimes there was more terror than security in the arrangement.

We fell asleep together that night on a mattress that we had placed on the floor of the bedroom. The accommodations were part of Jules's spartan lifestyle, which happened to match our modest standard of living. There was nothing fun about sleeping on the floor when errant cockroaches were always a possibility. That thought flickered into my mind after the lights went out. Exhaustion hastened slumber. During the course of the night, the bogeyman of childhood visited in the form of a nightmare that interrupted my sleep. The dream and the incidents that followed were so troubling that I recorded it the next day.

I was walking alone in Central Park. My mother had dropped me at the theatre, but somehow I lost my way. I had no idea which direction to find Lincoln Center. With my ballet bag over my shoulder, I tramped along in a straight line, figuring that sooner or later I would come out on either side of the park where I could catch a cab. My legs did not want to move fast enough. I knew I was late.

A phantom sun fell somewhere behind the trees. There was only dim light filtering into the path ahead of me. I felt a flush of wind scraping space. Leaves trembled as if a storm were approaching. I told myself that rain would destroy my hair. I hesitated on the path. My feet seemed to be entangled. When I looked down in desperation, I could see the ground was covered with tracks, human footprints. I heard something flutter in the brush behind me. When I turned, a branch whipped out and scratched my face. I worried that I might be bleeding and started to run, stumbling forward.

I came to a bandstand surrounded by empty wooden benches. I recognized the place, but still had no idea where I was supposed to be. I suddenly froze with anxiety. Mr. B was sitting on the edge of the stage. Wearing a dark suit that billowed in the breeze, he was framed by the set that rose behind him, as if he had been blown out of a huge seashell. It was too late for me to avoid being seen. He beckoned.

As I hurried over to him, my voice caught in my throat. Before I could explain why I was not already in my costume, he asked me for the name of the character I was playing. Unable to remember the ballet, I started to search my pockets for a schedule. He stood abruptly and demanded again that I name the character. "Dear, must have name to dance." I blurted out, "Concubine." I knew I was wrong immediately and corrected myself. "No, no, it's Columbine."

By this time I was talking in my sleep and awakened Jules at my side. I was still repeating the name of the character from *Harlequinade*. Jules heard me say the word "Concubine" and launched into a cross-examination. The relief that I felt at being able to remember the name vanished as I awoke to a barrage of questions. It was as if he had decided to complete the dream by taking the part of Balanchine. I was in no mood to be taunted by anybody. As we traded accusations and denials, Jules did his best to incite me, not allowing me to go back to sleep. I kept asking him, "Why are you doing this to me?" He pretended innocence. If deceit were drifting snow, we both would have been buried.

Drawing my legs up, I listened, with head on knees, to interminable conjectures and ruminations. With an air of professional objectivity, he pressed for details. "But I heard you say, 'Concubine,' quite clearly. I just want to get to the bottom of this thing. Honey, I need your help if we are going to make any progress here." Between screams and sobs, I begged him to stop. Never losing composure, not even raising an eyebrow, he told me, "Now just relax. If you don't calm down, I think I am just going to have to call the police." Too stunned for words, I bolted from beneath the covers and made my exit, slamming the door behind me. I took refuge on the couch in the living room and the night passed without further disturbance.

The incident caused me to dread sleeping in the bedroom. I often woke up on the mattress and crept into the living room, afraid that Jules would once again invade the privacy of my dreams. There was now a physical threat that I could not put out of my mind. What might he do to me in my sleep? It seemed that one or both of us might be insane.

I blamed myself. Having never told Jules about the trick I had used to win his affection, the breast alteration, I was dependent on him to affirm my femininity. But my need to feel desirable to a man always put me at a physical disadvantage. Every time Jules touched me in bed or a partner lifted me on stage, a fear flashed through me that I had been exposed. When making love, I entered a zone of pleasure that intensified my vulnerability. I was terrorized by the prospect of abandonment. My secret pinned me to my predicament.

There was no way to extricate myself from the situation other than to admit my duplicity. Some months later, when the discomfort and swelling of my breasts became unbearable, I had no choice but another operation. Preparing Jules for the shock, I sat at the kitchen table for the inevitable scene of my confession. After stuttering my way through apologies and roundabout rationalizations, I was astonished by his reaction. "Is that all? I thought you were going to tell me you were a transsexual."

I had set myself up for emotional blackmail. Confiding in the wrong man was an error in judgment that would be repeated many times. Like a harlot who turns to the arms of every man except the one who loves her, I lacked the ability to distinguish between those who loved me and those who loved to use me. When I began to see my relationship with Jules as a burden and tried to throw him out of my life, he turned the tables on me. It seemed to me that breasts were easier to remove than boyfriends.

During the fall of 1972, the New York City Ballet toured the Soviet Union, visiting Kiev, Leningrad, Moscow, and Tbilisi. This was the same year that the ABM Treaty consolidated the policy of nuclear deterrence, known as MAD (Mutually Assured Destruction). I had no idea at the time that those words might have implications for both my personal relationships and the strategic doctrines of ballet as practiced in the context of the Cold War.

Throughout the five-week visit, I decided I would act, in effect, as a spy. The mission I gave myself was to infiltrate the arsenal of the Russian repertory and to penetrate the Russian system of ballet training—to steal the secrets of the great Russian ballerinas. As farfetched as this analogy may seem, the political reality of the Soviet Union turned our tour into a diplomatic event and created an atmosphere of intrigue that enveloped us from the moment that we arrived. At times the air was so thick with suspicion that the natural curiosity of a Western dancer could have been interpreted as an act of espionage.

The trip was a test of stamina and spirit. Since I was flying into the unknown, my primary goal was to maintain control. I tried to plan for every contingency that I might encounter either on or off the stage. Before leaving New York, I rehearsed *Theme and Variations, Scherzo Fantastique,* the third movement of *Symphony in C,* and a minor role from *Dances at a Gathering.* The problem on the road was how to sustain the mental and physical discipline necessary to dance those ballets. I was apprehensive about not having the benefit of Maggie Black's coaching. As my approach to training and performance had changed under her influence, I had to bring her with me, at least on tape, carrying along a recorded workout guide to the routine of barre exercises and the format of the classroom. Steadfast in my refusal to attend Balanchine's classes, which he taught on the tour, I usually found a quiet place to conduct my own class alone. Such behavior was frowned upon, seen as an attempt to embarrass him.

By the end of the first week in Kiev, I was out of shape. I had gained weight from the Russian cuisine, concentrating on omelettes and the chicken named for our host city. The hotel accommodations had all the charm of a cell block. Rooming by myself reinforced the feeling of serving time in prison. My nerves frayed from travel fatigue and lack of creature comforts. I was more than homesick. Paranoia seemed to come with the decor.

The radio in my room became an object of personal obsession. It was a little black box bolted to the night table. I noticed first that it would tune to only one station. Spinning the dial adjusted only the volume. When I tried to turn the radio off, the crackle of static continued. There was no plug. I jumped to obvious conclusions. What bothered me was the possibility that someone might listen to me talking in my sleep. I decided to match wits with this infernal device. American ingenuity would win the day.

I grabbed the hammer that I used to soften my shoes. After giving the radio a few good shots, I gave up. It was still crackling. For a moment, I had second thoughts. Someone would hear me. I figured I had every right to smash a defective radio that was keeping me awake. At the same time, I knew that I had better make my sabotage look like an accident. I dumped two cups of coffee over the box. The crackles continued loud and clear. In a fit of passion, I tried to suffocate my tormentor with a pillow. The static was muffled, but the proximity of the box and the lamp on the table made this an unwieldly solution. I was almost ready to admit defeat when I was struck by a sudden notion, almost a brainstorm. The onset of menstrual blues may have contributed to the tactic: I shredded Tampax and toilet tissues, and wadded them in coffee; then I stuffed the wads into the little louvers in the side of the box that covered the speaker of the radio. The silence that followed afforded all the satisfaction of a curtain call.

A standard fixture in all the hotel rooms, the radio became the pretext for jokes at mealtime. Why would anyone want to "bug" us? Were we receiving special treatment? Was electronic surveillance customary? Was this Russian hospitality? The members of New York City Ballet certainly had nothing to hide. Company gossip included speculations about some of the more peculiar sounds that might be heard coming from our rooms at night.

We ate in a dining area off the hotel lobby. What had once been a ballroom had been converted into a cafeteria. Massive wooden tables were always filled with bread and cheese. Waiters in aprons stood around trying to look inconspicuous. The lighthearted attitudes of my fellow dancers told me that I was the only one who really appreciated the gravity of our situation. Rather than the guests of a foreign country, the others could have been mistaken for a dinner party waiting to dine with Mr. B at a Russian restaurant somewhere in the neighborhood of Lincoln Center. I decided not to follow the crowd. I had to prove that I was independent, that I could manage on my own. The reality was that ballet was the only sphere in which I had even a remote chance of fending for myself.

But I was lost as soon as I entered the theatre. All of the Russian stages were raked, slanted down toward the audience. The angle was just enough to throw me into a panic. How was I supposed to adjust my balance? Every time the steps moved down the stage, the momentum of my body threatened to toss me into the front row seats. With each leap, I seemed to soar to the balcony. Was this the secret of Russian elevation? Could the gymnastic feats of the Russian dancers be explained by a trick as simple as this? I had my doubts as soon as I tried to reverse direction. Moving up the stage was like trying to dance up Mount Everest. Turning on a diagonal twisted the ankles and strained the shoulders. The soreness in my back indicated that I was not even using the same combination of muscles that I used on a level stage. I would be defeated by the terrain of this strange land.

Although the audiences responded to the performances with enthusiasm, I was not dancing; I was running through a gauntlet of adverse circumstances. I dismissed all compliments. When I heard that the famous Russian ballerina Maya Plisetskaya called me "a first-class ballerina," I qualified her statement in my mind, adding the phrase "for an American." My national inferiority complex would take years to overcome. How could the Russians think that I was a ballerina when I stumbled across the stage? Were they blind?

Feeling like a failure, I tried to reassert control. I began to starve myself, limiting my diet to candy bars and coffee. This was the first sign of an anorexic syndrome that later would become an obsessive rule in my life. I was trying to disappear, to deny my physical existence altogether. By reducing the intake of calories, I broke down my destiny into mouthfuls. I wanted to live and dance on nothing. I wanted to empty myself out completely. Purification and punishment seemed to go hand in hand.

When we arrived in Leningrad, I was pale and depleted, as if death had donned toe shoes. My condition was deteriorating. On a sight-seeing trip to the Hermitage Museum, I removed my street shoes and covered my feet with a pair of paper slippers, a precaution enforced by museum officials to protect the marble floors. I saw almost nothing of the exhibits. At first I was distracted by Mr. B, who was escorting dancer Karin von Aroldingen on his arm. There was something incongruous about the picture they made, softly padding along in dainty footwear. Slow and deliberate, their movements could have been choreographed in advance. I tried to read his mind without success. Was this place—rebuilt from a palace that belonged to Catherine II —part of the heritage he carried around with him? I began to feel faint and ducked behind a column. I was in the throes of an infection that would cramp my stomach as well as my style for the rest of the tour. Catching sight of me doubled over, Mr. B craned his neck and gave me a curious nod as he and his partner passed into another room of the museum.

I recall a more disturbing incident that took place shortly thereafter. The company had been followed from Kiev by a fan, a Russian youth who had risked crossing domestic borders without proper papers in order to accompany us from city to city. He appeared again at a theatre in Leningrad while a rehearsal was in progress. I noticed him sitting at the side of the stage, talking quietly with a few of the dancers. Several members of the company had befriended him. He spoke a little English and gesticulated like a mime. In the middle of a sentence, groping for the next word, he was grabbed from behind and lifted off the stage by two uniformed policemen, who seemed to come out of nowhere. They dragged him through the theatre and out the exit.

The shock of this intrusion halted the rehearsal, momentarily freezing dancers in place. A group of us rushed outside to see what was happening. Without explanation, we were ordered to board our bus. Crowding to the back to look through the windows, we saw the young man loaded into a police car. We yelled to the police, "We see you! We see what you're doing!" Our words did not deter them. We watched in horror as the Russian policemen pummeled our fan in the backseat of the car, without pausing to question him. The brutality of the beating filled me with revulsion. It was so senseless. Some of us wept as the bus pulled away, shedding tears of rage. Some of the others pounded the windows with their fists. We protested in vain, shamed by what we had seen.

So this was Russian society. Language was obviously the least of the barriers here. Our presence certainly did nothing to alter the prevailing order of tyranny. What place could ballet have in a country such as this? How could anyone dance under a reign of terror? I wondered if any of those policemen would bring their families to our show. Were they in the audience that night? We never saw the young man again. Nothing was ever learned of his fate.

While in Leningrad, my friend Cathy Haigney and I made a request to visit the Vaganova School. Associated with the Kirov Ballet, the school is legendary throughout the ballet world for the training of classical dancers. To our surprise, the request was granted. No other dancers from the company expressed any interest in attending.

A security official escorted us through the school. We were permitted to observe a class of girls, six gifted students who appeared to be ten or eleven years old. The dance studio was like those in the West except for one crucial detail: the floor was raked. The Russian dancers trained in the same tilted world in which they performed. I knew that had to take a toll on their lower backs. It also seemed to explain their protruding chins and the exaggerated turn-out of their feet.

As the class progressed, accompanied by a delicate piece of piano music, I noticed that the children already knew the order of the exercises. Without checking in the mirror, they performed a series of basic positions, as if they had memorized the classroom syllabus. With each position, the placement of their heads, arms, legs, hands, and feet shifted in unison. They were expert at this drill. The teacher walked around and whispered corrections in their ears. Did she not want us to hear what she was saying? Was this classified information? She was a stout woman, reserved rather than stern, who clearly did not like being watched.

After finishing at the barre, the children marched into the center of the studio like little toy soldiers. They were adorable, wearing leotards and matching white ankle socks. Several had bangs and pigtails. One tiny cherub raced for a towel to wipe the sweat from her face. They were aware that they had an audience. After a few more floor exercises, they stopped and put on their toe shoes. Instead of using rosin to secure footing, the Russians wet down the floor, sprinkling water across the wood. One of the girls was assigned to take charge of the watering can, the kind used for flowers. After she finished her task, the students split into two groups. Moving from adjacent corners of the room, they performed bourrées on pointe, running elegantly in diagonal lines across the floor. That was the finale.

The exhibition concluded when the girls curtsied for us and the teacher praised her favorite. It was made clear to us that the rest of the class was strictly off limits for outsiders. What I had witnessed led me to believe that the Russian students were more regimented in their training than Americans. I carried away images rather than technique. I could imitate the bangs and pigtails, which I did upon returning to New York, but I would have to discover a deeper set of principles to create the form that I saw emerging in that class. I would not have the benefit of years of physical memorization to take on the style and shape that seemed to be the basis of the Russian theatre. I would never be a Russian ballerina.

Before leaving the school, I managed to peek into a studio where another class was in progress. Sneaking to a hidden vantage by the door, I peered at a group of older girls, fifteen or sixteen years of age. It was obvious why this class was not on the official tour. Most of these dancers had not been able to develop their talents. They showed no promise. Their placement made them look like parodies of Russian ballerinas. This group proved to me that the Russian ballet also produced its share of casualties. I wondered what became of those who failed, those who were rejected by the system. I laughed to think how I might have turned out had I grown up in Russia, how I might have been typecast and tracked within that system of training—straight to Siberia, no doubt.

Such a dismal fate seemed to be a real possibility when Cathy and I, accompanied by her husband, Ricky, subsequently visited the home of Soviet dissident ballet stars Valery Panov and Galina Panova, formerly with the Kirov. The couple had already decided to emigrate to Israel. As targets of an intensive KGB harassment campaign, the Panovs had become something of a cause célèbre in the West, championed by Clive Barnes and Patricia Barnes, among others. A plan was made for us to attend a small party at the couple's home. Our purpose was simply to offer moral support. After making our way through the streets of Leningrad, trying to hide our anxiety, we were greeted at the door of their apartment by Valery. I could see the strain in his face as he welcomed us and introduced his wife, Galina. With our entrance, the two rooms of their tiny home were filled.

Cathy, Galina, and I huddled together and devised a language with which to communicate, mixing a little English, Russian, and French, as well as the more universal gestures of our art. There was no problem of translation when Galina tried on a pair of toe shoes, offered as a token of friendship. I was amazed by the muscle tone of her body and the arches of her feet. By Western standards, she had curves. Her manner was totally ingenuous, a portrait of innocence. How could anyone forbid her to dance? She was a blond angel who seemed to have had the gates to heaven slammed in her face. I was dumbfounded.

We did not discuss the politics of defection, but matters of dance and female concern. We heard about the Kirov and her sorrow at having to leave the company. The state bureaucracy had offered her husband a job as a baker; he declined the position, which evidently had been designed to humiliate him. How they were able to make ends meet with their recent loss in status was a mystery. Certain quarters apparently supported them in their bid to escape. Valery seemed to be as concerned with my career as he was with his own predicament. He advised me to make sure that I read the right books, the Russian "classics." The Panovs' plight suggested to me that he and his wife were part of a tradition that was now in danger of extinction. There had to be a profound shortage of courage in a country that feared such people.

A few days later, I saw a notice posted in the lobby of our hotel. The members of the New York City Ballet were invited to tour the Kirov Theatre, the Maryinsky theatre of Balanchine's youth. We were also offered the opportunity to observe a company class. The notice announced that a bus would be available on Saturday morning of the coming weekend. We were scheduled to perform on that day, matinee and evening shows at a theatre called the Palace of Industrial Cooperation. There would be just enough time to make the tour and the shows. I was not about to miss the chance to see the Kirov dancers at work. I had seen Nureyev and Makarova, who were stars with the Kirov before they defected; and I had heard the names of Yuri Soloviev and Mikhail Baryshnikov, who were still with the company and reputed to be the great male dancers of the present generation. An invitation to class at the Kirov was too good to be true.

On Saturday morning, I climbed into an orange bus outside the hotel. I sat by a window, leaving enough room for someone to sit next to me. Then I waited . . . and waited. Nobody else boarded the bus. At first I thought I must have mistaken the day. A Russian driver informed me that this was the Kirov tour. There was no mistake—I was the only one who had chosen to come. It occurred to me that the others had been discouraged by Balanchine's dismissal of the Kirov Ballet as "old-fashioned and boring." After checking his watch, the driver closed the door. I figured I had stepped into the Twilight Zone. When the bus accelerated into traffic and spun around a corner, kidnapping seemed plausible. Finally arriving, I found myself on my own. No guide appeared. Wtih considerable trepidation, I walked into a foyer and approached a reception area. After making my inquiry, I was told by the woman behind the desk to wait. She knew nothing about the tour, but would check to see if I might be permitted to attend company class.

I stood by the wall, trembling and shifting my weight from leg to leg. The door burst open and a young man rushed by me. After exchanging a few words in Russian with the receptionist, he leaned over the desk to sign in. I stared at his back, wondering if this might be a dancer, one of the Kirov celebrities. He was wearing a heavy wool overcoat, his dark blond hair shorn at the collar. When he turned around, our eyes met for a few moments, then I looked away, unable to hold his gaze. He was cute, a little fellow, more boy than man. Out of the corner of my eye, I watched him dash down a hallway and disappear.

At last a guide appeared and led me to a studio where a men's class had already begun. I sat near the door along with several other observers, who never identified themselves. Surveying the class, I saw the same young man whom I had seen in the reception area. He seemed to be pleased with himself as he scrutinized his double in the mirror, leaning back from the barre. An elderly man sitting on my right whispered in English, "That is Mikhail Baryshnikov." I was not impressed. The diminutive size and strange line of his body did not recommend this Baryshnikov fellow in my eyes. In first position, his feet were turned so far out that his ankles seemed to roll over, like he was mounted on casters. His tights were pulled so high that his proportions seemed comically distorted.

As I looked around, I realized that all of these dancers had the same placement. The others were even more exaggerated. They appeared to be older character dancers. Many were wearing girdles to support their backs. Straining, pushing and pulling muscles into place, they actually seemed to want to look as if they might break down at any moment. Compared to them, Baryshnikov was a winner.

I was disappointed. On the one hand, these male dancers appeared to confirm Balanchine's description of the Kirov as old-fashioned. On the other hand, the physical strain of the technique reminded me of my early training at the School of American Ballet. I began to think that I was wasting my time.

Suddenly all of the older dancers moved to the barre, clearing the floor for Baryshnikov. The music swelled and he launched into a rehearsal of the variations from *Don Quixote*. I had never heard of a rehearsal taking place in the middle of a class; I had never seen a performance like this. I made a snap judgment: he was the greatest male dancer on the planet.

His talent was beyond superlatives. He vaulted into the air with no apparent preparation. His steps seemed to blur together without losing any definition; he was literally a motion picture. It seemed to me that he had somehow managed to weld technique and style into a perfect voice. The man on my right leaned over again, informing me with discernible Russian pride, "And, you know, he's just back from vacation, still trying to get over foot injury." I was transfixed.

Baryshnikov's immediate effect on me was very much like that of Natalia Makarova. I had a new set of standards, a new caliber of dance that I had to match. Their performances were not only expressive, but utterly explosive. I asked myself how I could learn from what they were doing. I assumed there had to be a connection between how they were trained and what they were trained for, a link between technique and repertory. Both dancers seemed to possess a genius for dramatic interpretation.

In the case of Baryshnikov, I assumed he had to know exactly what he was doing. His obvious gymnastic ability was subordinated to character, to the delineation of qualities which were not necessarily Russian, but appropriate to the national origin of the story behind the ballet. Baryshnikov's rendition produced a Spanish flair, a passion supported by athletic ability and by what appeared to be a series of artistic choices. Even the toss of his head produced a subtle effect. His hands were expressive right down to the tips of his fingers. He was a living spiral, a human corkscrew. He seemed to be creating the rules as he went along, rather than following them. With the climax of his performance, I tread the fine line between intense curiosity and infatuation, too intimidated to think of approaching him.

After the class, I thanked the teacher and departed in haste. I was devastated. I had so much to learn and nobody to teach me. On the way out, I passed through several studios, catching a glimpse of the company's class for women. I saw one of the senior Kirov ballerinas, Ninel Kurgapkina, demonstrating exercises at the barre. I was now hypercritical. As I surveyed the figures of the women, I was relieved not to see anyone who would cause further demolition of my ego. I dreaded each perfect example of Russian virtuosity. Each became a challenge and a threat. I was tormented by what seemed unattainable—the method by which to transform the body into an expressive instrument. As practiced and demonstrated by the Russians, such knowledge seemed as heavily guarded as a military secret.

In a more optimistic mood, I wrote a letter home to my sister Johnna, describing the impact of the Russian ballet: "There is too much to tell! I learned a lot about the use of the upper body from watching the good Russian dancers. I hope I can apply some of it when I get back. They know how to use their heads—beautifully! When it's right, it's right!"

Years later, I learned that Mikhail Baryshnikov—Misha—had been in the audience in Leningrad when I performed *Scherzo Fantastique*. During the intermission of the show that night, he reportedly offered a few comments to his friend Gennady Smakov, including the words "Not headed in the right direction." He was apparently referring to the ballet rather than to my performance, but the description might have been accurate either way.

When the company arrived in Moscow for the last leg of the tour, I was emaciated and seriously ill. During the afternoon stage rehearsal for opening night, several dancers informed Mr. B of my condition, telling him that I had turned green. He made no response. As I had no replacement, I kept my mouth shut and retreated toward the dressing room. Without an understudy, the program would have to be changed if I were unable to dance. Balanchine followed me and delivered a lecture: "Dear, you know, you have to go out there . . . 'specially tonight . . . you see, is first night in Moscow . . . big city . . . important people. Audience must see this ballet. Not important how you dance . . . matter of fact . . . don't even have to do the steps! Audience won't know, won't care, as long as they see what's on program. Is necessary, you, Gelsey, go out there tonight. They expect you and yellow costume. Just try to look nice, dear. Don't worry. Everything will be all right. Audience will be happy."

He advised me to rest until curtain and vanished. His speech made me think he had lost his wits, or that I had, for listening to him. I curled up on the floor and tried to nap. Later, I crumpled into a chair in front of a r. rror and began to put on my makeup. My complexion really did have a green tint. In the middle of applying eyeliner, I heard a knock at the door. I ignored it until I heard Mr. B's voice, "Gelsey, you in there?" I opened the door. He grabbed me by the arm and gently pulled me into the hallway. With a face full of concern, he asked me, "Dear, how do you feel?" I whispered, "Not too good." He put something in my hand, saying, "Take this. Is vitamin. Take now. You feel much better." I followed his instructions.

To my surprise, I did feel better. In fact, I felt terrific. I danced *Scherzo Fantastique* and actually enjoyed myself, twirling through the steps. I looked down during an entrechat six, fluttering through a series of complicated beats. I did not recognize my feet. They seemed to be pointing in the wrong direction. They were attached to my body. They had to be mine. I ignored the strange sensations passing through me. When the performance ended, my feet continued to dance—they had a life of their own.

Shortly after I went to the dressing room, in the middle of removing my costume, Balanchine again appeared at the door. "Dear, how you feel?" I was giddy, bubbling with enthusiasm. "Fine. Really. Fantastic!" Lowering his voice, he said, "Gelsey, if some other time, you feel not so good, tell me. I give you again this vitamin. You be okay." He put another "vitamin" in the palm of my hand and left.

On the following day, I relapsed into fever and chills. One of Mr. B's assistants approached me at the theatre and took me aside. He seemed to be worried, inquiring about my health. Then he offered a piece of friendly advice, "Gelsey, it's really not such a good idea to take more of those pills that Mr. B gave you. I mean, as long as you can dance without them, don't push your luck." A fear shot through me. I knew nothing about drugs and never considered the danger. But I resolved not to take another. I wondered

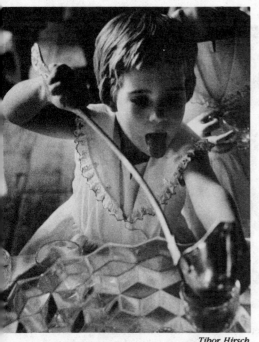

Tibor Hirsch

Gelsey Kirkland at six, 1959.

Ray Shaw

With brother, Marshall Kirkland.

As an angel, *The Nutcracker,* age nine.

Saratoga, New York, 1966. From left to right: father, Jack Kirkland; Gelsey Kirkland; mother, Nancy Kirkland; half brother, Chris Kirkland; sister, Johnna Kirkland.

In the studio, School of American Ballet, 1970.

Martha Swope

With sister, Johnna Kirkland (left), *Reveries,* 1969.

With George Balanchine.

Dina Makarova

As Firebird, with Peter Martins.

©*Farrell Grehan*/Life *Magazine*

With Balanchine and Karinska, costume fitting, *Firebird*, 1970.

Christopher Kirkland

Mimi Cotter

Dina Makarova

Before defecting from the New York City Ballet.

Dina Makarova

With Mikhail Baryshnikov, 1974.

Dina Makarova

With Misha at Howard Gilman's White Oak Plantation, Florida.

if these "vitamins" explained Mr. B's boundless energy. And to think I actually felt touched that he had shared his medicine cabinet with me. The pills were undoubtedly amphetamines.

Meanwhile, on the homefront, the New York *Times* reported Balanchine's triumph in the Soviet Union. The articles emphasized the enthusiastic response of the Russian audiences and quoted the choreographer: "When lots of dancers are twirling around, the masses applaud . . . They are overwhelmed by our ability to manipulate time. We have our special speed . . ."

We returned to New York by way of Poland, concluding the tour with performances in Warsaw and Lodz. Clearing customs at Kennedy Airport, I congratulated myself for stealing the Russians blind. I carried with me a wealth of images and impressions. I would break down the Russian style into bits and pieces that I could absorb into my body. I did not yet realize the difficulties I would have in deciphering their code of movement. Nor did I realize the personal cost that the trip had exacted from me. My first order of business was a scalding bath.

I could barely walk, and weighed less than ninety pounds, but I was anxious to dance and happy to be home. Upon returning to Maggie Black's class, I was surprised to find Natalia Makarova, who had begun to study with Maggie regularly while I was away. Natalia, whom her friends call Natasha, and I had met only a few times. After the class, she came over to me with an expression of bewilderment. "Gelsey, is that really you? I spend whole class vith you, and not even possible to recognize! Sooo skeeeny! Terrible! Tell me, vhut's happened? Tell me, pleeese!"

In my eyes, emaciation gave my upper body the swan-like definition possessed by Natasha. I did not have the heart to tell her that she had become my inspiration, that this was my new Russian imitation. Nor did I consider the possibility that I might have influenced her decision to study with Maggie Black. I felt only a surge of familiar anxiety, as if I were shrinking into my toe shoes. Natasha was the greatest ballerina in the world. How could I explain to her that the admiration she elicited was also the source of my deepest anguish?

Natasha was one of the first to advise me, informally, through a mutual friend, to leave the New York City Ballet. She suggested the National Ballet of Washington, D.C. (now defunct), which had a classical repertory, including *Cinderella* and *The Sleeping Beauty.* I had other ideas. My objections were rooted in fear.

Chapter Six

BETRAYALS AND DEFECTIONS

By the time I turned twenty, at the end of 1972, I had reason enough to make a move, to change the direction of my life and career; but I did not possess the maturity to follow my inclination. I was a timid rebel, held in a straitjacket of indecision. Each time I tried to take a step, I met mental and physical restraints.

My artistic rebellion was based as much on insecurity as conviction, as much on fragility as strength. I had to take extreme measures just to prove to myself that I existed. I continued to hope for some sign of approval from Balanchine even while resisting his authority. I wanted to win the respect of my greatest adversary. As he was perhaps the most popular figure in the world of American ballet, I needed his approbation in order to continue to pursue my career.

After performing the role of the Sugar Plum Fairy in *The Nutcracker* during the 1972–73 holiday season, I received an indirect compliment from Mr. B. He told my friend Cathy Haigney, "You know, her only problem is . . . didn't defect." He meant that I had not made the sensational impact of the Russian ballet stars who had defected. I wondered if he meant that I should have defected to the Soviet Union. Cathy assured me that Mr. B had intended a compliment. I knew he would never have said that face to face. I had hurt him in my own way too many times.

Early in 1973, I was invited to dinner by the Hungarian-born premier danseur Ivan Nagy, a frequent partner of Natasha Makarova, my idol. They had established their partnership at American Ballet Theatre. ABT, a company always in search of a home, sometimes appeared at the New York State Theater, the permanent residence of Balanchine's New York City Ballet. The two companies were to some degree competitive. The purpose of the dinner with a leading member of the competition was to discuss "my future." I was delighted that Ivan even thought that I had a future.

I joined him and his wife, Marilyn, at their penthouse on West End Avenue. I went alone by choice. As soon as I walked through the door, I sensed that I had entered the home of two citizens of the world. There was a cosmopolitan atmosphere created by the elegant furnishings and the works of art. There were paintings by Boulanger and Zupan. Here was a new life that might be mine if I had the nerve to follow the example of my hosts. Ivan had performed all over the world and collected memorabilia along the way. I was surprised to learn that his wife, Marilyn, was a former dancer. She was an attractive woman in her thirties, who seemed too self-composed and confident to have spent much of her life in a dance studio. Ivan, in his late twenties, was known for his portrayals in the traditional ballets that constituted the basis of the American Ballet Theatre repertoire. Having seen him dance with Natasha in *Giselle,* I knew he possessed special artistry.

Ivan encouraged me to move to ABT. He had danced for Balanchine one season in the late sixties and knew the frustrations that I was experiencing. He also knew that if I waited too long to leave City Ballet, it would be too late to make the transition. I was at a crucial point in my career, still young enough to adjust to the repertory that ABT had to offer. I was attracted to that repertory, which included a variety of styles: from the Romantic ballets of the early nineteenth century to the Russian classics of the late nineteenth century and the psychological dramas of twentieth-century choreographer Antony Tudor.

It was a mystery to me why some critics lumped such contrasting styles together with the term "classical." Although I danced the "classical" vocabulary of steps and positions, altering Balanchine's academic formula, I knew that I was not prepared for the technical and expressive demands of those ballets for which ABT was famous. As much as I dreamed of applying myself to the dramatic repertory, I did not want to make a fool of myself.

Ivan and Marilyn suggested that I had an artistic responsibility to accept the challenge, to expand my horizons. Their arguments were certainly persuasive. Their enthusiasm and flattery convinced me while I was in their presence, pumping me up into a little balloon. As soon as I left, I deflated completely.

With a touring company like ABT, I would be forced to depend more on my own resources. My mind clouded with fears at the prospect of being on my own. I was afraid to become the kind of dancer that I wanted to be. I was afraid that I would not be able to dance without the constant companionship and support of my coach, Maggie Black. I was afraid to leave Mr. B. I was afraid to fail.

I decided to wait. The episode that followed made me more vulnerable than ever. My dependency on Maggie Black touched off a crisis when she told me that she planned to move her studio to the West Village. I had grown accustomed to the convenience of her being across the street from Lincoln Center. I was especially upset to learn that she would be taking a vacation for a week during the move. I said nothing. While she was away, in order to cope with the disruption, I decided to return to the class taught by

Stanley Williams at the School of American Ballet. I missed Stanley. My body could not stand the strain of his classes on a regular basis, but I thought I could benefit occasionally from his emphasis on refinement and phrasing.

The lessons that I had learned from Maggie on placement and focus complemented what I had first begun to understand from Stanley's meticulous approach. When I returned to his classroom, Stanley noticed my progress. After class one day I tried to explain to him how I had changed through Maggie's instruction. There was a failure of communication. I did not know how to translate the vocabulary employed by Maggie to that used by Stanley or vice versa. They did not speak the same language.

When Maggie returned and opened her new studio, I knew I would have to tell her that I had been to another teacher. I also knew that she would be hurt, that she would think I had deliberately betrayed her. Maybe I had been unfaithful, but I now knew that I needed the freedom to move between teachers. I had no intention of discontinuing my relationship with Maggie, but I would not allow her to dominate me as she had in the past. This choice put our friendship on the line. She had the advantage of at least ten years of age and experience in her favor. I looked up to her. I had been happy to grant her a monopoly on my education, but that had to change. I assumed she would understand.

I approached Maggie privately in her studio. The moment of truth made me wish that I had never been born. I was still enough of a child not to be able to read the writing on the wall. She accused me of undermining all of the work she had accomplished with me, of being ungrateful.

After a long silence, she said simply that she did not think it was a good idea for me to come back ever again. I looked at her implacable face through my tears. There was something painfully absurd about the situation. For a moment I was struck by our mirror images. She had recently cut bangs like mine. We both looked like children. I begged to be forgiven, but she turned away. I let her have the last word as I walked out the door. "Don't come back. It's impossible, Gels."

I was too desperate to think. I walked uptown through the streets of Manhattan, oblivious to the world around me, grinding my fingernails into the palms of my hands. I went to a nearby health club. A young woman in the locker room pointed out that I had blood on my clothing. I stripped and headed straight into the steam room. I remember telling myself to fight back. After willing the tears to stop, I wrapped myself in a towel, body red and mind raw, and sat on a stool. I focused my life into a single question: how am I going to find a great teacher?

I saw an older woman who looked vaguely familiar, a dancer type, thin and muscular. Her tan skin and blond hair gave away her Swedish background. She introduced herself as Renita Exter, an instructor at Harkness House, a ballet school on the Upper East Side. I was familiar with the school because one of my frequent partners at City Ballet had studied there. Helgi

Tomasson was a beautiful dancer from Iceland who had come out of the original Harkness company. That company was known for the individuality and diversity of its dancers. I asked Renita to recommend a teacher. Without hesitation, she suggested one of her fellow instructors at the school: "David Howard. I promise you'll love him." I figured I had nothing to lose.

Several days later I called Harkness House and arranged to attend one of David Howard's classes. The school was located in a beautiful old building on Seventy-fifth Street, off Fifth Avenue. I was put off when I walked inside. The place was plush. Ornate chandeliers hung in the lobby. There was a marble stairway and a little elevator, its interior studded with jewels. The layout seemed too luxurious for serious ballet. My attitude changed when I looked at the photographs mounted on the walls. They were pictures of former members of the Harkness company. What encouraged me was the fact that all the shots were highly theatrical. These dancers were actors. The school must have been doing something right.

David Howard was British, a former member of the Royal Ballet. I heard his accent before I entered the classroom and expected him to be on the prim and proper side, maybe a bit too formal for my taste. I was in for a surprise. I was greeted by a slender man in his thirties. His face seemed both intelligent and sensitive. His manner was straightforward; he turned out to be anything but reserved when it came to dance.

I took a men's class. David's approach to technique was quite different from the way I had been taught at the School of American Ballet. Nor was he doing anything along the lines of Maggie Black. The class began with seven minutes of warm-up exercises, a therapeutic session at the barre. This was affectionately known as "The Hoop." All of the movements had a basic circular pattern, as if the body were an elaborate pendulum. The torso, head, and limbs were swung slowly through a series of long arcs. This was a comprehensive preparation of the body for the more strenuous exercises that followed.

As the class progressed, I became more and more intrigued. Instead of moving from one step to the next, these dancers were being taught to move through the steps. The men that I saw did not have an easy time with this concept. Nor did I. The connecting links between the steps were elusive. The movement was not broken down into individual positions or poses but treated as continuous fluid motion. It was like learning to swim. My body was so tense that I sank like a stone.

After this first lesson, I raced to catch up with David in the hall. We were both in a rush. I had to know his evaluation of my work. Breathlessly I said, "Excuse me, Mr. Howard. What do you think? I mean, how did I do?"

He offered a rather dry understatement, "Well, a bit stiff."

I was not about to let him off the hook. "Well, tell me what I can do about it. Can you tell me what to do?"

With a wry grin, he looked me straight in the eye. "Well, you could start by bending your elbows. That would make a world of difference, you know."

I immediately raised both arms sideways and bent my elbows, straining to give him what he wanted. "Like this?"

"Well, no, not really." With a look, I pushed him to elaborate. He explained, "You don't actually bend the elbow, you release it, which means you first release the shoulder."

David watched closely as I tried to translate his words into my body. Frustrated, I came back at him, "But what do I do as it's releasing? There must be something I should do while my arm releases down."

He seemed to be enjoying the dialogue. "Well, Gelsey, as you release your arm down, you have to resist against that with your whole body. Release and resist."

"Release and resist at the same time?" I was perplexed and refused to leave until I had mastered this elbow-bending business. We continued in the hallway until I got the hang of it. Before parting, I told him briefly about myself and asked him if he would consider being my coach. David accepted on condition that I understood he would never offer me the kind of relationship that I had developed with Maggie. He would not allow me to depend on him as either a teacher or a surrogate parent. In stressing the point, he was firm and sympathetic. After thanking him, I hurried away.

Our exchange inspired great expectations. I knew that I was going to be challenged with more than just another teacher's vocabulary. David seemed to be as curious about the cause and effect of movement as I was. His classroom corrections were not like those that I had received in the past. He was not simply telling me what to look like, he was telling me why and how to move my body in order to express something. I would have to fill in the something for myself. I was ecstatic. Someone had begun to help me answer a few questions.

My work with David began sporadically, between attending his classes and stealing time together in one of the studios at Harkness House. I had begun the rehearsal schedule for a new ballet by Jerry Robbins and continued to perform a number of the works already in my repertory. The thrust of the training with David was aimed at reversing bad habits by applying a new logic to my body.

David introduced me to the term kinesiology, the study of movement—a science that goes back at least as far as Da Vinci's studies of anatomy and mechanics. The word comes from the Greek *kinēsis,* which means motion. I would become a scientist, if necessary. With David, I felt that I was capable of understanding the laws of the universe, at least within my body. In that universe, the shortest distance between two points was not a straight line, but a curve. I learned that the motion of the body followed circular lines of muscular action, and committed myself to the acquisition of a "body of knowledge." I was about to acquire curves, which was exactly what I had always wanted.

I remembered the time at the School of American Ballet when the teacher had written the names of the positions and steps on a blackboard without explanation. Stored somewhere in the back of my mind, those words were dead nouns associated with static images. I was now given a set of action verbs which were related to concepts and principles of movement: oppose, resist, release, rebound, rotate, spiral, coordinate, etc. I kept these at the front of my mind along with David's verbal corrections. He always brought me back to the "compositional circle" within which I danced. I had only scratched the surface during the first month of training. But I kept saying to myself, why hadn't I been taught this way all along? Given my attachment to results, I immediately started to experiment in rehearsal. But my efforts were cut short.

I had been preparing for the Robbins ballet *An Evening's Waltzes,* set to five waltzes by Prokofiev. My partner was Helgi Tomasson, who had beautiful hands and an unusually expressive upper body. The ballet had no plot, but intimated a kind of ballroom melodrama. There were romantic undertones that rippled beneath the serene surface of the dance. Phrasing the steps with Helgi, I felt briefly that I was dancing underwater. For the first time, I was able to move as if weightless, while creating the illusion of weight. I had conquered gravity, at least for the duration of a few sweeping lifts.

When I arrived at one of the final rehearsals before the opening in May 1973, I was told that Helgi had hurt his back and was being replaced by John Clifford. I was not pleased with this turn of events. Switching partners was like looking up in the middle of a conversation to discover that you were no longer talking to the same person. While John and I were trying to coordinate a lift and slide on the stage, Jerry Robbins stepped into the picture. The choreographer was dissatisfied with the step. Perhaps it was too close to what Balanchine had done in *Concerto Barocco.* Jerry hit upon an alternative: "John, why don't you try lifting her straight up so she comes straight down before she slides."

I knew the danger: "Jerry, it's not possible to slide unless John puts me down at an angle. It's just not possible."

My complaint fell on deaf ears. Jerry commanded, "Just try." I tried to explain that I had done this enough times to know that gravity would not allow a dancer to come straight down and then slide at a right angle.

My new partner, John, picked me up and put me down as Jerry instructed. I had the helpless feeling that I was falling from a ten-story building. My foot jammed into the floor with a crunch loud enough to tell me that I was in deep trouble. My foot was broken. Clenching my teeth, I managed to walk off the stage without making a sound. Then I howled, my head full of tears. Jerry asked me if I was all right. Squeezing each word out through a jaw locked with rage, I said, "I'll . . . be . . . just . . . fine!"

The question that shoots into the brain of every dancer at the moment of injury repeated itself every day for the next six months: would I ever dance again? The doctor decided against a cast in order to prevent the muscles from atrophying. The treatment also prevented the bones and ligaments from healing properly.

I settled into the apartment with my boyfriend, Jules, and attempted not to move. I sat for hours on end with my foot propped on pillows. I knitted and played chess, but I did not really know how to deal with time. I plotted how I was going to transform my body, how I would realize my ideal of the perfect ballerina. I had the leisure to work my envy of the Russian ballerinas into a full-blown and fanatical obsession. Hearing that Natasha Makarova admired Botticelli and was a painter herself, I began perusing reproductions of Renaissance art. The drawings of Da Vinci made me wish that I had religious faith. I could see in the line work how the circular patterns of muscles were thrown into relief by light. The features of the women haunted me. The figures had weight. They seemed to move.

I thought of the long line of Natasha's neck. How did she do it? Da Vinci would have loved her neck. He would have been able to catch her at the height of a leap, when her arms and shoulders extended like the wings with which we were supposed to have been born.

I became more miserable by the minute. Without mobility, I devoted all of my energy to maintaining my appearance. I hobbled to the bathroom scale and balanced on one foot to check my weight several times a day. I went on a ration plan to stay at ninety pounds. In the morning I sliced one green apple into four pieces. Each piece constituted one meal, with a tablespoon of cottage cheese for dessert. I ate four "meals" a day. After several weeks of deprivation, I no longer had a concentration span long enough to read or even fight with Jules. Sex was out of the question. I was proud of myself for keeping my physical instrument tuned to perfection. I actually assumed the ascetic routine was part of the commitment that Balanchine had been advocating all along. My attitude toward him softened on the outside and hardened on the inside.

After several months, I was informed that the company was going to Germany and that Balanchine wanted me on the trip. I went to the theatre and found him backstage. I was on crutches. I figured he would take one look at me and send me home. The idea of travel mortified me.

Mr. B acted as if I were his long-lost friend. He put his arm around my shoulder and looked down at my foot. "Dear, you see, you come, and maybe it will be all right later." I tried to explain that even if the foot improved I would need at least a couple of months to get back into shape. Balanchine heard only what he wanted to hear. This was an important trip. The company would be recorded for television. I had to go.

Jules wheedled me into bringing him along. The trip was brightened by my old friend Meg Gordon, who had recently been admitted to the company as a member of the corps. Meg and I had tortured each other as children. She was familiar with my idiosyncracies and tried to keep a sense of humor about some of the more bizarre quirks. Our bodies were almost identical. We shared our clothes and our miseries on that journey. Meg was a nervous wreck about being out of line in *Serenade*, a minor catastrophe that had not been missed by Balanchine. While the company performed in Berlin, Mr. B sent me to a doctor, who sent me to another doctor, who injected cortisone into my foot. I sent a letter to my mother and capsulized the situation in one word: "DISASTER!"

The pain in my foot was gradually subsiding, but time had already run out. I would not be able to perform for the cameras. As Jules had been on his own most of the time that we were in Germany, I had no qualms about leaving him behind to do some shopping while I returned to New York. I was ready to be rid of him. I was ready to go back to work.

The company had only been back in town for a short time when my friend Meg received a telegram. She had been fired. The New York City Ballet was sorry to inform her that her contract would not be renewed. She and two other dancers were given no warning and no explanation. Nobody had the decency to tell them in person. I was never able to console Meg. She dropped out of sight for weeks. What could I have told her? For a Balanchine dancer, there seemed to be no future after Balanchine. I had seen the pain too many times. Those of us who remained were reminded how lucky we were.

A similar lesson was driven home when the dancers went on strike at the end of the year. That was the first time that I thought seriously about my lack of material security. I was making less than three hundred dollars for as many as eight performances a week and endless hours of rehearsals. The real worry was what I might do if my career were to end. What else could I do?

Mr. B interpreted the union action as a personal attack against his theatre. I read his response in the New York *Post:* "If the strike goes on we'll close the theatre and everyone will go home. The girls will marry and the men will go and work on the streets." As I had excluded the possibility of marriage with Jules, it occurred to me that I might have to go to work on the streets as well. The idea of moving to another company was far from my mind at this point.

After Jules returned from Europe with a new motorcycle, I tried to think of some way that I might encourage him to ride away and out of my life forever. He provided the pretext by making an advance to a lady who happened to know my mother and stepfather. My anger finally galvanized for a decisive break. When Jules threatened to make an ugly scene, my stepfather came to the rescue and evicted him from the apartment. Without the support of my mother and her husband, I probably would not have had the strength of will to defend my own interests. I was relieved to be on my own again, but I was not yet my own woman.

With my foot more or less mended, I returned to David Howard to begin the reclamation of my body. I had become a human yo-yo. I swung between creative and destructive impulses. I wanted to yank myself back into shape. David turned my recovery from the injury into an education in spite of my impatience.

At the beginning of our first session, he sat me down in a chair and told me to get up without using my arms. I discovered that I was unable to rise from a sitting position. The more I tried to pull myself up, the more frustrated I became, until we both burst out laughing. I could see that I was going to have to learn how to initiate the impulse for movement from my torso, which was the point David had intended. This meant starting from scratch.

I began to reeducate my body, literally muscle by muscle. I had the chance to erase those aspects of physical memorization that had been the core of my early training. This was a slow process of deciding what to retain and what to discard. At my level of expertise and anxiety, it was not easy to admit to myself that I had never learned the most important thing about my art. I had never learned where dancing actually originated inside the body; I had never learned where movement began.

There was a methodical progression from inside to outside. Each part of my body had to harmonize within a physical dynamic that was generated and coordinated from the torso. The impulse of the torso was the key to turning out the entire body. Turning out the body was the key to each of the basic positions. The basic positions were the touchpoints for balance between and through the steps. Each step was a moment in the physical transformation of my image on the stage. That image had to carry weight if anyone was going to be able to see me from the back row of the balcony.

I had arrived at the point where ballet meets mime. I was learning to move in the sense identified by the famous French mime Jean-Louis Barrault:

When man displaces himself he ripples the external world, as a fish ripples water. For man, the external world and internal world weigh on each other.

Both ballet and mime required the ability to create substantiality where none existed. I was no longer pulling myself through visual space; I was pushing through a medium in order to reveal my inner world.

David proceeded with ironclad logic and gentle fingers. His eyes seemed to be able to see beneath my skin, pinpointing tension that blocked the fluid action of my movement. The pain that I experienced in releasing the knots of muscular tension was different from the kind of punishment I had inflicted on myself during my early years. After working at the barre, David would instruct me to stand, sit, or lie down, enabling him to locate the strategic pressure points that were causing problems. While pressing his fingers relentlessly into each knot, he offered soothing words to divert my attention: "Think of warm tea, dear. Mmmm. Yes. Warm tea." The object was to relax, allowing the muscle to release. As soon as that happened, the pain dissipated and David exclaimed, "Good! Very good!"

Working at least four hours a day over a period of several months, we developed a Platonic relationship based on a constant dialogue of questions and answers. This was really the first time that I ever consciously associated dance with anything like the joy of spiritual fulfillment. Yet my questions were often motivated by the wrong intentions. Something seemed to fester inside of me even as I struggled to find a healthy way to move. I was still trying to mold myself into a static image that conformed with what I saw other dancers doing on the stage. I was still consumed by jealousy and envy.

I charged into one of the sessions and fired a barrage of questions, comparing myself to Natasha. She had recently told me that my thumbs stuck out. I fixed that immediately, but I knew there were other areas of my body that did not fit the image of a Russian ballerina. David patiently absorbed the shock of my latest tirade. I went on about her style, posture, upper body, extension, and coordination. "David, I want to look like that. Why am I stuck with this body? Why do I have to look like a bulldog? Have you seen her neck? I want Natasha's neck!"

David displayed a dry wit on such occasions, attempting to show me the folly of my ways. "Yeees. She does have a lovely neck. Beautiful. Now what are we going to do with you?"

I was hardly pacified. "Why does she look like that and why do I look like this?"

David redirected my obsession toward rationality. "Well, Gels . . . Natasha looks that way because she is Natasha. That is the way she actually is, that is her natural shape. And you are not that way, so you're going to have to think about how you're going to get that body of yours to move in the best way that is possible for you. Your neck will not lengthen by stretching it. The problem is not your neck, dear, but how you support the weight of your head."

He differentiated the way Natasha looked from the way she moved. The way she moved gave her the freedom to make artistic choices through her upper body, neck, and head. I was unable to move my head freely because I had so much tension stored in the back of my neck. I was straining just to hold my head up. By releasing the tension over time, my neck lengthened and my head dropped forward gracefully, redistributing weight. I had achieved a delicate balance. The difference in my appearance was startling even to me.

While I made progress outwardly, I carried on a secret life aimed at appeasing inward demons. These were voices that told me I was not beautiful

enough to dance or to deserve the attention of men. I was not satisfied with
the speed with which I was accumulating knowledge. Even though I was
now able to understand cause and effect in composing beautiful movement, I
was still obsessed with the superficialities of beauty. With the departure of
my boyfriend, Jules, I had to prove that I was still attractive to the opposite
sex.

During the same time period that I worked with David, I went through
another round of cosmetic surgery. I had my earlobes snipped off. I had
silicone injected into my ankles and lips. The injection of silicone was illegal
and dangerous, but what made the whole thing truly absurd was that these
changes were barely perceptible—not only from the balcony, but from the
front row.

I was adding to the collection of skeletons in my closet. I even tried to
hide having my teeth realigned. Then I used the dental work as an excuse to
hide the truth about my swollen lips. Whenever David brought up the subject of my health, I mounted a staunch defense. I shut him out along with my
family. My mother suspected the truth, which was enough to strike terror in
her heart. One day my stepfather called to express his concern. He told me
that she had awakened in the middle of the night, crying out, "Oh God, I
know what she's done! I know what Gelsey's done! She's had silicone put in
her mouth!" I assured them both that what I was doing was perfectly safe.

When I returned to Balanchine's stage, I had the facility to absorb ideas,
to move in a truly individual way. I also had the ability to make those ideas
speak dramatically within the plastic context of modern ballet. The role that
registered this change was Dew Drop in The Nutcracker. All of my new
knowledge was poured into the long run of holiday performances. David
frequently attended and coached me. This was actually the first time I danced
without pain.

In order to endow the steps with quality as well as technical precision, I
used my imagination, taking the name of my character quite literally—Dew
Drop. Mr. B never told me that I was supposed to be a piece of candy in the
so-called Kingdom of Sweets. I wanted to appear as though a drop of dew
had fallen on my cheek. I was going for crystal clarity.

The final touch that I added to this role might be credited to Margot
Fonteyn. She was not a model one could imitate anyway. There was no real
possibility for me to look like her. Margot's personal mannerisms were too
distinctive to work for me. David simply showed me how she managed to
light up her face, releasing all tension that inhibited illumination. I had to lift
the mask of intensity that clouded my features. The same laws of circular
motion governed the muscles of my face as the rest of my body. I spent
hours wiggling my ears. The facial muscles had to be fluid enough to separate from the bones—to make my countenance glow. I decided not to proceed with the face-lift I had contemplated during rehearsals.

The impact that I made was encouraging. Anna Kisselgoff wrote in the New York *Times* in December of 1973, "Gelsey Kirkland . . . seemed to score a personal triumph in leading the 'Waltz of the Flowers' with a new authority and manner." The real thrill came from one of my fellow dancers. In the middle of the bustle backstage, Peter Martins, the object of much hopeless infatuation, went out of his way to deliver a compliment: "Gelsey, I don't know what you're doing out there, but whatever it is, keep going—you're really on the right track!" Such praise was not to be taken lightly. I was in awe of Peter. He seemed to know what he was doing.

I continued my rampage through the New York City Ballet repertory during the winter and spring seasons. My technical confidence improved as did my ability to bring personal interpretation into the ballets, in spite of the limitations of the roles. The works included Robbins's *Four Bagatelles,* Jacques d'Amboise's *Irish Fantasy,* and Balanchine's *Monumentum pro Gesualdo, Symphony in C,* and *Tchaikovsky Pas de Deux,* and the pas de deux mauresque from *Don Quixote.* Writing for *The New Yorker,* Arlene Croce identified my struggle: "Another remarkable thing about Kirkland is that, unlike the rest of the New York City Ballet's ranking dancers, she hasn't depended on specially tailored roles to help her grow (and she hasn't had many); she seems to grow by herself."

I wanted to extend my progress on stage, however tentative, into an intimate relationship. There was always hope that a professional partnership might blossom somehow into romance. Moved by loneliness and desire, I passed through a series of inconsequential flirtations, beating a hasty retreat whenever things became too serious. The bedroom was a daunting proposition. I broke off a brief affair because I was unable to stand the pressure. I had too many secrets that had to be concealed.

At the beginning of 1974, I stepped into Violette Verdy's role in the Jerome Robbins ballet *In the Night.* This was another romantic abstraction set to Chopin. My partner was Peter Martins. I took special satisfaction in dancing with Peter in part because we were an unlikely looking couple on the stage. The critics complained at times that I was too short for him, or that he was too tall for me. Peter was Danish and looked like my image of Hamlet. In the company he was considered something of a prince and a playboy. My sister at one point had confided to me about her brief fling with him. That was a long time ago. His on-again-off-again girlfriend was a young dancer by the name of Heather Watts. Their melodramatic scenes made them into an ongoing item of company gossip. I was intrigued from a distance.

I flattered myself thinking I brought out the best in Peter on the stage. I felt that I inspired him to concentrate. I was good at eliciting concentration from most partners because of my serious nature. I always tried to give Peter a focus, but we rarely, if ever, talked about how we approached our work.

I resented what I had seen Mr. B do to him in the past. Peter was a great dancer and partner, a leading man blessed with a limitless facility. He was capable of moving with power, sensitivity, and intelligence. Yet, Balanchine seemed bent on making him disappear by giving him mincing steps. Every time I went out in the audience to watch Peter perform, there seemed to be one less step, something taken away that diminished his virtuosity. Some months prior to our work in the Robbins ballet, I noticed that he seemed to be walking through the "Diamonds" section of *Jewels*. He coasted until the very end. Then he flashed through a series of turns and off the stage. The final step was brilliant, as if he were trying to leave the audience with the thought that he could have done that from the beginning. At first I thought he was either injured or becoming lazy. Then it dawned on me that Mr. B had undermined him. Balanchine's emphasis on the ballerina took a toll, especially on those men whose masculinity might be a threat. Peter was being choreographically castrated. If ballet were woman, as Balanchine said, how would a classical male dancer, with obvious virility, fit into the scheme of things? I had a scheme of my own.

I was usually too intimidated around Peter for serious conversation. It was easier to play the role of coquette at times. I recollect dressing for a rehearsal in an outrageously provocative black sweater. I had teased my hair and painted my face with enough makeup to look like a courtesan from ancient Greece, or so I thought. After slinking into the studio, I caught Peter's eye. That flicker of interest was what I wanted to happen between us on the stage. The idea was to bring some romantic drama into the ballet. His reaction to my antics raised the question of ulterior motives. He taunted me, "You are really asking for it, aren't you!"

Some months later, in May 1974, I appeared again with Peter in *It's a Grand Night for Dancing*, part of the Promenades series presented by the New York Philharmonic at Avery Fisher Hall, also at Lincoln Center. Peter stepped in to replace an injured John Clifford as my partner. John had choreographed a little piece, a lighthearted romp to several tunes by Richard Rodgers. Romance was indeed in the air as Peter and I glided through the steps and turns, almost daring each other through the movement. After our little number, John tracked me down backstage. He said, "Well, Gelsey, what was going on with you two out there? Are you in love? I thought that's what it was—it had to be something!"

Having recently separated from his girlfriend, Heather, Peter took me out to dinner at the Russian Tea Room. I was falling in love in the fairy-tale sense, projecting my dreams into our partnership. By the time Peter took me to my apartment on the Upper West Side, we had begun to discuss the possibilities of a shared future. It seemed to me there was more than physical attraction. I was willing to overcome my fears on that score because of a deeper promise that might be fulfilled. After his brief visit, he left me at my door, tantalized. I blocked out the implications of his parting words: "Gelsey, I don't understand why you are so willing to give everything to me. Why are you trusting me with so much all at once?"

I figured I was the answer that Peter had been seeking. Like me, he seemed to be going nowhere with City Ballet, having reached the limits of progress with the company. He also seemed to have been going nowhere with his girlfriend, Heather, a young colt as far as I was concerned. I stopped only for a moment to consider the nature of Peter's attachments to Balanchine and Heather. I trusted our rapport, accepting Peter's encouragement as proof of a direction that we had chosen together. We began to make plans to leave the company. We talked about realizing our potential as artists. We talked about finding stories to dance together. Peter hoped we might perform *Romeo and Juliet.* He called friends in Europe to find a company that might be a vehicle for our dreams.

I slept occasionally at his apartment in the Sixties near Central Park, overwhelmed by the physical reality that bathed my senses. Peter seemed to be a Greek god. Our love and sexuality seemed to go hand in hand, even though I still felt a personal distance, a lack of intimacy. I figured time would bridge that gap. His attempts to make me feel comfortable were touching. He asked me what kind of food I wanted him to stock in the refrigerator. Such consideration was new to me. The surroundings flamed my fantasies. His apartment was a bachelor pad with a marvelous sunken living room and several levels of living space. The balcony effect transported me into a Shakespearean romance.

I remember waking one spring morning, hearing birds chirping outside, the sun sitting on a windowsill. I turned over and saw Peter watching me intently. I was naked and blushed. It never crossed my mind that he might think I was physically beautiful. How could anyone think that? He encouraged me not to move, but I was too self-conscious. I got up pulling the sheet around me. I was afraid that he was comparing me with the other women he had known. He seemed so sincere in his admiration, but I knew that I had to be inferior. His eyes might discover the truth unless I evaded them.

In June 1974, Peter and I heard that Baryshnikov was performing in Canada with a touring group from the Bolshoi Ballet. We decided to make a trip to Toronto along with Peter's friend, a fellow dancer named Victor Barbee. I put on sophisticated airs for the journey, high heels to match my high spirits. Escorted on the arms of two gallant men, I played the princess. We saw Baryshnikov perform the pas de deux from *Don Quixote,* the same ballet that I had seen in Russia. Misha's impact on male dancers could be devastating. His virtuosity sometimes discouraged competition. I think what dashed the aspirations of other dancers was the idea that they would have to work too hard to become that good. Even Peter, who certainly had the potential to equal Misha, seemed daunted by him.

It was Peter who invited Misha to dine with us that night. We were staying in the same hotel. After the formal introductions, we went to a nearby restaurant. As we were being seated, Misha stepped back and made an appraisal, patting me gently on the rear, "You know, would be perfect partner for me. This girl, perfect partner.'' He was like an adorable boy looking through the window of a candy store. I was not exactly thrilled. My concern was Peter. After laughter made the tension of the moment pass, I glowed inwardly with the thought that the greatest dancer in the world had considered me worthy as a partner. It was hard to tell if he was joking.

I hardly said a word through dinner. The men did the talking. Peter broached the subject of Misha dancing in the West. The two of them seemed to communicate well in spite of language difficulties, as if they were old buddies. On the topic of defection, Misha instantly turned his eyes away. Peter offered encouragement, as I remember, suggesting that Misha should think about leaving the Soviet Union. For a moment, I had the feeling that I was back in Russia, that someone might be listening.

We returned to the hotel together and headed for the elevator. It was at that point that I demonstrated my talent for saying the wrong thing at the wrong time. Conversation is always difficult for me in elevators, with the walls closing in as you look into somebody's left ear. I made an innocent attempt to say something mundane to break the silence, blurting out to Misha, "Do you have a big bed? I mean, is it large enough for you?" A. if I had just cracked the greatest joke they had ever heard, my two sidekicks, Peter and Victor, fell into hysterics. Misha stood with a deadpan expression on his face. Apparently he failed to understand the humor, much to my relief. When he got out, I laughed along with Peter and Victor at the absurdity of the episode. I was obviously not inviting myself into Misha's bed. The thought never entered my mind.

After we returned to New York, Peter and I resumed our lives and careers as before. We still planned to make a break from the company. The romance between us continued to flourish as far as I was concerned. Spending nights intermittently together, I soon became aware that there were some changes going on inside Peter. He seemed to be wrestling with some sort of inner conflict. I would never have pushed him to reveal his turmoil. I did not think the understanding between us called for words.

A message soon arrived in the middle of the night. It was more like a revelation had walked into the apartment while we were sleeping. I lifted my head at about four in the morning and thought I must have been dreaming. Someone was sitting in the room with us.

As my eyes began to focus, I recognized the intruder. It was Peter's old girlfriend, Heather. She was just staring at Peter and me, as if she were in shock. Peter woke up and quickly surmised the situation. With a scowl he jumped up and threw on his robe. He told me to stay in bed, that he would handle Heather, which he did. He grabbed her by the arm and dragged her out the door. From my position, I listened to them argue, unable to make out the exact words. I got up and put on my clothes, planning to leave the scene of the crime—and wondering if I were somehow the criminal.

On my way out, I walked into the middle of an altercation in the living room. Peter insisted that I stay and listen to every word that Heather had to say. He said that she was going to try to destroy our trust. Then he told her that he wanted her to stay as long as necessary to see the hopelessness of her cause. He wanted her to be convinced of our love for each other, as that was the only way for Heather to be sure that it was over between them.

Heather stood while Peter sat by my side. He began by encouraging her to tell me everything. "I'd like Gelsey to hear what's in that mind of yours."

Her accusations made the situation into more of a triangle than I had realized. "Gelsey, this is really ridiculous. I mean, Peter has never been attracted to anyone but me . . . not really. He doesn't want to sleep with anyone else. Isn't that what you've always said to me, Peter? You might try to be with someone else, but you know you only want me!"

This soap opera escalated into a psychodrama that continued until the sun came up. I said hardly a word. When Heather finally ran out of venom and steam, Peter asked her if he had made his point. She seemed to resign herself to the fact that he and I were a partnership, saying something to the effect that she hoped that we would be happy. When she walked out the door, Peter had the last word, "It's so nice to see you leaving here like a lady . . . finally!"

The incident left me with misgivings. I wondered how she had been able to enter the apartment. Peter and I did not discuss the matter. As bizarre as the event had been, Peter did seem to be committed to the reality of our romance and to our plans for the future. I felt sorry for him.

Shortly afterward, Peter decided to have a birthday party at his apartment for a friend in the company. On the night before the gathering, Peter asked me if I would mind if he invited Heather to join us. He assured me, "She promises to act like a lady." He had already made the arrangements. I simply hoped for the best.

A group of maybe twenty dancers from the New York City Ballet attended the festivities. It probably qualified as a bash for everyone except me. At one point, I found myself in the upstairs kitchen, chatting with a few guests. Heather entered and leaned against the counter opposite me. She went straight for the jugular. "Oh, Gelsey, do you know what Peter said to me at lunch the other day? He told me that making love to you was like masturbating." Turning to the others in the room, she added with a smile, "That's exactly what he said."

I was stunned with shame. It felt like something jagged had been thrust between my legs. I ran from the kitchen. Heading down a flight of stairs, I broke into tears and lost my bearings. People approached me, but I turned away and continued to run, bounding into a bathroom. I locked the door behind me. I figured that what she said had to be true, whether Peter had actually said those words to her or not. I was not somebody to be loved.

Peter tried to bang down the door. "Please, Gelsey, let me in! What did she do to you! Oh God, what did she do to you! Please! I've got to explain! Let me in!"

He sounded desperate, and it was his apartment. I unlatched the lock. He vaulted through the door, slamming it behind him and pulling me into his arms, all in one motion. He held on to me, tightening his grip. He tried to get me to look at him, shaking me. "Gelsey, you've just got to believe that I never said that. Heather twisted my words to hurt us." I looked into his eyes for some sign of hope. He must have seen that I saw none.

"Oh my God, Gelsey! You don't believe me, do you? She's actually done it. I mean, how could you ever trust me again!" Straining to keep his voice under control, he continued, "Well, you have got to know the truth. What I actually said . . . was . . . that . . . when I didn't make love with you . . . I masturbated—that was all I said!" I was now unable to hold on to a single thought.

My memory of what happened next is like one of those old movies in which the action is speeded up. Peter exploded into the air and out of the bathroom. He raced up the stairs, yelling, "Goddamn it! Where is she?" Then he raced back down the stairs, dragging Heather behind him. Bringing her toward me, he screamed at her, "You owe that woman an apology! How dare you! Apologize! Goddamn it!" She turned away with a cold smirk on her face. Peter started to get rough. She gave me a look that was enough to tell me that her next words were a lie, "Oh, Gelsey, I'm sooo sooorry." On that note, Peter became violent.

He dragged her back upstairs and their fight became so heated that they had to be broken apart. I was broken apart inside; the kind of feeling when you tell yourself that you will never be put back together again.

I did not leave. I moved just outside the door, ready to flee. Peter and Heather were already outside. I stayed at a safe distance. There was a taxi waiting. Somebody pushed her toward the cab. She screamed back over her shoulder. "Gelsey! Remember—I have the key! I have the key!"

I went back inside the apartment. Peter had already taken a seat by the balcony. He had his back to me. He seemed to be in a coma. I asked one of his friends if he was all right. The friend told me that I had better leave him alone.

I left. I ran through the streets until I came to the building where I had lived with Jules. My friend Meg had an apartment in the same building. She gave me refuge. I went on an eating binge for three days and had a condensed nervous breakdown. I could hardly put two words together to make any sense of what had taken place. Somehow it had been my fault.

After gaining a few pounds and losing a few marbles, I returned to the New York State Theater. I had to do a performance of a pas de deux in *A Midsummer Night's Dream*. I felt bloated and fatigued. Afterward someone told me that I had never danced with such feeling.

About a week later, I spoke with Peter on the phone. I was in the lobby of the theatre. I suppose I must have called him. We had avoided each other since the party. I was still in love.

Peter said he felt torn. On the one hand, he spoke of his adoration for me. On the other, he spoke of his responsibility to Heather. He said he had to help her grow up. He told me not to wait for him.

I slammed down the phone and decided to pay Peter a visit. His vacillation may have been based on the best of intentions, but I knew that I had been abused. Some of the blame had to be directed where it belonged. During my ride in the cab, I rehearsed what I was going to say to him. The scene was over as soon as I delivered my line. "Peter, I really have only one thing to say: the next time you have a problem, I would recommend that you think carefully before you bring someone else down with you." I was proud of myself. I had walked in and out without being deflected from a simple commitment to the truth. The cab had waited.

As soon as I stopped to think, I was more depressed than ever. I threw myself into my work and tried to put Peter out of my mind. The difficulty was that I did not know how to think of my future in ballet without him. His rejection did more than make me question my sexuality. I was trapped again in the dead end of the New York City Ballet. My romantic aspirations had never been separate from my artistic ambitions. I had pinned all of my hopes on one man and one partner.

On the Sunday following my break with Peter, I went to the theatre at Lincoln Center to work out. It was quiet. The building was almost deserted. While warming up at the side of the stage, I was told I had a phone call. It was long distance. The call was from an old friend, Dina Makarova (no relation to Natasha). Dina was a ballet photographer whom I had met years before when performing as a guest for the Long Island company run by André Eglevsky. She and I became friends and stayed in touch sporadically over the years. There was nothing unusual about hearing from her. On that particular day, Dina's voice had a ring of excitement.

"Gelsey, it's Dina. Listen, I'm calling from Canada on behalf of Misha . . . Baryshnikov. I've been called in to interpret for him. He's defected . . ."

I absorbed the shock with a scream. Dina advised me to keep my voice down and say nothing—the press had not yet been informed. Then she came to the point of her call: "He wants to know if you would be willing to dance with him."

My mind was reeling. I said only, "Yes. Is that all?" That was all. There was nothing definite. Nothing was set. Misha simply wanted to know if I would dance with him. Maybe. Perhaps. Someday. Misha himself then came on the line. His accent was so thick that I hardly understood a word he said, except for my name, which he repeated in a soft voice, almost a whisper, struggling to pronounce each syllable.

After hanging up the phone, I stood for a moment quite still. Then I shrieked, "I can't believe it!" Soaring through the theatre, I mumbled to myself, "Mikhail Baryshnikov just asked me to dance . . . this just cannot be true . . . this cannot be happening to me . . . Oh, my God!" I said to nobody in particular, "I mean this has got to be the greatest thing that has ever happened to me! What am I gonna do?"

The call had been only a feeler. I was not supposed to tell anybody. I would never tell just ANYBODY.

A truce was unofficially declared between Peter and me on the following day, after he heard the news that Baryshnikov had defected. This was Monday, July 1, 1974. After his last performance in Toronto, Misha had slipped miraculously through a crowd outside the theatre and eluded the KGB. Not even two weeks had passed since Peter and I had seen him.

Peter cornered me at the theatre to talk about this latest Russian bomb that had fallen on the ballet world. "Gelsey, I knew he was going to do it. I could tell that night at dinner. He didn't even say he was thinking about it—he couldn't—I mean, he was being watched. But I knew somehow that he'd do it. Didn't you think he would?"

I was more concerned about the fact that Peter and I were talking again. "Well, no, Peter, I hadn't expected him to defect." I was tempted to ask Peter if he still entertained the idea of leaving the company, if he thought about the practical realities that confronted us. Misha seemed to have had the courage to choose artistic freedom. Wasn't he an example for us to follow? Weren't we still in Siberia? I kept my mouth shut.

A few days later, Peter invited me out to dinner. I accepted. I was a bundle of nerves. I would have returned to him in a minute. Peter was still the perfect partner in my mind. We met at a Columbus Avenue bistro called The Red Baron. After ordering, Peter looked up and said, "Gelsey, I think there is something you want to talk about . . ."

I hesitated for a second, shaking my head, "No, not really."

Leaning across the table, he was nothing if not direct. "I think you want to talk about sex." It seemed to be Peter who wanted to talk about sex, though I was all ears. He filled me in about how I felt about it and what I should do about it. He had certainly thought the subject through. I knew he was trying to bolster what I had left of an ego. He encouraged me to take what I wanted, to be more aggressive. His thesis was that sex and love had no connection; sex was the connection to the animal inside of us. He had no trouble in luring me to his apartment to test his theory through experiment.

The seduction brought on a new wave of expectations for me. I was a child again. I thought of angels. I thought of the wondrous dance that we might perform with our lives. Peter had other ideas. While I was sprawled somewhere between bliss and fantasy, he changed the subject on me. What had just taken place had no bearing on what he was about to say. That was his point.

Something tingled in my spine as he began. "There is something you want to say, but you are afraid of hurting me. So I guess I will have to say this for you." His voice was suddenly gentle. "The other day someone told me that Misha had asked you to dance with him, and that you said it was the best thing that had ever happened to you. Well, Gelsey, it is."

I began to cry. There was no stopping him. "You didn't want to tell me because of our plans. You didn't want to hurt me. Well, you have to go. You have to dance with Misha. You've got to forget about us. We are not that important."

After a last embrace, I left, feeling like I had just been pushed onto the tracks and was skidding out of town. I wondered if he was acting out of nobility or cowardice. Had I been railroaded? Would he return to Heather? Would he stay with the New York City Ballet?

I performed with Peter again years later at a college gymnasium in New York City. We were doing an old number for each of us, *Tchaikovsky Pas de Deux*. Peter must have known about all those questions that had burned in my heart. Before the show, while we were warming up, he came over to me. He answered the look on my face. "You know, Gelsey, I really hate seeing you again. You remind me of everything I didn't do."

Chapter Seven

THE IRON CURTAIN

Somewhere along the line, I moved back into the Upper West Side apartment where my family had lived when my father died. I had the place to myself. The other members of my family had gone their separate ways: my mother lived with my stepfather on Fifth Avenue; my sister moved to Los Angeles to find herself, eventually joining the Los Angeles Ballet; my brother went to college in San Francisco. The apartment had been maintained over the years, kept exactly as it had been. Surrounded by the familiar objects and memories of childhood, I felt as if I was imprisoned in the museum of my past.

I was not really leading my life. I forgot why I had ever chosen to become a ballerina. It seemed that the role had been imposed on me. Without knowledge of the world outside ballet, I lacked the maturity of mind necessary to determine my own fate. Each experience came as an unexpected blow. Without knowledge of real human beings, other than the creatures of ballet, I lacked the ability to judge character. Each romance held the promise of fulfillment. Each failure drove me deeper into myself. My only refuge was a world of ideals. If I were unable to realize those ideals in my life, I could at least bring them to life on stage, but that was not enough to satisfy me.

I knew that my dance was both an act of will and a means of expression. Ballet was the only link that I had ever been able to make between thought and action. Simple logic told me that I had to make the same connection off the stage. I had to find a way to break through the barrier that separated art and reality.

I thought that making an exit from Balanchine's theatre might allow me to make a decisive entrance into the world. I was forced to accept the fact that Peter Martins would no longer accompany me. There was still nothing definite about the overture from Mikhail Baryshnikov, but my mind was set to leave the New York City Ballet—by myself, if necessary. All of my lingering doubts disappeared at the close of the spring season in 1974.

I began rehearsals for an upcoming production of a new version of *Coppé-*

lia, to be staged by Balanchine and one of my former teachers at his school, Alexandra Danilova. While *Giselle* was undoubtedly the great tragedy of the traditional repertory, *Coppélia* was the great comedy. Having seen the latter performed by American Ballet Theatre, including performances by both Natalia Makarova and Italian star Carla Fracci, I knew the ballet required an ability to act and dance in the classical form. I also knew that Balanchine would adapt the concept to his vision of pure dance. The story and the characters would be encased in plastic.

The role of the heroine, Swanilda, had provided memorable moments in Danilova's own career on the stage. The elderly teacher tried to pass on the secrets of the part, showing me the opening variation, but she was unable to explain what she knew, providing only a precious caricature of the role. I thought she had mistaken my character for that of Coppélia, the doll in the story. I made a pact with myself: I would leave the company before dancing in this production. Danilova's somewhat old-fashioned approach was to be wed to Balanchine's modern sensibility. I knew the inevitable outcome of such a marriage would be a stylistic travesty, a waltz of dolls. I had had enough of glorified triviality.

At the beginning of July, the company traveled to Saratoga for the summer season. While upstate, I exchanged telephone calls with Baryshnikov through his interpreter, Dina Makarova. Misha was still in Canada, waiting for permission to enter the United States. Each call was a variation on the same theme: his desire to dance with me. His future in the West was still uncertain . . . I had somehow become a part of his plans . . . He had seen me dance in Russia . . . He believed in me.

I believed in him as much as I believed in ballet itself. Misha was more than the ultimate romantic fantasy; he was a miracle, a rose that fate had cast upon my path. He seemed to be the living embodiment of beauty and truth. His very existence inspired me to clarify and confirm the direction in which I had been moving. Bursting upon the scene at the perfect moment, he offered the opportunity to share the gift of his genius. That was the dream that filled my nights. The possibility of a partnership with such an artist gave me the final measure of courage to confront Balanchine with the news that I would be withdrawing from the company.

I had to wait for the opportunity to catch Mr. B in private. During a relatively quiet afternoon in Saratoga, I found him walking in the hallway of the theatre and followed him into his office. He turned on me as soon as we were inside, as if he were in a hurry to be rid of me. "Well, dear, what's the matter?"

I informed him only that I intended to leave at the end of the summer. When he asked about my plans, I told him that I was uncertain, that I needed time to work things out. No words were wasted between us. There was no discussion of the matter. I was not invited to sit down.

He led me to the door, his arm around my shoulder. He must have been able to feel me shaking. "Dear, I understand . . . you see . . . when I was your age, I had to do everything my way. And now, you have to do everything your way."

Close enough for me to feel his breath on my face, he offered his parting shot, "You know, if you ever want to come back, you can . . ."

After I had taken a few steps into the hall, he added, ". . . if there is room!"

The tears came after I walked out of the theatre. I looked up into a blue sky and asked myself why I should be crying. What had I done?

A few weeks later, after Balanchine learned from the press that I would be dancing with Baryshnikov, he privately called me a "traitor." It seems that he thought, on the basis of our brief encounter, that I would be going up on a mountain to meditate. He assumed that sooner or later I would return, like a prodigal daughter.

Asked to comment on my departure for *Newsweek,* he hid his indignation. "She came to me first and said she wanted to try her own ideas . . . E eryone should. Why not? It's like marriage. People get married two or three times. I was married five times. Every dancer secretly wants to be Giselle." Balanchine could afford to be generous and philosophical about my infidelity —his *Coppélia* was a major hit that summer without me. I had no regrets about not appearing in that one.

My arrangements with Baryshnikov were dependent on his negotiations with American Ballet Theatre. Natalia Makarova had been instrumental in providing him with an entrée to ABT. If Misha and I were to dance together, each of us would have to join or guest with the company. He apparently had a picture of me with him and was as excited about the prospect of our partnership as I was.

After performing in *La Sylphide* for Canadian television, Misha arrived in New York to dance with ABT. He replaced Ivan Nagy as Natalia Makarova's partner in *Giselle.* I counted on Misha's success. Prior to his opening night, July 27, 1974, I sent the following telegram from Saratoga:

> MISHA,
> MERDE A MILLION TIMES.
> MUCH LOVE,
> GELSEY

"Merde" signifies "good luck" in the world of ballet. I would need the luck more than Misha. His performance in New York made him an overnight sensation. He was the drawing card for whom I would have to prove myself worthy.

For the first time in my career, I secured the services of a personal manager, Shirley Bernstein, sister of the famous conductor Leonard Bernstein.

Shirley was actually a literary agent who had known my father. While representing me, she always demonstrated an extraordinary tenacity of spirit. Prone to worry and given to fits of temper, I was not an easy client. My concerns were exclusively and obsessively artistic.

After Misha closed his deal, he recommended that the company hire me as his partner. Shirley then negotiated the terms of my contract. My salary doubled changing companies. I was to dance for six hundred dollars a week and appear in at least half of Baryshnikov's performances.

My bargaining position with the theatre was never strong. I was not Russian. I was not even European. My background did not impress the management. The artistic director, Lucia Chase, had never even seen me perform. She had been the principal founder of the company back in 1939. Her generous financial support over the years had consolidated her power. She did not favor Balanchine ballerinas. As far as Lucia was concerned, I was Baryshnikov's little partner, a prop he needed for his show.

I was encouraged from all sides to appreciate the opportunity that had materialized. My mother added her voice to the chorus that told me how fortunate I was to have the chance to dance with Baryshnikov. It did seem that I was on the verge of taking command of both my career and my life. The idea never crossed my mind that events and circumstances might have their own logic and momentum. It never occurred to me that ballet might be considered a business, that I had become a commodity in the theatrical marketplace. I thought in terms of pirouettes, not profits. I was in so many ways a little fool.

I remember the heat of that summer, the waiting and the pressure. After returning to Manhattan, I went on a crash diet and locked myself in the dance studio. Drowning in sweat day after day, I prepared for what I could only imagine would be demanded by the ABT repertoire. Unless I maintained my physical condition, I would have no chance to fulfill Misha's expectations of me as a partner. I would not let him down by allowing my body to slip out of shape. In my mind, I had already turned Misha into both savior and judge. My imagination soon endowed him with virtues that only a saint or a lover could possess.

Long before our first meeting in New York, I had considered the rather obvious possibility of falling in love. Just knowing that Misha had my picture with him caused me to jump to the conclusion that his interest might be more than professional. I was aware of his much publicized relationship with a young American girlfriend, Christina Berlin, whose father was a former executive with the Hearst corporate chain. Misha and Christina first met in England during a 1970 Kirov tour. She subsequently visited him in Russia, somehow managing to carry on the affair in secret. The official story, however implausible in retrospect, was that he defected for love. I knew that she joined him in Canada and later traveled ahead of him to New York. I did not know that he had proposed marriage to her shortly after the defection. The rumor was that Misha had already had a change of heart about the relationship. I hoped that I might be the reason.

At the beginning of August, I attended one of Misha's rehearsals at the New York State Theater. My friend Dina Makarova, acting on Misha's behalf, did her best to put me at ease. Her skill as translator was combined with a talent for discretion. Dina assured me that Misha was truly looking forward to our meeting, but she offered no revelations as to what I might expect from him, what the purpose of this meeting might be. She did not try to second-guess his motives or his plans. He was still suffering from the trauma of his defection.

Watching him rehearse the variations for his upcoming appearance in *La Bayadère,* I was stunned again by his technical virtuosity, the liquid purity with which he executed the steps. His body was more than an object of physical attraction, it was a fountain of wisdom.

When he finished, I was in a quandary. What was I supposed to do? In the hallway outside the dressing room, Misha was hemmed in by admirers and seemed unaware of my presence. I stood out of the way, trying to look voluptuous and finding myself ignored. He finally passed me on his way into the dressing room, saying only, "Vait here. Ve go to dinner." Leaving me with the image of his mischievous grin, he danced out of sight.

After what seemed an eternity, Misha reappeared at my side, all wistful and boyish. He had been given a scrap of paper on which was scribbled the address of our destination. I had no idea where we were going. Leading the way, Misha hailed a taxi outside Lincoln Center. Although he knew only a few phrases of English, he let me know that he was in charge. When I made an offer to help him with the language, he seemed not to understand. Even his bewilderment was charming. I told myself that I would have to learn Russian.

During our ride in the cab, language did not pose a problem. The silence was filled by the sudden touch of his hand. My heart fluttered in its cage. We were as shy as teenagers on a first date. He was twenty-six and I was twenty-one, but there did not seem to be any real age difference. When I felt his glance and looked into his eyes, I saw two shocking-blue stones, a vision of innocence and eternal youth. I imagined that we had already established an unspoken rapport, that we both knew how perfect we were for each other.

I must have lost myself. The next thing I remember is that we entered a small suite in the Essex House. Little did I know that our hostess for dinner was to be Natalia Makarova. I was hit by an immediate cold flash. Natasha's greeting was enough to tell me that I was not a welcome guest. The only warm spot in the room was occupied by my friend Dina, whose role as interpreter proved to be useless under the circumstances.

At the time, nobody bothered to explain those circumstances to me. The scene had a history to which I was not yet privy. I had no idea that Natasha had been Misha's first serious love, that she had broken his heart in Russia some years before. Nor did I realize that this dinner engagement was to have been their first private meeting since Misha's defection. Why in the world had he decided to bring me along? I was certainly aware that Misha and Natasha were matched as partners in New York. It seemed to me that she might want to have him all to herself, at least on the stage. Was I an interloper? Had Misha decided to play us off against each other? Was my presence intended to signal some sort of message to Natasha?

Caught unwittingly in a crossfire between my two idols, I tried to make believe that nothing was happening. I said to myself: this has to be the way sophisticated people behave. The four of us sat around a small table to dine. The conversation was minimal. I found that I was unable to eat—or breathe—in an atmosphere saturated with repressed hostility.

My mind kept wandering to Misha. Had he forgotten me? Was I being tested? Had I already failed? I tried not to look at him, at least not directly. Watching his reflection on the glittering surface of my silverware, I tried to pin down his image, which was the only clue I had to his personality. I was drawn into the mystery of him. He had the benefit of all my doubts.

After finishing his meal, Misha abruptly excused himself and moved to a couch across the room. Dina assumed a neutral position, sensing trouble. Natasha and I remained face to face, staring at each other across the table. I wanted to lie down and wait until the emergency passed. She placed one of her cigarettes into the end of a long holder. She was sexy, fathomless as the smoke that drifted into the air between us. Her composure was absolute. Her eyes sparkled like dangerous jewels.

"Sooo . . . Gilzey . . . vhut is this I hear about you and Peter Martins? Vhut! You just take men . . . pick up . . . and poof," waving her hand like a wand, "like that . . . already you don't vant anymore!"

Feeling as if my cheek had been slapped, I turned to Misha and laughed nervously. He was the one who had set the stage for this little scene, yet his face was a total blank. Content to watch and listen, he crossed his legs and flung his arms over the back of the couch. He made no comment. Turning back to Natasha, I said that I had no idea what she meant.

I was actually flattered to be characterized as the infernal woman, a fiction that somehow made me Natasha's equal. That was how I hoped Misha would see me. Apparently the rumors about my affair with Peter had twisted the truth in my favor. The irony of my newfound reputation, however absurd, provided a certain satisfaction. Still technically on the rebound, I was not about to set Natasha straight on that romantic score. Her inquiry might blow my cover.

Brushing off her questions and begging her pardon, I departed in haste. Misha followed me. There was no doubt that I was involved in both a competition and a courtship, that I was already vulnerable. According to the rules of the game, I now had to make a show of playing hard to get. After sharing another taxi, I went home alone.

I fell asleep that night with apocalyptic expectations. I interpreted Misha's choice to bring me to dinner with him as his way of announcing his intentions to Natasha. He might be dancing with her for now, but he was committed to the future of our partnership. Such a commitment had to come from the heart. I was about to take my first step into Paradise.

Misha and Natasha appeared in two performances at the beginning of August. The ballets were excerpts from two of the "classics" of the Russian repertory: *La Bayadère* and *Don Quixote.* There were rave reviews and standing ovations. A party was thrown at the end of the season by Howard Gilman, a businessman and multimillionaire. He was one of a number of influential friends who had gravitated toward Misha shortly after the defection. The party was given at Howard's magnificent penthouse on the Upper East Side.

Misha was the unofficial guest of honor that evening. He invited me to meet him at the party. When I arrived, I discovered that I was not his only date. He had also invited his erstwhile girlfriend Christina, whose status at that point was somewhat uncertain. I saw her as soon as I walked through the door. We had never met, but I recognized her at once from photographs I had seen.

I asked myself the obvious questions. What was she doing here? If her relationship with Misha was over, why had he bothered to invite her?

I knew just enough about the situation to maintain my buoyant sense of confidence. Misha had attempted to evict Christina from his life. His effort had failed. I assumed, in muddleheaded fashion, that he must have decided to use our appearance together at the party to confirm the eviction notice. The message would be delivered now in no uncertain terms.

I made excuses for his behavior. He was trapped. He was suffering from culture shock. He was still having difficulty adjusting to his new freedom. He had not learned yet how to communicate his feelings. My mental defense of his nobility concluded with the absolute certainty that we would be free from such problems. We would be able to express ourselves through the language of dance. We would share an understanding beyond words.

It soon became obvious that Christina was not my only adversary. Misha was surrounded by glamorous beauties. Members of both American Ballet Theatre and the National Ballet of Canada were conspicuously in attendance. The party seemed to have been contrived as some sort of elaborate contest with Misha as the prize. He attempted to keep the leading contestants separated, dividing his time and attention, dashing back and forth through the rooms of the apartment. My own passion was enough to keep me blissfully in the dark. What special suspicion could I have? I thought that I had already been chosen as the winner.

Although constantly aware of Christina's presence at the party, I had no intention of either speaking to her or speaking to Misha about her. On my way to the powder room, I noticed her slouched in a chair, obviously sulking, a dour expression superimposed over delicate features. Through glassy eyes, she watched me try to hurry by her. Before I could pass, she lurched to her feet and intercepted me. Clamping her hand on my bicep, she said we had to talk. She spoke with the voice of a woman who had been humiliated.

Hooking the elbow of a young woman whom I failed to recognize, Christina led us, a swerving triumvirate, through the crowded room and onto a terrace. I assumed the other woman had to be one of Christina's friends. Years later I discovered she was actually a Canadian dancer with whom Misha had already started an affair. The three of us huddled outside a glass door, like conspirators. Seeing us together, Misha quickly dropped out of sight. Christina blurted, "I think you both . . . should know . . . he's a difficult person. I'm afraid he's . . . difficult . . . he's . . . he's . . ."

I was in no mood to listen. As soon as she began to falter, I broke away and went back to the party. She was out; I was in. It was that simple. I discounted what I heard as the hopeless litany of a spurned lover.

Between the workings of my ego and my infinite capacity for playing the fool, I created my own version of Mikhail Baryshnikov. I thought he was a great artist; therefore, he had to have the same superior qualities as a human being that I had seen him reveal on the stage. Misha was nothing less than a hero. As that fateful evening progressed, his heroic attributes multiplied in my mind; his depth of character was unquestionable.

He said almost nothing to me. Against the background noise and music of the party, our courtship was a ritual carried out in silence. There was no need to speak. The aura of mystery around him was like a sponge capable of absorbing every projection of female desire and fantasy. I squeezed meaning out of each gesture, each furtive glance. I understood the sadness in his eyes. I understood why he had to guard himself.

The image of Misha as suffering artist magnified his appeal. His story created an automatic mystique. He had defected for freedom and, in doing so, had lost the freedom to return to his homeland. I felt sorry for him. If he seemed to be acting out the role of a Russian Don Juan at times, who could blame him? By dancing between amorous partners, withholding his commitment to any one in particular, he constructed his own iron curtain, drawn as a precaution against the hazards of love and attachment. In his case, the artist apparently had to separate himself from life as a means of self-preservation. I was not discouraged.

The party was not over yet. I prepared to leave early with Misha, his faithful interpreter Dina, and a jovial Russian dancer, Sasha Minz, a recent émigré who had been one of Misha's buddies at the Kirov. Plans had been improvised for us all to have dinner and discuss the future. As the elevator door was closing, Christina rushed inside. This was clearly an incident that Misha had not anticipated and his distress was obvious. When we reached the lobby, he told us to wait for him outside while he had a word with

Christina. What impressed me at that moment was his ice-cold expression. He was suddenly a stranger.

I waited as instructed with Dina and Sasha, loitering on the sidewalk. It was one of those steamy summer nights. Soon Misha came out of the building and walked toward us. He appeared to be lost, wandering somewhere between the sun and the moon. His expression was the same frozen blank. Looking up as if he were startled to find me, he said, "Is okay. Is nothing." There was another instant change. He came back to earth. He was Misha again, his face melting into a smile.

Taking charge of the situation, he urged us forward. Looking back over my shoulder, I saw the form of a woman walking in the opposite direction. It was Christina. She was alone. Some drops of light rain had begun to fall. I thought she might need help. A shiver ran down my spine as I recalled the scene on the terrace. What was I supposed to do? Pulled along by my companions, I tried not to think about her fate. She had become an outcast.

The four of us—Misha, Dina, Sasha, and I—went to a restaurant in the neighborhood. There was an unspoken understanding that Misha and I were together. I was enthralled. If our future was discussed at all, I was never included. Any serious exchanges were conducted in Russian between Misha and Sasha. The possibility that I might be the subject of their conversation was enough to satisfy me. I was more than happy to hand over my fate to Misha. I was ecstatic.

The next step seemed inevitable. It was a simple matter of logistics as to how Misha and I would make our exit. He whispered something in Russian to Dina and Sasha. I went along with whatever he said. I asked no questions. I learned later that he had issued a polite dismissal, announcing his plan to escort me home.

After leaving the restaurant, Misha said good-bye to our two companions in Russian. I said good-bye in English. Then the two of us caught a passing cab. I looked out the back window and saw Dina and Sasha watching us, a single expression of concern pasted across their two faces, colored by my own anxiety. Misha leaned against me as the taxi pulled out and accelerated into traffic.

We both lived on the West Side. We both knew we were about to share a bed as well as a cab. I invited Misha to my place with as much subtlety and nonchalance as I could manage. He had no trouble translating my proposition.

I was suddenly petrified. It was happening too fast. Hit by a whiplash of insecurity, I needed to talk to somebody. I needed an interpreter. How could I explain myself to Misha? He would misunderstand. He would be hurt. He would think that I had been teasing him. Our partnership would break up before it had even begun.

With the aid of a few convenient rationalizations, I blocked out the fears and threw myself into his arms. It was divine madness . . . It was love . . . It was bound to happen sooner or later.

Arriving at my apartment, I made sure to steer us away from my bedroom. The bed of my childhood had to be avoided. Thinking fast, I maneuvered us from the living room into my brother's old room. There was only a mattress on the floor. The room was small and unremarkable except for a strange little statue that my brother had given me years before as a Christmas present. Standing upright on a dresser, the figure of an ape could be seen holding a human skull in the palm of an outstretched hand. I saw this statue as a vague symbol of fallen humanity, forsaking the angels in favor of the beast. The ape was Hamlet in the grave scene, holding my skull, saying something like, "Alas, poor Gelsey!" I would not allow this grotesque object of art to witness the activities that were to highlight the evening. As I began to disrobe, I casually threw my blouse over it.

After groping with buttons, belt, and zipper, Misha appeared for a brief moment to be a statue himself, a pedestal of rumpled clothes at his feet. He seemed embarrassed, like a bashful god. I shared his discomfort and dimmed the lights to conceal my own naked form. Our embrace did nothing to relieve the pressure. This would be our first performance. We were both suffering from stage fright.

I retreated back into the refuge of fantasy, allowing my imagination to guide me through the seduction. We were two statues that had somehow come to life only to dance this intimate pas de deux. The choreography called for us to topple in slow motion onto the mattress. After sliding gracefully beneath the sheets and into each other, the next moment found us hopelessly entangled—like something out of one of those abstract ballets. There was an awkward frenzy of limbs, a struggle for balance and possession. I felt that I had to surrender at this point to his need for control, to his fantasy. My purpose in life came into focus as his fingers ran up and down the lashing curve of my spine: to please him, to give him pleasure.

Sensing what was expected of me, I waited for him to be done. I felt no need to fake what had not taken place, what could not have taken place in the time that had elapsed. After he came to rest in my arms, we both turned back into stone. It was over.

During the quiet interlude that followed, when I was lulled to sleep by the sound of his breathing, I thought I had hit upon the secret of male tenderness, dreaming in my arms. I felt his thoughts drifting through mine. If our encounter had been somewhat awkward, if at first there had been no sensual fireworks, it had created in my heart a still more profound endearment. Even then I knew the technique of love was for me nothing compared to that which had inspired the act itself. Satisfied to satisfy him, I was about to become an expert on anticlimax, both in the bedroom and on the stage.

In the morning Misha hurried away without breakfast. Looking the part of a dissolute angel, he said only, "I call you."

He was true to his word. Our romance continued as a fitful routine of nocturnal visits. After calling, usually late at night, he came like an orphan looking for shelter, only to vanish in the morning without trace or explanation. He seemed to be locked inside himself. The attempts at sexual expression were my only assurance of his affection. What promised to become an intimate bond of trust turned swiftly and imperceptibly into a kind of emotional bondage. I waited for his calls. I wondered why he seemed to want to keep me a secret. I kept all of my questions to myself. It had already become a matter of having him or losing him.

There was almost no trade of ideas between us during those first few weeks. There was only the dream of an exchange that might soon take place in the studio and on the stage. Whenever I tried to humor him, I was never sure if he was responding to what I said or to what he thought I said. This was unnerving. I knew that I needed another line of communication and enrolled in a Berlitz course to study Russian. Misha made no effort to speak to me in his native tongue. I never knew how to ask for his help without feeling like a pest. Without encouragement, I would never become fluent. I soon understood what Christina had been trying to say, that he was a difficult person. But it was too late to heed the warning; I was in love.

Although the years may have disfigured certain feelings and impressions, I can swear to the faith that held me to Misha. I took it for granted that we already shared both a point of view and sense of purpose toward our art. If we had begun on the wrong foot, I never doubted that the partnership would prevail as the ultimate expression of our love. I knew by heart the words of Da Vinci: "Great love springs from great knowledge of the beloved object." We just needed time to know each other, as dancers and as lovers.

There was another factor that seemed to guarantee our success: the indisputable fact that Misha was more advanced as a dancer than I was meant that his male ego could not possibly be threatened by me. His stature as an artist qualified him in my eyes as the greatest teacher that I could hope to find. As far as I was concerned, he had demonstrated a thorough knowledge of the classical form. He had to possess all the answers that I had been seeking.

Our romantic routine was interrupted briefly during that first month. Misha returned to Canada to perform. I went to England on a futile errand, to track down the manufacturer of my toe shoes for a proper fitting. I wanted to have a mold made for my feet. The retailer told me that my shoemaker (known only as "Mr. Y") was deaf, dumb, and "dying out." Discouraged from seeing him, I returned to New York to begin rehearsals.

Misha chose the ballets. These initially included the Kingdom of the Shades excerpt from *La Bayadère*, the pas de deux from *Don Quixote*, and, later, the full-length *Coppélia*. Misha also suggested that we dance Balanchine's *Theme and Variations,* included in American Ballet Theatre's repertoire.

For the most part, I would be walking into ballets that were closely identified with Misha's experience and cultural heritage. I interpreted his decision to include Balanchine in our repertory as a passing phase, a bug of artistic curiosity that Misha had to work out of his system. In spite of my doubts, I offered no resistance. Because I was experienced with *Theme and Variations* and rated myself as something of an expert on Balanchine, I was actually relieved to have at least one area of specialized knowledge to offer my partner. I should have seen his attraction to Balanchine as a sign of things to come.

The initial rehearsal period ran through September. The immediate challenge was technical. *Don Quixote* and *La Bayadère* were showpieces that had been lifted out of context, from the full-length versions of the nineteenth-century ballets. As such, I did not have to worry too much about plot, at least not right away. The problem was the composition of the steps.

Both ballets had been staged originally by Marius Petipa, the prolific French choreographer who established much of the Russian repertory. In a sense, I was leaping a century backward through history. In order to make that leap, I would have to transform myself. For me to fit the design of Petipa's aesthetic would require more than a simple change of image. The technical transition reflected the fundamental difference between Petipa and Balanchine, the distance between the traditional and modern approaches to the classical form. The years that separate these two choreographers might be measured by the change in expressive purpose of the dancer's body, from telling a story to dancing for the sake of dancing.

Petipa codified the vocabulary of classical steps which had become popular in Europe during the eighteenth and early nineteenth centuries, ordering movement and gesture according to a precise grammatical structure. But the Russian form seemed to advance without corresponding progress in content. Petipa's ballets, in essence, did not move beyond the limited thematic domain of Romanticism—fairy-tale formulas equating love and death. Such thematic currents merely coalesced within the more rigid form, establishing a kind of theatrical ideology and fixed style. The codification to some extent betrayed or fell short of what I would one day call the classical ideal of dramatic dance. Nevertheless, the bodies of the dancers still had to render a coherent dramatic statement.

By modifying Petipa's grammar and further shifting the emphasis from content to form, Balanchine altered the logic with which the steps had been linked together, ultimately transforming the process by which each step had been composed. The styles of the two choreographers contrasted most obviously in terms of the density and speed of the steps. Mr. B's dances were often packed with multiple combinations, intended to dazzle at high velocity. The relative simplicity of Petipa's design was actually far more complicated for me. A single step was truly brought to life only by revealing subtle complexities of character. I felt like I had been studying the game of checkers and was now being asked to play chess. I needed a strategy, a way to make each move or movement lead to the next.

In rehearsing with Misha, it became immediately clear that my covert attempts to inject drama into the Balanchine design had not prepared me for the technical demands of Petipa's ballets—even though the purpose of the steps was now explicitly dramatic. I had not yet developed a facility equal to those expressive demands. It also became clear that Misha was not a teacher. He was unable to explain either how or why he produced a step in the way he did. He was at a loss trying to verbalize his approach either in Russian or in English. At first this was a challenge rather than an obstacle to our partnership, not unlike the challenge of intimacy in our romance.

There was no teacher at American Ballet Theatre who possessed the specialized knowledge necessary to help me make the technical transition. This would continue to be a problem when I moved on to ballets that required mime and character dancing. The assumption was that such skills had somehow been included in every dancer's basic training. The theatre did not provide either understanding or sympathy for my predicament, a situation that was no different from the New York City Ballet. I had to find a remedy outside the company. Misha was willing to make enough of an effort at that point to follow me to David Howard's studio at Harkness House. We were encouraged by Mrs. Rebekah Harkness, an eccentric patroness who sponsored the Harkness Ballet.

Under David's watchful eye, Misha and I rehearsed the segments from *La Bayadère* and *Don Quixote.* As the weeks passed, I privately bombarded David with questions. Each ballet had to be investigated moment by moment. We slowed down films of Misha as well as various ballerinas who had performed my roles. Each step had to be broken down into the basic physical principles that had to be applied in order to compose the movement. Then the steps had to be phrased, according to the same principles, working off Misha's timing. When further refinement became necessary later in my transition, I frequently turned to Stanley Williams for his unique emphasis on placement of the feet, his sense of polish and precision complementing the kinesiological insights that I had worked out with David. I had to combine the verbal languages of these two teachers into a single conceptual framework. Assimilating David's pivotal ideas on initiating movement from the upper body enabled me to absorb Stanley's meticulous stress on the lower body. The entire process was a maddeningly complex problem of coordination.

I never received an explanation of the stories behind these ballets. No ballet master ever explained the steps in terms of the drama. I gleaned what I could about character and action from the films. My intuitive sense of the larger story slowly influenced my technical choices. The necessity of adding an interpretive signature to a work, at the same time remaining faithful to a literal rendering of the steps, underscored my awareness of deficiencies. My movement appeared arbitrary and artificial until I found a way to connect the lyrical passion of each character to the prosodic definition of the classical form.

The technical key for which I was searching—which would link the dance to the music and to the drama—was known as "legato." This was the special dynamic which seemed to allow the Russian dancers to move through the steps with such fluid grace, to bind all the steps within the overall concept of the ballet. The Russians themselves, including Misha, were unable to translate the verbal cues and corrections which they had received in their training into a comprehensive and intelligible idiom. They were often unable to communicate the knowledge that was stored in their bodies to American dancers, whose training was geared to a different aesthetic. Legato was an alien concept to Americans who had been conditioned for speed, blurring rather than binding the steps. In spite of my best efforts, I was no exception.

Rather than learning how to dance, Misha seemed to have been programmed to dance. He followed an elaborate set of rules that originated with the Russian classroom syllabus. In my adoration of his abilities, I continued to presume that he consciously understood the underlying logic of that syllabus and how it was related to the movements of his body. We did seem to converse beautifully when we danced, at least for the duration of certain passages, as if we were thinking along the same lines. If he were unable to explain how he was able to bind the steps together, how he had developed legato, he still provided a singular example for study. He suggested to David at a certain point that I be drilled in Russian classroom exercises, as if repeating words in a foreign tongue enough times would reveal their meaning. This was a hint of the frustration and the folly that lay ahead.

To create an effect that was essentially poetic—such as "walking on a cloud" or "floating in a dream"—I needed a specific language that could be internalized and translated directly into the body. As I began to build such a language, I discovered a disparity between what I felt and the feeling that a particular image communicated in poetic terms. I did not feel for a moment that I was walking on a cloud or floating across the stage. The real feeling was frequently in opposition to the quality embodied in the movement. Even a simple movement, like rising on pointe, demanded that I exert a force in the opposite direction, pushing down against the floor, resisting the inclination to pull myself up with legs and arms. Poetic inspiration, what seemingly lay behind the physical imagery of the dance, did not reveal the method of composition.

I had to start from scratch with each ballet. The trick was to channel the physical impulse from my torso through the rest of my body, coordinating all muscular action through a specific set of circular pathways that defined motion in the classical form, regardless of the particular national style. Guided by intuition and rigorous analysis, I isolated the integral patterns of movement, unfolding a continuous geometry of expressive possibilities for each dance. A particularly beautiful phrase might possess a quality that could be extended into a longer sequence of steps and gestures. A theme might emerge from this pattern to connect each phrase to the composition as a whole. Such a thematic concept ultimately had to be tested by painstaking trial and error.

At the end of the pas de deux from *Don Quixote,* for example, I performed thirty-two fouettés. This exasperating series of turns had to say something significant about the character, Kitri, even in this vignette. I knew only that she was supposed to be a Spanish peasant, won over by Misha's character, Basil, a mischievous barber. The thirty-two turns gave me the opportunity to measure her strength.

I calculated the exact capability of her spine, making her spinal column part of the long fulcrum that included her supporting leg and continued through the back of her neck and head. Each of the turns was a dare that I had to take to prove that the character had a backbone, a quality that both Basil and Misha might understand. The entire sequence of turns had to be performed in place, a test of precision and stamina. Kitri's spirit had to equal the brazen intensity of Basil's machismo, the quality captured in Misha's bravura display. Through my technical control of momentum and balance, each spiral spin seemed to kindle a spark, figuratively speaking, making these fouettés into a visual metaphor for the fire that burned in her Spanish soul. She was proud to dance. Her grace and dignity flowed through those steps. This entire concept would be expanded several years later when I performed the full-length ballet.

During most rehearsals, Misha offered corrections. For instance, in preparing for a lift, he advised me: "Just go up straight . . . strong . . . stay strong." Words such as "straight" and "strong" described the effect rather than the cause. He had a string of adjectives similar to those that my early Russian teachers at Balanchine's school had employed. Occasionally he broke the tension with a string of English four-letter words, delighted with his newfound command of the language. More often, he demanded repetition and speed: "Come, girl . . . quick, quick, quick, let's go!"

He tried to be helpful by pointing out how my dancing deviated from pictures he had in his mind of whatever ballet we happened to be preparing. Each picture was a static image; a pose that a ballerina had to strike in the course of the dance. He could describe each pose, or offer an imitation, but he could not tell me the process by which it was generated. This was a particular problem in the *Bayadère* excerpt.

The Kingdom of the Shades segment had been reset by Natasha in a version faithful to the traditional Russian staging. The libretto was a variation on the Orphic myth, transposed to India. A warrior, Solor, pursued his beloved, Nikiya, into the spirit world. This was supposed to be a world of Elysian bliss, a perfect realm of classical beauty, envisioned by the choreographer, Petipa, through the opium dream of the hero, adding more than a touch of Romanticism.

I knew that my character, Nikiya, was the spirit of a temple dancer—the bayadère. As a denizen of that land of the dead, her movements reflected the cold purity that Petipa infused into the steps. Her dance epitomized his academic style. In the imaginary world of Petipa, the plane of human existence was separated from the plane of human ideals—just as Solor, Misha's character, was separated from his beloved. I resisted the message of despair that seemed to permeate the story, that Solor's infidelity doomed his love for Nikiya to unworldly consummation. That was not my idea of love.

I made the ballet personal. Misha and I had to find each other through the steps. We had to create our own paradise on the stage, in this world, corresponding to the overall story of romantic betrayal, redemption, and reconciliation. The pretty picture dreamed up by Petipa—including the hypnotic maneuvers of the corps, a large group of shades in diaphanous white tutus setting the mood with a sequence of repeated arabesques—was only a pretext for the action between us, the lovers.

How could I be cut off from Misha? How could I be cut off from life? Was death supposed to be beautiful? What sort of psychological depth could a dead character possess? What in blazes was a shade anyway?

I instinctively rejected all of the supernatural female creatures that inhabited the nineteenth-century ballets: shades, sylphs, wilis, nymphs, swans, sleepwalkers, spirits. I wore the costumes but fought against the fanciful premises underlying these imaginary beings. I never really believed in them. They were not real. They had no power to move an audience unless I brought them down to earth and made them human. They had to enter my reality. My ideas and passions had to speak through them. In order to believe in Nikiya at all, she had to say what I wanted to say through the dance. If Petipa gave her beauty, I would give her truth. I wanted to dance away the illusions.

The choreographic style seemed to block my telling of the story. Each climactic pose, like a freeze-frame, seemed to break the film, disrupting the motion picture of the dance. It was impossible to recover momentum after extending into Misha's static definition of the position. Because most of the poses came after turning with Misha, I was stuck between his hands, held in a position that demolished everything I had ever learned about dance. My impulse was to break away from him.

During those awkward moments, the ballet seemed to die. I had not yet learned that the shape of the position was composed through an imperceptible continuation of muscular action inside the body, that the stillness had to be kept alive through a deliberate transition. In a sense, I had to rotate even when I seemed to be at rest. That inward rotation was in no way automatic or instinctual, requiring conscious control of breath. Misha, characteristically rolling his eyes, had no patience for this sort of problem. It was "my problem." This meant it was not a "real" problem.

During our early rehearsals of the Shades scene, I decided to try working his way, taking one of his classes. I hoped against hope that class might become part of our shared routine, something we might do together each morning. Reality quickly dashed that dream. His half-hour warm-up period was much too brief for me. After following him through a series of Russian barre exercises, I felt as if my knees had been smacked with a sledgehammer. I was amazed at how much damage could be done in so little time. My body simply could not be worked in the manner to which Misha was accustomed.

The strain was nothing compared to the distressing thought that rushed into my mind. The realization was unavoidable: my approach to ballet was not compatible with Misha's. I would never be able to create the correct poses that he demanded by devoting myself to the Russian syllabus.

The problem of hitting a pose seemed to point to a contradiction between the fluid legato that tied the steps together and the strict upper-body lines known as épaulement. The Russian syllabus was designed to instill a set of physical memories that precisely related the head, neck, shoulders, back, and arms to various images that the dancers performed on the stage. The mechanical reproduction of style from generation to generation seemed to preclude a conscious mastery of the compositional principles that related form to content. The expressive purpose of upper-body épaulement, for example, degenerated in many cases into empty affectation, disconnected from any poetic or dramatic intent. Thanks to years of training, Misha's upper body did what it was supposed to do. Mine did not. I had to discover the principles that would enable me to give the impression that I danced according to the same rules.

Misha was impressed with how hard I worked, but he never understood the nature of that work. He never asked how I improved. He explained everything with a Russian aphorism that roughly translated, "Talent is talent —you can't hide it in your pocket." I knew that I had an extremely modest talent, especially when I measured myself against him, but I had learned how to work, how to think, and how to develop as a dancer.

He looked at my unorthodox methods with the sort of wide-eyed skepticism that a superstitious peasant might display when confronted with a scientific marvel. Seldom did he voice either curiosity or approval. Knowing he had a history of partner problems in Russia, I was sure that he appreciated my efforts. He had been mismatched with various ballerinas. One of his former partners, whom I had seen, looked like a refugee from Roller Derby. My rating had to be at least passable.

As I drove myself to equal Misha's range of expression, to rise to his standards, I made myself more and more vulnerable to his criticism. It was as if I were dancing only to please him. My heart was always in jeopardy.

I recall an afternoon when Misha brought several of his friends to watch

one of our rehearsals of *Don Quixote*. I had been working in the studio prior
to his arrival. The toe shoes that I was wearing were too soft to support my
feet properly in the pas de deux he intended to show off. I knew that I
should have changed them, but he was in a rush. He certainly did not want
to be kept waiting while his partner changed her toe shoes. After he introduced me to his audience, I yielded without protest to his impatience. As
soon as we began to promenade, one of my toes jammed into the floor.
When I wobbled through my turns on pointe, Misha suddenly let go of me
and turned away, muttering in Russian under his breath. He refused to look
at me, prolonging the suspense and torture. Then he turned and snapped,
"Ve go again. Don't stop!"

Blocking out the grief as well as the physical pain, I made it through the
second try without committing any major blunders. Neither improving my
performance nor telling him that I was sorry was enough to exculpate myself. I had embarrassed him in front of his friends. He gave no sign that I was
forgiven. I stayed on edge for hours, until his mood swung the other way,
until his charm turned again in my direction. That was my signal that the
episode had been forgotten.

I was never able to steel myself to this kind of incident. His demands
could always be rationalized in such a way that I was at fault for not being
able to deliver. My only recourse was to dance to perfection, as he defined
the word.

Our progress in the studio was steady enough during the early rehearsals
for me to remain guardedly optimistic. I had become a part of his life. Our
dancing seemed to indicate that the curtain had begun to rise, that Misha had
begun to trust me, that he was open to a deeper exchange. Each gesture,
each movement, rapt and sublime, attested to our mutual love. I made sure
to make no demands. In spite of the lopsided nature of our relationship, in
spite of contrasting temperaments and approaches to ballet, the dances that
we created seemed to combine and enhance our individual gifts. We were
better than our material. I liked to think that Misha was as proud of me as I
was of him.

The romance continued at Misha's convenience. The nocturnal routine
began to vary. Sometimes I stayed with him at his temporary home, part of
the penthouse complex belonging to Howard Gilman. The atmosphere was
on the order of a hotel suite, all rather anonymous and impersonal. I felt
more like a privileged guest than a lover. The fact of the matter was that I
allowed myself to be turned into a servant, as devoted in the bedroom as I
was in the ballet studio. My passion seemed to justify all manner of sacrifice,
from the indefinite postponement of gratification to the constant deference.

During occasional bouts of insomnia, I secretly wondered if my previous
experiences had somehow ruined me sexually. Was I inadequate? Was I cut
off from myself? Even these doubts about my womanhood could be rational-

ized from the point of view of the studio. The physical performance of ballet
depended on a shared ideal gradually unfolding over time. Nothing had
been easy about our progress so far. Surely love was an art that required
both an expressive ideal and a period of unfoldment. Circular reasoning
always carried me back to a thought that I held on to when I finally fell
asleep: Misha himself was the ideal.

Even our insecurities seemed to balance. I usually made a fast exit in the
morning, like he did when he stayed at my place. I had the feeling that I was
invading his privacy. His homesickness was a constant complaint, the origin
of many of his darker moods. After one of my overnight visits, I found him
washing dishes in the kitchen and innocently asked him why he was doing
the honors. He cringed as if I had asked him if he were a member of the
KGB, as though I had begun an interrogation. Then he stared for a moment
at the dish in his hand, motionless, as if his mind had just boarded a plane for
Leningrad. Finally, with a baleful glance, he muttered, "I like washing d..hes
. . . sometimes." The gloom was impenetrable. I was shut out.

During the period of rehearsals, the veil of secrecy that surrounded our
romance lifted ever so slightly. Misha invited me several times to accompany
him to soirees attended by Russian émigrés and an assortment of American
friends. He asked me to come along on these occasions but usually ditched
me soon after we arrived. For the most part, Russian was spoken. I caught
only a few of the words, still struggling with my Berlitz course. Misha did
not attempt to help me, though he thought my efforts were cute enough to
warrant an occasional pinch on the cheek.

I met a Columbia professor at one of those gatherings, John Malmstead,
who offered some assistance with the language and cultural barriers. I began
to learn a Russian folk song, a contemporary tune that likened love to war.
Later, I performed this number for Misha, who had a consuming passion for
the modern poets of his homeland. He was touched with my rendition,
repeating his catch phrase, "Talent is talent . . ."

The Russian circle eventually included the famed musician Mstislav Rostropovich. Misha was introduced through an émigré, Remi Saunder, who
worked at times for Rostropovich and for Tiffany's. Remi became something
of a mother figure for Misha, slowly replacing my friend Dina as interpreter
and personal assistant. No détente was possible for the women who worked
for Misha. He seemed to like it that way, encouraging each female confidante to think that she knew what he needed. Flaring tempers were inevitable.

Misha had a special interest in cultivating the relationship with Rostropovich. The musician traveled back and forth to the Soviet Union, performing in both the East and the West. That was the kind of arrangement Misha
hoped to establish. The Soviets apparently made at least one overture in this
regard through Irina Kolpakova, a Kirov ballerina and former partner.
Kolpakova had political connections and had assumed some official responsi-

bility for Misha on the Canadian tour during which he defected. She later passed on a formal request for him to come home. The KGB even maintained Misha's Leningrad apartment for two years after the defection. The expectation that he might return was not unfounded, a contingency that filled me with dread.

Near the end of rehearsals, Misha invited me to spend a weekend with him at Howard Gilman's Florida estate, White Oak. The place was a magnificent plantation, thousands of acres located along the Florida-Georgia border. We traveled down on Howard's private plane. During the flight, I looked over at Misha and realized for the first time that this was the kind of first-class treatment to which he was accustomed. There was something in the expression on his face, a hint of impatience and annoyance. He expected people to wait on him. This struck me as odd, because I had been thinking of him all along as a tormented artist, a Russian dissident who had been persecuted. To think that he might have been spoiled, that he had been a member of an elite society, clarified his image somewhat. If he was no longer quite the hero I had imagined, he was more human. His flaws narrowed the distance between us. I felt less frivolous, less expendable.

The saving grace on that holiday was my friend Dina, who made the trip with us and kept me company. Misha frequently disappeared for long walks in the woods. I remember feeling out of place, having no idea how to deal with a vacation. I was afraid to break the work routine even for a day. There are photographs that prove that Misha and I played tennis, that we went fishing and horseback riding. Those memories have faded. I do recall being uncertain about the sleeping arrangements. I did not allow myself to make any assumptions. His mood fluctuated too much to be sure of anything. A moment of levity could lead without warning into a spell of melancholy. I waited at night for him to make the decision. A warm body seemed to be the one form of comfort that he was able to accept.

We returned to Manhattan just in time for a rehearsal. I was sore from riding. After a brief warm-up, I told Misha that I was going to take it easy at first. He looked at me like I was malingering. As we began rehearsing, he urged me, "Come on, girl! Don't stop . . . just do it . . . no problems. You'll see." What I saw was that his body bounced back from the layoff much faster than mine. I faked it as well as I could and refrained from complaining. There was no arguing with him. His opinion was that any dancer who needed more than a half hour to warm up was not a professional. He did not understand that we were not built the same way, that we had different physical needs. He would never comprehend that simple reality.

We were scheduled to open with the pas de deux from *Don Quixote* in Winnipeg, Canada, at the beginning of October, 1974, performing as guests with the Royal Winnipeg Ballet. I made my first mistake sometime before we left for this engagement. I called Misha by the wrong name. It was a slip of the tongue. I heard myself say, "Peter," before I could stop the word from popping out of my mouth. Misha threw it back in my face. When I tried to apologize, he shut me up, "That's your problem, girl!"

He claimed not to be hurt, but the temperature between us was as cold as the snow that greeted our arrival in Winnipeg. My next mistake occurred just after we checked into the hotel. I asked Misha what I should say about "us" if the press should ask about the romance. It was a reasonable question at that point. He replied with a strange voice, "Vhut you vant. It doesn't matter. Vhut you vant."

I had said something wrong. His harsh tone made me feel I was asking for his permission to publicize our private lives in order to push my career. His ability to twist my meaning made my head spin. I told him that I really did not want to take part in any of the interviews. The next thing I knew, he reversed himself. He pouted, cuddled, and sweet-talked me into going with him to face the press. I told myself again that it was the language problem. He had learned to speak English by watching television. He failed to connect my words with my feelings. I decided the safest course of action was to say nothing that could be misconstrued—to Misha or to the media.

The press asked him why he had chosen me as his partner. He quipped, "Just look at her . . . and besides, she's not a bad ballerina. I don't have to give her any advertising. What better partner could I ask for?"

I bubbled over with effusive praise, saying, among other things, "Just watching Misha dance makes me find more in myself that I want to express." That was true.

As a test run for our partnership, the performances in Winnipeg were successful, at least as far as the audiences and critics were concerned. As usual, I was in tears, disappointed with the technical side of my dancing. In spite of nervous miscalculations, I had an intuitive sense of how to turn our precarious personal rapport to dramatic advantage. Critic Marcia B. Siegel, reporting on the performances in Winnipeg, wrote in *The Soho Weekly News:*

> I was prepared for Baryshnikov to be astonishing, but Kirkland matched him. In a way, hers was the greater achievement; the publicity hypes Baryshnikov, plays her as an unknown Cinderella, yet she's as virtuosic as he is. The second night in particular she lit on one toe endlessly, swept into faultless turns in arabesque as if she had complete confidence in his being there to bring her out of them.
>
> I suspect Baryshnikov has a tendency to be too serious, and Kirkland's playful streak relieves that heaviness. Her delicacy complements his driving strength. Her exceptional control covers for his moments of recklessness.

The stage became the one arena in which I could challenge Misha with ideas and emotions. I could woo him through the dance. I could taunt him. I could joke with him. The intimacy that was lacking between us could be realized through the ballet.

He was not prepared to be matched in such a personal way. The first time I presented a rose to him during a curtain call he was unable to look me in the eye. I thought that I had offended him, that I had failed him with my performance. The truth was that he was unable to accept such an open display of love and gratitude. He was embarrassed by me.

When we returned to Manhattan, rehearsals continued. My stepfather sent me a typewritten note informing me that I was living on bank loans and that my credit cards had been suspended. He also reminded me that I had neglected to call my mother, concluding with a piece of advice that infuriated me at the time: "You must really start thinking of others who are involved in your life and love you. In the long run, they will have more permanence than the Peters and Mishas, or Jules." How could my stepfather put all of the men in my life, past and present, into the same category? How could he not tell them apart? For some reason, I kept his note. It would take ten years for me to appreciate his wisdom.

Back in the studio, Misha was ready to put me in my place. He seemed to adopt a more condescending attitude. I was not allowed to think for a moment that we were equals. I offered no resistance to being patronized by him as long as our exchange continued through the dance. There were times he did seem to embrace that exchange with such warm enthusiasm that I would have given him the world. There were other times, more and more frequent, when he reminded me with his cold intransigence that any trade between us required an official approval from him. The only sure way to get through to him was to make him think that he had come up with an idea, to flatter him with the sincere acknowledgment that he was my inspiration.

He predicted the future of our partnership and thereby dictated the terms. During a press interview at the ABT studios in midtown Manhattan, a few blocks from Carnegie Hall, he spoke through an interpreter: "Of course, no one knows now what the outcome of our partnership will be, and it may be presumptuous on my part to say so, but I believe in Gelsey, I think she'll come through beautifully, and I—I'll hold up my end." To hold up my end, I had to hide my means. I had to make him believe that I was working his way. His ridicule could be unbearable. In the same interview, he defined the root of our problem: ". . . You can't exist behind an iron curtain, an artist can't."

In preparing *Coppélia*, we frequently worked at cross-purposes, a basic romantic and artistic antagonism which happened to mirror the relationship of our characters in the ballet, Franz and Swanilda. This pair of rustic lovers put our own amorous folly into perspective, at least for me. Their ironic fate bolstered my faith that love would prevail for us. The dance itself was the first full-length story ballet that I performed. Conventions such as pas de deux, solos, and codas were subordinate to plot, focusing attention on the relationship between the principal characters.

Coppélia was staged originally in 1870 by the French choreographer Arthur Saint-Léon at the Paris Opéra. The plot turns on an ingenious comic device: a doll who comes between two human lovers. A high-spirited peasant, Franz, forgets his fiancée, Swanilda, when he unwittingly falls for Coppélia, a mechanical doll created by a mysterious toymaker, Doctor Coppélius. Rather than giving up without a fight, Swanilda steals into the toymaker's workshop and discovers the real identity of her inanimate rival. The heroine's action not only results in madcap havoc, but ultimately pushes Franz into a moment of truth. The doll is revealed for what it is, thus exposing his foolishness. The shared realization that they have both been deceived allows the love between Franz and Swanilda to mature. There is a reconciliation and renewed pledge of betrothal.

In *Baryshnikov at Work,* Misha described his character as follows: "The role of Franz is not terribly complicated. He is a flirt; he flirts with everyone. Failing to recognize Swanilda's will of iron, he assumes that she is just a silly little girl. Her caprices tickle his fancy, he is amused by her, fascinated by her, but he doesn't take her seriously—which leads to all his problems." My challenge in working on the ballet was to bring Misha to the same moment of truth that Franz experienced. I failed, but my effort brought Swanilda to life. Through her character, her actions, her gestures, I was able to spar with Misha. Her iron will had to be forged from a heart of gold. She had to love with boundless faith. She had to see through Franz. She had to hold on to her wits and her sense of humor. That was not always easy.

The role of Swanilda was taught to me by Enrique Martinez, the ballet master who had staged *Coppélia* for American Ballet Theatre. Enrique was kind and well-intentioned, but he was unable to elucidate either the characterization or the related technical demands of the part. Long sections of mime had to be incorporated into the dance itself. In addition, the choreography included character dances, a Scottish jig, and a Spanish bolero, that had to be fused into a single dynamic, along with Swanilda's impersonation of the doll. I had a language for dancing, even for acting through the dance, but not dancing and acting with pantomime. I was lost again.

When Misha came into one rehearsal wearing his street clothes, I figured maybe he realized I needed some help. I was in for another rude awakening. He had no patience for any questions that required him to explain how he made the mime and the dance fit together. His curt dismissal was subtle and effective enough to humiliate me without any overt sign of hostility. He did not take me seriously. When I showed him my initial attempt at the pantomime, he belittled my efforts through exaggerated mimicry. Then he left without changing his clothes. I went back to the films, back to my teachers, then back to the studio alone.

Misha was a perfect Franz right up to the moment of truth, at which point his portrayal indicated no recognition of the folly, no awareness of that dramatic transition. His face was deadpan. That became a target for me. But he never responded. He never discussed his role with me. According to his published account, Misha was more interested in playing Doctor Coppélius, the maker of dolls, the misanthropic buffoon, that character who epitomized the Romantic notion of suffering genius.

I was harboring some explosive resentment. The rehearsals of *Theme and Variations* were especially frustrating, mainly because Misha was stymied by the transition to Balanchine's choreography. In addition, the ballet master, Michael Lland, insisted that I give a performance faithful to Mr. B's original production, a role fashioned for Alicia Alonso. After a fair fight, I did it my way, compromising just enough to smooth over the ruffled feathers. I figured Alicia would have taken my side had she been around.

Misha apparently believed Balanchine's theory that the dancer must dissolve personal identity and passion in order to render the purity of the choreography. It was as if he tried to forget everything he knew about the art of dramatic expression. His natural patterns of movement broke down speeding through the steps. Without his usual control of breath and coordination, he danced from his waist down, fixating on his legs, giving each step equal emphasis rather than accenting and phrasing the steps within the larger musical sequences. When he lifted me over his head, I felt like I was being jerked into the air by a system of levers and pulleys.

Ironically, what I learned from Misha's dancing in the traditional story ballets enhanced my performance of *Theme and Variations* by bringing out the same musical qualities that now disappeared with his strained effort. I hoped his problems would make him appreciate what I was going through in trying to make the reverse transition into his repertory. I hoped that an ongoing dialogue would begin. That was wishful thinking. He refused to accept any help except for gratuitous technical details—like how many inches his arm should be placed above his waist or how high his leg should be raised.

He moved in this ballet like rigor mortis had set in, and the worst part was that he knew it. Misha's recognition of his own failure led to the grandest delusion of them all: he assumed that if he were unable to master Balanchine, then Balanchine had to be the greatest genius since Petipa, the true spiritual heir of the Maryinsky tradition in the twentieth century. This did not bode well for our future.

Misha and I attended the New York City Ballet on one occasion during this period. The ballets we saw escape me, but Misha's reaction made a vivid impression. He did not applaud the performance, but declared that Balanchine was an "absolute genius." Then he raved about how "beautiful" the Balanchine dancers were. Then he leaned toward me, saying, "But . . . Gelsey . . . you . . . you are the most beautiful of all! You are the most beautiful vun!" He was so sincere.

When we arrived in Washington, D.C., at the end of October, 1974, we were set to open a two-week session at the Kennedy Center. I gave an interview to George Gelles for the Washington *Star-News*. During the question-and-answer session, I was asked how Misha differed from the men at the New York City Ballet. My response went beyond either discretion or diplomacy:

> . . . First of all, he comes from a wholly different background. He has a Russian temperament, and all the Russians I have known have been moody. But he is extremely sincere. When we are working together, Misha is never, never a bastard. He can be impatient, or maybe very serious, but he is never rude. If I'm having trouble with something we work it out, and though he may make fun of me, he is never a bitch.

Between "bastard" and "bitch," the lady did protest too much. I hoped my partner would get the message. If he loved me, why did he have to denigrate my work? Why did he have to hurt me?

I never actually allowed myself to doubt his love. To have done so would have meant repudiating everything that we had accomplished. I did assume that he had trouble dealing with his own feelings, that he was afraid of that part of himself he had begun to share with me.

Whenever I questioned his sincerity, he seemed to come back with some new proof that I had misjudged him. In my room at the Watergate Hotel, he put his head on my knee and confided to me with sad eyes about his childhood in Russia. His mother had abandoned him when he was a boy. He had never recovered from the blow. She was the most beautiful woman he had ever seen. My heart went out to him again, as did my arms.

Years later, I heard various versions of the same story from other women, including one account of suicide. He brought up the subject again during a 1977 tour in Vienna, telling me, "You know, Gelsey, I really understand this Oedipal problem. I know I have this trouble. Is terrible." I did not have the nerve to ask him for clarification.

Before our opening in Washington, I overheard company gossip to the effect that Misha was interested in a young dancer, all-American and virginal. I was stunned. If the rumor were true, what was my status? I felt the first sting of jealousy when he made no effort to conceal his attraction. I was able to reassure myself with the knowledge that she was straitlaced and unlikely to succumb to his advances. What did I have to fear from a virgin?

In spite of occasional lapses, we still seemed to be the happy couple, a picture of young love in the midst of a mad whirlwind of sensationalism. The press featured us as an item in the nation's capital before we had even appeared on the Kennedy Center stage. We took time between classes and rehearsals for shopping sprees during which Misha assembled a wardrobe worthy of his place in the limelight. I played fashion consultant. It was not always easy to keep up the appearance of outward harmony. I felt like I had to disguise my own inner identity. I was always less than myself.

At some point, he dragged me and one of our fellow dancers, "Keith Hartley" to see the porn film *Deep Throat.* Misha's impulse on that night seemed to contradict the virgin theory. I found myself seething with silent rage as I sat in the theatre. This was not my idea of romance—much less a good time.

After shopping for cowboy hats, the giggles of my cohorts were cut short when Keith tried to light a cigarette for Misha and almost scorched him by accident. Without saying a word, Misha turned the episode into a nightmare. His face became a tragic mask as he continued to check for a burn that did not exist. Keith was not allowed to forget the misdeed. He was so contrite that I felt guilty for not coming to his defense. I knew how he felt. The incident was so absurd that I initially considered the possibility that Keith and Misha had staged the whole thing for my benefit. But the mood did not lighten. They did not laugh. It was no joke. Misha's behavior mystified me. I was afraid to touch him.

During the run of Washington performances, the exchange of flowers became a focal point of unspoken contention between us. A lovely bouquet was delivered to my dressing room on the first night, before we performed the pas de deux from *Don Quixote.* The tiny card said only, "To Gelsey— from Misha." The choice of words made me realize, with some consternation, that he had never actually told me that he loved me. On closer examination, the handwriting on the card did not look like his. This was not the kind of encouragement that I needed on opening night. I tried to put the flowers out of my mind. The thought behind them did not count. He did not utter the words "I love you" until 1980. By that time, it was a case of too-little-too-late.

If I had difficulty accepting Misha's backstage bouquet as a gesture of good faith, he had an equally trying time with my gushing appreciation during curtain calls. Clive Barnes may have been the first critic to comment on this curious aspect of our stage rapport. He accurately reported an event which took place after *Coppélia,* writing for the New York *Times* on November 10, 1974:

> . . . Gelsey was given a bunch of red carnations. She pulled one out, in the traditional ballerina gesture, to present it to Misha. Then, she obviously felt, to hell with it. She kept the one red carnation for herself and pressed the rest of the bouquet on a startled Misha. Fasten your seatbelts; it's going to be a fascinating partnership.

Misha never would have acquiesced to my breach of propriety if our dancing had not won such acclaim. I was pushing my luck.

The partnership between a Russian defector and an American ballerina

did seem to capture the imagination of the press and the public. What aston-
ishes me in retrospect is what little impact the reviews and recognition made
on my sense of self-esteem. I remember reading that early notice by Clive
Barnes on *Coppélia*. He offered a fair observation about my dancing with
Misha:

> She matched him. She even challenged him. What was important was
> that they were dancing together as if they had grown up together. Per-
> haps they had.

Such words were actually a source of dismay. I did not allow myself to
believe them because Misha had not said them. He withheld comment. He
knew we had not grown up together. He reminded me of that by his conspicuous lack of enthusiasm. Damned by faint praise and subtle disparage-
ment, I was deaf to all applause.

There were at least a couple of humorous moments and minor fiascos
before we left Washington. Misha had devised a number of dazzling steps for
his variations in *Coppélia*. As it happened, the ballet was scheduled for a
matinee and evening show on the same day. Misha had the evening slot. His
counterpart in the matinee was my former flame, Fernando Bujones. Fernando had recently won a gold medal at the prestigious Varna competition in
Bulgaria, one of those events in which ballet is judged according to Olym-
pian rather than artistic standards. Misha had won a gold at the first Moscow
competition in 1969. Fernando's accomplishment, a first for an American
dancer, had been overshadowed by Misha's entry into the company. Fernando was not to be outdone.

On the day when both of them were to perform *Coppélia*, Fernando stole
Misha's steps—stealing the thunder in the matinee. My disgruntled partner
was put in the position of having to come up with a new gymnastic twist for
his variations by the evening. I offered my sympathy as he confined himself
to the studio. His revised rendition of the steps seemed nothing less than a
miracle. Later, at the company's Halloween costume party, Misha imagined
having a last laugh, by wearing a bright T-shirt with the following words
emblazoned across his chest: I AM FERNANDO BUJONES—VARNA GOLD
MEDAL WINNER. Fernando appeared as Abraham Lincoln. I didn't bother
with a costume.

I had my own costume problems in *Theme and Variations*. Lucia Chase, the
artistic director, insisted that I wear a choker-style necklace for the part. I
thought the thing was a gaudy piece of paste that distorted the line of my
neck. On the night of the opening, just moments before my entrance, I
ripped the bauble off and threw it into the wings. According to eyewitness
reports, when Lucia caught sight of my bare neck in the opening variation,
she nearly had a conniption sitting in her box. She and I never did see eye to
eye, nor did I ever wear the necklace.

Dina Makarova

At the American Ballet Theatre.

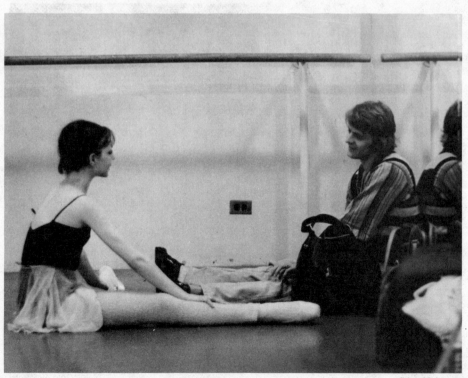

Dina Makarova

With Misha, in studio.

As Swanilda, *Coppélia,* 1974.

Not a doll.

William Reilly

With teacher David Howard, 1975.

Dina Makarova

As Giselle.

With Misha, rehearsing *Giselle*, 1975.

Not a Wili.

The mad scene.

With Ivan Nagy, *Romeo and Juliet,* 1976.

Max Waldman, © The Waldman Archives
With Ivan Nagy, *Romeo and Juliet.*

With Ivan Nagy, *The Leaves Are Fading*, 1976.

I limped out of Washington. My old foot injury had been aggravated by the hard floors at Kennedy Center and the unusual stress caused by the mix of the modern and traditional styles. With the latter, I spent most of my time turning on my left leg, a balancing act that was perhaps a temporary metaphor for my life. I was relieved to board a jet and shut out the world. I don't recall the destination.

In a city in the Midwest, walking along its Main Street toward the local theatre, Misha informed me that he would not be returning to the company tour the following year. He chose not to elaborate. I stopped myself from asking him about his plans. Our continued romantic affair in hotel rooms across the country alleviated my worries about the future, but not my immediate frustrations. There seemed to be no way to break through to him.

By the time the company toured and returned for a grand opening in New York City in December, I was out of shape again. It was impossible on the road to maintain the physical condition necessary for me to match Misha. The daily grind of company class, rehearsal, and performance did not give me the kind of tone I knew that I would need to fulfill all of the critical and promotional promises that preceded our appearance in Manhattan. I went into a panic. The prospect of friends and family seeing me flop filled me with a new form of anxiety. I was nervous about being nervous. I knew what would happen if I lost concentration on the stage. I also knew who would tell me about it.

During the week before our Christmas Eve opening, I broke into a rash. It was a hideous scourge. There was no way to hide the flaming red blotches that covered my back and chest. When Misha walked into my apartment for one of his nocturnal visitations, he found me in the middle of an uncontrollable crying jag. I expected him to turn around and leave, repulsed by a face full of tears and smeared mascara, but he surprised me. He was gentle. He stayed and offered consolation. He even sprinkled baby powder on my tender skin. This was the prince with whom I had fallen in love. I figured that his selfish act on the outside was just a front for the benefit of those who would never understand him.

With Christmas approaching fast, I went into a dither about what to get Misha in the way of a gift. I asked his friends what he might want. I was under the impression that he had been hoping to try some marijuana. That struck me as a little odd, but I supposed it would be like an American in Moscow who wanted to try some caviar. Not only was I naïve about drugs, but I had no idea where to purchase marijuana. After asking around the company, I did manage to find a dealer and procure a small amount of grass. But this present seemed somehow unworthy of Misha. It was too impersonal, inadequate. I did some frantic, last-minute shopping and found a ring in a Greenwich Village antique store. Then I began to worry. Would Misha get the wrong idea about receiving a ring from me? If he had trouble with flowers, what would he do with a ring? There was no time to change my mind.

The Christmas Eve performance of *Coppélia* at City Center was a minor disaster. It was one of those performances in which a little voice told me in the middle that I should go back to the beginning and start again. I did not have the punch in my steps for Swanilda to win Franz away from his doll fantasy. I was not the same ballerina who had performed in Washington. I made a valiant effort, perhaps, but I was unable to reach Misha. We danced away from each other.

Judging by the ovations and curtain calls, the audience had not noticed the flaws. The critics later proved to be equally enthusiastic. As soon as the show was over, the backstage area turned into a madhouse of excitement. I suffered the compliments from my fellow dancers with a painful lump in my throat and a pair of burning eyes. Misha said nothing. He made a point of avoiding me.

I broke down completely in the dressing room. The place was a shambles, my mind was smithereens. I was mocked again by the mirror. I saw a pitiful wretch changing out of her costume and removing her makeup. My mother and my friend Dina stood by me, trying to do the impossible, trying to boost my spirits. There was one terrible question that neither of them could answer: why had Misha abandoned me?

I had been invited to a Christmas party at the home of Misha's friends Helen and Sheldon Atlas. Helen was the publisher of *Dance News,* a critical newsletter that has since folded. Sheldon was a polymer chemist who taught at Brooklyn College. The couple had offered Misha a place to stay in their home when he first arrived in New York. Their apartment was located in the Eighties on Central Park West. I had assumed that Misha and I would be traveling there together. After all, it was Christmas Eve. We had just opened in New York. We were the talk of the ballet world. How could he leave me in the dressing room without offering so much as a word of explanation? I was baffled again.

My mother and I were the last to leave the theatre. The streets were packed with holiday traffic. I caught a taxi in midtown, leaving my mother on the sidewalk. She was loaded down with my flowers. I was still in tears as I watched her juggle roses and blow me a kiss. I had forgotten to thank her. I checked to be sure that I had packed both of Misha's gifts in my pocketbook, taking care not to crush the ribbons.

Bouncing on the seat of the cab, I made a futile attempt to pull myself together before arriving at the party. Inside the elevator of the apartment building, I took out a compact and touched up my face and hair. I pushed buttons for the wrong floors so that I had enough time to add a few drops of Visine to my red eyes. When the door to the Atlases' apartment opened, I was greeted by a reception line of grinning Russians. A loud chorus exclaimed, "Merry Christmas, Gelsey!"

The mirth was contagious. Misha was among those who had been waiting for my entrance. Encouraged by his cronies, he stepped forward with a broad smile, obviously holding something behind his back. Then he whipped out a brown paper bag and pushed it under my nose. "Here, Gelsey, for you! Please, open now." I heard snickers from the others. Misha whispered, "Is funny."

I was taken aback to say the least. Before I could remove my coat, the group huddled around me, unable to hold back giggles. I was tickled to be the center of attention. Misha evidently had gone to some trouble to arrange this little surprise. Looking at the bag, I wondered if Russian men knew how to wrap. I played along. I reached into the package and pulled out a baby nipple and a container of baby powder. Their laughter was uncontrollable.

In response to my bewilderment, Misha jumped around me like a dancing bear, saying, "You know, Gelsey . . . for cry baby . . . for rash!"

I failed to appreciate the Russian humor. I knew immediately the one thing that I could not do was show them any tears. Feeling my eyes welling against my will, I looked down and forced a laugh. Then I thanked them and headed through the apartment into the bedroom where the guests had piled their coats. Misha did not follow me.

My friend Dina came to my rescue, humoring me until I had recovered my wits. The question of the hour was what to do about the gifts that I had brought for Misha. After circulating and reconnoitering, I found him in the living room and placed my two little packages in his hands. He did not open them. He thanked me, but I had distracted him from a conversation with his Russian buddies. The iron curtain slammed in my face.

I beat a hasty retreat, feeling utterly rejected. I was sure now that he would misunderstand the ring. I asked Dina to explain to Misha in Russian that the gift was not to be interpreted as anything but a sincere token of my friendship, that there were no strings attached. She did her best. From across the room, out of his line of vision, I watched his face darken as Dina carried out the mission. He did not want to be bothered about me.

After another hour or so of being ignored, I was ready to leave. I made my apologies and said my good-byes to the host and hostess. I avoided Misha and the Russian crowd in the living room. I tried a shortcut through the dining room, only to find Natasha, seated with a group of ballet critics and friends at a large rectangular table. She was not about to let me make my getaway without giving me an exit line.

"Gelsey, vhut is this? You goink? So eeearly, you go? You go to bed?"

"Yes, I'm tired. Good night, Natasha."

"But you go now, all alone, by yourself? How can this be?"

I found the door without further delay.

Out in the street, I was unable to catch a cab. I started running down Central Park West. I ran about twenty blocks until I arrived at the home of two of my old friends, Cathy and Ricky, from the New York City Ballet.

They listened patiently to my misadventures. My fury was boundless. Their sympathy confirmed that my anger was justified, that I was not losing my mind even if my heart was breaking.

Fearing that I had ruined their Christmas Eve, I went to see my dear friend Meg. By then, most of my rage was directed against myself. I was hysterical. I had no way to fight back. I needed to be reminded of who I was by Meg's familiar face. She had seen me fall apart before. She knew what I refused to admit: he was a hopeless cause.

After a sleepless night, I was ready to join the Bulgarian ballet. On Christmas morning, I received a call from Remi Saunder, Misha's confidante of the moment. She invited me to a holiday dinner being given for Misha by Howard Gilman. It would be an intimate affair with just a few Russian friends and fellow dancers. I was most welcome to come.

My inclination was to bow out at this point. My mother stopped by my apartment for a visit, and I told the story again, showing her my pacifier and powder. When I mentioned the latest invitation, she had a daring idea. "Why not just go . . . and show him how well you can take a joke? Turn the tables on him, Gels. You can't take this sort of thing lying down!"

We hit upon a plan, farfetched and devious. I would return with his gift. Or, rather, I would wear his gift. I would turn that baby nipple into a piece of jewelry. With a pin, I attached it to my sweater. It was a stroke of absolute madness.

My mother, the former actress, coached me. I was to walk in wearing the pacifier and pretend that nothing whatsoever was wrong. Something was bound to happen. He had to respond. I would at least get some sign of life out of Misha. Embarrassment would be better than nothing. The tactic was no different than what I used on the stage.

Anticipating possible reactions, my mother and I howled with laughter, as close to each other as we had been in years. My life may have turned into a black comedy, but I felt less helpless. I changed into a black wool dress and attached the surprise. I took a final peek in the mirror, bundled up, and headed across town to the Gilman penthouse, resigned to whatever lay ahead.

Howard Gilman welcomed me with a kiss at the door. After we exchanged Christmas greetings, he helped me off with my coat and chuckled at the sight of my strange pin, saying only, "Gelsey, I'm so glad you could come."

I walked into the living room and planted myself on the soft cushion of a huge couch, near friends and fellow dancers. I received a couple of curious glances. There were only a few guests who had an unobstructed view of my dangling nipple. Misha breezed into the room, decked out in a dark suit. He wished everyone a happy holiday and sat in a chair on the other side of the room. He barely even noticed that I was wearing clothes.

I was fuming. After some drinks and casual conversation, the guests began to migrate toward a small drawing room where a pile of gifts had been stacked. Misha and I were left alone together for a few minutes. There was a long, awkward silence. Finally he cleared his throat and gave me a crooked smile. "Gel-sey, anysing wrong?"

He sounded like he had just asked me for a weather report. My tongue was burning with acid. "No, Misha, what could possibly be wrong?"

His eyes pointedly avoided my pin. "You upset about some-sing?"

"What could I possibly have to be upset about, Misha?"

He shrugged and turned away. After a few moments, tears were once again threatening to betray me. He suddenly twisted back toward me, brightening, "Oh, Gels, thank you for presents. Remi vill take ring to make smaller. Is very nice. Thank you."

As I nodded and looked hard into his face, we were called to join the other guests. Misha scooted out ahead of me.

In the drawing room, Remi, an attractive woman with a cheerful smile, handed out the gifts. She presented me with a neatly wrapped package. The card said, "To Gelsey—From Misha." I knew the handwriting had to belong to Remi. I unwrapped the package, still hoping I might find a note, anything that might acknowledge my existence, maybe just a word of appreciation about the work we had done over the past few months. What I found was a box of bonbons. My thought at that moment stuck to the roof of my brain: "What am I doing here?"

I made a pathetic effort to thank Misha for his thoughtfulness. As we marched into the dining room, I asked myself if this great artist had ever in his life touched another human being. Had we ever really danced together? I bit my tongue.

Misha and I were placed side by side at the table. A lavish setting had been laid out. Before anyone made a move, Misha patted my cheek, announcing for all to hear, "Pretty girl." He continued to pat my cheek and called to his devoted friend across the table, "Remi. Pretty girl, huh? Beautiful!"

That was all I could take. I abruptly pulled away from him and back from the table, protesting in a loud voice I hardly recognized, "Misha, stop it!"

"Gels, vhut happened?"

"Misha, do you know the story of *Coppélia*? Do you?"

He looked confused and gave me a vague nod. "Vhut happened? Vhut do you mean?"

"Well, Misha, you know the doll? Coppélia? The doll in the story? That's not me! I'm not that doll!"

I rose from the table and stared for a moment at the ring of shocked faces. Struggling to keep control, I said, "I'm sorry. I don't think I belong here. Good night."

I found my coat and my way out into the hallway. Misha came running after me just as the elevator door opened. He yelled, "Gelsey, stop! C'mon, Gels . . . vait. Please. Tell me, vhut is it? Some-sing is wrong?"

I stepped inside the elevator. "Just forget it, Misha."

"C'mon, girl, vhut is it?"

I held the door for my exit line: "If you don't know by now, I'm not about to tell you."

The door slammed in front of his face. As the elevator plummeted, I felt that terrible kind of relief that comes when you know you have broken your own heart for the best of reasons. With the knowledge that a long winter season was still ahead of me, I did not like the fact that my knees were shaking. That was not a good sign. One of Misha's Russian sayings seemed appropriate: "Love is not like a potato—you can't throw it out the window."

Chapter Eight

THE MAD SCENE

There were two volatile passions shifting inside of me: my love for ballet and my love for Misha. My New Year's resolution for 1975, to break off the romance and continue only the professional side of the relationship, was destined to fail. With each success on the stage, I was drawn back into seductive illusion. How was it possible that Misha's resources as an artist, so evident in performance, were different from those of his basic personality? Each time I tried to answer that question, I came up with a new and more elaborate set of evasions.

What was perhaps for him a casual affair was for me a prolonged catastrophe of heart and mind. I actually believed that I could lose every battle and win the war. Fighting for intimacy, I turned myself into a casualty of his convenient arrangement. As if to act out the death wish of nineteenth-century Romanticism, I tried to destroy myself for love, eventually running through all the fashionable forms of self-destruction.

We added three ballets to our repertory at the beginning of 1975: *Le Corsaire* pas de deux, the full-length *La Fille Mal Gardée* and *La Sylphide.* These became hits for us in rapid succession during the first couple of weeks of January. What we accomplished artistically in the ballets seemed to make up for my personal torment. I began to accuse myself of being selfish, of placing my own petty concerns ahead of the vision embodied in his art. One night while watching him perform a ballet by Roland Petit, *Le Jeune Homme et la Mort,* I was struck by a sudden notion: he may not know how he does it, but he does it like a god. My critical faculties broke down. How could I question his genius? Misha had transformed himself into an existential hero —he wore blue jeans, smoked a cigarette, and hanged himself on the stage. I thought the ballet tawdry, but confronted with both his technical virtuosity and stylistic versatility, my own classical ideals seemed to pale.

As a conciliatory gesture, Misha invited me to a party given by the Russian cellist, Rostropovich. The familiar pattern of indifference and neglect reasserted itself as soon as we entered the musician's home, a large duplex apartment. My partner instantly vanished up a stairway with several of his buddies. Happily, the elderly host took me under his wing, insisting that I join a small circle of Russian men who were seated around a table on the second floor. There was a raucous bout of drinking in progress. Misha was in the middle. Shots of vodka were poured and passed around to the guests. This looked to me like a Russian contest to see who would reach oblivion first and who would be the last to collapse.

I began to think that I had been better off in the past when Misha had excluded me from such rituals. I had no taste for vodka, but I desperately wanted to fit in for once with his friends. Sensing my predicament, Rostropovich hooked his arm around me and stole my glass, secretly downing its contents. Then he gave me a sly wink. He continued to drink from my glass as well as his own throughout the evening, saving me from the embarrassment of not being able to keep up with the rest of the jovial crew.

At the end of the night, Misha came reeling over to me. There was a glint in his glassy eyes, "Gelsey, let's go home . . . huh? Yes?"

To prevail over my hesitation, he purred, "A pochemu nyet?" ("And why not?") That particular rhetorical question seemed to justify any and all propositions. It was an invitation to share his solitude.

We went to his place on the East Side. I remember listening to muted sirens and horns, sounds of traffic that drifted in long after he passed out in my arms. The embrace had been nothing more than a matter of capricious inconsequence. The bedroom was pitch black, baffling my attempt to discern the features of his face. It was a marvel to me that he could sleep so easily. I wondered if my post-coital sorrow might disturb his dreams.

I squeezed my eyes closed and conjured an image in my mind of Misha performing the role of James in *La Sylphide*. At the beginning of the ballet, he slept in a chair—while my character, the Sylph, tried to get into his unconscious mind. It was a dark fairy tale. I was a beautiful figment of his imagination . . . I lured him away from his earthly lover . . . I made myself his obsession . . . I led him to ruin. That was the action I played on the stage. Did he believe that story? Did he believe that the purity of a man's ideals had no place in this world?

I sat up in bed and leaned over him. As a futile antidote for insomnia, I followed his dancing image through the entire ballet, picturing each scene, until I saw James place the deadly scarf around my shoulders. That was the climax: the moment that the Sylph went blind, doomed by his unwitting act, his inability to reconcile the real and the ideal. In the darkness of the bedroom, I called up the precise expression on Misha's face when his James realized that he had shattered his own life, his dream turning to nightmare. I found myself weeping. I hoped that one of my tears might fall on Misha's invisible cheek. He never stirred. I let my head drop back on the pillow and waited for dawn to light my way home.

I was soon abandoned. At the end of January, Misha and Natasha departed on a foreign tour. His absence played havoc with my insecurity, exaggerating my fear of permanently losing him as a partner. He sustained an ankle injury in Australia that put him out of the picture for the remainder of the winter. Meanwhile, I expanded my repertory, if not my horizons.

Kenneth MacMillan's *Concerto* and Alvin Ailey's *The River,* both successful on the stage, made me more cautious than ever about modern choreography. These ballets were exercises in liquid abstraction. Due to the apparent contrast of styles, most observers would probably not mention MacMillan and Ailey in the same breath, but I found an ironic strain of similarity, at least in these particular works. I employed the same recipe in each ballet: listen to the music; phrase the steps; wait for some glimmer of feeling to spice the movement with quality; blend in a few hints of drama; whip the concoction, not over-vigorously, with a wire whisk, straining out any residual meaning.

My partner in *Concerto* was Ivan Nagy, the premier danseur who had tried to bring me into American Ballet Theatre some years earlier. We also danced several other ballets during that winter season: the pas de deux from *Don Quixote, La Fille Mal Gardée,* and Michel Fokine's *Les Sylphides* (not to be confused with Auguste Bournonville's *La Sylphide* which I had performed with Misha). This was the beginning of an intermittent partnership that I treasured.

During the spring and summer, I made two trips to Europe at Misha's behest. The first journey took me to the Paris Opéra to replace an injured French star, Noëlla Pontois, as his partner. I skidded across a raked stage and back into Misha's arms. The city of Paris cast its legendary romantic spell, providing at least an occasional aphrodisiac. We performed the standard excerpts from *Don Quixote* and *La Bayadère.* I recall only that performance conditions were so trying for me that not much Petipa was left in the steps. As Petipa was no longer around to complain, Misha took the liberty of defending his choreographic interests, pulling me upstage by the back of my tutu during one performance. I had nearly fallen into the audience.

Venice was another story. The city of canals looked to me like a vast sewer system. I had visions of its polluted waters rising to cover the stage in Piazza San Marco where we were scheduled to perform. The whole city was supposed to sink within a few decades. I recall a gondola ride, more harrowing than romantic, certain as I was that we would capsize. I made several forays on my own into the marketplace. The women in Venetian society seemed somehow oriental—mysterious, precious, utterly subservient, yet hanging on to a subdued sense of dignity. I watched how differently they carried themselves whenever they came into the presence of men. I watched young mothers bustle through crowds, followed by more children than seemed humanly possible. The idea of maternity was both alien and wondrously alluring. It was, of course, out of the question for me.

On one of my excursions, while walking up the steps of a marble palace, I thought of the Chinese custom of foot-binding. I have no idea why I should have puzzled over that barbaric practice at that moment. Perhaps my feet hurt. As I continued to climb, my mind stumbled onto another disquieting thought: while toe shoes actually enhanced the expressive facility of the ballerina, the masters of ballet had devised a means for binding the brain. This was obviously not the sort of thing I could talk about with Misha, no more than I might bring up the subject of motherhood.

The production in Venice—"Serata a Quattro"—took place on July 3, 1975. The center of local attention was Italian star Carla Fracci, fondly known in her country as La Fracci. She and I switched between Misha and her frequent partner, Paolo Bortoluzzi. Carla danced the solo and pas de deux sections from the second acts of *Giselle* and *La Sylphide*. I performed the pas de deuxs from *Coppélia* and *Don Quixote*.

This outdoor spectacle concluded with multiple ovations and an unusual pageant apparently arranged by Carla's husband, Beppe Menegatti. A group of barefoot children joined us for the final ceremony. The urchins made a surprise entrance that was all too contrived, prancing around the stage while Misha, Paolo, Carla, and I posed at a makeshift barre. I saw Misha out of the corner of my eye, seemingly reluctant to take Carla's hand for the bow. Not to be undone, Carla took his hand and led him to the front of the stage, all of us bowing toward the cathedral across the square.

The ballets were almost overshadowed by the sheer bedlam of the curtain festivities. Misha was obviously infuriated, embarrassed by the whole display. At the end, he pulled me toward the exit. "Quick, Gelsey! Let's go." He continued muttering, "Stupid . . . stupid . . . just stupid!" I thought this was a bit much to do about nothing, especially when there was nothing to be done.

Before leaving Venice, I committed a minor artistic felony. This theft seemed entirely justified at the time. I had already made a Washington, D.C., debut as Giselle, and I was obsessed with work on the role. I was especially taken with Carla's exquisite costume, a long tutu that she wore in the second act of her celebrated portrayal. Her costume was nothing less than a mirror of the heroine's soul. The material flowed with the same line and quality of movement with which Carla had endowed the character. The hem was frayed, radiating behind her body like a soft flame. On one evening, when a group of us went out to dinner, I asked her for the secret.

"Carla, I wonder if you could tell me how I might get hold of some of the material that you use for your second act Giselle costume. It's really so beautiful . . . I mean, the way it moves!"

She leveled her dark eyes at me and drew a deep breath. "Ah yes, I buy from little old man. But he stop making. I don't know. Even for me, it is very difficult to . . . to get this material. But Gelsey, why think about that? You should think of the role—Giselle!—that is what matters."

Carla was sixteen years my senior; I felt like I had just been slighted by the older generation. She did not pursue the topic of Giselle. Like most dancers, she did not offer privileged information. I had no intention of imitating Carla's interpretation, but I did want to have the opportunity of cutting a figure from cloth of that quality and texture.

Not about to be put off in my quest, I sneaked into Carla's dressing room during a performance. I was astonished at how meticulously she had arranged cosmetics and toilet articles. The place was like a museum, or maybe a church altar. Photographs and keepsakes hung around her mirror. Each cherished item had its special place. I was discouraged to think of my own dressing room, which usually resembled a disaster area.

The costume in question was hanging near her dressing table. With great trepidation, I tiptoed over and tugged a tiny piece of material from one of the frayed inner layers. I took a sample the size of a quarter; it would never be noticed. Then I bolted out of the room as if I had committed the crime of the century.

Back in New York, I showed the piece of fabric to a designer named Carl Michel, a dear friend who had helped me over the years with all of my costume problems. The material turned out to be silk tulle. A facsimile had to be ordered from Paris via London. Not surprisingly, the management at ABT had no interest in my ideas about the costume for Giselle. Given the budget, the distinction between silk and nylon was denied. My taste in fashion for the spirit world of the second act became a ludicrous point of contention. I would not be caught dead in the starched rag provided by ABT. So, in the end, I invested a thousand dollars into my own costume without regret. It was Carl Michel who executed the unique design, a cut that fit my unusual physical requirements as well as my portrayal.

I had to have the final choice about every aspect of Giselle's outward image, which was, after all, an essential reflection of her inward being—each facet of her psychology had to be forged from a real quality in my own personality. That was the only way I could translate her character into my body. No details were minor in the physicalization of such a role. It was always a case of life or death.

I approached the part of Giselle as a detective. The meaning of each personal moment for the character was a mystery that had to be solved within the dance. The clues consisted of the story, the steps, and the music. The mimed sequences provided the key to the investigation, allowing the evidence to be ordered into a coherent interpretation of the entire ballet.

In preparing *Giselle* and a number of subsequent productions, I turned to mime artist Pilar Garcia, a woman who was recommended to me by my old friend Ricky Weiss. Realizing that I was awkward with pantomime and that nobody at ABT, including my partner, could teach me what I needed to know, I had no choice but to seek outside coaching. After our first meeting in Manhattan during the spring of 1975, Pilar and I became fast friends, sharing a specific approach in the studio. With her, I became more confident about a perspective of dance that included both drama and mime.

Pilar did not have what most people consider a typical dancer's body, yet she was able to create at will physical illusions of weight, size, and shape, at the same time opening up a psychological dimension of beauty and truth. She was able to move her large bones and broad frame with a nimbleness that took my breath away. Her range of characters as a mime was phenomenal. There was nothing mysterious about her method, which enabled me to add layers to the core of knowledge already established with my teachers, David and Stanley. The words of Schiller, first spoken on a Weimar stage in 1798, isolate the principle of mime that Pilar and I brought to bear on each ballet:

> Hard is this art, its praise is transitory;
> For mimes, posterity entwines no garlands.
> Therefore they must be greedy of the present
> And fill the moment which is theirs, completely . . .

To fill each moment in *Giselle* required as much cunning as modesty. The work with Pilar had to be done for the most part in secret, far from the eyes and ears of those who might be offended or threatened. She and I privately explored Giselle's motivation, attempting to make dramatic sense out of the traditional inconsistencies. Then I had to try to reconcile our findings with the company's staging and with my partner's portrayal, trying not to step on toes or egos.

It was assumed at ABT that a directorial concept emerged automatically from the steps taught by the ballet master. The emphasis in rehearsals was usually placed on stylistic rather than dramatic considerations. The story was glossed over. There was rarely any indication of a unified vision. Nobody ever discussed how the steps were illuminated through character and action. The premises of the drama were explained away as a matter of "tradition." The production followed the staging originally done for the company in 1968 by David Blair, formerly a leading dancer with London's Royal Ballet. Misha later introduced the Kirov staging, more or less replicating the Russian version done by Petipa in 1871. Meaning was gradually sacrificed in a misguided quest for "authenticity."

Giselle was originally choreographed by Jules Perrot and Jean Coralli and presented in Paris in 1841. The primary contributor to the libretto was the French critic and poet Théophile Gautier, who borrowed from a legend he had encountered in the work of German poet Heinrich Heine. The legend of the so-called "Wilis" tells of the spirits of young women who had died before their wedding nights. The plot line of the ballet covers two acts and moves through two planes of existence: from the bucolic reality of the fragile peasant girl Giselle to the ethereal realm of the Wilis.

The story in my mind went as follows. In the first act, after learning that her lover, Albrecht, has betrayed her, Giselle loses her reason and dies from the shock of a broken heart. The betrayal is twofold: not only is he an aristocrat disguised as a peasant, but he is already promised to another woman. In the second act, the spirit of Giselle returns to save her repentant lover from the curse of the Wilis, who have condemned him to dance himself to death.

The way I interpreted the role of Giselle made for a subtle clash with the way Misha interpreted the role of Albrecht. Our conflict did not seem to be limited to technical or creative differences. It was as if we were acting out the limitations of our own love through the ballet.

Deviating from a traditional portrayal of Albrecht as a philandering playboy, Misha chose to characterize his love for Giselle as innocent. His Albrecht was a prince trapped by circumstance. I had no difficulty playing off his charm and sincerity during the first act. Giselle projected all of her passion for life and for dancing onto Albrecht. Had I not already done the same with Misha?

The mad scene was Giselle's attempt, however desperate and deranged, to hang on to her love for him, even at the expense of denying life itself (in the original version, she killed herself with Albrecht's sword). There was a method to the madness that led from flesh to spirit, from the sword to the cross, foreshadowing the climax between the two lovers, the shared moment of epiphany that ultimately would allow Giselle to rest in peace and Albrecht to resume his life. The gist of my effort registered with Clive Barnes in his review for the New York *Times* on May 19, 1975:

> Her mad scene was abstracted and remote, given with a trancelike pathos, limp features and dead eyes. This betrayal and death was like the crushing of a butterfly, a perfect essay in Romantic mime. In the second act, where Giselle returns as a phantom to save her reckless lover, Albrecht, Miss Kirkland made an admirably fugitive and fleeting ghost. Few more experienced ballerinas have shown themselves so adept at distinguishing between the two acts of the ballet—at drawing the demarcation between flesh and spirit, substance and shadow.

The tragedy that haunted me throughout the graveyard scene of the second act was perhaps something quite different from what either the critics or the audience might have witnessed. Could any of the spectators have known that Misha and I were committed to two diametrically opposed visions of the climax of the ballet? Would anyone have suspected that we never even discussed the tragedy as it related to our characters?

What I experienced in the second act was Misha trapped by his earthbound love, unable to release himself from despair. Misha's innocent Albrecht was consumed by his thwarted desire. He played contrition and guilt to the back row of the balcony. The lilies that symbolized Giselle's love became for him a kind of magical fetish, revealing the depth of Albrecht's desolation, his inability to take heart from that love and let go. Misha described his point of view in *Baryshnikov at Work:*

> . . . the flowers are central to the end of the whole drama. When Albrecht is saved and Giselle has forgiven him but must return to the world of the Wilis, Albrecht desperately tries to hold on to her. The way of that world cannot be halted, but in strewing the flowers in a straight line from her grave Albrecht tries to save her for himself, to hold on to the final link between them.

I never allowed Giselle to become a Wili. The stage directions never specified that she return to that world of evil, but to her own grave, beneath the same cross that she earlier advised Albrecht to use as a refuge. As the originator of the story and a commentator on the ballet, Gautier drew a fine line between "her instinct as a woman and a Wili." That crucial distinction defines her spiritual struggle, not only to save herself, but to save her lover. Giselle, the woman, has to triumph over Giselle, the Wili. She has to fight to forgive Albrecht for his duplicity and to overcome the bitterness represented by the Wilis. By forgiving him, she not only purifies herself, but in effect breaks the spell of the Wili Queen. It is Giselle who enables Albrecht to survive until dawn—halting the reign of those illusory demons and hallowing the world of the human heart—giving him the chance to redeem his life.

I had to bring those qualities into the dance that would allow my character to buy time for her lover. Composing the movement was like walking a tightrope between the opposing dramatic forces of Albrecht and the Queen of the Wilis. Each gesture was torn between those poles, a complication fully appreciated by Martine van Hamel, whose marvelous portrayal of the Wili Queen enhanced my own performance. Giselle's dancing, set to the famous score by Adolphe Adam, had to be phrased with a sustained flow of nuance that would reveal her true nature. Without the sensitive support of my partner, that degree of control, that expression of Giselle's love, was in jeopardy at every moment. I had to contend with my own bitterness.

It became clear that Misha had no interest in salvation. His Albrecht seemed to be doomed to the same fate as his James in *La Sylphide.* Misha's eagerness to have me rush off the stage after our final parting underscored the point. He was inclined toward a melodramatic display of anguish, a solo portrait of defeated love. Fixating on the lilies, he staggered backward, strewing them, one by one, in slow motion. I looked for some way to penetrate the curtain of grief, to inspire a gentle ray of hope in my lover.

My Giselle was never able to soften the impact of his final gestures or alleviate the sense of doom. On one occasion, the front rows of the audience may have heard Misha hiss at me: "Get off the stage, stupid!" I wondered how he would have handled the last scene in the original version of the ballet, in which Albrecht withdrew with his fiancée, Bathilde, her head resting on his shoulder and the lilies clasped to his breast. Would he have accepted her consolation? Would he have pushed her off the stage or allowed her to forgive him? Perhaps Heinrich Heine, the man who gave us the Wilis, provides the answers as well as a lyrical portrait of Misha's Romantic hero:

> I've known it long: I saw you in my dream.
> Into your night no hope will cast a gleam;
> I saw the serpent on your heart's blood feed
> And saw, my love, the life you're doomed to lead.

I had rebelled for years against Balanchine's modern vision of the ballerina; it seemed that I had to revolt against Misha's Romantic image of womanhood as well. Between these two Russian men, my little insurrection in the name of love and reason was bound to be put down. I was easily disarmed.

The traditional, lithographic poses—the pictures of female passivity specified by my partner—were yet another source of tension, a tangle of thorns between us in the rehearsal hall. In New York, after I had suffered through Misha's accusations about being unmusical and unhelpful, I took him to Stanley Williams, a teacher whom he more or less respected. My idea was that Stanley would act as a mediator between us for the central adagio section that we were polishing for the second act. Misha's attitude was that he was doing me a great favor with my problem to consult my teacher. Stanley's reaction fell somewhere between being honored and intimidated in the presence of the Russian star. We made progress only after I encouraged my longtime mentor not to hold back his criticism. I had to drag it out of him. Stanley seemed to treat Misha with a deference that previously had been reserved for Balanchine.

Later, in Washington, D.C., the bottom fell out of our relationship in *Giselle*. The ostensible problem involved the final bit of partnering between Albrecht and the heroine. The lateral lifts at the very end require an exceptionally long and graceful arc. The impetus of the movement is completely dramatic, demonstrating the ultimate level of Giselle's control, compensating for Albrecht's nearly fatal exhaustion.

Technically described as a sequence of supported temps levés en arabesque, these lifts were the cause of violent fights between us over the years. Misha tended to bounce me up and down, like I was a duck splashing through water. He did not want any advice on how to improve his performance, especially since I was the one who had the focus in the scene. I knew there was a way for him to carry me smoothly. Ivan Nagy had perfected a technique with Natasha Makarova. The male partner, hidden by the ballerina, could get away with a somewhat unflattering "frog walk" in order to

support the female spirit through her flight in the air. I assumed that Misha
had a complex about his prince looking like a frog.

I scheduled an hour of private rehearsal time with Misha in order to work
on "my problem." He arrived late with his big pet dog and ignored me,
deliberately running through his solo variations without offering so much as
a nod. This was not a simple lack of etiquette. I was fuming at the side of the
studio as other dancers drifted into the room. Time was wasting.

He finally deigned to remember that we had an appointment to work.
When we arrived at the spot for those troublesome lifts, I had duck feet
again—splash, splash, splash across the floor. When I pulled away, he was in
shock: "Gels, it's fine! Vhy you stop?"

I decided to test him. "Misha, have you ever seen Ivan do this lift? He
stays in plié and moves sideways behind the girl, you know, so it looks like
she never touches the ground. Her feet skim across the floor."

Judging by his facial reaction, those standing around us might have
thought that I had called his mother some obscene name. "Buut, Gelsey, he
look terrible!"

Mimicking his whine, I came back quickly, "Buuut, Misha, the audience
won't even see you." Then mimicking his accent and swishing through the
air with my hand, I added, "You know, make like music. Graaaaduuual.
Smooth."

He mumbled harshly, "Ivan is silly actor. Can't do steps."

I changed my tack and pampered him. "Misha, maybe, well . . . I know
it's hard, but, can't we do it more like one long line, you know, like we've
done before . . . in New York."

Shifting his eyes for a split second to those watching us, he raised his
brows and came back at me with his most sugarcoated and cooperative tone,
"Sure! Any-sing you vant, Gels! I do best I can do!"

We tried again with the music—splash, splash, splat, splat, bang. This time
I was a crippled duck. My right foot twisted trying to resist and prevent him
from letting me hit the floor. He was going way beyond lazy and inconsider-
ate. He was being downright mean.

I just stared at him. I thought maybe this was just another bad joke. He
was suddenly so loud and sincere. "Vhut? It's how you said! No?"

Turning away, I let out an exasperated chuckle and murmured very quietly, "You bastard. What a routine."

I felt like I had been shot in the back by his screaming voice: "Vhut you
say, Gelsey? Vhut you say to me? Vhut!"

Over my shoulder, I tried to brush him off. "Misha, never mind. It's not
important."

"Vhut you call me? Tell me! Vhut you call me, Gelsey?"

The incident was obviously not going to pass. I faced him down. "Okay,
Misha. What I said was, 'You bastard.' "

I was actually calm, all things considered. Very matter-of-fact. That may have been what caused the bomb to go off. He turned to his dog and exploded, "Goulou! Goulou! Come! Let's go!"

Goulou was obviously well trained. I expected the wagging hound to help Misha on with his robe. My partner did that himself, flinging the luxurious garment over his shoulders like a cape and flying out the door of the studio.

The room was dead silent. I went back to working. My mental monologue went something like this: I am not guilty . . . I have witnesses . . . I have done nothing wrong . . . I am standing up for my work . . . Why should I be afraid?

Then I pondered what would happen in a court of law. Would anyone in that studio testify on my behalf? Would any of them stand up to that Russian prima donna? Would any of them risk losing their jobs? I was in trouble again.

After rehearsal time was over, I took the elevator down to the floor where dressing rooms and staff offices were located. When the elevator doors opened, I was met by the sight of a pacing artistic director, Lucia Chase. Crisis was written all over her face. As I walked by her, she screeched, "Gelsey! Gelsey! Come over here!"

She was always chasing me; she was always flustered about something. "Really, Gelsey! You can't call Misha names! Now look what's happened— you've upset him! You simply can't call him—"

I cut her off. I had no mercy at that point. I pulled my arm away when she tried to touch me. It was obvious that Misha had vented his hostility on her, and I did the same. "Lucia, don't you ever tell me what I can and can't say to him! I am the only one around here who has ever really worked with that man! Don't you dare tell me what I can and can't do!"

She gave up. I got the message in my dressing room that Misha was refusing to dance with me. He later changed his mind. A member of the teaching staff apparently gave him one of those lectures about how the show must go on, touching on three points. I heard a capsulized version that must have been revised for my ears: "First of all, you have taken advantage of her. Second of all, you asked her to dance with you. And third of all, you need her more than she needs you." It was one of the few times in all of my years with ABT that anyone came to my defense.

I was not so much pleased by the hearsay as by Misha's partnering in the performance that night. It was a relatively great *Giselle* for one incredibly simple reason: we had no choice but to try to forgive each other through the dance. I did it my way. He did it his way. That was what the ballet was all about.

Our truce lasted no more than a day. The next time I arranged for a rehearsal, he was late again. I heard that he was playing the piano in one of the other studios. After sending a message to him, asking if he intended to show up, he passed word back to me via one of the other dancers: "Misha says to go fuck yourself, and he'll be here in a minute." This was presumably

Misha's idea of a good joke to precede his belated appearance. His command of English never stopped improving.

At the beginning of August 1975, the company was scheduled to present one of its gala extravaganzas at Lincoln Center. I assumed that Misha would be my partner for this event. Only a week before the show, I learned second-hand that he had invited the French ballerina Noëlla Pontois to appear with him. I felt like the teenager who suddenly discovers that she has no date on the night of the prom. Somehow I found the nerve to extend my own invitation—to Rudolf Nureyev.

Rudi and I had never danced together. He graciously accepted and flew into New York at the last minute. We had just enough time to prepare the pas de deux from Le Corsaire. I did the solos in my own fashion and followed his lead through the rest of the dance, adapting myself to his specifications for a series of symmetrical poses that we performed together. He was at the time thirty-seven years old and set in his ways. I was in awe of him. To have tried to alter his course through that ballet would have been tantamount to throwing myself in front of a speeding subway train. His commitment to his approach was absolute.

Our performance was an unforgettable experience. The story of Le Corsaire is based on a poem by Lord Byron, who no doubt would have been delighted with the pure passion with which Rudi transformed steps into fire. It was not so much the raw energy on the stage that touched me, but the tender moments that followed the dance. Rudi seemed to be genuinely proud of me as a dancer. I had heard how difficult he could be with his ballerinas, but on that night he was the perfect gentleman. He showed me off during curtain calls as if I were an equal sharing in the art, not merely a necessary appendage to his artistry. I wished that he were ten years younger.

Later in the year, I performed the title role of his production of the ballet Raymonda. As a guest with the company, Rudi directed and provided his own version of the choreography (after Petipa). He also danced the male lead. He certainly had endeared himself to me, but he did not offer the kind of directorial answers that I needed. Determined to avoid trouble that might arise from creative conflicts, I, as usual, did my work on the sly.

According to the plot of Raymonda, Rudi's character, Jean de Brienne, was my romantic partner in a prearranged marriage. Before my character, Raymonda, met her intended husband, she danced in anticipation, waiting for his arrival, playing with a scarf. The choreography called for me to throw the scarf into the air, execute several steps, and catch it on the way down. No explanation was offered as to the significance of the actions surrounding the scarf. Was I supposed to be fascinated that this prop floated like an airy nothing? Was I supposed to be amused?

I was told eventually to watch the scarf as if I were intrigued by some ethereal quality it possessed, differentiating it elementally from the air. I might as well have tried to snatch an answer from the air. Nobody wanted to hear about it. After all, it was only one moment in the first act. It was only a dumb prop. It was only my problem.

I went to work on the story with Pilar, the mime artist, reconstructing the action and the motivation. On one occasion, working through the night in my apartment, she came up with an imaginative explanation for the presence of the scarf. This gave me a real scenario with which to animate the dance. We supposed that the scarf had been sent to Raymonda as a token of affection by her prospective husband, portrayed by Rudi.

As a symbol of his courtship, the scarf became the focus of my dance. Music, movement, and character fell into place with the given steps. The scarf was no longer a mere prop, but the amorous fetish of a young woman's imagination. It possessed the qualities that she fantasized in a lover she had not yet seen in person, and I treated it accordingly, teasing and wooing it into my hands. The moment informed my entire performance, but nobody in the company, including Rudi, knew what I had done. Only much later did Pilar and I learn that in the original ballet, the version performed a century ago, the scarf had been depicted just as we had imagined, as one of the gifts of courtship sent on the occasion of Raymonda's birthday.

Only one choreographer at ABT actually seemed to support my artistic inclination toward dance and drama. His name was Antony Tudor. I performed three of his ballets in 1975: *Jardin aux Lilas (Lilac Garden), Shadowplay,* and *The Leaves Are Fading.* Mr. Tudor usually had either the answers to my questions or the patience to seek the answers with me. In order to find the expressive key to a single step, we sometimes spent hours in the studio. His aim struck me as something of an enigma, an arrow that was its own target, psychological and physical, daring me to follow. I always shot for the dramatic heart of a moment, even in *The Leaves Are Fading,* a work that appeared to be plotless. Each Tudor dance that I performed was both a fantastic puzzle and a social portrait composed of intricate ballet images and mimetic gestures. Each detail held a possibility for revelation.

Mr. Tudor was one of those people who seemed to be able to see through me. The only problem was that I could never be quite sure what it was that he saw. His bald head and chiseled features gave him an arch demeanor, both stern and refined. His face lit up like a lantern whenever an image or idea caught his fancy. The back of his neck and shoulders had an uncanny way of communicating his attitude and mood. He could speak his mind through the slightest change of posture. A world might materialize instantaneously in the crook of his arm as he demonstrated a step, only to vanish with a sudden pause and a quizzical brush of his fingers across his cheek.

He demanded the utmost sensitivity from the dancers who performed his ballets. With a flash of caustic wit, he could cut down anyone. I recall his berating a dancer for tearing a "passion to tatters," the Shakespearean reference perhaps over her head, but the point well taken. The atmosphere during his rehearsals inspired reverence. A former British dancer, as well as a teacher and choreographer, he was in his sixties when he choreographed *The Leaves Are Fading*. That particular ballet was his first creation for ABT in a quarter of a century. It was more than an honor for me to work with him, it was both a challenge and a fair exchange. We worked together quietly.

I often wondered if Mr. Tudor had some insight into my relationship with Misha, especially during our rehearsals of *Shadowplay* (originally choreographed for the Royal Ballet in 1967). Misha was the "Boy with the Matted Hair," and I was the "Celestial." The dance was a kind of Zen Buddhist romp through the jungle of life, culminating with a balletic martial arts contest between the Boy and the Celestial. Rehearsing this cosmic wrestling match one afternoon in New York, I found myself temporarily sprawled on top of Misha. Mr. Tudor offered only a wry comment, somewhat disconcerting at the time: "You like that position, don't you?"

Whatever my position may have been, it was overturned during a tour at the end of 1975. We were performing in one of those small cities that defy memory. I made a surprise visit to Misha's hotel room in the middle of the night. I did it on a dare from one of the other dancers. The idea that I might descend on my lover without being invited was new and totally outlandish. I had acquiesced to his double standards for such a long time that to try to change the rules certainly meant that I was courting disaster. I was thrilled by the risk. I got the keys from the hotel desk and stole into his room. After creeping into the darkness and crawling into his bed, I heard only his sleepy voice, "Gelsey, vhut you doing here? You crazy."

He made no complaints in the morning. On the following night, however, he made a telling appearance at a party in the hotel. He was accompanied by a young beauty with whom he had been smitten for some time. The three of us ran into each other briefly. Surrounded by fellow members of the company, I thought the scene had a certain theatrical unreality, like a stage manager had called us to our places. Misha summed up the situation for those within earshot with a line that was both a command and a farewell: "Good night, Gelsey!"

I was crushed. The other woman, a dancer in the corps, barely figured in my rage. It was Misha who was laughing at me. Was I imagining things? The betrayal seemed to have been designed with deliberate malice, to teach me a lesson.

I said almost nothing to anyone for days. Prior to a performance, Misha approached me as I was warming up backstage. Out of the blue, without so much as a word of warning, he tried to fondle one of my breasts. Pushing at his arm, I was outraged, "Misha, what are you doing? Get away from me! If you want to fool around, find somebody else!" He was trying to be playful. He stalked away looking hurt. Was I oversensitive?

I doubt that his actions were ever intended to terminate the romance between us. He simply wanted to remind me who set the terms. He knew the exact location of my most intimate pressure points. Subtle humiliation was always the most effective way to keep me in line. The same kind of strategy applied to making decisions about our partnership. When I balked at dancing with him in a new piece to be choreographed by the avant-garde dancemaker Twyla Tharp, I was caught in a bind. I had no inclination toward that brand of entertainment. Misha let me know that I was missing the artistic opportunity of a lifetime and had to be ignorant not to hold the opinion that Tharp was the greatest thing to hit classical dance since the mazurka. There had to be something severely wrong with me not to want to be one of his partners in *Push Comes to Shove.* What ballerina in her right mind would turn down the chance to work with both Mikhail Baryshnikov and Twyla Tharp? I had to make excuses. I had to be sick.

The excuses and the sickness had only just begun. A major disruption of my life and career came in the form of an offer to star in a Hollywood movie about the ballet world. The film was entitled *The Turning Point.* The cast included Anne Bancroft and Shirley MacLaine in the major roles. The idea seemed to be that Misha and I would play ourselves in a thinly disguised subplot about an affair between an American ballerina and a Russian star.

The producers, Herb Ross and his wife, Nora Kaye, insisted that they were making a realistic film about the lives of dancers. Nora was herself a former ballerina. She had won acclaim as a dance actress in the early Tudor ballets. Herb, who would direct the film, was an experienced choreographer. I rejected their first offer for the simple reason that I wanted no part of Hollywood. My resistance soon collapsed. I was hit from all sides: what ballerina in her right mind would turn down the chance to be a movie star?

As I was drawn into the screen tests and script readings, I began to realize that I had committed a monumental blunder. The screenplay by Arthur Laurents was a soap opera. My character, Emilia, was an ingenue with nothing between her ears. The story had nothing to do with either the reality or the art of ballet, and the premise about how knowledge was passed from generation to generation of dancers seemed nothing less than artistic fraud. I made some suggestions. I was humored. I was told to trust the professionals, the filmmakers. I began to starve myself.

The first sign that I was out of my element came at a black-tie dinner in Los Angeles, organized to launch and promote the project. ABT happened to be in town on the Western leg of its 1975–76 winter tour. The festivities began after a performance at the Dorothy Chandler Pavilion. Nora Kaye had taken me to buy a little party outfit to replace my usual blue jean look. Herb escorted me around on his arm and introduced me as the new starlet. At a small dining table, I sat across from Ryan O'Neal and ignored the idle banter. An obvious flirt, he gawked at me. I turned away and refused to eat.

On the following day, Herb Ross called at my hotel and informed me that I had to telephone Ryan O'Neal and offer an apology. I was floored. He had to be kidding. Apologize for what? Herb was adamant: "Well, Gelsey, all I know is you upset him." I made no call. The word must have gone out that I was being uncooperative. That was the reputation that preceded me.

I had no words to explain myself to anyone. When the company toured San Francisco, I met briefly with my brother Marshall, who had stayed in the city where he had graduated from college, eventually landing a job with the San Francisco *Chronicle.* He had watched from afar as my career skyrocketed. I had been on a recent cover of *Newsweek* with Misha; I had been marked by *Time* magazine as one of the new beauties of 1975. Marshall was proud of me. He was mystified when I set him straight: "My success means nothing! I hate every minute of it! Ballet is a curse!"

I was more than bitter. On June 2, 1976, back in New York, I received the rehearsal schedule for the film from Nora. She sent the following note:

Enclosed is the new script and you will see that your part is very exciting and, no doubt, will make you a big star not only in the ballet but also as an actress on the screen. I am very excited for you and hope you are too.

That was the pitch. It was too late for me to withdraw gracefully. The problem was not merely selling out, but giving a false picture of my life to the world. I knew that people would see me as Emilia and make the assumption that the character was Gelsey. The coaching that I received to play the role only made matters worse: "Don't act. Just be yourself." Did they really think that I was Emilia, that little twit?

I was sucked into a Mutt and Jeff routine: every time I introduced an idea about the character to Herb, drawing from my own experience, and winning his tentative approval, he turned to Nora and hit a stone wall. I was unable to empathize with the fairy tale they had concocted to foist on the public. It seemed to me that the makers of the movie simply wanted to exploit my name and the superficial aspects of my story, without any concern for the truth. How could they have any idea what it was really like to dance with Misha, to make love with him? How could they know how I might feel about the hidden scars on my body being exposed to their cameras? How could they think that being a star had anything to do with my being an artist? How could they expect me to trust them?

As they discounted my words, I tried to show them the real nature of modern ballet by the only other means I had available: my body. I would blot myself out . . . I would vanish into thin air . . . There would be nothing left for the camera to photograph. This was not so much conscious design, though I entertained such thoughts, as a regressive slide back to the world of my childhood. I intensified the obsessive patterns established with my girlfriends during the early years of my training. I was simply returning to Balanchine, finding myself at the mercy of both anorexia and bulimia.

Receiving no support from Misha, who seemed to have no problem with the script or with the producers, I enacted my own private mad scene: I starved by day, then binged on junk food and threw up by night; I took injections of pregnant cows' urine, reputed to be a miraculous diet aid; I stuffed myself with laxatives, thyroid pills, and celery juice; I emptied myself with enemas and steam baths. During the wee hours, I often made desperate trips to the drugstore to pick up ipecac, the emetic that I used to induce vomiting. I became an expert with the technique of shoving two fingers down my throat. The blood vessels around my eyes erupted with the constant strain. These symptoms and diseases continued for months and, intermittently, for a period of years.

I knew that I was sick. I watched myself helplessly, always trying to pretend that I was in control. It was the sense of having dirty secrets that made me truly powerless. I was a prisoner inside my body. I was too ashamed to tell anyone. When I did happen to complain to a doctor about the constant vomiting, he suggested that I try wearing a tight belt to prevent the eating binges. Another doctor made the ingenious diagnosis that I was suffering from a potassium deficiency. No doubt I had iron-poor blood as well. I was told that I needed rest, relaxation, and food—the assumption was that my condition was entirely physical.

Herb and Nora suggested a health farm. I flatly refused. I told the press that I was looking forward to the experience of the film, that I was thrilled to be working with such wonderful people. I took a brief vacation and got a tan, cultivating a bronzed illusion of health. I had to look as if I were making an effort to help myself. I was terrorized by the possibility that someone might lock me away.

My weight loss had me hovering at eighty pounds. That gave the film producers ample reason to replace me in the role with Leslie Browne, a young dancer out of the School of American Ballet. She also happened to be the goddaughter of Nora Kaye. The unlikely turn of real events almost seemed to confirm the improbable plot of the movie, which had already begun filming as I accepted the rejection. Later in the year, the movie became a popular hit, and Misha was nominated for an Oscar. I was relieved to be out of the film, but at the age of twenty-three felt more than ever like a total failure.

Distracted and demeaned by the flirtation with Hollywood, I suffered from a profound shortage of joy throughout the spring and summer seasons of 1976. I pushed myself through *La Bayadère* and various ballets, both with and without Misha. We kept our distance. I had no stamina, no staying power. My second-act performance in *Giselle* actually improved, according to the critics. I must have looked like I had come back from the grave.

I was teetering on the brink during rehearsals for *The Sleeping Beauty* with Ivan Nagy. I stole the costume from the theatre in the middle of the night and had my favorite designer, Carl Michel, fix the shocking-pink number that had been provided for my character, Princess Aurora. The company threatened to take legal action against me.

Ivan and I opened without the benefit of a full dress and lighting rehearsal —the outcome of economics. Money had to be spent to cover rehearsal time. From management's point of view, Misha might have rated such an expenditure, but not Ivan. He and I had no time to adjust to lighting, props, and costumes. My disorientation destroyed the most beautiful section of the ballet, the famous Rose Adagio. Ivan's partnering saved the night for us again and again. After the curtain went down, the two dancers who played the King and Queen, Gayle Young and Sallie Wilson, told me that they had been in tears on the stage watching Ivan and me perform the wedding pas de deux. It was a dance about youth and purity. I wept as well.

I continued with my infantile regression, adding layers of eyeliner in a new phase of Suzanne Farrell parody. The gaunt, oriental effect occasioned a wry, telling comment from Mr. Tudor, "Gelsey, what have you done to yourself now?"

I finally had enough sense to visit a psychiatrist, an old Freudian who enjoyed listening to tales about my father. I confided my belief that nobody would ever be able to love me with the scars that I still carried from breast alterations. The doctor and I discussed the meaning of love. It seemed that I was losing faith in all of my ideals. I was demoralized. I was distorting my own creative process. I was defiant. I was not adjusting effectively to my social environment.

I absorbed the descriptive map of my mind provided by the good doctor and his books on psychology, but I had no idea how to chart a new direction. I was still lost. I took little consolation from the fact that I was a fascinating case. Compared to those that I read about in journals, I was somewhat unique. That was a perverse source of pride. I rejected the theory of penis envy for women, but thought it might be applicable to various men that I had known. Breast envy was another matter. That I could understand.

I sat in bed at night and thumbed through fashion magazines, memorizing faces and figures. This began as a game I played to beat insomnia. I wanted to be a gorgeous someone, anyone other than who I was. I clung irrationally to the idea that my body had been the cause of all my problems. I prayed for a perfect body. Please, God, make me into the doll that everyone wants me to be. I stared at pictures of models and imagined that I might wake up in the morning as one of them. I wanted to free myself from the weight of artistic choice. I wanted to make myself into a creature without substance. I wanted to lose my identity. I looked forward all day to the night when I could become a little pebble tossed into the dark pool of sleep. Those waters were magical. I was able to transform myself. I was able to dream my way into somebody else's body. I was no longer Gelsey.

My games had to catch up with me sooner or later. I have a stark memory of an evening in the autumn of 1976. I had so depleted myself that death was no longer an abstract concept. I lay in bed and listened to my heart skipping beats, certain that it was about to cease altogether. I buried my face in my pillow. The horror came up in my throat. I could taste the emetic that I had downed earlier in the evening. I murmured to myself, "Please don't die . . . Oh my God, I'm so scared . . . What am I going to do? . . . I don't know what I'm going to do!"

The phone rang and sent yet another wave of cardiac terror through my system. I was almost immobilized. The caller was a photographer friend. She insisted that I accompany her at the last minute to a lecture at the New School for Social Research. A psychologist from Sarah Lawrence College was giving a talk on the subject of inspiration. My friend would not take no for an answer. Fearing for my life, I somehow pulled myself together.

The lecturing psychologist, speaking with some warmth and humor, raised one of the questions that had been troubling me. Why did the inspiration of creative artists not carry over into their personal lives? Did that have to be true for all artists? Did their calling condemn them to loneliness? Stimulated mentally for the first time in months, I wanted to ask the psychologist if he had found fulfillment in his life.

Shortly after the lecture, I was introduced to him and vaulted foolishly into a romantic affair. I felt too worthless most of the time to return his affection. His attentive companionship made me painfully aware of my inadequacy. I would have made a better patient than a lover. In his thirties, he was the type who wore tweeds, a mild-mannered intellectual, distinguished and gentle. I could find no fault with him, but it was easier to cut him out of my life than to have him care for me. There had to be some essential part of me that had been lost. Every time I tried to recover that missing part by becoming involved with a man, I became more sure that it was irretrievable. I was simply a freak of nature.

I decided on more surgery to remove the scars from my breasts, embarking on another round of warfare with the looking glass. I had to meet with Misha to tell him that I would not be able to take part in the company's production of *The Nutcracker* that was planned for the spring of 1977. This ballet would be his first venture into choreography. I felt I owed him an honest explanation why I would be unavailable, but I was not looking forward to an encounter that would likely take the form of *True Confessions*. I had never had the courage to say anything to him about my mishaps with the mirror.

On a cold winter afternoon, Misha picked me up in a taxi. We were going to a nearby Columbus Avenue bistro for a drink. He was in high spirits. The cab bounced us around on the back seat. Misha swung over and put his head on my lap like a puppy, snuggling for more than warmth, "Oh, Geeeelsey, is really good to see you!"

I put him off firmly. This was business. He paid for the cab. After entering the restaurant and sitting at a table for two, I began to speak with a nervous stammer. "Misha . . . when I was young . . . I had some silicone put into my"—looking down at the zone in question—"breasts, you know, many women have this done . . . lots of girls . . . well, anyway, I did, and then I had it taken out, it just had to go, and I was left with these two scars that have always bothered me, and so I have to have another operation to try to fix myself up, and so, you see, well, it won't take long, but I can't start work right away on *The Nutcracker* . . . I'm sorry. I know how important this ballet is for you."

After my shaky start, I was nonstop. With a seriously confused look on his face, Misha leaned over the table toward me, "Vhut! Please, Geeeelsey, I don't understand."

I believed him. How many pairs of silicone implants could there be running around in the Soviet Union? He simply had no idea what I was talking about. I made two more attempts to explain, waxing eloquent on the nature of the female anatomy. I tried to make it less complicated, but he remained in a state of absolute bewilderment. The words "hospital" and "operation" did seem to register. "Geeels, you need some-sing? Vhut can I do? You need money?"

I turned down his generous offer and eventually let him put me in another cab. I was touched enough to second-guess his motives. Maybe he really cared after all. Maybe I had misjudged him. Maybe I was just never honest enough with him.

A surgeon at a New York hospital carried out the last series of misguided operations. The doctor was middle-aged and had bags under his eyes. He felt compelled on one occasion to give me a lecture. He asked me if I believed in God. I said something ambiguous about my belief in the human spirit and the creative act. He jumped on that like a favorite cocktail party opening. Working himself into a fever pitch, he tried to prove for me that all human emotions, including love, were nothing more than complicated neurological responses. Science would one day control them. My brain was a computer . . . My body was a machine . . . The universe was just a matter of chance. Was this his usual bedside manner? He concluded his rambling discourse with an invitation for dinner. Why not? He seemed to need help, and he already knew that I needed help.

He picked me up at my apartment one evening. Before we departed for our date, he took out a small vial of white powder. It was cocaine. I had never seen it before. He showed me how to sniff a narrow line of dust into my nostrils. He kept asking me how I felt, but I felt nothing whatsoever. I had never taken drugs of the recreational variety, not even marijuana, but I had no qualms about trying. After all, he was a doctor. This experience was quickly forgotten. It was uneventful. The drug had no real effect as far as I could tell. We went to a restaurant and I listened to his endless sob story. He was losing his wife. He was losing his home. He said he never slept. He never stopped talking. At the end of the night, I gave him something else to complain about—a cold embrace. He left me with his diagnosis: "You don't know what to do with a tender moment!"

I was still trying to put Misha out of my mind. I had no alternative but to dance. I had prepared myself for a comeback, struggling to repress my nasty dietary habits, never really dealing with the root of the problem. In February 1977, Misha and I were partners for several performances in Vienna. We agreed to dance Petipa's version of *Le Corsaire* and Balanchine's early dramatic work *Apollo*. I set two goals for myself before leaving for the engagement: not to eat anything and not to sleep with Misha. I lacked conviction.

Not long after arriving in Vienna, my partner and I went to a little café. He was moved by the sight of an old married couple at a nearby table. "Oh, look, Gelsey, do you see them?" He remarked on the simplicity of their lives, the way they held each other's hands. He lauded their loyalty, their purity of heart. I thought to myself, Misha is going sentimental on me. We were soon joined by two acquaintances of his, a foreign couple, maybe in their thirties. They talked about their philosophy of marriage as a convenient arrangement. They were evidently free spirits. I had no sympathy for their brand of low passion.

I piped up, "If we have to live with ourselves forever, why shouldn't we be able to devote ourselves to one other person? Is that so unreasonable? To love someone for a lifetime?"

Misha cut in, "You know, Gelsey, I like you . . . I really like you!"

The affection seemed to come from nowhere. Something familiar stirred in me. I had never harbored either the hope or the intention of marriage, but I did nurture the delusion that I occupied some special place in his heart. Having heard rumors about his affairs with other women, I supposed that he always came back to me for a reminder of that gentle part of himself, and that he valued our struggle in the studio as well as our splendors on the stage. There had to be some piece of him deep down inside that aspired, like me, to a higher kind of expression in our dance and in our lives. It was not a matter of personal fidelity, but faith in a shared ideal.

Later that afternoon, he came to my hotel room. He had been on the phone and received news about one of his projects. He was ebullient, dancing around my quaint little room. "Oh, Geeelsey, someday you vill dance any-sing you vant, anyvhere you vant . . . vill be vunderful! You still be dancing when I am old man!" He proceeded to enact a grand imitation of me as an aging ballerina, doing the last-act variation in *The Sleeping Beauty*. Next, he did himself as an old man with a cane, hobbling to the theatre to see me. He had me in stitches.

Offering yet another imitation from his rogues' gallery, he sniffled about as Balanchine, making a pronouncement about ballerinas. I tried to match his lighthearted mood and show my displeasure with his new character, "Oh, please, Misha, not *two* of you!" He missed my point. I did nothing to deflate his spirits. Such moments were too rare.

The mood inevitably changed and the scene culminated with yet another grave confession of Oedipal turmoil. His mother seduced me again, bless her heart. After a fleeting taste of ecstasy, I watched him grab his trousers and prepare to leave. The departure was cold-blooded. He dressed faster than any man I have ever seen, then skidded across the floor of my room like he was expecting a flood—splash, splash, splash—in a mad dash toward the door. I was unable to resist the impulse that coiled in my throat and let out a little laugh. "Oh, Misha, thanks for lunch!" The door closed on my sarcasm.

I thought my parting comment had rolled off his back, that he would give it no more thought than he had given the events that preceded his exit. It seemed that he had gotten what he wanted. We had plans to go out together that evening. I waited on a divan in the hotel lobby until he joined me. After planting himself beside me, he described a book of provocative photographs he had been perusing. Misha enthused over the sensuality, "So beeeautiful, just girls, you know . . ." I did not know or have the faintest idea why he chose the topic. I suppose he just wanted to set the mood for his non se-quitur. "Oh, Gelsey, by the way, that was not good joke this afternoon. Really!"

I gave him no warning. I simply charged away before he could say another word. It was something in his tone, a harsh note of condescension, as if I was being scolded for years of misbehavior. I tore into the elevator and literally punched the button for my floor. Tears were streaming down my cheeks. A real torrent. I slammed and locked the door of my room. I was in a complete rage, bouncing off the walls and furniture. He came banging after me:

"Gelsey, it's Misha . . . open the door! Open the door, Gelsey! I like you! Is important! Please, Gels . . . I really like you!"

I let him in with a sense of déjà vu. I had been here before. Maybe a million times. When he tried to hold me, I screamed, "Don't touch me! Just don't touch me!"

"Gels, vhut's wrong? Please, is important you tell me. Vhut's happened vis you? I don't understand."

I spluttered through more ridiculous tears, "Nothing seems to work with you! Nothing I do! No matter what I say, it's wrong! I mean, first I try to be serious and that's bad—Oh no! None of that!—and now I try to be like you, so casual, make a joke about the whole thing, take the pressure off you—Oh no! Bad joke! Bad taste!—I mean, what do you want from me, anyway? What do you want, Misha? Do I have to dance myself to death for you?"

He left me alone. On our opening night in Vienna, we walked into the theatre, the Staatsoper, a couple of hours before the show. The place was empty. We had nothing to say to each other. I went to my dressing room and began to prepare for *Apollo*. Five minutes before curtain, a little man with a mustache walked in and placed a wad of money on my dressing table. This was the local custom of payment in advance. I understood at that moment the real nature of my calling: I was a dancer and a member in good standing of the oldest profession in the world.

The performances were received warmly enough. The Viennese audiences apparently had not changed since the time when Beethoven said of them: "One must not speak at all about artistic judgment: their interest is confined to horses and ballerinas." Nobody seemed to care that my two female cohorts in *Apollo,* ballerinas from the local company, did not know how to dance that ballet. These young women were both blessed with good intentions, but they had not had the opportunity to rehearse adequately. I was shocked to discover that they spent most of their time at home. They prepared meals for their families. They had children and cooked. They went from the kitchen to the stage.

Boarding a flight back to New York, I doubted that I had a future. How could I dance without love? What reason was there to pursue dreams that had no place in life or on the stage? The world of ballet was defined for me in the broadest of terms between Petipa and Balanchine, between the fairy tales of the nineteenth century and the decorative fantasies of the twentieth century. Misha had broken into that closed world with his body. I was so sure that he held the key to the next century. To the extent that I recognized the success of our partnership, I credited him with drawing the best out of me. He was the ultimate challenge. The possibility for dramatic expression in the classical form had come into focus for me only with him. He had become the reason I danced.

How could I have understood Misha if I failed to comprehend my own art in the context of a ballet world that was stacked against me? He and I were actually dancing against each other. As long as he was in my way, I was blocked from my course, from myself. I was unable to pass through him. He was not the cause of my decline, what the press called my "emotional turbulence." He was a convenient excuse.

Later in the year, I replaced a pregnant Natalia Makarova as Misha's partner in a Jerome Robbins ballet called *Other Dances.* Relatively speaking, I was in top form. There were two dazzling solo variations for each of us. The audience often interrupted our performance with ovations. This sort of distraction had always been frowned upon at the New York City Ballet—it was one of Balanchine's pet peeves. Robbins himself seemed to like the casual effect created by dancers entering to watch other dancers, dancing through the audience response.

That is probably why on one occasion, in the production with ABT, while Misha was soaking up an ovation following one of his solos, I happened to make an entrance that stepped on his applause. The clapping died down as soon as the audience noticed me. Misha left the stage. He was incensed and hissed at me from the wings, "Stupid girl! Stupid girl!" I was not professional. I had stolen his applause. Some things would never change between us. Some things would always be unforgivable.

Chapter Nine

UNSEEN MALADIES

Just before the ABT spring tour of 1977, I was shocked into a phase of personal reform. My manager, Shirley Bernstein, informed me that my mother had been hospitalized at the Memorial Sloan-Kettering Cancer Center in Manhattan. During a taxi ride to the hospital, Shirley told me that my mother was suffering from some kind of liver ailment. The doctors had diagnosed a probable malignancy. I was supposed to prepare myself for the worst.

In a darkened hospital room, I saw my mother's long, tawny hair spill across a pillow, her face turning toward me. My heart cracked at the sound of her voice. "Gels, it's okay. I'm not afraid to die."

It was my mother who consoled me. She had managed somehow to make peace with herself. "Just cry. It's okay. Just cry, Gelsey."

Her courage purged me of self-pity. In her desperate hour of need, she gently insisted that I continue with my life. I decided that if she were able to deal with a mortal crisis, I could certainly dance on the upcoming tour. Anticipating a futile operation and maudlin scenes of family grief, my mother squeezed my hand and sent me away.

Motivated by the terror of losing her and by the certainty of my love for her, I committed myself to surmounting my problems on the stage. In Chicago, I danced with a resurgent spirit. On my mother's birthday, March 15, I performed *La Bayadère*. She was still in the hospital. I telephoned her from the theatre to wish her well and express my gratitude for the inspiration. A few days later, a critic for the Chicago *Sun-Times* reported on my progress in *The Sleeping Beauty:*

Gelsey Kirkland, partnered on Sunday night with his usual elegance by Ivan Nagy, came closest in looks and character to the young princess. Slim as a reed and light as a feather, she practically skimmed across the stage in her second-act variations, every extension of her pipestem legs indicating that she is returning to top form.

As if to answer the prayers I had uttered through my dance, the doctors told my mother that the previous diagnosis had been incorrect. The operation had revealed only scar tissue from an old bout with hepatitis. The lesson of the episode was not so much undercut as underscored by the false alarm. Upon reflection, I jotted down a number of practical resolutions: "I will stay at 92 pounds . . . I will go to class every day . . . I will be polite . . . etc." Brute force and willpower enabled me to improve my physical condition. I rationalized a plan to turn my own internal scars into a source of strength. I would conduct an exploratory operation through my art. I would heal myself through the dance.

The plan looked good on paper. I even looked good on the stage. There was only one catch: I was treating the symptoms, not the disease. I had no idea how to cure myself. I swallowed homeopathic doses of misery. I made an art of suffering. My failure of critical insight coincided with a failure of courage. I was afraid to take a public stand within the ballet world. I was afraid to challenge the prevailing aesthetic as well as the popular authority figures. Rage festered inside me. Returning to the stage was like renewing my contract with a familiar devil. I was selling my soul on an installment plan.

Mentally divided and conquered, reveling in the sheer agony of my discipline, I tore into the New York summer season of 1977, performing *La Sylphide, Giselle, La Bayadère, The Leaves Are Fading,* and *Les Sylphides.* The limited partnership with Misha was still a powerful drawing card for the company, but we were moving in opposite directions. As I dove into another Romantic classic, *Swan Lake,* partnered by Ivan Nagy, Misha prepared for a guest appearance in Balanchine's *Prodigal Son* with the Chicago Ballet.

During rehearsals for *Swan Lake,* I gave an extensive interview to John Gruen. It appeared in the New York *Times* on June 5, 1977. The writer noted that I was "a moody, introverted girl . . . filled with self-doubt . . . endlessly self-critical and, at times, on the verge of despair." He must have caught me on a good day.

Asked about the turmoil of the preceding year, I observed:

Suddenly, the physical problems became mental problems, and I didn't know which were caused by which. It was frightening to feel myself changing and perhaps losing what I had. It was a fight, but I'm feeling much better now.

Skirting the more personal issues, I contrasted Misha and Ivan as partners, choosing my words with as much accuracy and diplomacy as possible:

You see, with Ivan, it's a shared experience. I don't feel there are two egos in the room. We both have lots of patience, we experiment together, and we learn from each other. Also, he has a great sense of humor, which I don't have most of the time. It's totally different than working with Misha. I mean, Misha is totally impetuous, and if I have something to say, it just never hits the right spot, and vice versa.

After watching Ivan and me work under the direction of Enrique Martinez, the writer asked about my rumored intention to return to Balanchine's New York City Ballet. My denial was honest. At the same time, I felt obligated to speak favorably of my early experience with Balanchine and Robbins. What would the audience and the critics think of a ballerina who did not worship the idols at the New York City Ballet?

If the nostalgic homage I paid to Balanchine was somewhat disingenuous, it was also professionally pragmatic. I recoiled at the thought of being considered one of his creations, and later refused to take part in an interview for a book devoted to his ballerinas. Yet in struggling with the traditional story ballets, I sometimes invoked his name to bolster my argument against blind adherence to the nineteenth-century tradition. In trying to play both sides off against each other, I found myself caught in the middle.

When called upon to dance Balanchine's ballets, however infrequently at this stage of my career, I fashioned my performances with technical insights I had gleaned in dramatic works, disregarding his stated intentions and his training. I avoided the over-extensions, the broken wrists, the swayed hips, the flapping arms, and so forth. His ballets felt like so many variations on a familiar theme. From a dramatic point of view, it was as if I were playing the same character in each of his dances. That character was ice-cold and aloof, moving within a single band of the psychological spectrum. Even certain details of costume, such as a pair of rhinestone earrings, reappeared like a meaningless leitmotiv. As always, the challenge was primarily physical survival. My body continued to warn me against taking punishment for the sake of an aesthetic in which I did not believe.

As the actress delivers the lines of the playwright, so the ballerina dances the steps of the choreographer. I pushed the limits of interpretation as far as they would go. Yet my personal statement had to fit into an imposed vision of the world. No matter where I turned, I found myself inside a pretty picture that someone else had rendered. Discontent drove me forward with the faith that eventually I would find myself and my own world. I had a tentative compass in my work with Mr. Tudor.

My long-standing reservation with regard to Balanchine, that he did not speak to me in any compelling artistic sense, seemed to apply in a different way to Petipa. Most of the fairy tales seemed to be saying essentially the same thing. That disturbing realization included the irony of all ironies: it was Balanchine who had described them as silly stories. How could I admit my growing disillusionment with the traditional repertory without admitting that Mr. B had been right all along? Had I been wrong in leaving the New

York City Ballet? I was not about to reverse my course or retrace my steps. Why should I have given up the method of artistic discovery that had afforded all the breakthroughs that I had accomplished?

The Petipa formula, in actual fact, provided little more than a flimsy, narrative pretext for gymnastic feats. My passionate commitment to endowing the movement with substance and quality, to expressing some aspect of psychological truth, was frustrated by the material. There were too many gaping holes in both character and action. The dance itself simply did not hold much water, to say nothing of flesh and blood. The moral of the story usually disappointed the idealistic side of my nature; all of the exotic supernatural devices grated against my penchant for some sort of realism. Such was my perplexity as I immersed myself in *Swan Lake*.

The dual role of Odette/Odile—the good and evil swan princesses—usually represents a milestone in the career of a ballerina. My debut in *Swan Lake* at the Metropolitan Opera sold out weeks in advance, intensifying the pressure for me to live up to the expectations of the public. I barely considered the fact that I had become a box office attraction without Misha. My partner, Ivan, met me more than halfway on every choice I made during the rehearsal period. The production was originally staged for the company by David Blair, after Petipa and Ivanov. The music featured the familiar strains of Tchaikovsky. In the end, the great surprise for me would be the set designed by Oliver Smith.

My conception of character was contradicted by the scenario of the story. I wanted to play the white swan and the black swan as two intricate facets of a single personality. They were actually supposed to be identical enough in appearance to deceive the eye of the smitten Prince, with Odile disguising herself as Odette, their paths crossing briefly in the third act. In my effort to emphasize the psychological drama of good and evil, the two swans had to be technically linked in such a way that each of their gestures and actions originated from the same impulse and shape, differentiated only by movement qualities—marking the distance, for example, between love and lust. To have carried out such an interpretation of character to all its logical conclusions would have required me to revise the libretto. Taking such liberties was always a risk.

As it happened, I did alter the ending. I knew that the case of mistaken identity leading the hero, Prince Siegfried, into infidelity was a bum rap, a bit of sorcery lacking both justice and credibility. I balked at the image of the Prince and the white swan, Odette, reunited for a final boat ride across the serene waters of eternity after each had chosen suicide. It seemed to me that their stand against the evil spell of Von Rothbart should serve as the climactic moment, a shared resolution of hope and power. The vow of eternal love was the salient point, not sailing into some clichéd sunset.

In the studio, I suggested my idea to Ivan. "If we have to die at the end, we should be together. It's the action before our dying that matters. It's the love that breaks the spell, not the death."

His eyes flashed with excitement. "Gelsey! You know, I have always felt uncomfortable with that moment. This is the first time anyone ever felt the same way. It always seemed so strange to go out separately, for me to go running after you."

We worked out a kind of tableau, with Ivan's Siegfried folding his arms over my Odette, both of us emphatically defying the power of Rothbart with our love, then throwing ourselves into the lake. Without the benefit of a full dress rehearsal, Ivan and I opened on June 10, 1977. My technical aspirations were thwarted by the need to adjust to lights, props, and orchestra. Bronchitis contributed to the feeling of spatial disorientation, as well as my lack of stamina. By the time I spun through my thirty-two fouettés in the third act, I was a dying swan, just trying to stay with the music.

Our final scene in the fourth act was a travesty. When I mounted the platform where Ivan had agreed to join me for our last stand, I discovered that the space was too small for the two of us. The designer, of course, had no idea that we had changed the staging. As I saw Ivan dancing up the platform after me, I turned back to him, as if to wave good-bye, saying in low voice, "See ya later." Then I jumped off into the lake, a pile of mattresses hidden from the audience. After I landed, Ivan came tumbling over on top of me. Our bumping heads summed up the whole experience.

The audience loved the performance. The critics were kind, one of them crediting me with a "miracle." In my mind, it was just another disaster. I read a review by Arlene Croce, who made a fascinating attempt to analyze my artistic predicament. After pointing out in detail, almost step by step, how I had succumbed to a tendency toward "technical overkill," she stated:

> Kirkland has recovered her strength after a year of dancing and looking like her own shadow or not dancing at all. The audience that mourned her was entitled to its jubilation at this debut. My feeling is somewhat less than jubilant. Kirkland has returned to her Ballet Theatre form, and she can do better. Putting aside errors of conception and execution, which she can correct in future performances, Kirkland is in possession of a clear victory. But there is still room to doubt whether she is on the road to artistic fulfillment. I've mentioned the lack of guidance at Ballet Theatre. Kirkland aggravates the problem by a tendency, noticeable even in her New York City Ballet days, to aspire to a type of grandeur on the stage which is extraneous to her own true path of development. It's as if she wished to be any other kind of ballerina than the kind she is . . .

What kind of ballerina was I? Modern? Lyrical? Dramatic? Romantic? American? Russian? What was my true path of artistic development? Who was qualified to guide me? What kind of ballerina did I really want to become?

I had no role model. I had no real image of the classical artist. With only the support I found within myself, with only my limited education and modest experience, my perspective was not strong enough yet to articulate adequately. The kind of grandeur to which I aspired might have been clear, in principle at least, to choreographers such as the Frenchman, Jean-Georges Noverre, and the Italian, Salvatore Viganò, to those ballet masters of the eighteenth and early nineteenth centuries who sought to realize a dream of dance that expressed the progress of the human spirit, a ballet that conveyed emotions and ideas as powerfully as the other arts. My progress as an artist seemed to stall in a world indifferent to such aesthetic judgment. I was stifled on a stage that valued form over content, beauty over truth.

I was chasing a myth. I might have found kindred spirits among those artists from other fields, from other eras, those who celebrated a sublime marriage of Eros and Prometheus, those who created a symbolic wedding of heart and mind. That was my ideal of artistic grandeur: to kindle the fire of love, to steal the very soul of my audience, to dance with such intelligence and constant conviction that no eye could remain dry, that no throat could hold back the virtue of its laughter. For better or for worse, that was also my ideal of a good time, of entertainment.

Had I been able to speak as well as dance, I might have won the support of those who, like me, longed for a dance that portrayed the human drama with more depth and diversity. Such a dance was a seemingly impossible dream. I never uttered such ambitious words about my art, even to myself, without feelings of absolute loneliness and derangement. The fanatical extremes of my commitment isolated me. I had not yet reached back far enough in time to know that I was not alone. With few exceptions, I had no intimate or intellectual allies. The audience and critics surely sensed my vulnerability, if not my disenchantment.

I had only a vague suspicion that the expressive possibilities of the classical form—the dramatic potential that I sensed in the studio and on the stage—might extend beyond both the modern and traditional repertories. My basic dissatisfaction did not prompt me to try my hand at choreography. If nobody embraced my approach to being a dancer, except perhaps Mr. Tudor, why should anybody have supported me in my attempt to compose a ballet?

My approach was tolerated in the ballet world, very often appreciated, but only rarely understood. Inside the theatre itself, I had to fight tooth and nail every step of the way. I was humored. I was manipulated. I knew only two things with certainty: my personal fulfillment and artistic destiny were inseparable; my true path of development was yet to be decided.

I failed to foresee the consequences that would arise from the clash between my inner needs and the outer world. That was perhaps the fundamental cause of my disease, the ultimate source of all my maladies. I suffered from a chronic failure to take full responsibility for my vision, within a professional and social context more or less inimical to that kind of grandeur to which I had dedicated myself.

I was at a loss, held under the spell of those men in my life from whom I sought approval. I could neither appease them nor resist them. Nor could I read their motives. It was one thing to measure Siegfried and Rothbart on the stage, to tell the noble from the base, to unmask good and evil, and dance free from deception; it was quite another thing to gauge character in the real world. If I were unable to discern the identities and intentions of those around me, how would I ever reckon with the swans of my own personality?

At twenty-five years old, I was one of the walking wounded, ready to attach myself to the first gentle heart to beckon. His name was Richard Schafer, a soloist with the company, tall and ruggedly handsome, confident about his masculinity. We had known each other since the early days at the School of American Ballet. Our friendship took a turn toward romance on an ABT European tour over the summer of 1977. I may not have solved any of my cumulative problems in the course of the relationship, but I realized that sex was not really one of them. Nor was it an ultimate solution.

Richard provided both aid and comfort. For once, I did not have to feel like an enemy between the sheets, like a prisoner of war. The sense of shame lifted from my body. I was no longer quite so servile. I remember listening one night to the sound of bedsprings, creaking with each sudden shift of body weight, the mattress sagging and swaying beneath us. We were in a hotel room somewhere in Vienna, the first stop on the tour, perhaps the first night that we spent together. After the groaning of metal and flesh had subsided, after the silence had enveloped us, I heard bells chime in the distance. I thought of a church. I thought such naked happenings had to be holy. Why else would bells have tolled at such an hour?

I wondered how it was that I was able to watch myself perform right up until those moments when my mind seemed to slip into the shadows. I wondered what it was like for a man to be with me and where this new coupling would lead me.

We toured for eight weeks, traveling on from Austria to Greece, Romania, Italy, Germany, Denmark, England, and France. Companionship almost made life on the road bearable. Richard's practicality and common sense gave me a base of stability. His humor broke the tension and relieved the tedium. The pain of the daily routine was balanced by the pleasure of our nights. Between the physical extremes, I maintained a precarious equilibrium. Romance had to fit into a strictly regimented schedule. The hope that this love might somehow withstand the vocational hazards of dance seemed remote, but that did not diminish the intensity of my longing. I was still a dreamer.

There was a threat to the relationship from the beginning: I still had not come to terms with Misha. Our combat continued on the stage, as did our success. His image frequently intruded into my thoughts. Until I separated my artistic purpose from his, I would be haunted by the failed intimacy, the unfulfilled dreams. I knew that I was using Richard to prove that I was free from the past, which meant that I was not free at all. His support provided the competitive edge that I needed to match Misha. I hated the competition.

In retrospect, I suppose Misha must have thought at times that I was trying to undermine him. That was never the case, at least not consciously. Yet it is true to say that my art undermined his, and vice versa, precisely to the extent that our visions were irreconcilable. It was only a matter of time before our clash became more personal and more violent.

My repertory on the tour included *The Leaves Are Fading* and *Giselle*, as well as various showpieces. The highpoint was Athens, where the Tudor ballet became a living monument in the Herodes Atticus Theatre, where the moments of the dance seemed to be immortalized along with ancient ruins and azure skies, an apotheosis of eternal love and wisdom. The lowpoint was Paris, where the spirit of Giselle was dampened in the courtyard of the Louvre, where dancers and spectators were drenched outdoors, if not drowned, by torrential rainstorms, an overcast of gray clouds providing an incessant drizzle for the entire three weeks spent in the French capital. I saw no silver linings. The weather seemed appropriate to the emotional tempest with which I had to contend.

In spite of the threatening Parisian sky, Misha and I met one afternoon to rehearse for an evening performance of *Giselle*. The problem was maintaining the fluidity of the lifts in the second-act pas de deux. These were the same lifts that had caused trouble in the past. To put it as gently as possible, Misha's partnering was careless. He seemed to be more consistently interested in his solo work. Who could blame him? Certainly not Giselle. It had to be Gelsey's problem. How could any male dancer put up with a ballerina who called for his undivided attention when he lifted her into the air? What ballerina would dare complain about a moment when the man had complete control, when she was utterly vulnerable? What woman would risk a flare of temper or breach of trust that might land her on the moon?

I tried to be polite. We had reached the point where even the most innocent question could be interpreted as a personal attack. A number of fellow dancers were watching us work. I knew that I was taking a chance by stopping in the middle of the adagio. I had tried to say the same thing so many different ways. Sometimes Misha tried to improve his partnering, sometimes he made no effort at all. There was no predicting his reaction. On that occasion, he gave me no chance.

"Vhut you vant now, Gelsey! Ve never did before that vay! Vhy all of sudden you change! Tonight is performance . . . and you vant change! I don't understand!"

Biting the inside of my lip to keep calm, I could taste the blood in my mouth. "Misha, we have done it this way before—at least when we did it right! Remember how we used to come down later? Listen, I know that it's tiring, I know I'm a pain, but just let me show you with music . . ."

Misha insisted that he was doing the best he could do. I insisted that he could do better, and that he knew he could do better. Things got nasty.

"Gelsey, you know, you respect no one!" He was stalking away from me, always a sign of his disdain. "You don't respect your partners! You don't respect your teachers! David! Stanley! Your mother! You don't respect your mother! You don't even respect Richard!"

He might have included me on the list. He must have. I yelled back, not about to let him get away. "That is not true! None of that is true, you bastard! How the hell can you say that when you don't know what respect is! How dare you!" I was shrieking by this time. "Why don't you ask them! I love them—do you know what that word means? Go ahead and ask them!"

He was not done. I had given him the perfect opening. "You treat them like shit!"

I felt like I had been dropped from a great height, like I had crashed to the floor of the stage. I screamed bloody murder and went at him.

Richard rushed between us before we could come to blows. Without taking sides or allowing himself to become any further involved in the dispute, Richard pulled me away. He prevented me from flying at Misha and inflicting the physical damage I had in mind. Had I hit the target I had chosen, we would have been equal adversaries.

As I recall, the performance that night was rained out. I was not open to consolation. I am sure I made Richard feel quite miserable. How could he understand what I failed to understand myself?

Before leaving Paris, I performed another *Giselle* with Ivan. The raked stage was slick from rain. When I made an entrance in the second act, my toe shoes had no traction whatsoever. My feet came out from under me, and I slid on the back of my tutu, skidding most of the way across the stage. Coming to a gradual halt, I found myself looking up into the astonished face of Martine van Hamel, the Queen of the Wilis. Someone with knowledge of baseball and an American sense of humor yelled, "Safe!"

The tour soon drew to a close, but the blowup with Misha continued to torment me. As former lovers, we both possessed knowledge about each other that neither of us ever really wanted. My loss of control revealed another aspect of my vulnerability, a nerve that he could touch whenever he chose to do so. Each time I exposed myself to him, I gave him the means to turn the situation to his advantage. As long as I cared about him and assumed good faith on his part, he effectively controlled my temper. He knew how to fluster me, how to incite me, how to make me into the shrew, the nag, the villainess. The various lifts in our repertory became more than so many points of mutual contention. They marked the dividing line of power within our partnership.

Who knew when he was lifting me properly, when he was investing his soul into the image we created on the stage? Who was qualified to judge the finer points of his partnering? Who could accuse him of lacking respect either for his partner or for the dance? Who would know when he deliberately hesitated, when he dropped me too soon, when he tilted me ever so slightly, just enough to distort the line, just enough to jar me? In his heart of hearts, only he would ever know for sure.

Back in New York City, later in the year, we rehearsed *Other Dances* one afternoon for a surprise audience provided by Misha. Meeting me outside the ABT rehearsal studio, he greeted me warmly and asked, "Oh, Geels, do you mind if a friend vatches?"

How could I mind? His friend was Liza Minnelli, who sat in a chair at the front of the studio. Her presence was somewhat intimidating. I was on my best behavior. After a brief introduction, Misha and I began to work on the ballet. The pas de deux began very quietly. We walked forward in silence, hand in hand, stopping for a moment and letting go of each other. Then the piano began to accompany us. We moved through the delicate phrases, sensitive to each breath, each physical stress, as if the male and female of the species could mirror each other through the dance.

The technical challenge with this piece was to make each phrase flow from the preceding phrase without any disruption, matching the tonal quality of the music. It was smooth sailing until we came together for a lift. The painstaking refinement of the passage had already been accomplished in a few previous rehearsals. I was expecting to be swept gently into the air. Much to my surprise, Misha heaved me up and set me down with all the subtlety of a garment worker unloading a truck—I was just another hanger on the rack.

The entire shape of the lift disappeared as Misha dumped his load. My position was precarious. What he had done would not be noticeable to an eye not educated to the level of refinement required. We stood only a few feet in front of Liza. In my mind, it was the kind of jolt that had to be corrected, audience or no audience. I stopped on a dime. I looked at my partner for an explanation. He offered none.

"Misha"—adding a little chuckle to keep it light—"that lift, you know . . . Come on, Mish . . . you know . . ."

"Vhut? Some-sing wrong? Geels, vhut you vant? Explain me, please!"

"You remember. It's not up and down. You know, it's more of an arc. More gentle . . . quiet . . . like the music. I think, maybe, you put me down, well, just a bit too early." He knew exactly what I meant.

"Any-sing you vant, Geels. I try."

We took it from the top. I knew that something was not quite right, but I kept hoping. When we came to the lift, he did it his way, with a wonderful touch of pantomimic exaggeration. He created the illusion of weight, like he was hoisting a ton of raw meat onto a butcher's shelf. He looked like he was making a superhuman and noble effort to please me. I stopped again. Both my voice and my temperature were rising.

"Misha, come on, the lift should be more gradual, even though it's short." I tried to show him with sign language. "It's a curve, not up and down! You know . . . not landing so fast. Could we try it again?"

"Sure, Geels. Vhutever you vant."

The pianist followed my cue. We tried just the lift. It was exactly the same. He was not about to show his special audience that he knew what I meant. I was losing my composure rapidly.

"Why are you doing this, Misha? You know how it used to be! You never just lifted me up and down like this! You know what I mean! It's not even close . . ."

"But, Geels, I try best I can. Really. Please try, maybe again, explain me. Show me. Vhut is it you say? Really, I don't understand."

"Misha, I've told you what I want, but it's getting worse . . . as if you're doing it wrong on purpose!"

With a look of shocked innocence, he protested, "No, is not true! Geels, vhy you say such a thing? I try best I can, but this business you talk-king—I don't know vhut is it. You must try again explain me."

I was ready to beat him up. Then he added, putting his fingers to his lips, "And, please, Geeelsey . . . voice. Keep voice down. Easy. Explain me in nice voice. Please. Soft."

I started to follow his instructions, but I knew the game he was playing and felt my control slip away. "Misha, you're trying to get me mad! It's not up and down! Is that so difficult to understand? Why are you making it so . . . I just don't see why . . . I mean, I've already told you . . ."

He put his fingers to his lips again. "Shhhhhhhush . . ."

I felt like the girl in *The Exorcist,* my head taking a full spin, rotating through a full three hundred and sixty degrees. I ran out of the room, a terror, afraid that I might vomit green slime. My face was blood red. I was livid, slamming my way into the bathroom. I paced around trying to stop the tears, repeating to myself, "Damn him . . . damn him . . . damn him . . ." Then I looked in the mirror, commanding the image I saw, "Stop it . . . stop it . . . stop it." I had to pull myself together before they sent out a search party to find me.

I banged my head against the concrete wall three times, saying aloud after each thud, "Stop!" Then I splashed cold water in my face and wiped my eyes. When I returned to the studio, I found Misha and Liza conversing quietly. Undoubtedly Misha apologized behind my back for my behavior. Somehow we ran through the rest of the rehearsal. I doubt that I made any more complaints. My humiliation was complete. I had three lumps on my head to remind me of the incident for at least that many days afterward.

I did not change my tactics with Misha. I intensified my demands over the next year. I was not turning the screws simply for myself, but for the sake of the partnership, which seemed the one consistent expression of virtuosity in my life. If I had to pester, cajole, threaten, and shame him into making an effort, that was my obligation. My first concern was the artistry that passed between us. In my zeal for perfection, I was repeatedly seduced and stymied by his incomparable flair for showmanship.

In spite of all our differences, in spite of the agony and the rivalry, Misha did complete the unique picture we made on the stage. He was both the irresistible force and the immovable object. It was as if the purpose of my dance was simply to engage him passionately and technically and, in doing so, to draw more out of him than he was willing to give. There was an essential drama in that engagement, a romantic paradox, which, at its best, went beyond the choreographic limits of our repertory. I still loved the dancer, so much that I continued to believe that if I scratched away at the surface long enough, I would find the artist, the man, the human being.

There was a cost in working at cross-purposes, one that I never really took into account: a constant attrition of spirit. Even with the reward of perceptible improvements, the fights were demoralizing. The only way that I could make sense of struggling with such a man was to assume that he really did know what he was doing. I was still telling myself that, behind the mask of indifference, he had to appreciate my unswerving commitment to the art. He knew that I made the same kind of demands on all my partners over the years. My meticulous attention to detail pushed them to deliver and sparked at least a few moments of real splendor. The subtlety that I built into performance could not be produced by the last-minute rush of adrenaline that came from simply stepping onto the stage. The hours of studio time were my antidote for mediocrity.

New York City was the only place where I was able to maintain a support system of teachers and coaches. The routine of daily practice and preparation kept me shuttling in taxis all day. In addition to classes and rehearsals at various studios in the city, I regularly visited health clubs for swimming, whirlpool treatments, and sauna, and more specialized facilities for massage and physical therapy. The expenses added up, so that I was always broke. Whatever discretionary dollars remained in my personal budget went into practice clothes, wigs, cosmetics, and a myriad of related items, including costumes whenever the need arose. I never pushed for salary demands above what was necessary to cover the day-to-day cost of living in pursuit of my career.

Richard and various friends encouraged me to take more interest in my financial affairs. "Gelsey, what do you do with your money? How much do you make? Where does it go? Why should you be making a fraction of what Misha makes? Don't you know that he gets thousands of dollars just for one performance? Don't you realize that you're a star?" I ignored such questions. When I attempted to establish my independence, assuming responsibility for my accounting, I found the easiest way to deal with all the problems was to erase the credit column, to live in debt. I usually knew what I was spending, but rarely what I was earning. From 1977 to 1978, I averaged between six and seven hundred dollars per performance, according to a complicated contractual arrangement covering the thirty-six weeks of the year during which I rehearsed and performed with the company. The fine print of the contract contained a marvelous clause:

> It is expressly understood that in the event of war, riot, rebellion, blackout, fire, floods, strikes, force majeure, or other similar or different causes beyond the control of the respective parties hereto, neither party shall be held liable for the delay or suspension of performances and employment occasioned thereby.

Was the theatre unaware that I was at war? Was management oblivious to the riot inside of me? My cause was in so many ways beyond the control of any interested party, including those who loved me.

Although Richard and I never actually lived together, I often spent the night with him at his apartment, two floors in an old brownstone building on the Upper West Side. He shared the place with his father and an occasional boarder from the company. When we wanted more privacy, Richard and I stayed at my apartment in the Apthorp. He called me Kirkland. I called him Schafer. I liked being on a last-name basis.

I liked the fact that he told me he no longer needed marijuana to fall asleep at night. That was somehow significant. I surprised him once at the dining room table, finding him with a joint and a small amount of cocaine. Curious, I asked him what he was doing. Disturbed by my intrusion, he allowed me only a puff of the grass and barely a taste of cocaine—not enough to really have any effect as far as I could tell. I appreciated his concern. Richard wanted to protect me, to shelter me from any influence he thought might be unhealthy.

Most of my friends and my activities were localized in the neighborhood of Lincoln Center, within twenty-five-blocks of the theatre. I tried to avoid being alone. I still had anorexic tendencies and experienced occasional bouts of bulimia. Between the romantic routine and the work schedule, I was able to suppress, at least temporarily, those self-destructive impulses that jeopardized my life and career.

With the passage of time, the conflicts with Misha did seem to clarify somewhat, even if the bitterness did not diminish. There was less ambiguity about our personal lives. His romantic involvement with Jessica Lange became rather well known, in light of which Richard's emotional support did wonders for my self-esteem and provided a cushion of security.

Misha's relationship with an actress did not seem to make him any more receptive to the sense of drama that I tried to bring into the dance. He did not mellow with love, even with a woman whom he reportedly worshiped. I had little doubt that he was a prince who would probably always be given to dalliance, that he was no more constant than the moon. Neither his attitude toward me nor his approach to the dance changed. I have no recollection of conscious jealousy with regard to Jessica. I must have thought too much of her and too little of myself.

The affection and the animosity that I felt for Misha, the love and the hate, were too deep, too long-standing, and too thoroughly entrenched in the dance to be explained by a concept as simple as jealousy, or as obvious as the wrath of a spurned woman. Was I the green-eyed monster, or was I jealously guarding the province of my art? Was a man who was incapable of amorous fidelity somehow blessed with a noble and unwavering faith in the artistic sphere? Was a man who dissembled as a matter of course, even with those closest to him, to be trusted on the stage? To be once in doubt was to be forever resolved: I would never let him get away with less than his best effort.

Rather than disentangling from each other, the psychological twists and turns of the dance kept us knotting into each other. Most of the knots were mine. Misha merely cinched them.

In September 1977, I made my debut in his stage production of *The Nutcracker,* performing at the Metropolitan Opera, followed in October by the televised production for CBS, filmed in Canada. Not only was he my partner, he had assumed the role of choreographer as well. The pressure on him must have been intense. It was obvious that he was not entirely comfortable with the additional responsibility. His difficulty with verbal communication and his impatience turned him into a caricature of himself. To withstand his assault on my psyche, and to avoid threatening him in his position of power, I turned secretly to my own director.

My friendship with mime artist Pilar Garcia flourished through the years in spite of the fact that she never won either recognition or acceptance with ABT. Working in the shadows on my behalf, she was an unsung heroine as far as I was concerned. Misha apparently saw her as someone who might subvert his authority by the influence she had on me. His mocking imitations of my work made it painfully clear that he thought my collaboration with her was an unnecessary and ridiculous waste of time. Ironically, Pilar and I did bend over backward to fulfill his vision in *The Nutcracker,* trying to follow through dramatically on his intentions as much as we could discern them. Only years later did I learn the full extent to which we had superimposed our own interpretation onto his design.

Misha's concept of the ballet was not altogether clear but was laden with wondrous possibilities. Drawing from various versions handed down since the time of Petipa and Ivanov, Misha effected a transformation. The familiar childhood dream of Christmas became a kind of adolescent fantasy, marking the heroine's first taste of adulthood, almost a coming-of-age. The focus of the action was Clara's encounter with the Nutcracker Prince, orchestrated by her magician godfather, Drosselmeyer. I had danced in Balanchine's version of the ballet enough times to appreciate Misha's attempt to explore a different theme, that of maturation. Where Balanchine had invited the audience into a child's dream, surrendering to candycane and sugarplum nostalgia, Misha asked the audience to consider what happened to the child after the dream came to an end. What was going on in that little girl's brain? I had a different answer than my partner intended.

Misha invented some brilliant steps, dazzling in their simplicity, especially those that he choreographed for himself, such as the fight scene in the first act—when Misha's Nutcracker Prince fought to save Clara from the Mouse King. The task was to flesh out the story—to make Misha's choreography articulate that story, to bring the drama ever closer to the spirit of the Tchaikovsky score. I first had to figure out what story Misha wanted to tell. The focus was obscure. The steps by themselves did not add up to a cohesive drama. Writing for *Dance Magazine,* critic Tobi Tobias commented on my portrayal of Clara:

> Kirkland's realization of the role—in which she appears less to dance and act than to live—does wonders, too, for Baryshnikov's production, focusing ideas and feeling that are implicit, yet only half-effected in his choreography, and explicit in the score.

To realize that role, I had to have Pilar disguise herself and sneak into the rehearsals. Later, with the blueprint of Misha's staging in mind, she and I retired to a private studio, sometimes stealing into the Met in the middle of the night. We invented the narrative details, down to the names of the minor characters, specifically relating each personage in the ballet to my character. We took each moment apart and put it back together with the steps, defining the entire plot line with spoken word and gesture. Then I went back into rehearsal alone and approached Misha, as gently as possible, with some of those ideas that Pilar and I had worked out together. I always asked for his permission to make changes. After all, it was his ballet.

Whenever other dancers in the cast were open to my way of working, I pursued and clarified ideas with them. Alexander (Sasha) Minz, who played the part of Drosselmeyer, was usually agog with enthusiasm about my insights into the relationship that might be established between our characters. By emphasizing the innocence of Clara's affection for her godfather (conceiving of him as a favorite uncle), we effectively downplayed whatever sexual or Freudian connotations Misha may have had in mind. Sasha, who had danced with the Kirov back in the "good old days," proved to me that there was nothing inherent in the Russian cultural type which was closed to new ideas, to a fair exchange. He requited my overtures with humor and warmth.

After a number of performances, I gave an interview to critic Tobi Tobias for *Dance Magazine*. I credited my success to a book entitled *Beyond Technique*, by the Danish dancer Erik Bruhn, and to my previous work with choreographer Antony Tudor; but I omitted any reference to Pilar. I was terrified that mentioning her name would antagonize Misha and the ABT management.

The critic offered a precise formulation of the theme that I tried to develop in *The Nutcracker:* ". . . the ecstatic vision of perfection, surrounded by dark threat . . ." That might have been the story of my life. Only in retrospect is the irony apparent: Misha, the Nutcracker Prince, the dancer, was an ecstatic vision of perfection; Misha, the personality, the choreographer, was a dark threat. My idealism grated harshly against his cynicism. As stated in *Baryshnikov: From Russia to the West,* a book written by one of his friends, Gennady Smakov, Misha's intention at the end of the ballet, when Drosselmeyer banishes the heroic Prince, was to say to Clara: "That's it, my dear, get used to the fact that in life there is no place for dreams."

The light of my character created shades of meaning at odds with that sort of cold, cruel fatalism. My Clara was still looking for the Prince in the last scene, even when the curtain came down. She may have lost him, but she would never lose her dreams, her ideals, most especially her ideal of love. She would grow into a woman of imagination. She would be wise enough to defend her place in the world. No man would ever strip away her love of virtue and perfection. I gave her the benefit of the lesson that I had learned in working on the ballet:

I let Clara's world become alive for me—her reality and her terrific fantasy. In a way it felt like a childhood I was able to go through, that I never had. I think it taught me to trust my imagination.

In Canada, filming the ballet over the course of a week, the friction with my partner, who styled himself as a television director, created enough sparks to burn down the set. When Misha suggested that I carry all of Clara's Christmas gifts during the first act—when she says good-bye to the party guests—I was desperate to change his mind. Did he want to turn her into a greedy little brat? Didn't he know that one gift had already captured her imagination? Didn't he see that the Nutcracker was the key image of the whole story?

I had some difficulty getting anyone to take me seriously, given my wig and costume, which did make me appear to be all of twelve years old. I tried to stay in character, even as I made the demands of an actress, saying that I felt Clara should hold only the Nutcracker. I must have looked like a little princess, peevish and pouting, making a royal stink about carrying the other presents. Fearing perhaps that this Clara might throw a real tantrum, Misha relented, with a comment that caught his attitude, "Vhut you think, you are Sarah Bernhardt?"

I did not adjust well to shooting scenes out of order. I was kept in the dark about camera angles. Who knows how many takes were required to cover the lifts in the first act? If I were to float across the stage—or the screen—that quality had to be composed with exquisite grace. It was a matter of pride. From Misha's point of view, I must have been making trouble again.

The frustrations were maddening. The stage was too small. The tape of the music was too slow. There were recurrent crises with costume, hair, and makeup. I filled my eyes with special French drops, causing each blue iris to sparkle and the whites to match the falling snow—washing out the tears and the redness. I flew in Pilar and found lodging for her. I did the same with my hair designer/stylist, Patrik Moreton—my wig, abused on the set, had turned into an electrified mop, full of static and starch. Patrik, who was a faithful friend indeed, came to the rescue, managing to salvage the piece that he had designed.

I lost money on the production. By the time I returned to New York City, I had spent almost all of the six-thousand-dollar fee that I had been paid to dance. Residual payments diminished. There was a more enduring form of compensation: the residual satisfaction of having made a Christmas gift for all those fans whose mail I never had the time or heart to answer.

If I were tilting at theatrical windmills, what better ballet could I find to pursue my quest than *Don Quixote?* Rehearsals for the full-length version ran through the winter of 1977, and the production opened on March 23, 1978, at the Kennedy Center in Washington, D.C. Misha was again billed as the choreographer. With *The Nutcracker,* I had missed the opening and some of his initial directorial machinations, passed on through a ballet master, but in *Don Quixote,* I got the full treatment. He was assisted graciously by Elena Tchernichova, a former dancer at the Kirov, too devoted and too dear to even think of altering his course. She contributed a great deal of what she recalled from her Russian past.

When I first heard that I had been cast in the production, I tried to pull out. I did not think that I was suited for the role of Kitri. I lacked the bulk and the muscular power. The pas de deux that I had done was nothing compared to the three-act ballet. I found Misha in the ABT rehearsal studios one afternoon and asked him to find someone else for the part. Lounging in a director's chair in the middle of the studio, he sat me on his lap and patted my cheek. I was his doll again. It felt like his fingers were searching the zone between my shoulder blades for a key—to wind me up.

"Misha, I'm afraid I'll let you down. I mean, I'm just not right for this role."

"Oh, Geels, no! You be very good in this ballet. Everything will be okay. You'll see. Believe me."

With his benediction and slap on my backside, I toddled off, apparently back in his good graces. I knew that he knew that Kitri was out of my range, that a particular type of Russian ballerina had filled the role historically, epitomized by Maya Plisetskaya, who possessed an extraordinary flamboyance and a spectacular arsenal of technical fireworks. Americans were simply not taught the kind of style and bravura required for the part. As such, Misha could be assured that his Basil would dwarf me, that I would make an adorable soubrette, bending to his will, ready to be clipped by his barber.

With my cheeks burning, I made up my mind before leaving the studio to be more than very good. I would make myself into a Kitri that he would never forget. She had to be worthy of Basil. She had to be his equal. She had to be able to win his heart and dance him off the stage.

I had to be out of my mind. The role of Basil was part of the Russian tradition built into Misha's body. He had performed the ballet at the Kirov and intended to speed up the production for American audiences. It would be a showpiece for him, and a downfall for me. I did not have the gymnastic ability to meet the dramatic challenge.

I called Pilar immediately. We set to work on the story. I watched the films of Maya Plisetskaya and turned to my teachers. Maya had a special leap that seemed to capture for all time the joyous elevation of Kitri's spirit. This was an awesome jump, a kick-jeté in which she soared so high and arched back so far that her head actually touched her back leg, like a beautiful curved explosion in the air. I would master that leap. The rest of Maya's unique portrayal, her overall interpretation of the role, was useless to me. That was Maya's personality blazing through the dance, wild as a flame. I would have to find my own Spanish fire and transfuse it into my blood.

I went to a dancer by the name of Maria Alba and applied myself to the Spanish folk tradition, taking a crash course in that style of dance related to the ballet, including the technique of the fan. I learned that the flourish of the ruffled skirt for the Spanish dancer was more than a simple act of flirtation. It was as provocative and as calculated as the unfurling cape of the bullfighter. These were touches that had to be absorbed into the classical form. They had to be reconciled with both Misha's choreography and my conception of character.

How would Kitri, a woman trapped in domestic drudgery, a woman with dirt under her fingernails, a woman with a streak of mischief as deep as her pride—how would such a woman hold her skirt? How would she unfold her fan? How would she walk? How would she have her way with Basil? As Maria told me, "A Spanish woman is always in control with a man."

As I watched Misha during rehearsals, struggling to convey his wishes to the cast, I wondered why he and the theatre were so dead set against providing the dancers with the educational resources that I had at my command. So much time could have been saved with a mimetic breakdown of the drama, and so many problems could have been avoided with instruction in the specialized style of the ballet. The corps of matadors could have looked like matadors instead of traffic cops. Why were Pilar and Maria not available to everyone? Why did the three of us have to hide most of our activities? Why did I have to sneak them into rehearsals? Our sneaking around in the middle of the night to find studio space at Lincoln Center eventually came to the attention of George Balanchine, who had a note placed at the door of his New York State Theater, instructing the guard to bar me from the studios. Of all people, Mr. B was not going to stop me.

As early as the fall of 1977, Misha told me in passing that he wanted a "mock death" that would serve as the climax of the second act, the so-called Tavern Scene. I had no idea why he had decided to confide his plan to me. Did he want help? As rehearsals continued, frequently interrupted by tours and performances, I waited to see how Misha would put his plan into action. At the beginning of 1978, with only a rough outline of his scene, I invited some of the other members of the cast to attend a series of secret rehearsals, with Pilar. Misha was out of town at the time.

I assured the other dancers that I would take full responsibility. I would run the risk of offending Misha. The choreography and direction were his territory. I was forced to invade because nobody had any notion what to do in the scene besides stand around. The action was undefined. The mock death of Basil was a great comic device, but Misha had not been able to follow through with the logic of the situation. If he possessed the imagination, he seemed to fall short in terms of initiative and patience. Nobody had the nerve to tell him. Nobody questioned his judgment. Who cared whether or not this emperor wore any clothes? He was born to be a centerfold.

His Basil faked a mortal wound with a barber's razor, but how was that action to be supported by the rest of the characters? How would the story be resolved? Was Kitri privy to the ruse? Was her father, the innkeeper, going to permit her to marry Basil simply because the barber was about to die, or because Kitri begged the old man for mercy? What about the others on the stage? What about Gamache, Kitri's spurned suitor? What about Don Quixote? What about Sancho Panza? What actions were they to play?

Rehearsed by Pilar, who effectively set the mime, the members of the cast were able to discover the answers to such questions. With Sasha Minz as Don Quixote, Frank Smith as the Innkeeper, and Victor Barbee as Gamache, the scene came together. The moment of reckoning arrived when Misha joined the company on tour. We had to show and tell.

Misha and I had already clashed. When his Basil slobbered kisses on my Kitri in an early rehearsal of the first act, smothering me, coming across more like a Russian schoolboy than a Spanish barber, he made it clear that he would take no corrections from me. I tried to be nice and explained that Kitri would scoff at such behavior. Later, in the third-act pas de deux, he mocked my stylized Spanish arm positions. "Must do classical positions!" I knew all about the positions that he favored.

Rigmor Mydtskov

Beyond Technique. With Erik Bruhn.

Gala, 1980. Lucia Chase points to the front row, from left to right, Agnes de Mille, Marcia Haydée, Gelsey Kirkland, Igor Youskevitch, Alicia Alonso, and Anton Dolin. Anthony Dowell stands behind Alicia Alonso.

With choreographer Antony Tudor, *The Leaves Are Fading.*

Nina Alovert

Roy Round

With Georgina Parkinson.

As Clara, *The Nutcracker,* 1977. With Alexander Minz as Herr Drosselmeyer.

The lift. With Misha, *Le Corsaire,* Vienna, 1976.

Dina Makarova

Don Quixote Pas de Deux, 1975.

Martha Swope

As Kitri. *Don Quixote,* 1978.

William Reilly

With Misha, *Don Quixote,* 1981.

Val Mazzenga

With Patrick Bissell, Chicago, 1981.

Lanna Swindler

Under the influence.

Judy Eng

As Juliet.

Judy Eng

With Anthony Dowell, *Romeo and Juliet*, London, 1980.

I knew what to expect when I hit him with our mock death scene. Misha was sitting with some production people in the studio. He called for a run-through with music and I piped up, shaking in my toe shoes, "Misha, um, well, I've worked some things out in this scene, and I've asked Victor, Frank, and Sasha to do a few things . . . so, so it makes more sense. I promise, it was all my idea. I mean, they're just doing what I asked. Really!"

He looked at me like I was speaking Chinese. I gave him no chance to cut me off. "Let's just go through it like you said, and I'll show you what I'm doing, what we're doing—I'll explain as we go, okay? And then you tell us what you think about it, okay?"

"Vell, let's see . . . but quick, Geelsey. Please, ve have only little time."

We took our places. The pianist accompanied us with the Minkus score, plunking along with my exhibition. I ran around the studio like a madwoman, miming the action, verbalizing the logic:

"Okay, Misha! I run to you—'What have you done to yourself?' I cross myself—'Almighty God!' I fall to my knees in grief—'Oh, my poor, sweet Basil!' Then my eyes catch sight of the razor—'Blood!' I must get rid of the horrible weapon. I throw it away. I continue to grieve over your body. Wait! I think I hear your heartbeat. Yes! You're still alive—'Quick! Water! Someone help me! Water!'

"The jug of water arrives, and I take the first slug myself. Then I lift your head to help you drink, and surprise! You pop up and kiss me. I sit up in shock. I try the same thing again, and you kiss me again—'Aha, you rascal!' I squeeze your hand to let you know that I know what you're up to. I drop the jug and take both your hands in mine—'Don't worry, my darling, I'll take it from here!'

"So, Misha, that's all pretty much like you wanted. I'll just need to have someone fetch the water.

"Now, as Sancho trips over you, I see Gamache standing over us. I rise and block his way—'Not another step!' I scold Gamache. I accuse him of causing you to commit this dreadful act, knowing that my father can hear every word. I run to Don Quixote. I beg him to help—'Please! Look at what Gamache has done!' Then I walk back toward you. I turn to Gamache—'Be gone!' I kneel over you. I whisper to you. I fill you in on how things are going. Then I see my big chance. I run back to Don Quixote—'Oh, dear man! Please! Look at this poor soul dying! We just want to be married! Please, help! Before he dies!'

"Don Quixote gets my point. I run back and kneel by you. I plead with my father. I cup one of my tears in the palm of my hand and hold it up to him—'Papa, please! Have mercy on his soul!' Papa sees my tear. He turns for a second, torn between Don Quixote and Gamache. Then Papa turns back to me and gives us his blessing, and boom! You jump up! We did it!"

I looked at Misha. His face was a rigid mask, just the hint of scowl playing across his lips. Before he could so much as breathe a word, I said, "Misha, let us show you one more time . . . so quick, you won't believe it! Okay? It really does make sense. Ready, guys? Music!"

We were off to the races again. Misha threw in a line, something like, "Please, Gelsey, less talk-king. Just do. Please."

When we finished the second demonstration, Misha walked to the center of the studio. "You know, Geelsey, I think will be funny if I put foot up. You see it and push down. Let's try." We did. It was funny. A real comic touch. He never said another word about the work. There was never an expression of gratitude or a compliment to anyone.

Weeks later, the scene was recorded in dance notation, preserved for posterity. It was now Misha's property. I asked Pilar if she minded not getting credit for the hours she put into the mime. "I'm not worried about it, Gelsey. Without the underlying motivation and logic, it will never look the same again, anyway." I went to my dictionary and looked up the word "humble."

In scene after scene, Misha and I did not see eye to eye. I could have strangled him when he insisted that I make an exit for a costume change without supplying any narrative motivation for my leaving the stage. Pilar and I made up our own scenario, sending me off to find first aid for an injured Don Quixote. The most important detail, overlooked by my soaring partner, was the title role, a minor character in the ballet, but an absolute symbol of classical virtue ever since Cervantes wrote the book. Misha could ignore the white knight, but I would turn Don Quixote into an ally for Kitri, a tenuous link between earthbound realism and starry-eyed idealism. The choreographer would never even notice. His story never had a focus. It was as if Don Quixote had been reduced to a circus freak, an excuse for the festivities.

During our first stage rehearsal on tour, I unveiled the explosive leap that I had taken from Maya. I cleared a space and worked through my first-act solo, incorporating the kick into Kitri's steps. I was awkward at first, but my intention was obvious. Misha's voice found my ear, "Gelsey, vhere did you get that?" He knew exactly where I had gotten it. His disparaging tone gave me the impression that I had just invaded Russia, that I was crossing the border into his homeland. I decided on a sneak attack. By the time we opened, he would not know what kicked him.

I decided to perfect one of the steps for which Misha was famous. This was a hitch-kick that he displayed in various ballets, vaulting into the air like a pair of human scissors. Kitri had nine of them in the first act. On one afternoon, Misha saw me in the studio, my knees bleeding from my repeated attempts to stay aloft. I was working with my teacher, David. Misha offered him a wry comment, "She steal my step!"

I may not have stolen the show, but I did more than hold my own. It was like a *Rocky* fantasy. Each act was another round. I attempted to be less effusive during the flower ritual of the curtain calls. I conspired with Pilar to commemorate the opening night by presenting Misha with a fan, passed along privately, which eventually found its way onto the wall of Misha's New York City apartment. When I saw the gift mounted there years later, a torrent of mixed emotions rushed through me. I still had no perspective on the events that bound me to him, the fantasy and the reality.

There was a triumph to be shared. Clive Barnes observed in the New York *Post,* March 27, 1978:

> Gelsey Kirkland as Kitri demonstrated that she is one of the five or six great ballerinas in the world. She is a young Plisetskaya, a young Fonteyn, a maturing Kirkland. She pounced on the dances with exultant smiles and total, taut and wary elegance. She is gorgeous—a new queen in the first reality of her realm.
>
> Baryshnikov was, of course, himself fantastic. We have never seen a dancer quite like him. His is a unique flame . . . His genius as a dancer is emblematic and his sense of drama is unequaled. Everyone is going to tell you in the history books how high Misha jumped—and he did jump high. But the important thing is how graciously he acted.

The ballet caused a media sensation across the country. Writing for *Time* magazine, April 3, 1978, Martha Duffy credited me with a "bravura triumph" and lauded Misha's accomplishments with both the ballet and the role:

> He has a hilarious, hollow-eyed mad scene in which he stabs himself—a sort of male Giselle. No choreographer-dancer is more generous to his colleagues than Baryshnikov in *Don Q* but his acting makes it Basil's story . . . Playing it, he says, taught him a great deal: "Technical control, mime, how to use a cape, how to give a flower to a girl, how to be funny, touching, a lover . . . a lot." He is giving those gifts now to the ABT dancers . . .

Those words made me laugh and cry. I wondered what Misha's response might be if I were to ask him to show me how to present a flower to a man, how to use a cape, how to be funny. I tried to believe that he was generous, that he was gracious—that the words written about him were true. I tried to make the image of him true in my mind. He had taught me more than he would ever know. He had to be everything they said he was.

I was not amused when I appeared on the cover of *Time* magazine, May 1, 1978. I was disappointed by the picture. Misha told me that I should feel honored. I was supposed to be proud—Kitri, flying through the air with the greatest of ease, clutching her fan, hanging from the masthead. Even my sister Johnna had something to say about it. She offered the cryptic observation that if the corpse of Aldo Moro had been discovered any earlier, I would have been buried inside the magazine. (The Italian political figure had recently been kidnapped and was the subject of a news story in the same issue.)

I had reason for seeing the *Time* magazine spread as a bitter irony: Misha was leaving. He called me one evening to break the news that he would be joining the New York City Ballet at the end of the season. He had decided to go with Balanchine. He simply could not live any longer with the artistic management at ABT. That was all. His last words, just before he hung up, buzzed in my ear like a winged insect: "Maybe someday I come back, Gelsey."

Our last performance with ABT that season was Balanchine's *Theme and Variations*. The situation was almost unfathomable. The ballet was to have been Misha's swan song with me, the culmination of the partnership, the sad and ultimate anticlimax.

There was an overriding tension. Fernando Bujones had inserted a series of double turns into his variation in the pas de deux from *Don Quixote*—the same series of tours and pirouettes that appeared in Misha's second solo from *Theme and Variations*. Both ballets were scheduled for the same night. There was a provocation implicit in Fernando's choice, almost a challenge to duel. He knew that all of Misha's turns moved through the air in one direction. By turning left and right, Fernando probably thought that he was outdoing Misha, however out of place the turns may have been for *Don Quixote*.

Misha was in a real fix: he could not change his turns because they were actually Balanchine's, that is, the turns were technically part of the given steps of Balanchine's ballet. With an old ballet, any dancer could get away with altering the choreography, but not when the choreographer was still alive, and certainly not when the choreographer was the head of the company that Misha was about to join. To make matters worse, the show was scheduled to be televised "Live from Lincoln Center" on PBS. The telecast would include both Fernando's *Don Q* and Misha's *Theme*.

Misha and I rehearsed during the afternoon before the performance. His improvement in the Balanchine ballet was readily apparent. Nevertheless, we had one of our knock-down-drag-out scenes when we practiced one of the lifts in the coda. As soon as he hoisted me over his head, I could feel something coming. He jerked me down like he was a Santa Claus whose bag was stuck in the chimney; I was the bag, about to spill. I stopped and gave him a quick correction, pointing out the exact trajectory that my body should travel.

"Gelsey, ve never did before like that!"

"Oh, please, Misha, I am not asking for the impossible!"

He looked like he was going to spit in my face, or worse. "Gelsey, you really don't know vhut the hell you talk-king about in this ballet!"

The snarl did not daunt me. I was determined not to lose control. "Misha, this time I really do know what I'm talking about. Why don't you fuck off!"

That did it. The fact that I held my ground drove him up the wall. He crashed into a nearby chair, his voice booming across the studio. "You go tell Lucia that you refuse to dance vis me! Now! Right now! Go!"

Enjoying his fury, I looked him in the eye, keeping my voice ever so low, "Misha, it seems that you are the one here who doesn't want to dance. So I suggest you go tell her yourself."

His look was homicidal. He jumped up and stormed at me, by me, and out the door. I had refused to follow orders.

After I finished rehearsing my solos, I gathered together my belongings and headed to the dressing room. Lucia Chase caught me by the elevator. "Oh, Gelsey! What happened in there? Oh, dear! I knew it! I should never have let you two rehearse! I knew it!"

I was still calm as I walked with her down the hall to a yogurt and hot dog stand. Misha had flatly refused to dance with me. What was she going to do? I watched her hands tremble as she rambled on and on. What could I say?

Later, I overheard a ballet master pleading with Misha in the wings: "Listen, you'll never have to dance with her again—never! You're leaving anyway! Just this last time—that's it! Please!"

I heard Misha mumble something. Unable to make out his words, I went back to my dressing room. A messenger soon came to tell me that the show would go on as scheduled.

In the midst of chaos, my friend Dina Makarova stopped by for a chat. I kept my suspicions to myself as I began to put on my makeup. Fernando had lifted Misha's turns. Did Misha want to bow out to avoid the embarrassment? Could he have been that calculating? Had he deliberately started the row in order to force me to withdraw from the performance—to give himself an out? Only he would know for sure.

Misha did not acknowledge my presence on the stage. We were fortunate that this was a Balanchine ballet. At one point in the pas de deux, with the music swelling, I reached out to him with my hand—straining to touch him in what might be our last dance, our last moment. Tears were threatening to mar my smile. He was absolutely cold, unrelenting. His forced look was enough to exile me to Siberia.

In the studio the next day, Mr. Tudor came over to me. He said, "Gelsey, you know what part I really liked? That place where you smiled at him."

Weeks later, my boyfriend, Richard, took me out to dinner with an agent. The conversation was unsettling. I listened to all the talk of lucrative possibilities, like concert tours and dancing for a stint with Béjart's company. They told me that my future had never been brighter. I must have downed at least one toast to that future. Out on the streets of Manhattan, I came apart with angry tears. I aimed my words at Richard like so many arrows: "Don't you know that I'm nothing without Misha? Nothing!"

Chapter Ten

DRUGS POISON HER
THAT SO FELL SICK OF HIM

Misha's move to the New York City Ballet sent shock waves through the world of dance and caused considerable speculation in the press. He accepted a drastic cut in salary in order to join a company where no star could shine brighter than Balanchine. For seven hundred dollars a week, Misha lived out an artistic fantasy that had been part of the baggage he brought from Russia. Presumably he wanted to broaden his experience. I watched from afar and sometimes from the audience as my former partner performed more than a score of new roles from July 1978 to October 1979. I listened to the rumors that had me following him back to City Ballet. I was sick, but I was not that sick—not yet.

The critics pointed out the risk that he was taking, that his schooling and stylistic trademarks would be out of place in Balanchine's theatre. How would Misha adjust to being just another pair of legs? How would he perform his tricks? How would he distinguish himself within the more impersonal and mechanical choreography? How would he cope with a system that seemed to put all the emphasis on the ballerina?

I had expected Misha to outwit Balanchine. When the reverse turned out to be the case, I was surprised and disappointed. Unlike those rare dancers, such as Edward Villella, who managed to become stars at City Ballet, Misha never really stole the show. Quantity undermined quality: he sped through dance after dance. Strain undermined his health: he came down with tendonitis. He fell into all the familiar traps. Nobody in that company would wise him up, though I understand that Patricia McBride, his most frequent partner, suggested that he see a doctor.

I could see that Mr. B was cramping Misha's style, sometimes miscasting him, always putting him in his place, never giving him the direction that might have enabled him to stand out. Misha played the game by Balanchine's rules, failing to make a distinctive mark as far as most of the critics were concerned. Most of the performances were passable but did not show him off to advantage. He seemed to trust Balanchine's theories and steps more than he trusted his own vision as a dancer. He never made the roles his own.

When I saw him in *Prodigal Son*, wearing a new costume, one of the most ridiculous designs ever executed for man, beast, or dancer, I asked myself if he had any idea that Balanchine was making a fool of him. The line of his body was totally obscured, as if Mr. B wanted only Misha's feet to show. I knew the choreography. I had seen Eddie Villella perform the same ballet years before. Eddie turned the same physical action and Prokofiev score into a revelation of the biblical story. When I saw Misha crawling on his knees across the stage and tapping his cane on the beat, I asked myself how such a dancer could have missed the drama. Had Balanchine advised him not to act?

Misha's steps and gestures were empty. His movements were not filled with that special combination of passion and truth that might have moved the audience. I shed no tears of joy. His character did not come across as the penitent son returning to the arms of his father, but a pathetic creature, the kind of boy only a mother could love. His abject humility did not hold the promise of paternal reconciliation. Misha's Prodigal Son lost his pride so completely that redemption robbed rather than restored his dignity. Was this a choice made by the dancer or an oblique reflection of reality? Was Baryshnikov throwing himself at the feet of Balanchine?

Misha came closer to asserting himself in *Apollo*, but the rug was cut out from under him. Like *Prodigal Son*, this ballet dates from the 1920s, when Balanchine was still telling stories. In the revised version that Misha performed with City Ballet, the choreographer stripped down the drama along the lines of pure dance, removing the last traces of plot and character development. The dancer pumped some emotion into the title role but could not rescue the ballet from its creator. It seemed to me that Balanchine had a last laugh at his own Russian past—at Misha's expense.

My impressions were certainly not shared by Peter Martins, who watched from the inside and shared a dressing room with Misha. Peter wrote in his book, *Far from Denmark*:

Misha stayed for two years, and I think of it as a glorious period. Then he was offered the artistic directorship of American Ballet Theatre, and he accepted with Balanchine's encouragement and aid. Balanchine gave Misha *Prodigal Son* and *La Sonnambula*, ballets that Misha excelled in for us and that Misha presented in exciting productions with ABT dancers. Their firm friendship continues. Misha had gotten what he wanted: he had had his experience.

Peter and Misha appeared together in Balanchine's *Union Jack* and in Robbins's *Dances at a Gathering*. In a moment of whimsy, I was amused by the image of them as a male partnership. What irony that Peter would one day be the head of the New York City Ballet, and that his Russian pal would one day be the head of American Ballet Theatre—and that both would follow the same path in and out of Lincoln Center, looking for footsteps that had vanished like the stars who once danced for those companies.

Although I did not understand why Misha had gone to Balanchine, I did resign myself to his absence. I tried not to hope for his return. He would never come back on my behalf. His initial attraction to me had been based on my image as a Balanchine ballerina. He had to sense that I did not quite fit that image. By jumping companies, he had a whole theatre full of Balanchine dancers. I hoped that Misha would learn to appreciate, however belatedly, the nature of my transition, my struggle with mime and drama, my lack of theatrical education, the deficiencies of my early training.

In retrospect, I see the inevitability of his dancing away from me, the absurdity of my thinking we were moving in the same direction. While he devoted himself to modern choreographers, I committed myself to the more traditional masters. As if driven by demons, he experimented with Roland Petit, Glen Tetley, Alvin Ailey, John Neumeier, John Butler, Robbins, Balanchine, and so forth. Relentlessly pushing for refinement, I passed through Petipa, Perrot, Saint-Léon, Bournonville, and so on. Misha's course always mystified me. He seemed to be an impossible act to follow. As our choices became more emphatic, the common ground between us was bound to fall away.

Not long after Misha departed from American Ballet Theatre, Ivan Nagy made his exit as well. Ivan eventually would become the director of the Santiago Ballet in Chile. I was left without a suitable partner. If I were nothing without Misha, I was surely less than nothing without Ivan.

Lucia Chase sat me down in the theatre one afternoon. She was pleased to have me cornered, pinned down for the question of the hour. "Gelsey, who would you like to dance with?"

I had no idea what to say. I let her decide, though I tried to rule out Fernando Bujones. I had nothing against Fernando personally. There was certainly no antagonism. But his fixed notions about technique told me that he would be resistant to my ideas. Drained of motivation, I could find no reason to make choices about partners and repertory. My voice cracked when I tried to explain myself. My criteria and my passion fled in the same instant. Over the next year, I found myself matched on the stage with various male consorts.

In the fall, I was cast by Mr. Tudor in a new ballet called *The Tiller in the Fields*. Like his previous work, *The Leaves Are Fading*, the music was a composite of Dvořák pieces, and the set was designed by Ming Cho Lee. My new partner was a young dancer by the name of Patrick Bissell.

I thought Patrick might be too inexperienced for the part. Several years my junior, he had been pushed into some major roles before his time due to the shortage of male partners in the company. Huge and handsome, he was a raw talent, eager to learn and open to suggestions. It soon became apparent that Patrick had the potential to become a brilliant partner.

Mr. Tudor apparently saw something in the incongruous picture: Patrick towered over me, like a hulk. I played a gypsy sprite, a wild seductress who taught a lesson of love to the youthful giant, a strapping peasant boy whose heart had not yet lost its virginity. The ballet was a pastoral romance with an unusual twist that called for my character to become pregnant. The gestation and birth of the ballet in the studio seemed to parallel its romantic theme. We were an unlikely pair. We came from different worlds. There were communication problems.

Patrick's streetwise mentality was a bit of a stumbling block. He spoke a language that was alien to some of the more subtle requests made by the choreographer. At a rehearsal just before the premiere, I tried to translate the specific movement qualities—such as the mimetic indication of sunshine falling on Patrick's back and neck—into images from the world of boxing. Patrick could relate to athletics. I did an imitation of Eddie Villella, whose rough-and-tumble background seemed to offer a key to his amazing grace and projection on the ballet stage. Then I tried to show Patrick how to distribute his body weight and move through the intricate phrasing of the dance itself. He accepted my lead just as his character accepted paternity.

In my eyes, Patrick's improvement was dramatic. The ballet was at least a moderate success, though my swollen belly troubled some of the audiences and critics. I most enjoyed the punch line of Arlene Croce's rather mixed review. She described the moment when I revealed that I was with child: "My first thought when Kirkland pulled open her sweater was: Can a baby become pregnant? Kirkland isn't Lolita; she's Tudor's constant nymph."

During the winter, in spite of my initial reluctance, I established a partnership with Anthony Dowell, a visiting artist from London's Royal Ballet, a premier danseur cast from the aristocratic mold for which that company was famous. Anthony's nobility was more genuine than I had expected. He had to be gallant to put up with me. He was not fazed either by my way of working or by my occasional outbursts of temperament. With characteristic patience and curiosity, he gave himself to the methodical process that led from studio to stage. His humor released my dormant wit. Our laughter was more than a mutual recognition that we had pleased each other through the dance. His wry perceptions reminded me to appreciate the ludicrous, to gently scold myself for past and future follies.

The moments of joy had a way of slipping through my fingers. After dancing the pas de deux from *Don Quixote* in New Orleans, we performed the full-length ballet in Washington, D.C. Pressure and nerves got to me during our first appearance at the Kennedy Center. I thought that my dancing had disappointed Anthony in the first act. I rushed off the stage and vented my frustration on the conductor. I became a terror for anyone who tried to come near me. Natasha Makarova made a surprise visit to my dressing room between acts to offer her congratulations. I screamed and slammed the door in her face.

Natasha refused to speak to me for a year. Her reaction was justified. The lack of communication between us may have been unnecessary, but it was nothing new. Nor was it unfounded. Chronic misunderstanding inhibited friendship between us.

The upshot of the performance was a muscle spasm that crippled Anthony at the end of the last act. He thought that he had disappointed me. When the dust settled, we had a few good chortles over the review, appearing in the Washington *Star,* December 7, 1978:

> So exciting was Anthony Dowell's debut in "Don Quixote" at the Kennedy Center last night, that when the English dancer disappeared just minutes before the final curtain, it briefly seemed he had flown up and away . . . But until the injury, Dowell's performance as Basil the Barber, with Gelsey Kirkland as the all-knowing Kitri, was the sort of triumph artists and audiences only dream of. And the beginning of a partnership rich in promise . . .

In looking back over the years, I am intrigued by the reactions that my partners had to my personality and methods. Trust was always difficult to establish and maintain. Sometimes it was impossible. Without an alliance in the studio, the work was without gratification regardless of what happened on the stage. Misha was perhaps a technical exception. One of the more trying cases was that of Peter Schaufuss, who came along shortly after Anthony.

Peter was an exceptional talent out of the Danish school, whose path I had crossed years earlier at City Ballet. I remembered him as a kind of juvenile delinquent and hoped that he had grown up. Scheduled to perform *The Nutcracker,* we clashed at the start of rehearsals. There was never a chance to cultivate a rapport. Evidently he was not accustomed to a female partner who had ideas and made demands. I could see the tension building during our first afternoon in the studio. After offering him several corrections, I was put on the spot. He yelled at me, "I'm not stupid! You only have to tell me once!"

His face lit up like a red light bulb. I tried to figure another way to explain the problem to him. He obviously did not absorb the idea the first time. The concept was pretty simple: his partnering was too rough for a prince. I walked to the piano and leaned against it. What could I tell him? His lifts were the kind that belonged in the weight room of a gymnasium . . . I was not supposed to be a barbell . . . He was not supposed to be Arnold Schwarzenegger.

The truth was that he was too fatigued to lift me and too proud to say so. I gave him a merciless glare. He strolled over and stated with ironic nonchalance, "You really hate men, don't you, Gelsey!"

I thought he deserved a slap, but suspected he might enjoy it. I kept a tight lid on my temper. "No, Peter. I don't. It's a shame you see it that way."

The incident made me wonder why I was dancing. For the remainder of the rehearsal period, I was careful not to perturb Peter. I said almost nothing to him until the day of the stage rehearsal. Then I made a point of reminding him several times about the lifts. He exploded. "Jesus! You've said that already!" He went on to tell me what kind of woman I was, and I let him know what kind of partner he was. The air was clear enough. His performance was fine. It cost me more mental anguish than I cared to think about.

Years later, Peter became the artistic director of the London Festival Ballet. I made a request to dance with his company, and he responded with an invitation to be his partner again. Only money and the muse who watches over this book prevented a rematch. There is always hope.

I understood the vocational plight suffered by my partners. I could sympathize with them to a degree. On the superficial level, the job of the male dancer often seemed to offer nothing more exciting than to lug around the ballerina. There was a tendency for men to see it that way. The ballerina became a burden, an annoying obstacle to overcome in order to get to the more serious solo work. I was damned if I allowed myself to acquiesce to that point of view. A relationship had to be constructed in each case. The lugging around had to be made into the stuff of drama; the technique had to be on a par with classical poetry.

Partnering is the heart of each ballet. When that heart is empty, the dance becomes at best a gymnastic exhibition, a sport. One of my subsequent partners, an Australian dancer by the name of John Meehan, paid me one of the kindest public compliments when he said, "She taught me more about partnering than I ever knew before." He also said that I had not compromised myself as an artist. That was not true.

The decline of my spirits through the winter of 1978 and 1979 was hastened by the breakup of my romance with Richard. The two of us became partners for a few unfortunate concerts outside the company. Richard was a soloist whose talent and technique were not fully developed. His dancing lacked focus. He did not have the drive and the will to perfect each moment. I doubt that he ever had that kind of desire. He worked as hard as most dancers, but that was not the key to virtuosity. My half-hearted coaching did not inspire him. My love did not work any miracles. I was afraid that his frustrations would lead to resentment. I was afraid that he would leave me.

How could I tell my lover that we were not suited as partners? How could

I help him improve without hurting him? I desperately wanted to avoid any competition. Rather than wound his pride, I failed him. As if to make sure that he looked better than me on the stage, I starved myself and impaired my ability to perform. Unwittingly protecting his feelngs, I fell back into my sick routine. I became so thin and so weak that I could barely dance at all. As I recall, we did the pas de deux from *Don Quixote* with a regional company somewhere in the Midwest. My appearance was an embarrassment. It was also the death knell for us.

Richard agreed that we should have a serious talk when we subsequently arrived for the ABT season in Washington, D.C. We met in the restaurant of the Watergate Hotel. I began by stammering incoherently. He came to the rescue. "Gelsey, I think you want to say that we shouldn't be together right now—that you want time to think."

I avoided the real issues. "It's just that I'm such a mess. I think I should be alone for a while."

We both knew it was over. Our hearts were broken without explanation. He left me in the hotel and went out to his car. I heard from a friend that he wept as he drove away. He never knew how my love had betrayed us, how I was the one who led us astray. Neither of us ever considered the motives of the agent who had encouraged the concert business in the first place, who used Richard to lure me to the stage—knowing that my name sold tickets. I had no control over the strings that were pulled.

Some months later in New York, Richard came to my dressing room during an intermission. After trading a few trivial tales, I asked him if he wanted to have dinner after the performance. I wanted his company. I had a faint hope that I kept to myself: maybe we could make amends. His tone was almost haughty.

"No, I can't. I already have plans. I can't break them. You know what that's like, Kirkland. I mean, when you're determined to do something, nothing can stop you!"

He was mysterious. He seemed to be snubbing me. I felt like I had no right to ask him about his plans, but he volunteered the information. "I'm going to try some heroin tonight. I've been wanting to for a long time and tonight I'm doing it."

He could see the shock on my face. There was anger in his voice as he explained how his friend, a doctor, would help with the injection. I knew the friend as well, a shady character who had insinuated himself into the lives of several dancers in the company. The image of a syringe plunging into Richard's arm was enough to make my insides somersault. "You mean you'd rather do that than have dinner with me?"

I tried to make it sound like he would miss the time of his life. His look shut me up. His soft eyes turned sharp, arrogant. His words were calculated for maximum effect.

"You know, Kirkland, you've always done exactly what you set your mind to do . . . and now, that's what I'm doing. Of all people, you should understand!''

He left abruptly, without waiting for a reply. Was he lying? Was he trying to make me feel guilty? Was he trying to prove that he could take a risk? Did he think heroin would make him an artist?

I was scared to death for him. I wanted to be the reason for him not to do it. The word "heroin" had only poisonous connotations. How could he be so stupid? How could I stop him? He put me in an impossible position, but that was his whole point. He was saying that I had no right to interfere. He was saying that I could not stop him from being himself, or even from destroying himself. He was making a fool of me.

My life is riddled with so many "should haves" and "might have beens." I should have followed him. I should have confronted him with my feelings. I should have talked some sense into him. Things might have been different. I have no idea whether or not Richard had his experience. Had I known half as much about drugs as I knew about my art, I might have set him straight.

By the spring of 1979, I had fallen so far into malaise that I could see no way out. I had become so injury-prone and so undependable that bets were placed in the front of the theatre on whether or not I would perform. I languished. I became a complainer. I blamed my art for all trials and tribulations. I had no inspiration, no friends, no lover, no support, no muscular power, no prospects, and no grasp of the problem. I did not even have the sense to quit.

In April, I achieved a popular success with the Australian dancer John Meehan in the ballet *Three Preludes,* choreographed by Ben Stevenson and set to Rachmaninoff. This adagio duet was a showpiece that turned into a crowd-pleaser. Yet the victory was hollow. I was not pleased even when Clive Barnes effused in the New York *Post:*

> Kirkland—looking all the time intensely as if she was about to break into tears immediately—with her fantastic extensions, her perfect line and her grace, seemed to be going out of the way—as well she should—to show what greatness in a ballerina really was.
>
> Meehan—totally up to the moment—partnered with a cool yet eager grace. And Kirkland sailed in orbit through the stars. This is one hell of a dancer—watch her and gasp.

I knew how to fight for a ballet, but I did not know how to fight for my life. I was fading fast.

In May, I ran out of rationalizations. It happened in the middle of a performance of *The Nutcracker.* Anthony Dowell was my partner that evening. Moving through the familiar steps, I was lost in mental monologue, silently muttering to the cadence of Tchaikovsky: Gelsey, what are you doing out here? . . . You know, and your body knows that you're a sick girl . . . You don't have a joyous bone left in your body . . . Do something about it before you go screaming off this bloody stage! . . . No! . . . No! . . . No! . . . You can't let Anthony down!

As he held me in a lift, I felt my left leg knot in pain. By the time he lowered me to the floor, I was yelping under my breath, "Oh, God! My leg! My leg!" We exited at the end of the act. I hobbled into the wings and crumpled onto the floor, hyperventilating and cramping. I knew that I was dancing a lie and I was ready to lie in order not to dance.

My condition was not serious. I could have continued the performance, as I had so many times in the past. I chose to make what seemed to me the decision of my life at that moment: I groaned and exaggerated the severity of the cramp. With the blessing of the artistic director, I was replaced in the performance and began an intermittent leave of absence that continued for more than six months—until I finally found the courage and the wisdom to tender my resignation.

From the first day of my unofficial sick leave, I was pressured to return to the theatre, to resume my career. Why was I playing hooky? Why was I being selfish? Why was I wasting my talent? Why was I turning my back on my accomplishments and my audience? Why was I so unhappy?

I expected my mother to understand. Surely she could see that I was killing myself, that for me ballet was suicidal. I was devastated when her maternal pride prevented her from comprehending my desperation. I was ready to disown her. When she quietly voiced her concern and asked how I planned to support myself outside ballet, I flew into a rage. In my irrational state I had a fleeting impulse to throw her off the balcony of her Fifth Avenue apartment. After a traumatic session of tears and confessions, we embraced, as if to encircle the distance between us with our arms.

I whispered, "Mother, I just want you to be my friend."

She winced. "Gelsey, I'm so afraid you might not want me as a friend."

How could we cut the umbilical cord without severing the long-standing bond of affection? How could we learn to love more wisely? She had never been one of those ballet mothers who lived vicariously through her daughter's career. She had her own life. I admired the daredevil spirit with which she rode her bicycle to the office, pedaling each day through the streets of New York City. She was her own woman. Yet she held me in such high esteem as a dancer that I felt worthless as a daughter. I had only sporadically taken her into my confidence and included her in my decisions. Having never asked her how to pursue my career, how could I ask her how to end it?

My manager, Shirley Bernstein, continued to negotiate with management on my behalf. She and I eventually met with the company manager, Joyce Moffatt. Joyce was a businesswoman. Shirley was a businesswoman. I was an unfinished piece of business. If I were to return to the stage, I wanted the right to bring my own teachers and coaches into the studio. I wanted to stop sneaking in the middle of the night. Shirley took my side, pointing out that my request was neither unreasonable nor unprecedented. Joyce seemed to be sympathetic. She offered encouragement to the effect: "Well, Gelsey, all you are really asking for is the freedom to direct yourself within ABT, which is what you have been doing all along anyway."

Joyce later took the matter to the artistic director, Lucia Chase, and communicated the official response to Shirley: "Out of the question."

The negotiations turned to salary, repertory, and schedules. Shirley brought back an offer for more money than I had ever received. It must have been more than a thousand dollars per performance. I refused again and again. Without giving me artistic support in the theatre, how could they expect me to dance well enough to deserve that much pay? I actually felt that the amount they were offering was more than I would ever want. The money was a curse. Without sufficient rehearsal time, without even a guaranteed dress rehearsal, the repertory and schedule were insults to my intelligence.

I hit another stone wall when I tried to break the theatrical convention of signing autographs after every performance. In Florida on one occasion, to avoid being hounded by a mob of fans, I ran a mile in my toe shoes through a field of mud and back to my hotel room. I wanted some privacy after scrawling my signature across the stage with my body. I asked management for the right to sign autographs at my discretion. My request was rejected. There were just too many ludicrous details for me to sign on the dotted line. I was ready to find an umbrella concession and sell hot dogs outside Lincoln Center.

The cumulative frustration and unfortunate turn of events caused me to fall out with Shirley. At about the time that the dancers' union (American Guild of Musical Artists) went on strike in the autumn of 1979, I went to an "artist representative" by the name of Barna Ostertag. Barna turned my life around in a few short months. I virtually moved into her office at Forty-second Street and Fifth Avenue. We had no contract. She had no typewriter. The relationship was based entirely on our verbal agreements and scribbled notes of trust.

In her late seventies, Barna was a former actress, totally eccentric and radiant, with a deep, guttural laugh that seemed to shake her entire body and endeared her to me instantly. I saw her as someone to emulate, a woman who proved that internal grace and character demolished all outward forms of beauty. Small in stature, she had a pair of gigantic eyes that missed nothing and watered easily whenever something touched her. Her simple attire was set off by a passion for gold jewelry. She wore no makeup other than her bright-red lipstick, applied with the same infinite care with which she enunciated her words. One of her hands usually waved a cigarette holder, tapped to make a point, which was always well-taken. We talked endlessly.

Barna encouraged me to find my voice, as well as my value as an artist and a human being. I spoke out during the strike—when the ABT management locked the dancers out of the theatre for ten weeks. I went to meetings and gave my support to the only just and honorable cause, realizing that many of my fellow dancers earned far less than I and suffered from the same chronic insecurities and abuses. I tried to articulate what I knew to be our shared needs and aspirations. I gave an interview to writer Suzanne Gordon which later appeared in her book, *Off Balance*. For the first time, I made waves in public and addressed some of the problems of my training under Balanchine, identifying the passivity and guilt instilled by his system, the legacy that I was still struggling to overcome.

The material and professional issues of the strike-lockout compelled me to look at the stage of the real world, not simply to understand it in some abstract sense, but to act to change it—to alter the circumstances of my life. That meant bringing my ideals to bear on the theatre itself. I was somewhat ambiguous about my progress:

> It's taken me a long time to realize that what brought me to where I am is my ability to use my mind and to concentrate; to see that if I brought that to other areas of my life, it would be no different. But when you spend your life only dancing, you feel that there are too many steps to take to get to where you want to be, and so you question taking that first step at all.

My activities and personal growth led to my formal resignation from ABT in January 1980. I had made an appointment to see Lucia Chase. We still had not agreed on the terms of a contract. Barna coached me before the meeting, advising me to remain standing, to look down on Lucia, not to flinch in the face of what was called "the corporate structure." On my way to Lucia's office, I ran into Mr. Tudor, who advised me to find a knife and stay with the theatre—even if that meant stabbing the artistic director. His joke strengthened my resolve.

I eventually stood before Lucia with the schedule that she proposed for the coming season. I knew exactly what I had to say. Once I began to speak, I gave her no chance to cut me off. "Lucia, here is your schedule. I have thought about it carefully. It is not acceptable. If this is the best you can do, well, it's just not good enough. It never has been. You have never really listened to me!" Her expression was that of a mother about to slap the hand of an unruly child. "Lucia, please don't say anything! I'm tired of you talking, and I'm tired of trying to talk with you. You've never made me feel needed or wanted here. And most of all, Lucia, most of all, I feel unloved! You've made me feel just so unloved!"

I started for the door and turned back to her astonished face. "What I'm saying is that it is impossible for me to stay here. And, Lucia, that means I'm not coming back. I resign!"

On the following day, Lucia spread the story: "I just don't know what happened. But I do know that she did not break down with me this time—she broke up with me! That's what she did! She broke up with me! She said she felt unloved! Can you believe it?"

While on the outs with ABT, I received a letter from Mr. Tudor. He sent along some belated criticism of my performance in *Swan Lake,* reminding me not to flap my arms, not to fall into personal melodrama. His deeper purpose was to defend the world of the theatre. He counseled me not to lose my reverence for the stage. His sentiments made me burst into tears. I wrote him a brief message, unable to adequately express my gratitude for his thoughts and concern, saying that I had no words. He sent back a card emblazoned with the image of a lone red heart. There were no words whatsoever. He even omitted his signature. I kept that card with me through years of uncertainty and dissipation. It survives only by act of God. A fire has scorched its white, rectangular border. Its edges have burned and frayed away entirely. But the heart remains.

With Barna in my corner, I tried to reorganize my life and career, to put the past behind me, to prove my independence. At the beginning of 1980, I made plans to perform in Europe. I wanted to see if drama was still alive on the stages of Stuttgart and London, if my classical orientation would find a home in those places. My instincts told me that something had to be rotten in the American ballet world—something besides me. The training of the dancer not to think may have been appropriate for those ballets that encouraged the audience not to think; but I was a thinking artist. It was too late for me to change, or so I thought. There had to be some theatre where I could work and continue to learn without feeling like either a freak or a criminal.

My first trip took me to the Stuttgart Ballet. Scheduled to dance *Romeo and Juliet,* I was looking forward to working with Marcia Haydée, the artistic director of the company. She was a Brazilian ballerina who created the role of Juliet in John Cranko's 1962 version of the ballet. Her talents were prodigious. Her career as a dance actress had carried her to the head of a company. That accomplishment alone was inspiration for me. I rated myself a poor actress and hoped that she could further my education. I was disappointed to learn just before arriving that Marcia was ill and would not be available to coach me in the part. Nevertheless, I was determined to follow through on the commitment. My attitude was on the order of nothing-can-stop-me.

I was welcomed to the company by Marcia's frequent partner, Richard Cragun, who had been her Romeo in the original production. He did not take part in rehearsals, but his enthusiasm set the tone. Birgit Keil taught me the ballet, and Egon Madsen partnered me. This was a company of angels. I had my problems living alone in a local hotel and dealing with the language barrier, but I did not encounter any obstacles in the theatre. I directed myself without feeling like a misfit. Nobody questioned my methods. There was exchange between the dancers. There was give-and-take, which seemed to make up somewhat for the lack of guidance. The death of John Cranko, the choreographer, in 1973 was still felt by all. The company that mourned him was searching for direction. So was I.

The role of Juliet was a momentous challenge. I suppose that I never felt fully prepared. My rehearsal period was short, lasting just about a month. The nuggets of Shakespearean gold had to be plucked from the air, reconciled with the Prokofiev score, and technically transmuted into movement and gesture. The other dancers were not especially strong on technique, yet each had a unique sense of character and flair for projection. The emphasis was on drama. I had no complaints.

The performance was quite a success. After Marcia came to the theatre and watched my portrayal, she came backstage to say that Cranko would have loved me. I accepted her compliment without a fall from grace. To accept my own dancing without making apologies was major progress. I had taken a first tentative step toward finding value on the stage and in my life. I was proud of myself.

Back in New York, early in 1980, the rumors were confirmed that Misha would be taking over American Ballet Theatre as artistic director. I had not had contact with him for months, not since an East Side party, a formal celebration of some kind. Several dancers had attended, along with a select assortment of luminaries. I saw Misha with Jessica Lange and joined them briefly. They were sitting out of the way. When I approached, he introduced me cordially, then sank back into his chair, keeping a low profile. She was funny as well as gorgeous. We shared a few laughs about nothing in particular: the atmosphere, the situation, the pretense. We were in a fit of giggles when Misha leaned forward and gave me one of his suffering-artist looks, a pout followed by a wan smile. Perhaps we had excluded him from our conversation. Perhaps I had intruded. His face was too serious. Was he giving me a hint? I stood and backed off, bidding adieu, wondering how Misha was able to handle himself around her.

Elsewhere at that party, there were drugs in evidence, though I took little notice. A dancer friend was escorted into the men's room for a "special surprise." His prolonged absence made me curious enough to ask about him, but my question elicited only evasive responses. I caught the drift slowly. Whatever was going on was none of my business. I usually felt like a visitor from another planet when I attended these affairs. I was on the defensive socially. Protocol had to be spelled out for me.

I recall moving down a reception line, shaking the hand of Henry Kissinger, the guest of honor that evening, without knowing exactly who he was. Later, a nebulous character by the name of "Dexter," who turned out to be a drug dealer and discreet mover in Washington social circles, asked if I had any interest in the former Secretary of State, if I found him attractive.

My dumb expression must have said it all. The fellow explained, "But Gelsey, Kissinger is to politics what Baryshnikov is to ballet." I saw no connection and had no interest. I could only imagine the minds and corridors of power—narrow, winding, and cold—certainly no place for a ballerina. That logic applied to my refusal to dance with the latest defector, Alexander Godunov, at a White House gala under the Carter Administration. I was accused of being unpatriotic as well as temperamental.

With Misha's assumption of power as artistic director at ABT set for September 1980, the press was once again rife with speculation. How would he manage the company and continue to dance? Would he change the policy and the artistic direction of the theatre? The news of my return to the company, along with the latest gossip, appeared in *People* magazine, June 9, 1980:

> . . . Misha . . . has gone out of his way to win back Gelsey's feet, if not necessarily her heart. They were recently seen arm in arm at a Broadway opening, and now an ABT spokesman reveals that Kirkland will return to the company this fall. And the romance? "Gelsey says they're only friends now," confides an intimate of both. "She's not stupid enough to mess with King Kong's girlfriend"—Jessica Lange, currently Misha's steady.

I was unaware that we had any intimates in common. The opening was for Twyla Tharp's company. I attended with Misha and one of his friends, Charles France, a truly rotund and opinionated balletomane who worked at ABT. I sat between the two of them at the theatre, listening to their twitters and stereophonic stream of "oohs" and "ahs." Misha and Charles had become a Twyla Tharp fan club. They were titillated by her brand of "cynical chic." I tried to chime along with them, all the while thinking that I had missed something, like the point. I was just so unsophisticated.

After the show, we went uptown to a restaurant, joined by Rhoda, another ABT functionary, a young woman who worked in the front office. Misha was like a kid with a new toy, chattering about his ideas for the company, many of which had come from the mouth of Charles France, a regular Mr. Right. They talked too fast for me. I was still unable to tell the difference between what I wanted and what I thought Misha wanted me to want. I smiled, then more or less closed my ears. I was more than optimistic. With both the strike and the Stuttgart experience under my belt, I had enough confidence to resume the partnership with Misha—and to assume that we would work out any problems.

My stomach shrugged at the first sight of food. A number of colorful dishes were laid out before us. The cuisine was Japanese. The restaurant was a favorite of the "Saturday Night Live" crowd. The four of us—Misha, Charles, Rhoda, and I—were seated together around a small table. My mind wandered. I hoped for a new beginning. Misha had come to his senses. He had flunked out of the New York City Ballet and returned to the company and the tradition where he belonged. He held the future in his hands. That was the way I saw it. His excitement about Twyla meant nothing to me. His friends meant nothing to me. I was relieved that he was out of Balanchine's theatre. If only I had possessed the power of second sight, I might have foreseen the tribute Misha paid to Mr. B in an interview for the New York *Times,* June 12, 1985: "I appreciated his moral point of view toward the theatre . . . It gave me a kind of confidence that if you ask from the dancers what you think is right for the theatre, it will be right."

I snapped out of it when Misha asked me if I still smoked cigarettes. Both of us had kicked the habit off and on. I grimaced. He said, "Oh, Geels, me too." We were getting along fine. We were chums again. I played with my silverware and waited for the conversation to bounce back in my direction. I must have appeared anxious to leave. I was fidgeting blatantly.

"Gelsey, you know, you should try some-sing, just to relax. I had most fantastic . . . um, um . . ." Misha gave a quick look over to Charles. "Vhat vas it?"

Charles shook his head, a double negative, his lips puckered and brows knit. I interpreted the signal as an indication that the subject should be dropped. None of my companions could believe that I had never even tried sake.

I was miffed at Misha just for implying that I was too uptight, that I was a female and a dancer with too many anxieties for my own good. At the same time, I was envious of Misha and the life he seemed to lead. His tone carried a note of condescension. His advice and testimony touched a familiar nerve inside me. It was as if he always expected me to be happy for him, to applaud his good fortune.

His extravagance rubbed me the wrong way, especially when he talked at length about artistic sacrifices and ascetic deprivation. There seemed to be no experience that he would deny himself, no experience that would ever be denied to him. Misha was the Playboy of the Western World all of a sudden. I was ready to catch a cab and find my way home. Our parting was amicable. He promised to stay in touch. I tried to keep my mind on the work ahead. After being dropped off unceremoniously on a street corner, I wondered again how he rationalized his life as an artist on and off the stage. I must have missed Misha's statement to *Time* magazine, May 19, 1975: "The stage is a form of opium for me—a psychological feeling I must have, I cannot be without." I never thought about ballet that way. I was not bound so much to the stage (where I was often disappointed) as to the studio, to those feelings and ideas that came with each breakthrough in my understanding.

Shortly after the Broadway opening, Misha took me to visit his Czech friend, film director Miloš Forman. I recall trying to keep up with Misha's brisk pace as we walked to our host's Manhattan apartment. I felt like I was skipping as well as tagging along. The only other guest was the actress Nastassja Kinski, a shocking beauty who greeted us as we moved behind Miloš into a spacious living room. She was dressed entirely in white, like a voluptuous apparition. Misha cruised over to her. I took a place on a couch opposite them. Miloš landed at my side, announcing, "You know, you are actually quite a pretty girl! Really!"

The line did not exactly sweep me off my feet. I suspected that he had taken lessons from Misha. The two of them did seem to have a great deal in common, though Miloš was at least a generation older. His eyes were the sort that had seen it all and gone a little bloodshot. The lids had a way of closing, like tiny hoods of skin. I had not yet mastered the art of taking nothing seriously—though I managed with him. I played the part of the straight woman—strictly deadpan, mostly bored. I guessed that I was out of my depth. I went along with the coarse jokes that passed back and forth between Miloš and Misha. I tried not to be a wet blanket.

Just a few years later, when I saw the movie *Amadeus*, which Miloš directed, I recognized the humor—and wished that Mozart were still alive to give us his review. If only the composer had been around that night when Misha and I made our visit. I could have used the music and the wit, to say nothing of moral support. Maybe the Hollywood mentality put me off. Miloš had pinned a cartoon to a wall off the living room. Cut out from the pages of a newspaper or magazine, the graphic depicted some sort of naughty, nonsensical phallic symbol. Misha and Miloš stood in front of it, squirming and squealing, like boys shoulder-to-shoulder at a peephole. I heard that same laughter again, in the movie, coming from the mouth of a fictional Mozart.

Later in the evening, the four of us—Miloš, Nastassja, Misha, and I—went to Elaine's, one of those swanky restaurants favored by celebrities and other "influential" people. Misha was irrepressible, jumping up from our table to regale us. If he had possessed a gift for iambic pentameter, he might have been playing the part of Mercutio. Queen Mab must have placed a tack on his seat. He recited no poetry, but seemed to be talking about nothing, wagging his tongue and rambling on and on with a story that defies repetition. I blushed, thinking that he was making a fool of himself. Miloš and Nastassja apparently found him amusing. It crossed my mind that Misha and I never laughed together.

I picked at my food. He pushed me to eat. Reaching for his style of comedy, I accused him of always trying to force-feed me. My lead balloon sailed by unnoticed. Nastassja spoke briefly of the challenge of acting. Miloš and Misha gave her their rapt attention. I was sure that both of them would volunteer to give her lessons. The moment passed.

Outside the restaurant, on the sidewalk of Second Avenue, I said my good-byes. Misha broke away from the others, "Geels, vait, you vant to come to my place?" Seeing me hesitate, he added his nod to my freedom of choice, "Is up to you."

It was always up to me, woman of the world. "Well, I don't know, Misha. I mean . . ."

He encouraged me with a new and warmer twist, "Gels, I'd like you to come vith me," adding again, "but is up to you. Vhut you vant!"

I accepted the invitation. His apartment was nearby on Park Avenue. He had recently redecorated it. I had misgivings about the visit, but my immediate concern was finding a topic of conversation. I did not think he had seduction in mind. To fill the awkward silence, I complimented him on the way he had used the space. I even complimented him on his new boots, seeing his heels slip across the floor. I remember feeling slightly disoriented, as if I had walked off the edge of an Escher print. It was not the modern decor but the situation. We eventually sat on his bed, groping for physical meaning as we had in the past, a reflex action that led nowhere. Our course had not yet reached the point of shedding clothes, when reality intruded.

If my life were fiction—a movie or a play—the audience would be asking about now why I had allowed myself to go with him. How could I be such a fool? That was the question, word for word, that passed through my mind when the telephone distracted him. I did not have the answers then. Not having the answers may have been reason enough for my action. Sometimes we meet someone in this world who is everything that we love and hate and cannot stand all at once, and we throw ourselves at the feet of such a person, expecting to find . . . what?

Misha padded out of the bedroom and into the kitchen. I heard him pick up the telephone. I knew almost immediately who was on the line. It had to be Jessica. Misha kept his voice low. I waited for him. The situation had reached the height of absurdity. She was on the phone; I was on the bed. After a few minutes, I knew what to do. I got up and prepared to leave. I could see King Kong's sad face pressed against the window.

I walked to the kitchen on my way out. Still talking on the phone, Misha motioned me to wait. I was embarrassed. I turned my back to him. After hanging up, he said, "Geelsey, come on. Vhere you going!"

"Misha, that was Jessica, right?"

"Vell, yes, but not important . . . Please, don't ask questions . . . Let's just have nice time . . ."

He sat and sighed. I stood over him. "Misha, I have no questions, and I'm not making any judgments. I'm leaving because I think the most important thing is that we try to work together again . . . and . . ."

He cut in, "Please, Gelsey. No lectures. Please, I don't vant to hear."

"I'm not lecturing you, and I'm not angry. I'm just doing what I have to do. To me, the main thing is that we work together . . . Misha, look, I like you—that's why I'm going home. It's better this way."

I headed toward the exit. He rose and walked behind me. When I heard him call my name, I turned around. He was leaning against a doorframe. His voice was softer than any whisper. "Gelsey . . . Gels . . . I love you."

I waited through a few heartbeats. "Gels, I really love you."
I said, quite gently, "It's a little late."

I buried his declaration of love in the back of my mind, along with a million other conflicting impressions. The timing was perhaps more than just a little coincidental. Had he changed? Did he have an ulterior motive?

I was scheduled to dance Kenneth MacMillan's version of *Romeo and Juliet* with the Royal Ballet in the summer of 1980 and to return to ABT in time for Misha's first season as artistic director. A month or so before my departure for London, I agreed to spend another evening with Misha, this time in the seclusion of his home in Connecticut. I was to be his house guest.

The ostensible purpose of our meeting was to discuss business. We had not yet talked over the repertory and schedule for the coming season. We had not come to an understanding. He drove us out of Manhattan. I was curious about his intentions, at the same time daunted by the prospect of being alone with him, even just for the one night. I planned to listen to what he had to say before offering any ideas of my own. He played two roles now: dancer and director. I would not only be dancing with him, but for him.

We exchanged pleasantries for an hour or so in his car. He avoided the subject of our partnership. What passed for communication between us was nothing more complicated than the road signs and the traffic. Just the fact that he had a driver's license impressed me. It was another symbol of his continuous and awesome mobility. He wheeled into the driveway of our destination with obvious pride.

His country house struck me at first as medieval—heavy, dark, and oppressively cold. My imagination conjured pictures of romantic doom. There had to be a tower and a maiden in distress. He took me on a walking tour of the grounds. The exterior looked like a stone fortress, surrounded by trees and foliage. The sun had fallen, but a fine mist of light clung to the roof and treetops. He was apparently in love with the place. Maybe it reminded him of a dacha, one of those country homes of the Russian elite. I walked across the threshold with a nagging sense of foreboding.

The interior was stylishly austere, covered everywhere with dark wood and evening shadows. I dumped my overnight bag in a guest bedroom he showed me on the second floor. In spite of the mild temperature and season, Misha busied himself lighting a fire in the living room. I watched him poking logs in the fireplace and tried to make myself comfortable.

I was determined to follow his lead for the moment, to let him run the show. His appetite postponed any serious talk. He improvised a meal between the kitchen and the dining room table, complete with candles and a bottle of wine. I recall feeling tiny, like a child, sitting in a huge, straight-backed chair. The alcohol dulled my mind and made my skin tingle. I luxuriated. The gloom lifted, and I relaxed for the first time in his presence. He was not ready to turn to business. He said that he most enjoyed spending time alone in the house, that he had few friends now. I appreciated his effort to make conversation. His tone was confessional, nostalgic, touching.

After we moved to the floor of the living room, I asked him, "What about Jessica?"

His liquid eyes caught the red glow from the fire. "Vell, ve are good to each other." He seemed to imply that love should aspire to nothing more. "Geels, you seeing somebody?"

I was embarrassed to admit the truth. "No. Well, nothing serious."

The exact moment escapes me, but we fell into each other's arms again. It was an act of consolation, another surrender to shared loneliness, almost dispassionate this time. Later, as we traipsed up the stairs toward his bedroom, he murmured, "Geelsey, I never thought this vould happen, did you?"

"Never."

Nothing changed between us. The emotional spiral for me may not have been as violent as it had been years before, but my feelings were just as confused as ever. I had no real expectations. Pleasure—without promise, without meaning—was a kind of pain. I lay awake, thinking of a night long ago, one of our first nights together in my apartment, when Misha took a swing at sweet nothingness, saying, "Geels, I can see forever in your eyes." Forever—what did that mean? Good to each other—what did that mean? What did any of it mean?

In the morning, I tried to lighten the mood by playfully pulling him, still half-asleep, into the shower. I teased him into a few wet smiles and giggles. After we had dressed and eaten breakfast, I waited for him to get down to business. Time was running out. He seemed content to putter around in the kitchen. I knew better than to ask him why he was doing the dishes.

"Misha, we still haven't had a discussion about next season, and we have to go soon."

"Oh yes, vell, let's go upstairs. More cozy."

We moved to a small sitting room on the second floor. He lit another fire and turned on the stereo, a piece of music by some French composer who had captured his fancy. Misha seemed to be distracted and hunting for more distractions. I stood nervously, waiting.

I had prepared with Barna. I did not expect to settle everything, but to begin a working dialogue, an ongoing exchange. If our partnership were to develop, if we were to avoid the problems of the past, both Misha and I would have to make a serious commitment to the future. The question really was how much he valued our partnership and what place and priority it would have in his company. We had excelled with those ballets that constituted the primary tradition upon which ABT was founded. Would he use our partnership to enrich and expand that tradition? How much did he really want to dance with me?

He sat in an armchair; I sat on the floor and looked up at him. With a deep sigh, he began, "Gels, tell me, vhut you vant to do?"

"Misha, I think the most important thing is that we dance together as much as possible, that we find . . ."

"Yes, I'd like that too, but you must also think of who else you can dance vith. I can't always dance vis you. And also, the ballets you vould like to do vith others."

I was crestfallen, not just by what he said, but by how he said it. He had lifted me into the air with his words. He had turned the conversation toward me, but away from us. I did not know how to face him outside the studio. My eyes avoided his. I could feel beads of perspiration collect in the hollows under my arms, tickling as they rolled down my sides. When he rattled off a few suggestions about repertory for us, I denied the deeper implications. Misha would use me at his convenience, when and where he saw fit. But at least we would be dancing together. We had to start somewhere. As long as he was vague about the details and specifics, I could continue to delude myself. As long as I believed that he knew what was best for me, I would remain under his power.

I should have known that he was intent on building a theatre—not a partnership. He impressed me with all his new responsibilities and succeeded in winning my sympathy. I smiled and listened to his reassurances. I hoped for the best. It is not too much of an exaggeration to say he had wrapped me around his little finger by the time he uttered his familiar, closing line, "Don't vorry, Geels. Everything be fine. You'll see."

When we returned to Manhattan, nothing had been set as far as repertory and schedule. The personal and professional spheres had mixed in such a way that he had the advantage. He had wooed me back on his terms. I waited for him to put together a tentative plan for the coming season. Meanwhile, over the next few weeks, he occasionally stopped by my apartment in the evening, usually just to tell me about his day, to confide, to complain, to mull over the problems of his new job. We were apparently "friends." He always left early. What had happened between us in Connecticut was never mentioned.

This was a transitional period, with the artistic directorship changing hands, from Lucia Chase, the venerable and veritable mother of the theatre, to Misha, who elevated Charles France to an administrative position of considerable power. One night, Misha sat in my living room, brooding with such a morose expression that I had to ask what had happened. "Oh, Gels, is so terrible. Today, I fire someone. First time. I don't like do this—I don't like this part of job. You ever have to do this?"

Admitting that I had never been in that particular position, I offered my sympathy. Misha had begun to transform the company, getting rid of dancers whom he considered either too fat or too old. His preference in ballerinas was simple and straightforward: pretty, young, thin, long legs, good feet. He seemed to be attempting the impossible: to combine the look of the New York City Ballet (the taste of Balanchine) with the typecasting system of the Kirov (the concept known as "emploi"). The first step of his plan was to shape the corps, devoting his attention to the younger, less-experienced dancers. I thought that was a little like building a house from the roof down, but said nothing.

This was to be a company in which no star would shine brighter than the director. Certainly no dancer would speak louder than Misha. Meetings were arranged with various members of the company, during which they were informed by Misha how they fit into his plans. I recall his visiting my apartment and belittling some of those dancers with whom he had met. He dismissed them and the demands they made. They were thought of as squabbling children. I wondered why he chose to take me into his confidence.

I did not appreciate being privy to his directorial dilemmas. I felt twisted. I wondered if he would talk about me in the same fashion, behind my back, if I were to disagree openly with his judgment. Rather than defend the interests of the others, I adopted a sort of watch-out-for-myself attitude. I felt selfish and two-faced.

Aside from seeing lesser talents promoted and gifted dancers wasted or discarded, I was demoralized by Misha's show-business attitude. I had no desire to give my regards to either Broadway or Hollywood. I had spent most of my life developing a technique, a means of expression, that had virtually nothing to do with that style of entertainment. Though Balanchine had glorified Fred Astaire, I never understood the attraction. I felt somehow inadequate for failing to swoon for Fred Astaire. He was certainly a great partner for a waltz, always smooth and clever. But what did his debonair ballroom manner have to do with the kind of ballet I was pursuing? Misha's idolization of James Cagney caused a similar reaction. What was Cagney to him, or he to Cagney?

I was more than stupefied—I was traumatized. Cagney was the symbol of a broad show-business tradition with which Misha was infatuated, a childhood crush later consummated with his April 1980 television special, "IBM Presents Baryshnikov on Broadway." Tapping and singing were added to his list of talents. His versatility was showcased, highlighted by his partner of the hour, Liza Minnelli. The event was one more indication of the direction he had chosen. I was losing him simply by not following.

A forking path seemed to have been built into my head, dividing artistry and showmanship. I saw so many showmen, and so few artists. Misha attempted to wear both hats. There were those critics who were disappointed by his descent into more frivolous entertainment. A pillow could have been stuffed with his show but I found myself envious of his popularity. At the same time, I was disappointed in the personal sense. He was moving away. He no longer fit the image of the dancer with whom I had fallen in love. Who was he?

During this period, when Misha was turning to me as a friend and confidante, I came down with a case of menstrual blues one evening and decided to pay him a call. I had never before had the audacity to ask him for his company on the spur of the moment. It was an outlandish impulse. I needed to talk. We still had not come to terms. The communication between us had been mostly one-way.

Wearing his bathrobe, Misha met me at the door and led me into the bedroom. I sat in a chair. He flopped on the bed and turned his attention to the television set. He was watching a tape of his special, which had aired a couple months earlier.

Shifting his eyes from the screen, without turning his head, he asked me, "You see already, my show?"

I replied, "Oh yes, I've seen it all right."

"Gels, vhut you think? You like? I think is pretty good."

He was fishing for a compliment that I had already paid him. After clearing my throat, my voice quivered, "Misha, I thought you were wonderful, and, actually, that's why I really don't want to see it again. I sort of had something else in . . ."

He jerked his head toward me. My eyes had become puddles. "Gels, vhut is it? Vhut's wrong?"

I was squeaking. "Misha, well, you see, when I look at it, I'm reminded of who I have to go out on stage with. And I don't want to compete with that person. I can't dance with . . . that . . ."

"Gels, come on, girl! Is just fun! Is nothing!"

"Misha, Misha, it's just so hard for me to always be happy for you—do you understand? I don't know how to explain this to you. It's not nothing. How can you . . . It's so . . . It's just that I have to work so hard to come close to the kind of . . ."

"Don't be silly! I have to vork hard too. I don't understand."

I had flustered myself. I had passed the point of no return and had to leave. "Look, I really do think you're great in the show. But, I guess I really better get home . . . I'm sorry. Thanks for letting me come."

Trying to hide my face, I braced myself in the doorway of the bedroom. "Gelsey, you okay?"

"Yeah, I'm fine. Really. I just need to get some sleep. I'll find my way out." I yelled back from the exit, "Thanks again, Misha!"

He let me go. The entire visit must have lasted no more than two minutes. I walked who knows how many blocks down Park Avenue and found a cab. Why could I never find the words? Why did I even try?

Shortly after this interlude, sometime in May or June, I prepared to depart for London. By coincidence, Misha was scheduled to perform with the Royal Ballet at the same time. The Fates seemed to have nothing better to do than to take turns goosing me. Misha would be dancing MacMillan's *Romeo and Juliet* and Frederick Ashton's *Rhapsody*. His partner would be a ballerina named Lesley Collier. I would be dancing *Romeo and Juliet* and Ashton's pas de deux from *The Dream*, based on *A Midsummer Night's Dream*. My partner would be Anthony Dowell. I hoped that Misha would think to mount the Shakespeare tragedy with ABT someday—to match us as the star-crossed lovers. The idea thrilled me.

I was packing when the phone rang. It was Misha. He wanted to drop off the schedule for the coming ABT season. He was pressed for time and asked me to meet him in front of my apartment building. I went downstairs and waited on the sidewalk until he appeared. He was in a hurry to tell me that he was in a hurry. He abruptly handed me a few sheets of paper and started to rush away. Without looking at me, he yelled back over his shoulder, "Gels, don't vorry, is not finished."

As soon as I scanned the schedule for the upcoming tour, I knew why he had been anxious to get away: he was afraid to face me, for good reason. I was not to open with him in some of the major cities. He was bringing in a French ballerina by the name of Dominique Khalfouni. Why had he failed to mention this little surprise, either out in the country or at any time in these past few weeks? Why had he misled me? Why couldn't he have just told me the truth, like a responsible human being?

I later tore the pages of the schedule into tiny pieces and tossed them, like confetti, out the window of my bedroom. I knew now that he was capable of deliberate deception. I knew how those other dancers felt, those whom he had dumped. As I finished packing my bags, I told myself that time was on my side. I would work out a strategy with Barna. I would play a waiting game. I would outlast Misha.

I was well received by the Royal Ballet. The attitude in general was one of benign neglect. There were a few stuffy types who looked askance at my approach and even my casual mode of dress. The classic line: "But this is the way it is done, dear!" The founder and living legend of the company, Dame Ninette de Valois, stopped briefly at one of my early rehearsals. She was a real grande dame, the last person whom I would have anticipated as an ally. Someone at the studio apparently ridiculed me about some trivial matter. Unbeknownst to me, Dame Ninette ruffled and came to my defense, exclaiming, "Leave her alone!"

The choreographer, Kenneth MacMillan, was more of a challenge. During a rehearsal of the ballroom scene, he hid behind a pair of dark glasses and sat at the front of the studio. His hair was fashionably shagged over his ears. His image fell somewhere between aging movie star and hit man for the mob. Watching him out of the corner of my eye, I was already intimidated.

When I crossed by him, he leaned forward in his chair and slapped down my arm. He offered no explanation. I was stunned. I assumed that he wanted a less affected, more natural style of movement. He may very well have had a point, but his etiquette was not exactly cricket. My indignation carried over into the remaining rehearsals and performances.

The overbearing manner of the choreographer ironically gave me a motivational angle on the character, a valuable key to the romantic tragedy. I used my anger. Juliet was surrounded by pomposity and arrogant power, by family strife and civil warfare. Her love for Romeo and her death gathered meaning in that dramatic context. Was her world so different from mine?

MacMillan's version of the ballet, like that of Cranko, departed from the play by leaving out the resolution over the grave. The families did not come together at the end. That crucial level of significance had to be built by implication—through the interpretation of the role, through the rationale behind Juliet's suicide, through each of her relationships. The choreography had to be filled with a mimetic infusion of Shakespeare. I tried to develop the quality of Juliet's maturing love as she met with each reversal in the plot —as I met with each reversal in the studio. The choreographer seemed to relish the duel. I often went home in tears, frustrated, fighting against a feeling of total worthlessness.

I stayed initially in a hotel. I began drinking wine in the evening as a balm for my jangled nerves. The loneliness was unbearable. I usually dined by myself in a local restaurant, then retreated to oblivion. I was just another tipsy sleepwalker.

This dismal routine changed when I later moved into the home of a former principal dancer with the Royal Ballet, Georgina Parkinson, who was preparing to return to ABT where she had been working as a ballet mistress. She and her husband, Roy Round, a photographer, and their young son, Tobias, made a place for me in their lives. I was for a while part of the family. Georgina had danced the role of Juliet, as well as the role of Rosaline. She privately gave me the benefit of her experience and offered comfort during each crisis.

Georgina suggested that I should take heart from the fact that Kenneth MacMillan had shown such interest in me, attending all of my rehearsals. I had arrived just around the time when his irreplaceable inspiration, Lynn Seymour, a phenomenal ballerina and dance actress, was on her way out. I ran into Lynn in the dressing room one afternoon. She offered me a cryptic warning, "Be careful around this place."

My way of being careful was to devise several alternatives for each moment in the ballet and bring them into rehearsal each day. I composed a range of interpretive possibilities, letting the choreographer decide between them. I adopted Juliet's talent for dissembling—intentions, feelings, and ideas. Kenneth might have been her father. Though he was ingenious and elegant in his way, I still felt like a sack of laundry, tossed around the studio. That was the price of refining his ballet.

Anthony Dowell was a wonderful Romeo, always attentive and resourceful. He and I also whipped together Ashton's pas de deux from *The Dream* for a gala. I later stepped into the breach with Wayne Eagling, another Romeo, an engaging dancer whose scheduled partner had sustained an injury. All of my performances at Covent Garden were unanimously hailed by the critics. The British audiences gave a rousing series of ovations. The response was overwhelming, a triumph, seemingly a highpoint in my career. I shed joyous tears during the curtain calls, but I knew there was contradiction between my work in the studio and my appearances on the stage.

Writing for *Ballet Review,* Dale Harris credited me with "the gift of bodily eloquence, the ability to communicate the essence of any dramatic situation simply through the mimetic quality with which she invests all her movements." There was really no gift. To achieve that ability, to speak through the dance, to articulate something beyond the steps, was the precise art for which I struggled. I was baffled by the continuous resistance that I encountered. It was as if the modern theatre itself no longer valued that kind of expression.

I saw very little of Misha in London. He stopped briefly at my stage rehearsal and offered me a comment on the opening of my balcony scene: "Looks silly." Only years later did I learn that he had actually paid me a compliment behind my back, saying that I was "incomparable." If only he had communicated his true feelings to me.

On another occasion, he went out of his way to show me a film of a Russian pas de deux that he was considering bringing to ABT. He thought the piece would be great for me. I thought it was a study in banality, a really stilted heirloom. I softened my opinion for his ears, but he must have been able to sense my aversion. Nothing ever came of the idea. He pushed me to see another film of one of his former Russian partners, apparently for the sole purpose of praising her upper body. Was he hinting that I needed lessons in the Russian style, in épaulement? Did he think my Juliet needed upper-body work?

Misha's performances with the Royal Ballet did not win the usual raves. His notices were low-key. I heard complaints that his Romeo was overly glib, more suited to the lights of Broadway than the streets of Verona. Even Kenneth MacMillan asked me, "What's happened to Misha?"

The estrangement bewildered me more than his dancing. He seemed to be a different person than the one I had visited in Connecticut. That journey was already part of another lifetime. Georgina joked that Misha was professionally envious of me. How could that be possible?

After returning to Manhattan, I moved with Georgina into an apartment in the Olcott, a building on West Seventy-second Street. Sometimes I shared a bedroom with her nine-year-old son, Tobias. He was adorable. I treasured our time together, my glimpse into his childhood. His innocence kept me honest, disarmed, delighted.

In the late summer or early fall, I received a long-distance call from Patrick Bissell, my partner from *The Tiller in the Fields*. He was dancing as a guest artist somewhere in the British Isles, maybe Edinburgh. His call was way out of the blue. He said, "Gelsey, I'm thinking of coming into New York and wanted to know if I could see you—if I come. There's something I've been wanting to say to you for a long time. Please, will you see me?"

I was taken aback. "Well, sure, Patrick."

He sounded like he was whooping for joy. I knew of his current relationship with a dancer by the name of "Teresa." The call made no sense whatsoever. His tone definitely implied some sort of romantic lunacy. He mentioned something about his rehearsing with Natasha Makarova, about my return to ABT. His excitement was contagious. I was curious.

He arrived within a couple of days and visited me at the apartment. His mouth seemed to produce more words than he was able to speak. I got the idea that I was the main reason he had come to Manhattan. He would be in the city only for one night before returning to Europe. He was ebullient. It was the middle of the afternoon. I had no misgivings about inviting him to sit in my bedroom. That was where I retreated for privacy. He reminded me that we had first crossed paths when he lived in Richard's apartment, a couple of years earlier. Without batting an eye, Patrick told me that he had had his eye on me since that time. Then he made an unexpected pass, which I nervously deflected.

I was both shocked and flattered. His ardor compensated for a lack of subtlety. He certainly had come a long way to tell me his feelings. I had no doubt that he was sincere, though I wondered why he had waited so long to reveal himself. I jumped to the assumption that he had broken with his girlfriend, Teresa. That seemed so obvious that I saw no reason to inquire for confirmation.

At twenty-eight, I felt like the older woman. He needed me. That was a refreshing change. I needed to be needed. I was intrigued enough to test his infatuation. We agreed to see each other that night. He had a few errands to run in the meantime. Before departing, he made a polite point of greeting Georgina and her son. Patrick had known Georgina for at least a year or so. With a twinkle in his eye and an arm around my shoulder, he requested a favor. He was being mysterious again. He said that his visit was supposed to be top secret—nobody was supposed to know that he was in New York. He later asked that we refer to him in the future by a code name, "Cheddar." The whole idea seemed hilarious, charming.

When he returned that night, the three of us sat around a coffee table in the living room. Patrick did most of the talking; Georgina and I did most of the listening. He told us about a new ballet. He said the two female roles would be perfect for us. Patrick fancied himself an impresario. He was full of big ideas.

Interrupting himself, he took out a tiny white envelope and asked if we wanted to try something. I was unsure what he meant. Georgina instantly recoiled, "Oh no! Not me!"

It was cocaine. I had qualms, but only because of Georgina's adamant refusal. She added words to the effect, "Once you start with that stuff, you can't stop." My two brief experiences with the drug were hardly memorable, not even worth considering. There had been that doctor and Richard, years before. If what they had given me had really been cocaine, then Georgina had to be exaggerating. Still, she seemed so certain.

Without hesitating, Patrick placed a mirror on the coffee table. His opinion meant more than Georgina's at that moment. What would he think of me if I demurred? His insouciant dismissal of her warning was enough assurance to convince me to go along with him. It was not supposed to be addictive—no more dangerous than alcohol.

He dished out a small pile of white crystals on the mirror and chopped them with a razor blade, dividing the powder into straight lines, maybe an inch long, like tiny snowdrifts. Then he took out a dollar bill and rolled it, end to end, showing me how to use it as a straw to ingest the cocaine into my nose.

Patrick prompted me. "Here, Gelsey, just start out with a little."

Georgina watched me, her arms crossed, uneasy. Inserting one end of the rolled dollar bill into one of my nostrils, I leaned over the mirror and sniffed deeply, like a little vacuum cleaner, sucking up one of the lines. My nose burned, and my eyes watered. I felt no other immediate effects. After a few minutes, I was not quite myself. I seemed to be just slightly lightheaded, giddy. That may have been my imagination.

Patrick suggested that I rub a small amount of cocaine on my gums and lips. I followed his instructions. The taste was bitter. My mouth became numb gradually. My teeth became anesthetized, as if I had received a shot of novocaine at the dentist's office. (A year or so later, my friend Pilar Garcia would send me a poem by Emily Dickinson, ending with the two lines: "Narcotics cannot still the tooth/That nibbles at the soul.")

Over the next hour, the drug seemed to creep up on me. We were out for fun. We were rollicking. That was the spirit of the evening. The entire night was supposed to be an adventure. Distressed at the idea that someone had brought drugs into her home, Georgina informed Patrick that he would not be welcome to stay the night. By the time he and I said good-bye to her and found a taxi, I had no cares in the world. No worries, fears, anxieties, nerves, nothing: only bliss, a fantastic sense of well-being.

We checked into the Hilton Hotel in midtown and went straight to the room. Patrick closed the curtains and sat down at a small round table. He unloaded his drugs and his paraphernalia—razor blade, mirror, dollar bill—informing me that he had seven grams of absolutely pure cocaine, the kind that sold for a couple hundred dollars per gram. Purity, he explained, was everything. If a dealer adulterated or "cut" the cocaine, mixing sugar or some other substance, the potency was reduced. Patrick was a connoisseur. My education had only just begun. There was Peruvian "flake" and Bolivian "rock," indicating the geographical point of origin and consistency of the cocaine. The quality apparently varied like wine. It all sounded exotic. Every word sounded exotic by now.

The euphoria of cocaine was different from the intoxication of alcohol. Entirely different. I was not drunk. I was able to speak without the least difficulty initially. I was voluble, even fairly coherent. I experienced a strange kind of mental clarity. My mind seemed to revolve and whirl, like a merry-go-round, I thought, with each turn yielding a big brass ring. I was a child again. My thoughts seemed to organize themselves without conscious effort. Introspection always brought me back to the same place, the one and only ecstatic conclusion: I was in complete control. Little did I realize that the "I" was the drug.

My usual apprehensions and inhibitions about being with a man for the first time vanished. I was at ease under the circumstances. Patrick was an unknown, a stranger. We had worked together, nothing more. He continued to dish out larger and larger amounts of the drug at roughly twenty-minute intervals. The lines were longer and longer, maybe several inches now, what he called "Bissell lines." My body glowed. I felt as light as a feather. I could taste the "coke" in the back of my throat, dripping down from my nasal passages. We joked that "things went better with coke"—a reference to the free advertising provided by the Coca-Cola Corporation, which had, at one time, actually used the drug as one of the ingredients in the secret formula of the soft drink. "Coca" was the name of the plant from which the narcotic was processed, retained in the famous brand name.

I was able to laugh at anything; cocaine made me an instant cynic. No joke was too coarse or too insipid. The world was an ongoing, outrageous gag. Patrick and I suddenly spoke the same language. We were on the same wavelength. I talked about everything, from breast alterations to difficulties with Misha. We continued the conversation and the drug ritual, endlessly, deliriously, snorting more cocaine whenever the euphoric high was on the verge of dissipating. I could already sense that a law of diminishing returns applied. As I became fatigued with the passage of hours, more lines were necessary to lift my spirits. The pleasure of the high was evanescent, elusive. What went up invariably came down. There was an undercurrent of anxiety that always led to the next line.

My mouth became extremely dry. The muscles in my jaw seemed to be constricted. I had trouble speaking. A flash of intense confusion threw me for a loop. I seemed to black out for a moment. Was it the drug or me?

Patrick offered me a Valium, but I refused. I did not want to take any real drugs. We did more coke. At about the time the sun came up, we took a shower and had sex. It was playful. It was erotic. It was a movie. It was mindless pleasure. It was modern romance.

I had at long last liberated my primal and animal instincts. Sigmund Freud, who was no stranger to cocaine, would have been proud of me. I was a purely libidinal being. I was polymorphously perverse. I was the ultimate hedonist. I thought of the friendly advice that Peter Martins had given to me years before, that sex should be purely physical. I was surely nothing but physical.

Time—was suspended, obliterated by the hypnotic beat of rock and roll, a form of musical accompaniment that I had never appreciated before. Place— was boundless, yet concentrated within the carnal reach of that hotel room. I was living for the moment. I was transported. I counted myself the queen of infinite space, if I counted at all.

I could see forever in Patrick's eyes. There was magic on the face of the mirror. I was under the influence of a powerful spell. Was I falling in love? Did I love Patrick or cocaine? Or, did I love Patrick for giving me the cocaine? Or, did I love the cocaine for giving me Patrick? I was never quite sure. I was sure that I wanted more of whatever it was.

We continued to babble for most of the morning, snorting almost all of Patrick's stash. He was running low. I was entranced by the mundane. Designs on the wallpaper became an apotheosis of beauty. Patrick began making calls to Europe. He needed a story to cover for his absence. He was to meet Teresa wherever he was scheduled to dance. She was apparently still in the picture, still his girlfriend. The notion of me as the "other woman" somehow became thrilling. We concocted a tale about a sister in Europe who was sick, who had detained Patrick somewhere. The logistics of the lie became a matter of absorbing interest. He must have called the theatre. He asked me if he sounded convincing. He was convincing. I believed every word he said.

Patrick miraculously pulled himself together, packed, and left to catch his plane. I was sorry he had to leave. I was sorry that he had left me none of his cocaine. I went home. I was exhausted, but sleep took forever to come. My body was utterly racked. I lay on my back and stared at the ceiling of my bedroom. I was vanquished.

Several days later I received a letter that Patrick had posted from Europe. The last line read, "I intend to pursue you at any cost." During the period of his absence, I thought of him, infatuated. I thought of that night, of the experience, but not of the cocaine. I thought of him as a potential ally in the theatre, a partner who seemed to agree with me that the direction of the company was misguided. He boasted that one day he would take over the theatre. He had mentioned concert possibilities for the two of us. I still did not recognize the power of the drug.

While he was away, I moved to an apartment down the hall from Georgina in order to have privacy to carry on the new romance. On the day of the move, I sat with Georgina's son, Tobias, in the bedroom we had shared. He wanted to know why I was leaving. His eyes tore me apart. I blabbered some sort of explanation, feeling like a total hypocrite. His words touched my heart and my conscience.

"Well, Gelsey, I don't suppose anything I say will change your mind. If you have to go, you have to go—you know best."

He was precocious and flippant. Did I know best? I tried to make myself feel better by telling him, "But, Tobias, you can visit me any time you want." His eyes were saying good-bye forever. He gave me chills. I figured he knew something. That child knew something about "Cheddar"—something that part of me knew as well, something that part of me denied.

I thought I was madly in love. In retrospect, none of the emotions seems to have had any reality, as in a dream recalled. The bond between us was only chemical, the images created by an idled brain. Yet at the time, I assumed that what I thought and felt under the influence had been me, or a part of me that Patrick had elicited. The delusion of the drug was absolute, impenetrable. My life had already become a function of induced need, of fantasy, of craving. But why was I vulnerable? Why did I surrender? Why was I, of all people, unable to understand or resist? That I was unable to ask such questions is the gist of an answer.

Patrick and I had consumed an extraordinary amount of cocaine on that fateful evening. When he returned, we picked up, more or less, where we left off. Both of us were scheduled to dance with ABT. We were scheduled, in fact, to open as partners in a pas de deux called *Pas d'Esclave* on the upcoming winter tour. By the time we began to rehearse that ballet, its title had taken on a certain irony: it was a dance of slaves.

A routine began that had Patrick moving between my new apartment in the Olcott and the place he shared with Teresa at Sixty-second Street and Columbus. Patrick also stayed with his friend "Oliver Stone," a fellow dancer who had an Upper East Side apartment. Ollie quickly became the third member of our "cocaine klatch." There were other dancers and theatre personnel involved with drugs at various times—an ever-increasing number —but in the beginning I knew and cared only about Patrick. He was my "connection." I was hooked on him and on the coke, which we also referred to as "blow." I suspected the name derived from the expression "blow your brains out," which was what we did.

When Patrick first returned from Europe, I indulged only when he stopped by my apartment. He was the one who picked up the drug, usually buying from a dealer—supposedly a middle-aged painter—who had a loft in an office building a couple blocks from ABT's downtown studios. There were nights Patrick spent hours in the loft, playing a card game called "Trumps." That was his story, anyway. I was never sure where he was. He had a million stories.

I had not been introduced to the dealer. I was thus completely dependent on my lover to provide for me. Patrick insisted that cocaine was not something to be done every day. It was supposed to be a "recreation." He warned me, "You know you're in trouble when gobs of skin come out of your nose in the morning." He also said, "Shooting up is best for sex. One day we should do it together." I had an aversion to needles. I would never inject cocaine, though I would follow Patrick's lead in other ways.

At about the time rehearsals began in the fall, Patrick left town for a short concert tour. Without the prospect of his visits, I decided to buy a quantity of the drug on my own, a private stash to keep in reserve. Since cocaine is an appetite suppressant, I conned myself, rationalizing the purchase as a dietary aid. It seemed a preferable form of the diseases from which I already suffered. I thought of it as a kind of cure. Just a couple of years later, Patrick would suggest to my mother that I see his doctor and offered the opinion: "Taking cocaine is better for her than taking ipecac to throw up." Even I knew that what he said was preposterous. It was a lie that previously I had fed him. I found my own excuses most difficult to believe when they came from somebody else's mouth.

When Patrick left town, I borrowed a couple of thousand dollars from an old friend of mine. Then I asked Ollie, Patrick's sidekick, to make a visit to the dealer for me. I hoped to get about half an ounce, maybe a dozen grams or so. Ollie was reluctant until I offered to split it with him. He was afraid that Patrick would find out. I promised never to tell.

I went to Ollie's apartment to pick up the goods late in the evening. The two of us went through four or five grams in approximately that many hours. We were drinking beer, sitting on the floor of his living room. The cocaine seemed to increase my tolerance for alcohol. I clearly remember getting up, feeling off balance, and sitting down again immediately. The next thing I knew I was looking up into Ollie's terrified face. He was holding me at an angle off the floor, saying, "Gelsey? Gelsey? Gelsey?"

I said, "What happened? What have I been saying?"

Stricken with fear, he asked, "Don't you know?"

I barely knew my name. He told me that I had been raving about what Misha had done to me. I noticed that I was across the room from where I had been sitting. With horror and confusion in his eyes, he asked, "But, Gelsey, don't you know what you did?" My head was throbbing, and my mouth felt like it was encased in ice. He answered my silence, "You had some sort of attack!"

The attack had been a brain seizure. Neither of us even knew at the time. Ollie described what had happened. I had been going on about Misha, then suddenly shrieked and collapsed on the floor. My body had become a rippling mass of involuntary twitches and constrictions. I had come close to swallowing my tongue. Ollie's description was somewhat vague. He had trouble explaining, as he was suffering from a kind of lockjaw himself. The full picture emerged later.

The gravity of the incident did not really hit me. After all, I had been unconscious. I had no real recollection. But I made Ollie promise never to tell Patrick.

I went home and doubled up in my bed. I was sick and fatigued. I slept off the episode. I continued with cocaine the very next day. I assumed that moderation would prevent any recurrence of the mysterious attack. Each line reassured me.

All of this occurred within the first month of intermittent use. There were other warning signs that I missed or ignored. Soon after Patrick began to stay with me, I noticed that he had come down with a case of boils. The angry red sores on his back and neck were hideous, but I did not suspect that deteriorating health might be related to cocaine abuse. Certain aspects of Patrick's behavior were not easy to explain away. His occasional disappearances were followed, on his return, by wild fabrications. Once he came back after several days with a hospital wristband and a prescription for Thorazine. He complained of an ulcer. His new medication was a mind-bending tranquilizer, the kind that would make an elephant forget.

The frequency of deception between us increased. Our relationship seemed to be laced with lies, yet we continued to see each other. I wondered what excuses he gave Teresa. She appeared in the hallway of my building one evening, searching for Patrick, who remained hidden in my apartment, watching quietly through the peephole. On another occasion, I chased him to her door. He emerged with a smile on his face, cool as a cucumber, snickering, as if to say, "Nothing you're saying means anything, Gelsey, you're high!"

He apparently had some difficulty deciding between Teresa and me, a chemical and emotional dilemma. I was his drug partner—she seemed to exert a sobering influence. He went back and forth several times over as many months.

The dissimulations were nothing compared to the weapons that he brought with him into my apartment. He usually kept a hatchet under the bed and a knife under the pillow. After raucous nights of snorting contests, he would pace in front of the door of the apartment, clutching a can of Mace. Ollie and I sometimes watched him for hours. We were astonished and mystified, as well as under the influence, soon realizing that so much cocaine had accumulated in Patrick's system that he was suffering from paranoia. I waited for him in bed and subsequently discovered another side effect of heavy cocaine abuse: each sexual encounter was marked by an excruciating need to release tension, which became more and more difficult.

In the wee hours, we often walked his dog, Barney, a Saint Bernard. We used to stroll along the walled border of Central Park. Patrick stopped frequently, asking me to be still so that he could listen for danger. He was sure that he had heard something, that someone was following us. This became another one of our bizarre rituals. The fear gradually became contagious: I was afraid to ask what had frightened him. Muggers? Police? His shadow?

In a sense, all fears were justified. One night at Ollie's place, Patrick and I began snapping at each other. I was fed up with the paranoia and the whole scene. In a brief moment of sanity, I screamed at the top of my lungs, "All you really care about is that coke!" He came back at me with a fury, "Look who's talking!" He was holding forth a plate of cocaine in his hands, like exhibit "A". I slapped it away, spilling the stuff all over. He watched, mouth open, as the dish flew through the air and crashed. He looked like he had seen a ghost. I backed off, lowering my voice, pleading for mercy, "Patrick, it's just that I care about what happens to you! Don't you understand? I can't stand to see this happening!"

He lunged at me and grabbed my shoulders. Then, like the Hulk, he lifted me violently into the air. I thought he was going to throw me out a window, and begged him to let me down. The incident blew over, like every other incident. We made up. I could see that his personality was changing, but I could not see the changes in my own character. It was not simply madness. It was the method of the drug, the mirror between us. We carried that mirror into the studio.

I remember vividly the first time that Patrick and I rehearsed under the spell. We spent time running between the studio and the bathroom. My entire life seemed to have relocated into the bathrooms of Manhattan, a toilet stall affording the privacy necessary to bring the habit out into public. I staked out conveniently located facilities in nearby restaurants and hotels.

We were working on *Pas d'Esclave,* a fragment from the full-length ballet *Le Corsaire.* I was hamming my way through in the tradition of the Bolshoi. The run-through with Patrick was fantastic. I was struck by one extraordinary fact, an unprecedented occurrence: I had not stopped. I had not paused to analyze my work even once. It was painless for the first time. I felt no need for refinement, for perfecting each moment, for tedious argument. I did not have to think about the dance. I did not have to think about my partner, about the drama, about the steps. I was dancing by instinct. I made no creative breakthroughs. I simply relied on the twenty years of knowledge and experience that I had to fall back on. All of the sudden, after all those long years, Balanchine's advice not to think made sense.

The lesson was driven home for me on the following day. I rehearsed without the benefit of the drug. I looked like a bundle of mannerisms, an empty bag of tricks. How had I managed the day before? There was only one explanation: the drug provided all the answers. I no longer had to fight for my ideas. I no longer had to fight to express anything. It was that realization that led me to the dealer. I wanted to arrange for a steady supply. I planned to ration myself on about a quarter gram a day.

I went for the first time to the dealer's loft, a study in bedlam and clutter. Paintings and materials were strewn everywhere. There was a Ping-Pong table in the middle of the chaos. The entire place looked like a work of modern art, something that might be found in either a gallery or a junkyard. Was that Ping-Pong table supposed to be an object of art, or just a table?

Part of the hovel was reserved for the drug trade. I saw the lines of the dealer's face in the mirror, on which he offered lines of merchandise he sold to support his habit, that of painting. I figured he had to be wealthy. He had to be getting rich just from the business he had going with me and my partner. The dealer said that he only used a quarter gram a day. That was the limit he set on his personal consumption. I was impressed that he placed such constraints on himself. It seemed an extraordinary measure of discipline.

I explained my problem in detail . . . I needed the cocaine to work . . . The drug made the work bearable . . . I was no longer a misfit in the studio. I gave him a real overview of the ballet world and my predicament. He was reluctant to undertake the responsibility of supplying me on a regular basis. He had a sense of the danger and perhaps a pang of conscience. He also understood the dilemma that I encountered in the studio, so well, in fact, that he offered a piece of incredible advice: "Gelsey, it's really you, not the coke. Next time you rehearse, just pretend you are doing coke. Just try to act like you did when you rehearsed on the drug."

He was telling me to pretend that I was under the influence—not to dance more expressively, but to avoid the problems I had in the theatre, to avoid being an artist. That was the secret of my addiction. I did not want to escape from the world—from Misha, from his theatre, from Balanchine and his theatre, from the whole world of dance—I wanted to fit in for once, to conform. Only the drug enabled me to work and dance that way—without conscience.

I eventually overcame the dealer's resistance to my idea, telling him that cocaine would prevent me from poisoning myself with ipecac, that I would control my weight with the daily dose of blow. He saw me as a lady in distress.

The problem was that I could not completely kill my conscience, even with the drug. I was ashamed. I withdrew from my friends and family. How could I face them? I resented them. They reminded me of what I had become. I had to keep my dirty secret from them at all costs. I was addicted. I was a junkie. The guilt was agony. Even when I admitted to myself that I needed help, the shame and the fear overwhelmed me.

The drug did not in any way enhance my dancing. I remember when Misha came to the studio to watch me rehearse a solo from Pas d'Esclave. He came by to coach me. I could hardly see straight. I was sure that he knew. I was shaking. My nose was running. I buckled over on pointe. One of my ankles kept collapsing under me as I tried to hop. I apologized and started over, again and again. Misha never said a word. Was he blind? Had he never seen the signs before? Had he never seen the wadded tissues and bottles of Dristan, the knowing glances that passed between the dancers who shared the secret and the habit?

Complaining and worrying about Misha and the theatre was a pastime I shared with Patrick. He bragged about taking Misha into the men's room at Johanna's Restaurant and offering him some lines. That was supposed to mean that Patrick "had something on Misha." He had set Misha up. A waitress had seen them go into the rest room together. Patrick told the story to our dealer, who laughed and said, "Come on, Patrick, you have nothing on the guy. What do you think you have?" And, of course, Misha has recently denied ever taking illegal drugs.

Patrick looked like a kid mobster who had just had his favorite tommy gun taken away from him. I was his moll. His story had a long lasting and disturbing impact on me. When Misha later told me "you have to know how to separate work and play," I assumed that he was chiding Patrick and me for not being able to control ourselves. That line—separating work and play— would be key to the theatre's policy with regard to drugs for the next several years, sealing my fate.

The dealer later asked me, pointing to Patrick, who was unshaven and slumped in a chair, "Gelsey, look at him! What are you doing with him, anyway? I mean, it's not like he's Nijinsky! I know what your problem is— you need motivation and you picked him to follow. One day Patrick is going to walk to a bridge and jump. And you will trot after him and jump—just because you have nothing better to do. Come on, Gelsey, look at him! What are you doing with that?" Patrick just grumbled. I did another line. So did the dealer. So did Patrick.

I thought about the gun that the dealer kept in his loft. I had come into a world where violence was not imaginary. That may be reason enough not to mention the dealer's name. The drug trade is a hierarchy of retailers and wholesalers, cutthroat and organized. Why risk retaliation from someone at the bottom of the pyramid? This moonlighting painter, however dangerous, was certainly no mastermind. Perhaps someday he and his kind will be brought to justice. Or maybe his own lifestyle will be the end of him.

Patrick pointed out one day that my daily consumption would be interrupted by touring. He also raised the shocking possibility that the dealer might not always be dependable. Sometimes the stuff did not come in on time. It had to be smuggled. There were, after all, risks and uncertainties in the drug trade. That was news to me. I desperately sought several other connections around the company. Every time I heard the news of a police crackdown or bust of dope dealers, I worried that my supply might be cut off. It was as if I were part of a criminal conspiracy. In retrospect, I suppose that I was.

With the season and the tour closing in fast, I was desperate. The rehearsal process was an ordeal in itself. I watched Misha edit *Giselle* in the fashion of a Hollywood movie, streamlining the production for the modern audience. He consulted during one of the early rehearsals with Nora Kaye, who had been one of the producers of *The Turning Point.* I kept waiting for the credits to roll at the end, when Misha strewed his flowers at the grave. I had already relinquished my ability to complain about such artistic matters but that did not stop me from trying.

When he decided to bring in Balanchine's *La Sonnambula* for the company and cast me in the lead, I asked to have Allegra Kent coach me. She was the one dancer most identified with the part of the Sleepwalker. If I had to dance the ballet, I wanted her insights, whatever they may have been. I suggested the idea to Misha. He humored me for a while, but his final response was an abrupt dismissal, "Oh, Gelsey, she's too crazy." I had to settle for Misha's chosen assistant, who was pulled from the New York City Ballet. In the past, I would simply have gone outside the theatre for coaching, to Allegra or to Pilar. But with the drug mentality, I had neither the initiative nor the pride. I blamed the director for both his lack of direction and mine. I was more powerless than ever.

There were so many nightmares. Patrick and I saw so many sunrises, staying up sometimes for three days in a row. We were frequently late for rehearsals and classes, or missed them entirely. On one occasion, I came late to rehearse with Georgina, who was working as ballet mistress. She said she would go through anything with me. But how could I confide in her? How could I ask her for help?

Georgina was hurt by my request for her to leave the studio. I wanted fifteen minutes to work on my own. She informed Misha, who accused me in his office of wasting my friend's time and not respecting my elders. I blew up, throwing a wadded ten-dollar bill at him and offering a snide comment, "Will this take care of it?" He threw the bill back at me, yelling, "Ve don't vant your money—ve vant you on stage!" He had every right to throw me out of the theatre and never allow me to return, but for some reason, nothing happened. Georgina and I tried to make amends and finished the rehearsal.

There were warnings from management about punctuality and dependability to both Patrick and me. Drugs were never mentioned. Bissell seemed to have both the ability to clean up his act at a moment's notice and an unsuspected talent for diplomacy. I thought he might be stabbing me in the back. I also knew, or part of me knew, that I had become my own worst enemy. On a bleak afternoon in early December 1980, I called Joyce Moffatt, the company manager. She was at home, an apartment in midtown. I needed to open up to someone. Someone had to know the truth. Someone had to help.

Joyce received me warmly. She always did. She led me down a long hall and invited me to sit with her. She was on the young side of middle age, kind in her way, always very professional. I began to tell her about Patrick, about Misha, about everything under the sun. I doubt that I made any sense. I had already committed a thoroughly absurd error in judgment, a typical cocaine blunder. I had decided to bring along a kitchen knife that Patrick had been keeping under his pillow. It was the only piece of damning evidence that I could think of to show her, to make her believe me. She had to see how far gone we were. As soon as Joyce saw the knife, she bristled and made it clear she did not want to know about any personal matters. Then she encouraged me toward the door. I was defeated. Later, she would informally suggest a doctor. By that time, it was too late for me to seek help voluntarily.

I knew that I would never survive the tour. Within a week or so after my meeting with Joyce, I decided to resign from the company. I met again with Joyce, this time in her office. The first thing she said was, "Well, we're certainly wearing a lot of makeup today, aren't we?" It was an innocent comment, but I was thrown. I told her that I had to leave the company: there were too many "artistic" problems. Joyce called in the executive director of the American Ballet Theatre Foundation, Herman Krawitz, the man who had hired Misha. I repeated my artistic complaints regarding *Giselle* and *La Sonnambula*. I told him that Misha never listened to me. Herman was professionally sympathetic. He asked me about *The Nutcracker*, if I weren't "grateful" for all that Misha had done for me. I was outraged.

Herman, a proper administrator, convinced me to meet him and Joyce downtown for a meeting with Misha at the ABT studios. I took the subway and found a quiet spot to prepare chemically for the showdown. The meeting was a scream. When we began to talk about the artistic direction, I threatened to storm out. Misha said, "Look, she leaves, just like child." I turned around fuming. I made a point about *La Sonnambula* and Allegra Kent that hit him between the eyes, and he stormed out. I said, "Look, who is the child now." Herman and Joyce did their best to assure me that everything would work out. Not to worry. I acquiesced. I was a bomb, ticking.

Misha and I were scheduled to dance the Robbins ballet *Other Dances* in Boston the following night. After leaving Herman and Joyce, I was approached by Charles France. I followed him into his office where he told me that a new costume had been ordered for me. I was informed that I "simply" had to wear mauve rather than blue. It seems that Misha had lost his blue boots and had only a mauve pair in reserve. I had to match.

Charles pointed to a picture on his desk, a photograph of one of two dancers who had recently been fired by the company. "Isn't it a shame! Look what can happen if you're not careful," he said, indicating the picture. Both of the dancers had been heroin users. The drug had caused their bodies to bloat. I had noticed that they wore long-sleeved garments to the studio, but I had not suspected the problem at first. They were fired for breach of contract, for not upholding the professional standards of the company. They had been warned; they failed to heed the warnings. I did think it was a tragedy. Heroin was a horrifying drug.

Charles had apparently tried to get one of the unfortunate dancers into therapy. He seemed to have the best of intentions. I had not yet heard the rumors that he had his own occasional indulgence with a different substance —an indulgence shared with two other dancers. These two friends of his would be pushed too rapidly within the company—in my opinion—with a reckless disregard for their talents. Charles apparently was another one who knew how to separate work and play.

I stayed up most of the night with a seamstress and the rest of the night by myself. On the following day, I made a mad dash to pick up the new costume, and more cocaine, and nearly missed my flight to Boston. I arrived at the theatre at the last minute. Misha was waiting for me, leaning against a piano. He glared at me. He had every right to be furious. He was tapping one of his mauve boots on the floor.

This was my first performance under the influence of the drug. I was a total wreck. I was dying. Both my brain and my body were out of order. He had to have known. Misha had to feel the hesitations, the cold detachment. I felt like I was stumbling. I remember the final moments, my last turn and jump onto his shoulder. I landed with what sounded to me like a dull thud, as he took my weight. We were now even for every past lift. I was entirely to blame, and I knew . . . I knew. I was more than embarrassed. Misha said nothing.

Nobody else noticed. The Boston *Globe* reported on December 6, 1980: "Kirkland is like some lyrical phenomenon of nature, a willow bending beside singing waters." The Boston *Herald American* was even more confusing:

In "Other Dances," to the music of Chopin, he [Misha] leaped and bounded and spun through the air impressively, but not dazzlingly. Miss Kirkland, on the other hand, created a great stir. A small wistful waif in a diaphanous brown [sic] tutu, no bigger than a child, she floated in from some glen in Fairyland, took to the air as if there were no such force as gravity, coming down from time to time to nestle in Misha's strong arms. Lovely. A nice way to end a grand gala.

What was I supposed to think? I tried not to. But I knew. Line after line, I knew. I had conned the audience.

Three days later, on December 9, rock star John Lennon was gunned down by a disturbed character who happened to be involved with cocaine. At the time, I was at the home of my friend and hair designer, Patrik Moreton. We were within earshot of the fatal bullet. Patrik interrupted my sentence about Misha to say, "What was that?" Later, after hearing the story on the radio, I raced across town to Ollie's apartment. It was big news, a tragedy that seemed to be wired into the brains of everyone I knew.

After opening the front door, I found Ollie and Patrick Bissell standing by the fireplace of the apartment. I announced what had happened, but neither of them showed the slightest interest. As I walked across the living room toward them, I could see that Patrick had something in his hands and was banging away on Ollie's arm. I had a hard time believing my eyes. When I saw the bruises on Patrick's arm and realized what he was doing to Ollie, I attacked.

Screaming like a madwoman, I jumped on Patrick and tried to wrestle the thing out of his hands. "He's your friend! What are you doing to him! Stop! Give that to me!"

He picked me up over his head and walked toward the front door. I cried out and frantically tried to wrench myself free. I kicked and yelped, "Let me down! Let me down, you bastard! Ollie! Help!" Ollie was paralyzed.

Patrick released me, none too gently. Then he started banging his own arm with the needle. I went at him again, and he pushed me away, rushing into the bathroom, slamming the door behind him.

I beat on the door and pleaded with him. I was scared for his life. There was no sound from the inside. I tried to kick my way in—I made a hole straight through the wood. At that point, he opened the door. He was pitiful, saying slowly, "How the hell am I gonna cover this one up?" His arm was a mess. He was scheduled for a dress rehearsal of *Pas d'Esclave* with me on the following day in Washington, D.C. His costume was shirtless. I scolded him. He snarled, "Who the fuck are you to talk about my behavior? You do what you goddamn please, don't you!" What could I say?

The three of us—Ollie, Patrick, and I—stayed up late indulging in the usual fashion. The two of them guzzled down Valiums. They were able to sleep. I caught not a single wink. I had not yet been clued to the fact that America's popular prescription drug could be used to balance the nervous energy that gradually accumulated with cocaine. My mind buzzed for hours, like a radio that would not turn off.

In the morning, I woke Ollie and tried to rouse Patrick. He seemed to be stone dead. He had taken a barbiturate of some kind. I set out with Ollie, who had an earlier rehearsal in Washington, and prevailed on him to accompany me to the dealer's loft. After replenishing my stash, I returned to wake Patrick. Ollie left for the airport.

After I shook him, Patrick opened one of his eyes and said, "I know what you did! I saw you!" He was accusing me of failing to wake him and sneaking out to buy more cocaine. He unnerved me. We debated the logistics of taking action, of dancing, of not dancing. Should we call and cancel? Should we go and try to make the stage rehearsal? Patrick advised me not to call, not to go. He tried to seduce me. The phone rang. It must have been his manager. With time running out, Patrick suddenly announced, "Let's go! We're gonna dance." With my head spinning out of control, I was instructed to meet him as soon as possible at Teresa's apartment. She was already in Washington. I had to go to my place to pack. It was futile. Exhaustion and paranoia had taken a heavy toll. Patrick and I were both in trouble. Or so I thought.

When I arrived at Teresa's apartment, I felt and looked like an escaped convict. A street thug. A murderess. Wearing a smart shirt, Patrick stood with his manager, who was clad in a business suit, briefcase in hand. My partner in crime had transformed himself. He had shaved and bathed and recovered. He looked ready for a court appearance with his lawyer.

Patrick and I rushed to the airport, en route to Washington. At his request, I bought a ticket for his dog, Barney. Rush. Rush. Rush. We were already hopelessly late.

Unbeknownst to me, the decision had already been made to fire us. After arriving in Washington, Patrick revealed a number of surprises he had up his sleeve. He first ditched me for Teresa. She had been waiting faithfully for him to arrive and looked glamorous in her fur coat. The two of them made a pretty picture. She would provide a respectable cover and perhaps an alibi. They rushed away for a meeting with the company brass, Herman Krawitz and Joyce Moffatt. Either Patrick or his manager had already arranged for him to tell his side of the story.

The story came out like this: Patrick had made no effort to make the rehearsal because he knew that his partner did not intend to show. That tale may not have prevented his dismissal, for "breach of contract," but it might help get him rehired. Who was I to pass judgment?

Patrick and Teresa presumably retired to their hotel room. I waited the rest of the evening to see Herman and Joyce. I raced frantically between hotels, the Guest Quarters, Howard Johnson's, and the Watergate. I met with the two company officials in their room in that hotel remembered as the location for political conspiracy. I was broken. They were merciless, ice cold, and very professional. I blathered about the pressure, about the way the theatre treated its dancers, dancing them to death and throwing them away without gratitude. I told them how my partner in *The Leaves Are Fading,* Charles Ward, told me not to apologize for making demands on him. Chuck had listened to me. Why could Herman and Joyce not listen to me? Why was Misha not present? I was humiliated. But I had no right to talk. I was out of practice in the honesty department.

Drugs were not discussed. They were not to be discussed. That subject was strictly taboo as far as the theatre's managers, administrators, and directors were concerned. That was "policy." The official story was that Patrick and I had been fired for missing rehearsals. The board, rather than Misha, assumed responsibility for the action.

The theatre was attempting to protect our civil liberties, although nothing was mentioned about that at the time. I learned years later that neither Herman nor Joyce wanted to invade my privacy or infringe on my rights. Their intentions were as pure as the driven snow. What could my personal life and problems possibly have to do with the business of running the company? They had nothing against me. They thought of drugs as they thought of alcohol. Show business was full of hard-drinking, hard-luck cases.

How could the theatre afford to deal with the drug problem? How could the theatre afford to deal with a public scandal? How would such a scandal affect the reputation and box office of a major cultural institution? How would a scandal affect Misha's directorship? Why should the theatre accept either the responsibility or the financial burden of providing professional counseling and care for those dancers affected by drug and alcohol abuse? What kind of policy could be formulated to cope with drugs and protect both the theatre and the dancers? How could management, which was not immune to abuse itself, either implement or enforce such a policy with the dancers?

I never heard any of those questions asked at the time. I suspect that they were asked, perhaps whispered privately. I know they had some bearing on the events that followed. Had they been asked openly, I might not have wasted the next three and a half years, driving myself to death's door.

Faced with unemployment, I had only three questions: How could I get more cocaine? How could I get the money to continue to get more cocaine? How could I find Misha?

I wanted to apologize to Misha. That night, I went back into the Watergate, snuck past the front desk, and wandered through the hallways—listening for his voice and looking the wrong way through the peepholes of various hotel rooms. I was out of my mind. I thought that I heard Patrick and Misha talking behind one of the doors. I fled.

I made plans to fly back to Manhattan. On my way out of the Watergate, I saw Patrick. He asked me, "Sure you don't want to stick around to meet my mother?" I guess he was having a family reunion. I hurried away and back to New York. After borrowing money, I bought more coke. Then I flew back to Washington and made an appointment to see Misha.

After more waiting and worrying, I met with him in his hotel suite. Our encounter was formal, distant, and brief—what might have been expected under the circumstances. We sat across from each other. I think he realized the effort that I was making, though he did not appear comfortable. I began, "Misha, I'm just here to explain something to you. Have you ever heard the word 'scapegoat'?"

He nodded, and I continued, doubtful that he knew the meaning of the word. "Well, I used you as my scapegoat. I just pulled any old problem out of the trunk and tried to use it to put all of the blame on you . . . to cover for myself. Do you understand?"

He nodded again. I swallowed the lump in my throat and tried to hold back a gush of tears. "Well, Misha, I have to try to get better. And I just hope, well, that you are still around to dance with if I do. That's all I really wanted to say."

He said he understood. We said our good-byes. I left, thinking I had taken a first step, looking forward to the next line.

Chapter Eleven

A BORDERLINE CASE

After my meeting with Misha, I went into hiding at the Howard Johnson's Motor Lodge in Washington, D.C. I was exhausted, ashamed. Two days later, I was awakened by a maid and uniformed security guard. The room looked like it had been ransacked. The sheets had been torn. The headboard of the bed and adjoining nightstand had been broken. Still fully dressed, I slowly recollected that I had been searching for a place to stash the coke before "crashing"—that is, before the mental and physical crash that came as the effects of the drug wore off. I had ripped the room apart and passed out.

When the hotel employees found me, the coke was still in plain sight, an open envelope at my side. In a panic, I scooped up the packet and stuffed it into one of my pants pockets. I tried to explain that I had overslept, as if that were not as obvious as my runny nose and red eyes. I was guilty. I was ready to confess to everything and go to jail. Yet neither the maid nor the guard seemed to have noticed the incriminating evidence. After they left the room, I scrambled to pack, petrified that they might call the police.

I needed a line. With my heart banging in my chest, I locked myself in the bathroom and inhaled several quick blasts of confidence. Deciding against a shower or a change of clothes, I rushed to check out. I boarded a plane for New York. Had I been followed? Had anyone from the company seen me? I spent the flight making trips up and down the aisle of the cabin, reassuring myself in the miniature rest room, the walls closing in at thirty thousand feet.

Back in Manhattan, I moved into the Upper West Side apartment of a friend who happened to be out of town. When Christmas arrived, I went on a holiday coke binge, lasting several days. The euphoria turned to paranoia on the eve of my twenty-eighth birthday, December 29, 1980. In the middle of the night, I paced at the front door of the apartment. I shook with fear, recalling an incident that had occurred about a year earlier. I had been approached in the studio by a deranged fan, a bespectacled young woman who seemed harmless enough at first. She later harassed me, somehow finding my phone number and repeatedly calling my apartment. Her only purpose was to warn me that Misha was plotting to assassinate me. The memory spooked me. I was now crazy enough to believe almost anything.

On the afternoon of my birthday, John Hemminger, the husband of one of the dancers at ABT, called to wish me well and to check on my condition. He told me that one of his friends, a rock musician, had recently died of an overdose. Was I taking care of myself?

I did not know John well. I thought he was a sleazy character, the sort who might otherwise be called a smooth operator. Some months later, I would not think twice about sharing my habit with him on occasion. He had his own coke connections. The chain of buyers and sellers seemed to be endless.

I had become a little monster, but the metamorphosis of my personality had only just begun. I had new friends and new beliefs. Not only had I been introduced to the drug, I had been indoctrinated into a way of thinking, and I had been initiated into a social world. That world was not located at the fringe of society, but at the center of the respectable mainstream. In the company of fellow users, I did not have to feel ashamed, or defeated, or depraved. I was not alone anymore.

My life and art disintegrated. Not only had my privacy been invaded by the drug, but my integrity had been violated and compromised. My thoughts and actions bordered on the criminal, however deluded I may have been. The criminality and consequent dangers were offset by the glamour and romance, by the perverse thrill. It seemed that I was getting away with murder.

My personal values changed with one sweeping moral collapse, a dissolution that continued over many months. The changes were no more perceptible to me than an alteration of mood. I was simply doing my own thing, living according to the modern code: "sex, drugs, and rock and roll." I was a latecomer to the Age of Aquarius. My artistic license, however fraudulent, seemed to justify each act of degradation. I gave myself to each experience.

My lack of education does not explain the tragedy. There were deeper causes that made me a willing victim, an accomplice in my own destruction, even a villainess. My downfall was not only a triumph of the monstrous side of my personality, but the seductive and vacuous side of our culture. Maybe I should have known better. Maybe our culture should have known better. If I were poisoned, who poisoned me? Had I chosen to poison myself? Why would I make such a choice? Why would anyone encourage me to make such a choice? Could anyone be that evil? I was not yet capable of asking such questions.

Cocaine still seemed to be a godsend. The social setting of the dance world had insulated me, and I had isolated myself. I mistakenly identified my artistic ideals as the cause of all my maladies. The drug allowed me to adjust, to adapt to anything and anyone. I saw my firing as an unfortunate failure of control. I had not been careful enough, a judgment made by the drug itself.

My flight from creative responsibility was a misguided attempt to stay with the theatre. I belonged to the theatre, just as I belonged to cocaine. At the mercy of the stage and the white powder, I stepped into a new series of vicious circles. My delusions were reinforced by the personal and professional rationalizations of those individuals who tried to help me. My compulsion played into the hands of those who manipulated me, who pushed me inside and outside the theatre. What would I not do or pay to relieve the pain of my existence?

Everyone told me to continue to dance. My mother, who knew nothing about the drugs at first, was afraid that I would lose the last threads of my identity if I left the stage. That was the point of view of those who truly cared. That was also the point of view of those who cared for my ability to make money—for them. The intentions mixed, always leading to the same conclusion: I had to dance . . . I had to make money . . . How else could I afford cocaine? . . . How could I dance without cocaine?

At the beginning of 1981, I moved again, into another apartment on the West Side, this one in the Upper Eighties. It was gloomy and huge, a hole in which to bury myself. I tried to put up a front, a veneer of normalcy and health. I kept the refrigerator filled, as usual, with toe shoes. My mother especially had to be deceived. Whenever she visited, I made sure the place was immaculately clean, hiding any sign of drugs, of disorder. I tried to impress her with my independence. I was on my own again.

My mother expressed her concern one afternoon, driving through Manhattan to drop me at my place. She was secretly worried that I might be depressed, that I might even be suicidal. Knowing without doubt that I was troubled and erratic, she suggested that I seek counseling. I sensed her unspoken fears.

Seething with hostility, I said, "Don't worry about me! I know what I'm doing! I know all about suicide . . . The most convenient way for people to kill themselves is to find someone to do it for them . . . All you have to do is fall in love with the right person!"

My outburst had a ring of truth. I managed to put her off and reassure her. Looking back at these difficult times, my mother remembers that I often sounded quite convincing, that I seemed to be making progress.

In order to give the appearance that I was helping myself, which I half-believed, I began seeing a psychiatric social worker who had an office in the neighborhood. She was young, intelligent, and sincere. I missed about as many appointments with her as I had earlier missed rehearsals. She knew less about dance than I knew about psychology.

The analyst offered no insights into my problems, but she did provide a sympathetic ear. I never informed her about my secret life. Before walking through her door, I usually snuck a line from my pocketbook, then sat uncomfortably through the session. Did she realize that I was drugged? The symptoms of cocaine use surely distorted the tales I told about my traumatic past. She probed the surface of my stories. I marveled at how easily I could mislead her.

There was no way that I would ever deal with the underlying problems as long as the drug made my decisions for me. My judgment was twisted even when the coke was not in my system. Running out of funds, I became desperate and melancholy, sometimes having to remain straight and cranky for days. I planned my entire routine around that next line, whenever it might come. The drug had become more essential for me than the dance.

I could foresee the dismal end of my life and counted on being utterly numb when the time arrived. The only drawback about death would be my inability to indulge with my nose in the grave.

I had drifted away from Barna. She called me one evening in January. Her tone was firm. "Gelsey, things are not working out between us." I was actually relieved that she made it so easy for me. She was in the way: what I had cherished about her for so long had become a threat to my continued affair with the drug. After hanging up the phone, I spoke to the walls of my living room: "I could never be like her anyway. I tried, I tried, and look what happened." She was too honest, too dear. I needed someone to whom I could lie with impunity.

I turned to Patrick and his manager, Alex. Speaking on Patrick's behalf after the dismissal from ABT, Alex had pinned the rap on me—as reported in the Washington *Post* back in December. While I remained intimidated and silent, the public statements from the other side confirmed a cynical philosophy that I now saw as the key to my survival. Alex had exactly the kind of professional scruples and business sense that would keep me dancing. His intentions were calculated enough to fit on an accountant's ledger. I would use him, and vice versa. In fact, over the next couple of years, Alex would know me well enough not to want to know what each cash advance was being used to finance. When Patrick moved into a new apartment, Alex would ask me if he were dealing drugs. I had no idea.

Thanks to Alex, I performed for a television audience of six million in the second week of February. The occasion marked the ninetieth anniversary of Carnegie Hall. I danced *The Dying Swan,* a three-minute piece originally choreographed by Michel Fokine for Anna Pavlova. Set to Saint-Saëns's score, an excerpt from *Carnival of the Animals,* the ballet was a study in despair, of resignation to death, yet another mirror of my life and times.

Reviewing films of Maya Plisetskaya and Natasha Makarova, I rehearsed over a two-day period, a whirlwind. The technical challenge, coordinating upper- and lower-body movement, was akin to patting my head and rubbing my stomach at the same time. The drug turned simple pathos into something grotesque. The show was successful. I was accompanied by the famous violinist Isaac Stern and by Lise Nadeau on the harp. The piece actually had been intended for cello. Nobody seemed to mind. Nobody even seemed to notice the strange look on the face of my swan. I felt like a cooked goose.

There was evidently a place for junkies in the ballet world. Alex set up a series of concerts, sometimes teaming me with Patrick. We performed the *Don Quixote* pas de deux for the Eglevsky Ballet. I was plump with the weight gained from sweets and eating binges that became part of the drug routine. A review by Arlene Croce, dated February 23, 1981, was searing and only too accurate: "It was the saddest exhibition given by a dancer whose artistry is increasingly placed at the service of a gift for mimicry. She's dancing the public's idea of Gelsey Kirkland as a star." I had become a cheap imitation of myself. In fact, I was working entirely by imitation.

Patrick and I continued our escapades even as he continued to see Teresa. I remember a night during this period when he brought a syringe to my apartment. The injection of cocaine was supposed to be a grand prelude to sex. I was still hostile to the idea, but more curious now, after about six months of nasal ingestion. Patrick wanted to demonstrate the safety of the procedure.

He tried the needle route alone in my bathroom and emerged looking like a mummy, his skin gray, almost translucent. He rasped, "Where's the garbage? You can't do this, Gelsey! The coke is too strong to shoot! I thought it might be! I'm throwing this needle out! Where's the garbage?"

Patrick kindly deposited the syringe in the trash and advised me never to try shooting up the drug. I did not need to be convinced. To stave off an overdose, he immediately did some push-ups, drank a beer, took a hot bath, and gulped down a Valium. He was lucky. So was I. The mechanical release of sexual tension followed. What passed as tenderness was nothing but shared vapidity, like an endless tango. I was cast in what was by now a familiar role.

Sometime in February, I visited Patrick in Toronto, where he danced *The Sleeping Beauty* with the National Ballet of Canada. Oblivious to borders, I carried along a few illicit grams. Patrick was not pleased that I had taken such a risk. He reproached me for being less able to abstain than he was. How could I leave home without it?

As I recall, we sat in a hotel room. He had no complaints as we performed the usual ritual for several hours. Then he shoved me around, for whatever reason. I retaliated, slamming a hamburger into his face. It was just a spat between what he called "special friends."

Later, in a more jovial mood, we briefly visited Erik Bruhn, the Danish artistic director and former premier danseur. Erik's words have stayed with me: "Enjoy yourselves while you can—it won't last forever!" I remember wondering if that noble Dane knew something.

Early in March, Patrick and I danced *Swan Lake* at Indiana University. He was arrested one night at the local hotel where we were staying. He had been mixing alcohol and pills. He must have been looking for trouble. Wearing no shoes and waving a liquor bottle, he instigated a brawl in the lobby, breaking glass on the desk clerk's counter. I later heard the police had taken my partner away. The following morning, I went along with an official from the local company to bail him out. Patrick's only complaint about the "misunderstanding" was that the cops had not allowed him to retrieve his shoes before carting him off. He was still in his stocking feet.

Later in March, Patrick and I were scheduled to dance at Goucher College in Maryland. Our stash of cocaine mysteriously vanished just before the performance. I suspected Patrick of foul play. I refused to perform, having already gone into the bends of a crash. Finding a replacement, he performed without me, an apparent act of show business heroism.

Both Patrick's arrest and my non-appearance were well publicized. There should have been no question in anyone's mind that both of us were operating at severely diminished capacity. We were absurdities. Nevertheless, Misha made the first overtures to rehire us at the end of March.

Reluctant to return, I rejected the first two offers. To the best of my knowledge, drugs were not mentioned during my contract negotiations. Alex, the manager, had been working diligently to have us reinstated. Both of us were back in the ABT fold by April, scheduled for the summer season.

The news of our reprieve reached us in Seattle. We were guesting with the Pacific Northwest Ballet and decided on a celebration. It was arranged that a pair of black character shoes would be sent to Patrick by Express Mail. Inside the shoes a supply of cocaine had been concealed by a friend of Patrick's, a doctor, the same charlatan who had supposedly volunteered to help my former lover Richard with an injection of heroin. This doctor was also the one who had arranged for Patrick and me to perform at Goucher College. Here was another link between the dance world and the drug world.

At the beginning of April, I gave an interview to Ken Sandler for the Washington Post. I made several true statements that rebounded to my disfavor. I said that Misha was "resistant to my ideas," that I had fought for years for better coaching, more rehearsal time, and so forth. I also said that I was no longer committed to perfection: "If I do less than my best, it's still perfectly valid. I think it's more important to dance than not to dance." Such was the pact I made with the devil.

Misha responded by telling the press that I was a "chameleon," that my contradictory public statements were meaningless. He did not say that he encouraged my change of colors. I did not say that cocaine enabled me to avoid the misery, the agony that existed in a theatre that rejected perfection in favor of expediency and box office receipts.

I recently spoke with a former member of management, who estimated the number of alcohol and drug cases, those as serious as mine, to have been a dozen at the time. That manager saw fewer than I did. Even so, twelve dancers out of ninety, or a hundred, was a percentage then roughly in line with the national figures. There seemed to have been a rise in the number of dancers who used cocaine, marijuana, amphetamines, barbiturates, and so on. I knew choreographers, conductors, musicians, teachers, stagehands, and costume people who were also involved, suffering from the same cultural disease. Had I arrived at the party late? How long had this been going on?

The company was divided between the majority who did not use drugs and said nothing, and the minority who abused drugs and said even less. Over the next couple of years, some of the critics wondered about the artistic direction and demoralization of the company. Was there a connection between drugs and the decline of the theatre? Since writing this book and interviewing a number of dancers, I have heard conflicting reports about drugs in the theatre. A New York psychiatrist confided to me that "the ballet world is riddled with cocaine," due probably to lower prices and increased availability. But one of the stars at ABT told me, "Cocaine is no longer sophisticated. None of the soloists or principal dancers does it anymore. Marijuana is another story." One member of the company is now regularly tested for cocaine abuse, though no policy seems to have been implemented for the company as a whole. Perhaps my experience has already contributed to change, at least for my generation.

I know the impact that I had on the morale of those around me. I know that cocaine directly and indirectly affected the aesthetic itself. The fate of the theatre had to be related in some way to a company mentality that was susceptible to drug abuse. The "infantilization" of dancers, their prolonged immaturity and dependency, made them especially vulnerable.

The voices of moral authority in the theatre demanded only punctuality and physical performance. In light of the continuous pressure and stress, the occasional lip service paid to moderation was meaningless. Starvation and poisoning were not excesses, but measures taken to stay within the norm, both professionally and aesthetically.

Drugs were usually available, even on tours. Some members of the company had become small-time dealers. I was told that a member of the corps held or carried a stash for one of the stars on the road. That was only a rumor, but I had no reason to disbelieve it. The dealers were warned by at least one influential member of management not to allow things to get out of hand. One of the dealers was told to stay away from me. I was out of hand.

Back with ABT, I counted myself lucky to be dancing with Misha again. During April, we performed *Other Dances* in Washington, D.C., and New York. I was high. One of the critics credited me with turning the pas de deux into "the epitome of Romanticism." I remember the first curtain call. I pulled a flower from a bouquet and held it for Misha. He accepted it without incident. At that moment, I knew how to keep peace between us: maintain outward passivity and obsequious grace. How long could I hold that pose?

On May 2, we returned to New York's Metropolitan Opera House for *Giselle.* The critics observed that Misha had changed his interpretation of Albrecht. The character was now a cynical aristocrat, toying with Giselle. The irony of art mirroring life was painful. On stage, Misha did not even watch me dancing my solo in the first act. I was still trying to win his heart, to forgive his betrayal, to find redemption. My performance, under the influence, was full of wobbles and wavering balances, a million minuscule miscalculations. Without real inspiration I would never reach my partner. He treated me as if I had the plague. My mad scene improved in terms of realism, though, overall, the kind of heroine I had shaped years before was beyond me. The audience roared. Anna Kisselgoff wrote:

> Still—"Giselle" is a ballerina's ballet, and Saturday night was clearly Miss Kirkland's triumph. She gave us a most touching Giselle, a frail childlike soul whose shattered world was inevitable.
>
> Her first act provided the only mad scene in this series to reach beyond formulas and touch the heart. Filled with pain, it presaged the particularly sad spirit of Giselle in Act II, with its sisterhood of ghostly Wilis.

Shortly after the performance, I spent a night trapped in the elevator of my apartment building. Stuck between floors, I sat and fell asleep. It was only a question of what calamity would happen next. I had moved in with designer Carl Michel. Carl was a sober friend who believed that sooner or later I would pull out of my nosedive. He fretted about my occasional spells of drugged amnesia, when he had to remind me who and where I was.

My still stalwart friend from the School of American Ballet, Meg, worked for me during that summer. Herman Krawitz had always thought I needed an assistant, someone to wake me on time, someone to get me to rehearsals and performances. Meg was a joy, a real trooper. She suffered my abuses without complaint, playing scapegoat on my behalf even with Misha.

I went to Mexico for a concert that would finance my habit for the rest of the season. When I returned to New York, Patrick hired a limousine to pick me up at the airport. I already had alcohol and Seconal in my system. Patrick provided cocaine for me and the chauffeur. The driver, a talkative wheeler-dealer, bragged of his own drug connections and exclusive clientele. His list included not only rock stars and movie stars, but various citizens above suspicion, a Who's Who of hip young professionals. The chauffeur was pleased to have two dancers to add to his directory of "beautiful people." We drove downtown and visited our dealer's loft.

Patrick and I were in hysterics by the time we arrived. I laughed so hard that I was concerned for my safety. I sat in a chair while Patrick and our host played table tennis. I fought against a queasy feeling, listening to the ball bounce back and forth. I was losing control, unable to brace myself, unable to cry for help. I blacked out.

When I opened my eyes, I was being walked around the Ping-Pong table, guided by Patrick and the dealer. I had had another brain seizure. The dealer was angry and wanted me to leave right away: he feared that I would die on the premises. Blaming Patrick, he said, "I told you to go easy on her with that stuff."

Patrick suggested that we go to Teresa's apartment. During the ride, he told me what happened. I had let out a bloodcurdling scream and flipped myself into the air, falling into convulsions. Patrick and the dealer had wrenched open my mouth and grabbed my tongue. My throat and jaw were sore and bruised. I was still soaking wet from the cold shower my companions had given me, grateful that Patrick had saved my life.

As we barged through the door of Teresa's apartment, Patrick asked her to pardon the intrusion and tried to explain that I was sick. As she was aware of my drug problem, her reaction was quick and to the point: "I want her out! Now! How dare you bring her here! Take her to a hospital! Take her anywhere. Just get her out of here! This is my house!"

Patrick picked her up roughly and set her outside the door. Eventually, she took refuge in the bedroom. While I ate and recovered, Patrick played the role of tormented soul, torn between two women. Then he took me home. Over the summer, he tried to commit himself to Teresa. He even attempted to straighten himself out. He resented me for being a bad influence. I knew only one way to hang on to him. He taught me everything I knew in that department.

Alex tried to keep Patrick and me apart, booking us separately, knowing that we were trouble whenever we were together. Patrick urged me in his way to reform, that is, he ridiculed me. He tried to limit himself to alcohol and marijuana. His holier-than-thou attitude struck me as diabolical. He told me, "You're just like my mother—maybe you should try Valium or primal scream."

Patrick moved into a new apartment near Harlem. Sleeping over on his couch one night, I nearly burned the place down. Several firemen broke through the front door and woke us. I hoped one of them would ask me to marry. I wanted to be saved. My partner had to have oxygen. The smell of smoke lingered for days.

On another occasion, I had an optic seizure while opening Patrick's refrigerator. The inside of the Frigidaire turned into a kind of black hole, sucking me into the icebox. I screamed and flipped. Patrick took me to New York Hospital and found me a neurologist. A subsequent brain scan revealed nothing.

The summer was a continuing story of embarrassing performances and oddly mixed reviews. There were ultimatums from management. I was still missing classes and rehearsals. I stayed up for days and collapsed. Who could wake me?

I put Misha in a terrible position, especially when the critics were favorable. Preparing the Ashton ballet, *Les Rendezvous,* I was supported in my choice to provide a lighthearted mood for the ballet by Georgina Parkinson. My irreverent cynicism was perhaps an unconscious attempt to imitate

Misha's style of humor. I chose what I thought he would think was appropriate for the ballet, a camp approach.

I was incapable of innovation or inspiration. I could barely breathe. In the studio, mucous flew from my nose on sharp turns. After my first performance, Misha let it be known privately that my dancing, specifically my interpretation, had disgraced the theatre. I was dreadfully embarrassed. He seemed to think that I had deliberately chosen to make fun of him.

A review of *Les Rendezvous* by Jennifer Dunning appeared in the New York *Times,* June 6, 1981: "Miss Kirkland sailed through the difficult turn sequences and the piquant inflections of the ports de bras with perfect control and an almost whimsical air."

I talked recently with one of the company managers, who had once tried to discuss the drug problem with the artistic director. He refused to hear anything about it. Apparently, he did not consider it a medical problem. He might have been trying to protect me. He might have been trying to protect the theatre. Perhaps he received legal advice. I can only guess.

Was Misha guarding my civil liberties? Was my former lover worried about invading my privacy? The conspicuous failure of anyone to speak about the drug problem unsettled me and caused me to believe any rumor about management. What did I know? I was busy trying to convince the powers that be that I was better and worth their trouble. Who was I to believe? Misha's ability to separate work and play became questionable to me whenever he blew his nose in the studio. My attitude became more hostile toward him. But Misha was still the ultimate authority for me. As incredible as it may sound, I was still trying to please him.

At the end of the summer, my contract was not renewed. Patrick met with management and fingered me as his problem. His song and dance apparently won sympathy and another reprieve. He told me later, "I said whatever I had to say to get rehired." That included tales about my seizures. Supposedly, he had been trying to save me from myself even as I lured him from the straight and narrow. I was out in the cold.

Alex continued to arrange concerts for me. As sick as I was, I must have been a real problem to handle. Nevertheless, he kept me in tow, cajoling me and assuring others that I was dependable. I was both a name he valued to attract other clients and an erratic burden.

Chicago was a new lowpoint. Patrick and I were included in the "International Festival of Stars," scheduled for the end of June. We were to dance the second act pas de deux of *Giselle* and the pas de deux from *Don Quixote.* The show was organized by an enterprising woman named Geraldine Freund. She was unspeakably ancient, wealthy, and bizarre. She prayed for me. Her husband, a physician, informally suggested I probably just needed the right medication. What did he know about me? Everybody had advice.

The performances were horrifying. Patrick and I lost control entirely on the stage. We were staggering from days and nights of debauchery. With one arm, he lifted me into the air and almost fell over. Dancers yelled from the wings, "Put her down! Put her down!" Some of those dancers wept.

Shortly after that debacle, we went to Philadelphia. Our performances improved technically. Patrick tried to convince Natasha Makarova and her assistant, Dina, that he was misunderstood. His message was underscored by an apparent attempt at suicide. At the hotel where the dancers were staying, Natasha was awakened in the middle of the night by a call from Patrick. He was in bed, covered with blood, having inflicted a few superficial wounds. The rescue squad patched up my uncooperative partner, who broke a bottle and tried to resist treatment. He performed the next day with a bandage on one of his wrists.

In Denver, performing *Giselle* with Patrick, I appeared to be relatively in command on the stage. My dresser for the occasion supplied the coke. I made a special effort to hide my dark secret because my half brother, Chris Kirkland, had organized the performance at the Elitch Theatre. Local critic Irene Clurman noted my "breathtaking inspiration" and wrote, "Kirkland's featherweight dancing and effortless balance and Bissell's heroic overhead lifts were heartstopping . . ." Someone should have taken a long hook and jerked me off the stage.

In September I was scheduled with Danilo Radojevic, another ABT principal, in New Orleans. Our appearance was intended to promote a new ballet company. The trouble began when I ran out of coke. A musician gave me an amphetamine, a pill called a "black beauty," something similar to the vitamin I had received from Mr. B years before. During the intermission, two local managers stormed into my dressing room to complain about my dancing in *Tchaikovsky Pas de Deux.*

When they entered, I was half-dressed, snipping my toe shoes with a pair of scissors. I screamed for the intruders to get out. A doctor in the house decided I was homicidal and probably psychotic. The man who organized the performance, Brooke Cadwallader, came to my defense. He knew me well enough to know that I was harmless—to others. I was prevented from continuing the scheduled program.

In late September or early October, I had another brain seizure in New York. I was rehearsing with Patrick in Robert Denvers's studio near Lincoln Center. Alex was present. I heard him on the phone speaking with a level voice: "She's out of control." His office was a block away. His associate, Isabelle, arrived and they accompanied me by taxi to New York Hospital.

I was both terrified and relieved. I assumed the truth would finally come out, that I would finally get some help. I stayed at the hospital for three days. My mother visited. Sitting in a wheelchair, I told her, "I guess I always knew this is where I would end up."

The neurologist suggested that I be moved to the Westchester Division of New York Hospital. He was a fan of mine. He said, "It would be a shame to lose what you love most." The Westchester facility was supposed to be better equipped to deal with me. I assumed I was going into some kind of detoxification program. My mother and my friend Dina Makarova drove me out of Manhattan. Before leaving, I raised some money and stopped to pay off a debt to a dope dealer. My mother felt like she was driving a getaway car. My mind was clearing. There were moments of lucidity. Excited about the prospect of reclaiming myself, I wanted my slate to be clean.

I had sworn off cocaine for seventy-two hours. The withdrawal symptoms took the form of lethargy and a craving for sugar. In the back seat of my mother's car, I ate candy and slept. To my mother, my behavior was bizarre. When did I ever eat chocolate? She was already traumatized and stigmatized by the knowledge that her daughter was a drug fiend.

We turned into the parking lot of a suburban estate. My mother and Dina escorted me into the reception area of the main building. The three of us were in for a rude awakening: it was a psychiatric hospital. That shock was followed by a more appalling realization: I was going to be locked away.

We were met by two doctors and a social worker. Mind games started immediately. My mother and I were pitted against each other. She was afraid and confused, obviously unable to handle me. She had no choice but to commit me or to convince me to voluntarily commit myself. I was enraged that the responsibility for my recovery had been taken away from me. My mother said, "Gelsey, I wish you wouldn't make me do this."

I grabbed a pen from my mother's trembling hand and signed my name on the official admitting papers. She was in tears. I was livid. Little did I know that my behavior was evidence to be used against me. I was already under observation. So was my mother.

I knew without question that I was in the wrong place. I had expected to join other addicts who were fighting to overcome drugs. Instead, I had been confined in a mental ward, surrounded by people who were seriously disturbed in other ways. It seemed that I had been coerced and institutionally railroaded. The hospital staff did not explain my rights to me. I had not read the paper that I signed.

The next day, after interviewing Dina privately, one of the therapists, a middle-aged woman, tried to turn the two of us against each other. Dina had briefed the therapist on my personal history and on the ballet world. Having worked for Misha and Natasha, my friend had always been close to the action of my life. I had always confided in her.

The therapist ushered us into an office. She twisted Dina's words for my benefit and began a provocative line of questioning: "Miss Kirkland, are you angry about what your friend said about you? Are you mad that she is leaving you here? Do you feel she is deserting you?"

The transparent attempt to incite a confrontation failed. Having seen the resentment I felt toward my mother, perhaps the therapist hoped to elicit a similar reaction from me with my friend. Dina may have been in a state of confused anguish, but she was not easy to manipulate. I knew that she had to leave for Europe to join Natasha. When Dina returned after a few weeks, she was one of my only regular visitors. I felt neither abandoned nor betrayed, simply alone.

I avoided most of the other patients. Some of them could barely put two sentences together. Some of them walked around like zombies, tranquilized by heavy doses of medication. Some of them did not move at all, as if constrained by chemical straitjackets. Some of them seemed dangerous, lurking in the doorways of their rooms. My decision not to mix with this crowd was seen as antisocial behavior. Valium was prescribed for me. My subsequent choice NOT to take drugs was seen as "resistance to therapy."

After a few days, I did make a friend among the inmates. His name was "Mickey." In his early forties, he seemed an adorable character. He looked like a cross between an Italian leprechaun and a lightweight boxer. Mickey confided that he was homosexual and formerly a heroin user, that his mother had seduced him as a child, that he was often depressed. While working for General Motors, he had run naked one day through the plant. He had a wife and two kids, a family in the Bronx, as well as a gay dealer and lover known as the "King of Harlem." I would later meet the entire family.

In the cafeteria one afternoon, Mickey tried to set me straight: "Let me tell you, Gelsey, you are going to be here for a long time! You should have seen the expressions on their faces when they brought you in. I mean, you are their little treasure now! They can't let you out. If they let you go and anything happened to you, now they wouldn't look too good, would they? And just think what they can do with you while you're here. You're famous. You've got a name. Careers are riding on you. Reputations are on the line. I mean, medical history is being made here."

Mickey informed me that I did have the legal right to check out of the hospital if I gave seventy-two hours' notice. I gave notice and crossed my fingers. After three days, a therapist convinced me to leave on a temporary pass rather than check out. Playing for time, she advised me to reconsider while on the outside. She told me that if I still felt the same way after a few days at home, I would be free to go. I believed her. She said she would hold my room while I was gone. I promised to bring back pizza for everyone.

In Manhattan, I attended a meeting of Alcoholics Anonymous and tried to put my life in order. I stayed away from drugs. I stayed away from anyone who might tempt me. A musician with whom I had had a brief affair visited me one evening at my apartment. It was the first time he had ever seen me straight. The fact that he was still interested in me was encouraging, a boost to my ego. We conversed quietly. The possibility of living without cocaine became more appealing.

By the time I returned to the hospital, I was determined to check out permanently, to seek counseling and treatment in Manhattan. I was confident that I could make progress on my own. I intended only to retrieve the personal effects that I had left in my room. I had a taxi waiting for me.

Walking into the hospital, I realized that I had forgotten to bring the pizza. It was late on a Friday afternoon. My room had been cleaned out and my belongings stored. The staff apparently had assumed that I would not be returning. My therapist, Dr. "Elizabeth Spoke," said that I would have to stay, at least for the weekend, as it was too late to do the paperwork to release me. Incensed, I remember thinking that her name sounded like spook. I had been entrapped.

Dr. Spoke made me aware that the hospital could commit me, that a case against me, a psychological profile, was already being compiled. That was the subtle threat, that I would be permanently confined by the state if I did not agree to stay for another weekend, another week, another month. My room and belongings were restored to me.

I later asked the therapist, "What is a good patient? What do I have to do to get out of here?" She replied, "A good patient is someone who says, 'Please, help me. I know I can't help myself.' Miss Kirkland, you really must cooperate with us."

I was ready to volunteer for a lobotomy. A week or two after my return, Mickey was discharged by the hospital. He had refused to go along with his doctor's plan to place him in a halfway house. We agreed to see each other someday on the outside. I was now more alone and more desperate than ever.

I received some advice from one of the other patients, an elderly woman who had been spewing word garbage when she first arrived. Her medication seemed to have taken effect. She was able to make sense to me: "Look, dear, you just watch me—how fast I get out of here! You see, I've been here before. My husband had me thrown in here. Did you see how I acted when I came in? All out of control. Well, you have to make it seem like you're getting better. So, it's good to start off really bad. Now they've given me their rotten drugs. I take them like a good girl. And I tell the doctors how much I need their help. I thank them. I tell them how they changed my life. And I'll be gone . . . in no time. You'll see. But you will never get out of here, dear, not the way you're acting. You'll learn. You have to play their game, doncha know."

The clinical setting was highly structured and regimented, a behavioral maze, a glorified zoo. The house rules made for custodial order rather than therapeutic dignity. Dignity was a word too subjective or too imprecise for the doctors. PC—Physical Contact—was strictly forbidden. I was once reprimanded for an innocent hug. Innocence was another vague word. I was under SO—Special Observation—checked every half hour or so by my keepers. My resentment about being watched, about having no privacy, was seen as symptomatic. Scrutinized, I was increasingly self-conscious about each gesture and movement.

I spent a month climbing the walls and submitting to psychological tests. My response to the Rorschach inkblots must have disappointed my therapist. I saw only insects and flowers. I guessed at multiple-choice questions. I probably exhibited a fascinating range of phobias. My mother was told that I was suffering from "extreme narcissism." It took no genius to see that I was concerned about my body image.

I was most intimidated by the chief psychiatrist, Dr. Otto Kernberg, the man ultimately responsible for my case. He reminded me of many of the choreographers I had known. During our first meeting, a kind of preliminary evaluation, I faced him in front of a small audience, a group of his colleagues, sycophants as far as I could see, which was not far. Kernberg asked me to look him in the eye and describe my problem to him. He was close enough for me to see the hairs in his nostrils, flaring ever so slightly. I stuttered and blushed. Was that blush a sign of social inhibition or an attempt to attract attention?

I recall thinking, if this patronizing character wants to make me over into his image and likeness, I would rather be dead. I was familiar with the condescending attitude, the cold neutrality, the forced smile. I gave him all the symptoms and ammunition he needed. My vacillations and discomfort at this public performance fit neatly into a syndrome that happened to be his specialty.

He asked me, still nose to nose, "Do you understand how serious your problem is?"

"Yes."

"Are you sure?"

"Yes."

I was told that I could return to the ward. Later, a therapist told me that Dr. Kernberg did not think I really knew how serious my condition was. That was reason enough to hold me. I was told that I was potentially dangerous to myself and others. My mother had informed the therapist about the episode in New Orleans, repeating the rumors that she heard. Had I not threatened someone with a pair of scissors? The prospect of a life sentence hit me. I shouted, "I never did that! Look, I admit that I may be dangerous to myself, but never, ever, have I harmed or threatened to harm anyone else —Oh no!" Technically, of course, I had given drugs to others, but that was the problem I knew I needed to solve.

Truth seemed to be an alien concept here. I was at Kernberg's mercy. Was he qualified to doctor my soul? Did he deserve my trust?

The doctor was recognized as an authority on "borderline cases." These were cases that fell somewhere between neurosis and psychosis. Funded by the Menninger Foundation and the National Institute of Mental Health, he had done years of research and authored a number of scholarly studies on the subject, including *Borderline Conditions and Pathological Narcissism.*

The borderline condition had to have been clear in my case. How else can

I explain Kernberg's behavior? The criteria for making a diagnosis had to be definite in his eyes, not gray, but black and white. Why else would he keep me locked up?

My behavior and personal history seemed to define his category. I lacked self-esteem and longed to be loved. I admitted that I felt worthless and, at the same time, expected to be treated with some respect, held in some regard as an artist, as a human being. Why did I have such an enormous need to control my own fate? Did I think I was special because of my suffering? Did I think I was entitled to dispensations?

I had ambivalent feelings about all of the significant people in my life. My mother. Balanchine. Baryshnikov. Were they good or bad, or were they good and bad? Why could I not accept them? I exhibited the same ambivalence toward the doctor and his staff. I withheld my trust, yet acted at times as if I appreciated their efforts on my behalf.

Such contradictions supposedly indicated that my personality had not integrated at some early stage of development. The same observation might have applied to virtually every dancer I knew, whether anorexic or addicted or not. Two out of every ten were trying to starve or poison themselves to death—why? Most dancers seemed to accept the popular aesthetic as well as the authority figures of the ballet world—why? Most of them adjusted—why? What made me different? What made me fight?

My mother was pinpointed as part of the problem. She sometimes came to the hospital to join in my sessions with a therapist. My mother and I were drawn into the leading questions. Our defenses were stripped away.

It was an absurdly simple con game. My mother was guilty for bringing me up to be a drug addict. I was guilty for being a drug addict and causing my mother such grief. Our feelings of guilt were yet another aspect of the problem. Nobody mentioned the fact that the drugs were pushed on me and on our culture. Nobody mentioned the possibility that the ballet world might have had some impact on my behavior, my choices. The blame was divided between mother and daughter. We fell for it.

During one of these encounter sessions, my mother broke down. The therapist accused her of harboring delusions of grandeur about my father and his aristocratic background. The implication was that my mother had deceived her children. "Mrs. Kirkland, you want Gelsey to love you, you expect her to love you, but what have you done to deserve her love? You see, you are in so much pain yourself that there is no room for your daughter's pain."

My mother was so upset that she was told to leave the room. I was astonished by the doctor's hypocrisy. My mother felt humiliated. The therapist had asked for her honesty, and then told her to take it elsewhere. The treatment was cold-blooded.

With my insurance due to run out sometime after the first month of my stay, I had another meeting with Kernberg. The scene was a replay of our earlier encounter, with a smaller audience, two therapists, including Dr. Spoke.

Dr. Kernberg began by informing me that his colleagues were in complete agreement with what he was about to say. "What I am going to tell you will cause you to become enraged, Miss Kirkland." I was angry already, simply because he presumed to know my reaction in advance. "But you are a very smart girl and I think you should be told. What you have is a disease that is so complicated that we don't even have a name for it."

He probably meant a borderline condition, for which many labels were bandied about. He paused, reading the impact of his words, then continued: "You are so completely self-destructive that, if you leave now, you will be dead within six months. Your only chance is to stay with us for two years. Even then, well, there is no guarantee, but we feel this is the only chance you have."

My temples were pounding. I had to clench my teeth not to burst. The doctor turned to the others. "Do you agree with me?"

They gave him their vote of confidence. The plan was that I would stay at the hospital and perform in New York. The perverse beauty of the idea was that my occasional performances would pay the bills. There would be someone with me at all times, a nurse waiting in the wings.

He let me know he was in control. "Now, of course, you might try to fight this decision in court and, as you are clever enough, you might convince a judge. But you really should just be grateful that you are someone who can go into the city, do your gig, come back, and be able to pay for your stay with us. Not everyone has that opportunity."

His use of the word "gig" rankled me. His sweeping prognosis stunned me. My vision was blurring when he asked, "Is there anything you want to say?"

I looked at him with sincere hatred. I hated everything about him, everything he represented. Neither his intentions nor his rationalizations would ever redeem him. I had to say something. I was not about to let this man have the last word. I forced myself to focus. "Yes, I do have something to say. And that is . . . that . . . there is something I have that you can't see. It is so small that only I know it is there." I was shaking from head to toe. My voice was cracking. "What it is . . . is hope. A little grain of hope. And no one can take that away from me."

He blinked a couple times and said, "That is an illusion."

To the extent that I accepted Dr. Kernberg's dire prognosis, I was a hopeless case. His words were a demoralizing source of doubt for the next couple of years. As much as I hated to admit it to myself, he had predicted my rage. He therefore had to know something. Part of me believed him, much as I believed the illusions of a magician. Here was a highly respected physician saying that I had a disease that was probably incurable. I would always be an addict. I would always be self-destructive. Part of me knew that his desire to modify my behavior was based on his own inadequacy, his own need to control, his own limited analytical vision. But, as long as I was bewildered enough to believe him, as long as I was unable to see through him, I was still vulnerable.

He had seen me only twice. A therapeutic alliance on his terms would never have been possible. After that second audience, I returned to my room and snorted a line of Sweet 'n Low. I called a psychologist friend of the family for his advice. His name was "Stewart." He had had an affair with me years before. He had counseled my mother. The two of them eventually came to the hospital for a meeting with Dr. Spoke, a social worker, and the other female doctor who had been present for Dr. Kernberg's production.

The atmosphere in the office was formal and tense. Sitting across from the others, I felt somewhat detached. While my fate was being discussed, I stared out the window. There was a tree, its bare branches holding more life and interest than the faces of the hospital therapists. I tuned in when Stewart put them on the defensive. He said, "If you don't yet know that this is a person who will break before she will bend, then you know nothing about her at all."

I could hear their armor clank. He continued, "Listen, I would love it if Gelsey could trust you, she needs somebody to trust, but can you honestly say that she has any reason to give you her trust?"

Stewart managed to touch the conscience of at least one of the doctors. Dr. Spoke offered a curt apology to me. When another therapist was asked if she agreed with Dr. Kernberg's prognosis, she admitted her doubts and the basis of her opinion: "We have our politics too." Her reluctance to express her uncertainty about me to Kernberg himself reminded me of fellow dancers who kept their mouths shut when a choreographer or director could place their jobs in jeopardy.

Even with the candid admissions, Dr. Spoke and the others would not release me into my mother's custody. My mother had been trying to find a more suitable place for me. She looked into a detoxification center in New Jersey. She was told the cost was $40,000 for six weeks. Then she asked Herman Krawitz at ABT for financial assistance. She was begging. She offered to assist ABT by raising a grant from Time-Life, a little bribe that was rejected for legal reasons. The theatre claimed no responsibility. That was the bottom line.

I had no further recourse. At a private session with Dr. Spoke, I sat and stared at her feet. I refused to speak. Not to be deterred, she asked questions that sounded irrelevant to me. Frustrated at getting no answers, she finally made a direct statement about my resistance. I blurted, "You know, Dr. Spoke, maybe our problem is that we have nothing in common. I mean, I never did like your shoes."

Subsequently, I decided to play along with the clinical routine. Remorse would be my ticket. Tears won me a pass to take a dance class in Manhattan. At the beginning of November 1981, I improvised my escape.

I called the manager, Alex, for his assistance. I chose not to turn to a loved one, not wanting to endanger anyone close to me. Dina was trusted to drive me into Manhattan, but she did not know of my plan. After taking class, I went into hiding. Alex put me in contact with a lawyer, Jonathan Lash, who in turn had me see a specialist at Bellevue Hospital, Robert Cancro, M.D., professor and chairman, N.Y.U. Medical Center, Department of Psychiatry.

The legal system worked for me. The Westchester hospital decided not to go to court. One of the officials told Dina that they would do everything in their power to see that I never danced again. Unfortunately, they did not do enough. The hospital experience and my return to the dance world touched off the next phase of my destruction.

Meanwhile, I visited Dr. Cancro for weekly sessions of counseling. He can be credited with keeping me alive during this period and educating me about the drug, about its insidious power. I did not give him the chance to do more than that. He knew that the drug caused me to lie to him. Soft-spoken and middle-aged, he gently taunted me not to fulfill Dr. Kernberg's predictions, not to surrender. Cancro did not seem to believe I was an addict, though he knew I was enslaved.

In the weeks following my escape from the hospital, Alex may have believed that I was off drugs, although my requests for large cash advances began again in December. Aware that I was seeing a doctor, he sent me off to dance in Taiwan and Italy. By early 1982, I was dependent on Valium as well as cocaine. I had begun an unlikely romance with the heroin user that I met in the hospital, Mickey, who introduced me to the hellish world of Harlem "shooting galleries."

Though I never tried injecting heroin, I frequently accompanied Mickey to a junkie haven, a shooting gallery located at 127th Street and Lenox Avenue. This was a two-room apartment where addicts could buy or "cop" heroin and find someone to shoot them up. Some of them injected themselves. The place was bare except for an old Frigidaire, rotting mattresses, and a table. I found a home-away-from-home in the company of fellow victims, who were eager to supply me with my drug for a price. They accepted me as the poor little rich girl who was slumming her way toward certain death. I watched them search for veins in their necks and groins. They had no inhibitions. Mickey told me, "You're a junkie just like me. There's no difference between us."

I was terrorized on a number of occasions. I witnessed a hit man break in with a gun, demanding his fix. I was once stopped on the street by cops who wanted to know if I were "clean." When a bust was anticipated, I escaped with Mickey by leaping across the roof of the apartment building. Meanwhile, the antagonism between us became more violent. Living under a constant threat of physical abuse, I knew where I was headed, even as I continued to perform.

I told Alex that I was no longer capable of performing physically demanding, bravura roles. I was strictly lyrical. Promoted by Alex and traveling with Mickey, I danced in Puerto Rico and Venezuela. On April 11, 1982, the drug story broke in Florida. I inadvertently told a reporter for the Miami *Herald* that I was recovering from drug abuse. It was a month after John Belushi had died of a drug overdose. Major revelations of cocaine use in the sports world had come to light. My telephone interview with Laurie Horn was reprinted across the country. I was seen as something of an isolated case in the dance world. The theatres did not follow the example of professional sports teams. ABT, for example, said nothing and implemented no policy.

I was too intimidated to speak about the circumstances of my fall. "It's just something that's happening in epidemic proportions . . ." I lied that some trauma had brought about my reform. I did not mention Patrick. Nor did I mention that I was still hooked. Patrick would later tell *US* magazine that I had caused his problems, denying any use of illegal drugs. Such was the compelling voice of cocaine.

On April 24, 1982, Alex coached me for an interview with *Time* magazine. The notes survive. He advised me to say I had recovered, that the problem was stress-related, that I had used cocaine only half the time that I actually had. He was concerned for my appeal at the box office. The *Time* writer, Paul Grey, probably realized I was faking. The story was killed.

Three days later, I was scheduled to appear in Los Angeles with Canadian danseur Frank Augustyn. Rehearsing Ben Stevenson's ballet, *Three Preludes,* I insulted my partner. At the last minute, he withdrew from the ballet. But, I refused to cancel. Like a madwoman, I raced around the dressing room, secretly doing lines and trying to refashion the whole piece as a solo. I improvised on the stage, a Dionysian nightmare.

Gillian Rees wrote for one of the local papers: "Kirkland should not be dancing. One wonders why, in view of her problems with drugs and her subsequent inconsistency, the L.A. Ballet bothered to invite her." Alex told me that the choreographer, Ben Stevenson, had telephoned, saying he hoped to go down in history as the man who took his ballet away from Gelsey Kirkland. His indignant response was more than justified.

Alex tried to tempt me toward Hollywood, and film directors Bob Fosse and Robert Altman. I resisted somewhat, but I was desperate for money. During August, the manager arranged a television appearance for me in Canada in the Canadian Broadcasting Corporation's "Pavlova." One of my legs swelled to twice its normal size, a reaction to the cut in the cocaine. Out of control, I broke with Alex at that time. That was probably the kindest thing I ever did for him.

During the summer, while I was still spending time in Harlem, I decided to try to return to the New York City Ballet. I was exhausted from touring and wanted a stable base of operations. I went to see Balanchine. Maybe he would remind me of what I lost along the way. I caught him in his office at the theatre one afternoon and asked him to think about taking me back. He looked very old. He was sniffling as usual. I was sniffling. I did not know that he was already afflicted with a rare disease that would claim his life the following year. He said, "I see. Well, maybe, dear . . . I don't know." We agreed to meet the following week. He asked me to "surprise" him.

I showed up unannounced as requested. We sat down. He began talking, obviously uncomfortable. "You see, dear . . . you have to want just the theatre, just this place. Nothing else. You know . . . is like . . . well, like bums in the street. They want to be there." He raised a finger. "They want, you see."

He seemed to get stuck. I knew he was beating around the bush. I would later find out about the drug problem in his company. "Mr. B, I think what you are trying to tell me is that I came here hoping you could save me, but that is something I have to do myself. Right?" He looked relieved, his eyes thanking me for understanding.

I continued, "Just out of curiosity, you remember, Mr. B, when I came to you and said I was leaving, years ago . . ." He nodded slowly. ". . . Well, I was scared to tell you about my plans, you know. I was a chicken. Actually, I heard you thought I was a traitor. Well, anyway, I've always wondered what you would have said if I had told you and asked for your advice. Not that I would have listened, but what would you have said to me?"

He brightened at once. "Well, dear, I would have said, 'Don't go!' You see, everyone makes such big deal about Misha. But, really, he is just good dancer. Good feet. But we have many good dancers here." He paused and gave me an ironic chuckle, gloating. "Yes, good feet. Excellent for man." I knew at that moment without doubt how much Balanchine had enjoyed putting Misha in his place.

My face reminded Mr. B of the purpose of my visit. He said, "You see, if I take you . . . then what will I do with others who must dance. Everything in theatre is done certain way now . . ."

"I understand."

As we walked toward the door, he said, "You see, dear, anyway, is not smart enough for you here."

He kissed my cheek, and I left. He apparently could not resist telling the newspapers that he had turned me down. Soon thereafter, Patrick Bissell and I guested again with the Eglevsky Ballet, now run by Edward Villella. Eddie, a dear friend, was supportive. The newspapers called it a comeback for me. It was a fraud.

In October 1982, I broke up with Mickey. I had to flee from my own apartment under physical threat. On the same day, I ran into Misha at Robert

Denvers's studio. He greeted me like a long-lost friend, saying, "Gels, you know, I miss you. There's no one to give me hard time anymore!"

I was rehired by Misha and ABT in November. I ran into him again at the studio. He voiced his concern, "Gelsey, please don't die—ve need you!"

Chapter Twelve

DANCING ON MY GRAVE

I was "needed" by Misha and ABT for another couple of years. During that time, I occasionally fantasized about my funeral. I imagined Misha standing over my grave, belatedly realizing what had been good about me. The fantasy was not far from reality: I was dying. That I was a dancing corpse should have been clear to anyone in the company, to anyone who knew me.

My return to the theatre was an exercise in futility. I spent all my time trying to look good, trying not to be late, trying not to take too many five-minute breaks, trying not to make noise in the bathroom or dressing room when indulging, trying not to lose my purse or stash, trying not to be seen with the other users—trying not to get caught. The company itself had changed. Most of the younger dancers tended to look alike. The older dancers privately complained about misdirection. I was one of the disheartened old-timers.

I remember late-night conversations with my friend Dina. She recorded some of her recollections of the times we spent together in the living room of her apartment:

> You would read to me from Nijinsky's Diary—his reflections while he was in the asylum and how misunderstood he was. You kept relating yourself to his fate. Our conversations would eventually turn to the past and to those people you had been involved with, and how they affected you. We spoke a lot about your father, and so much pain and anger came to the surface. There was so much self-hatred in your words. You were convinced you deserved no better than your present state.
>
> Yes, I was determined to save you. How, I didn't know. I am stubborn by nature. I knew your tendency was to turn away from people that you considered "good," that you didn't "deserve them," or so you said. But if you kept coming back night after night, I felt that was a good sign.
>
> Our conversations dug deeper and deeper. At times you seemed pos-

sessed by an uncontrollable demon. You would look at me with those piercing eyes and scream, "Don't you understand, I want to die!" I felt I had to answer you back to give you reasons for living—no matter how you would reject them.

In our discussions, I felt ballet was the key to many of your problems. The profession you had dedicated so much of your life to was now gradually destroying you. You no longer had that obsessive desire to work, to explore, to test yourself to the limits of your potential . . . All the self-discipline and ambition were gone. Now there was a desperation and obsessiveness of another kind, another motivation, which was more frightening than anything you had done to yourself before. As I woke up to the reality of the situation, I realized there was no point in encouraging you to dance . . .

Whenever Dina left the room to make me tea, I would sneak a few hits of coke, too ashamed to allow her to see. The drug kept me talking, or did my talking for me. She never let on that she knew.

Near the end of 1982, I moved into my mother's Fifth Avenue apartment, its living room windows overlooking Central Park. She made the couch into a bed. I piled my suitcases under a piano. There was always a clutter of toe shoes, tights, leotards, and leg-warmers. In various nooks, I stored my drug paraphernalia—straws, bottles, "pyramid" papers for packaging, grinders, and spoons. I hid my cocaine and Valium under a cushion. Somewhere along the line, my kleptomaniacal tendencies caused my mother to lock up the silverware. I stole change from my stepfather, rationalized as emergency loans. He figured I was a lost cause.

My mother did not pry. Our schedules kept us apart in the daytime. We often exchanged notes, madcap rhymes to inform each other about comings and goings. On my birthday, she let me know that she understood some of my drug jargon. Her card read:

December 29, 1982

ODE to G.K. AT 30

1952: ABORN
1982: ACORN

From little acorns
Mighty oaks do grow
Provided they don't
Lie too long in "snow."

M.

She was confused by my hostile reaction to her humor, unaware that I was still drifting through the lower depths.

I continued to visit Dr. Cancro. He wanted me to stay with ABT until I realized that I did not admire Misha as much as I thought I did—until I was able to see that Misha did not love the art form in the same sense that I did. Dr. Cancro encouraged me to dance. He assumed that as long as I was dancing, as long as I was on the stage, I was not doing drugs. That was a false assumption. I had as much opportunity to destroy myself at ABT as I had in Harlem.

I never really leveled with Dr. Cancro about the extent of my abuse. He raised an eyebrow when I told him I was spending a couple of hundred dollars a week on my obsession. The real figure was at least three times that amount. On more than one occasion, he suggested that I try to kick cocaine temporarily. "Gelsey, you might think about putting it on the shelf for a couple of months. At this point, Johnny Carson would probably do the same thing for you as cocaine."

More than a simple analogy existed between the psychological effect of the drug and that of television. Sexuality was another part of the picture. I no longer had sex without the drug. The doctor tried to make me appreciate the transition I would have to make if I were to go straight. "You might be a lousy lover for a while."

The drug had taken over the sexual act just as it had the creative act. Cocaine was like a third person, always in control, always manipulating from that gray area between mind and body. I listened to Dr. Cancro's advice but was unable to take action. I could no more envision a future without cocaine than I could imagine throwing myself from a speeding automobile. I was locked in the fast lane.

Both love and reason were impossible. On the first tour with ABT at the beginning of 1983, I became involved with a pianist, "Dwayne," who was more fond of grass than coke. We shared our habits briefly. The mixture of marijuana and cocaine threw me for a loop. The disorientation was intensified by my change in musical taste. To psych myself to work each day, I began listening to Michael Jackson's recordings, and the soundtrack from the movie *Jaws*. The music had a way of galvanizing my anger so that I could put myself through each day. A Walkman tape-player enabled me to shut off the world.

In Chicago, Dwayne took me to a Stockhausen concert. Both of us were stoned on powerful marijuana. Three orchestras blasted at each other on the stage, a dissonant confusion of voices all very sophisticated and complex. An academic type sitting next to me claimed the music gave him "a natural high." I too was mesmerized by the density of sound, like a strident argument eventually resolving itself arbitrarily. Dwayne told me the performance was "perfect." I agreed.

When Dwayne provided the piano accompaniment for *Other Dances*, for which I was matched with Misha, the tempo of Chopin seemed to have been altered by Stockhausen. Dwayne's indulgence, whether deliberate or not, made it impossible for me to phrase the movement. I fluttered and skittered across the stage, catching his eye. My body language let him know I was furious. His feelings were hurt. He apparently took his music seriously. The headline in the Chicago *Tribune,* February 14, 1983, claimed, "Baryshnikov-Kirkland reunion shows flashes of old magic." After the show, Misha advised me, "Gelsey, you must apologize to Dwayne. He is suicidal!"

I answered Misha with a cynical chuckle and promised to do as he said. I actually did offer an apology, trying to make Dwayne see that it was I who was the pathetic one. Soon thereafter, I dumped him. I preferred to keep my private life more or less empty.

Random promiscuity had advantages which I found irresistible. Sex could be exchanged for coke; coke could be exchanged for sex. I was no stranger to such physical transactions. Had I not always been asked to sell my body?

The problem on tour was where to buy the white powder. In a paranoid fit, I had flushed my stash down a toilet in Washington, D.C. I subsequently found several new connections through fellow users in the company. Dealing drugs was one way for dancers to afford their own habits. One of my suppliers offered to carry my stash for me, calling it my "medicine." When I telephoned a stage manager in the middle of the night on one occasion, trying to track down a Valium, he told me, "Go to a hospital! You belong in a hospital!"

None of my "friends" who provided coke ever considered that they might be complicit in murder. Nor did I ever think that returning the favor might have endangered their lives. We were simply having fun, putting each other out of misery. Drugs filled a vacuum in a company without inspiration.

The company traveled to Miami later in February. The city was one of the main entry points for the drug into this country, and the price there was relatively cheap. I heard that one company official issued a warning to some of the dancers and dealers to be "careful." This was a call for moderation. The idea was to stay out of trouble. (A year later, I followed Charles France through a luggage turnstile at the airport in Miami. He turned back to me and giggled, "Welcome to the home of Scarface!" He was referring to the title role of the fanciful Al Pacino movie about the cocaine underworld. I was not amused.)

En route to San Francisco at the end of the month, I made a coke detour through Manhattan and arrived late on the West Coast. The following letter was delivered to me at the San Francisco Opera House:

February 25, 1983

Dear Gelsey:

I regret that I must put you on formal notice that your chronic and continuing cancellations of rehearsals, and your failure to properly prepare for performances is not acceptable and therefore, should any further incident of this kind occur will cause the termination of your contract. [sic]

You have been repeatedly warned that your disregard for your fellow artists, ballet masters and pianists has been a source of great distress to all of us and that it is improper professional behavior. We have made every attempt to encourage you to fulfill your obligations to the Company, and to meet the terms of your contract. However, as a result of your most recent incident, that is your failure to appear in San Francisco on Tuesday, February 22nd, your subsequent failure to appear on time at a scheduled rehearsal on Wednesday, February 23rd, and your 6:30 cancellation of a 6:30 rehearsal on Thursday, February 24th, I feel the situation has deteriorated to the point that I must give you this formal warning.

I would like you to see me at 2:15 tomorrow, Saturday, February 26th, in my dressing room. Please disregard your rehearsal which is scheduled for 2:00.

Sincerely,

Mikhail Baryshnikov

Subsequently, Misha found me in the theatre and asked me to follow him through the backstage door. Once outside, he picked up the theme of his letter. His tone was sympathetic. "Gels, I think that dancing is too painful for you."

Those words hit a tender spot. He continued, "Look, I help you. Ve think of graceful vay for you to resign . . . to stop. Really, I think of good vay for you and for company."

He did not mention that which was unmentionable. I did not accept his offer. I must have wanted to prove that he was wrong. He did not push the issue of my resignation. His warnings were hollow. I did not yet realize why that was so.

I received good reviews in San Francisco and prepared for a performance of *Giselle* in Los Angeles, working with Georgina Parkinson, whose allegiance as friend and ballet mistress was constantly put to the test. My rehearsals were scheduled in the evening. There was a space problem in Los Angeles. That was the least of the problems.

A few days before the performance, I was to meet Misha for a rehearsal at the theatre. He was late. I knew he was in one of the offices. I knew that he knew I was waiting for him. Was he trying to teach me a lesson?

I finally walked into the office and found him sitting at a desk. He was motionless, slumped in a chair, a blank expression on his face. I was not about to lecture him on punctuality. Seeing me, he snapped out of his revery and walked past me toward the studio. Before reaching the door, he stopped dead in his tracks. As if struck by a sudden thought, he said, "Gels, have you asked Peter Martins if he take you back?"

I was stupefied. "No, Misha. I haven't."

He was flippant. "Vell, I'm sure Peter take you into company if you ask him."

Misha was suggesting that I might return to the New York City Ballet. Balanchine had recently been hospitalized; Peter Martins was the heir apparent. Surely Peter would welcome me with open arms. "But, Misha, that is not where I want to be. This is where I want to be."

He did not reply. I took the hint as an insult. He further incited me by lauding one of the dancers at the New York City Ballet, insinuating that she might make a preferable Giselle.

The tension escalated at rehearsal. Georgina and a pianist were present. Misha requested that I rehearse my solos first, like some kind of impromptu audition. I resisted. I had expected that we would be working on the adagio sections together. I had not warmed up enough for those solos. Misha relented.

As we began to rehearse a pas de deux, I could tell he did not want to be in the same room with me. We kept stopping and starting. I blamed him. He blamed me. When I complained about one of our old sore points, he barked, "I do best I can do . . . You must jump to help me lift!" I knew that jumping would destroy the fluid quality of the passage.

I was terrorized—partly because I was high, and partly because we never could communicate. We continued to the point where the atmosphere was way beyond unpleasant. Back and forth. Then we came to a series of diagonal lifts. I was trying to correct his phrasing. He was trying to tell me that I was doing the steps wrong anyway. Suddenly we both stopped, facing each other. I tried to figure another angle. He brought down the ceiling: "And don't stare at me vith those daggers!"

I closed my eyes, squeezing back tears. He stormed away. Neither Georgina nor the pianist said a word.

On the following day, Misha canceled our rehearsal. I met with him and Charles France in the office. I was told that I was being replaced in Giselle, that I was not prepared, that I had not rehearsed properly. I accused the two of them of manipulating me. Charles shot back at me, "Oh, Gelsey, you're no better than you were in your Harlem days!"

I was stunned. That was too close to the truth for either of them. "Well, it seems like the two of you have really figured things out here. But if you don't want me to dance Giselle, you are going to have to take it away from me—because I am ready! I am prepared! It's you, Misha, who's not ready to work! You have taken everything away from me. You came from Russia and took everything! You can take Giselle away too! But, I'm going to let it be known exactly what happened here—exactly what's happening in this company! There is no way I'm going to let you get away with this!"

I was on my feet, still screaming. Heading for the door, I resigned and promised to go public with the whole story. I walked to a restaurant next to the theatre. I knew that I would never carry out the threat. I was much too intimidated to tell the truth to anyone, let alone the press. Nevertheless, I did intend to leave the company. When I returned to retrieve my belongings from the theatre, Charles encouraged me to reconsider, to work things out with Misha. "Just talk to him, Gelsey."

I did. I told Misha I deserved another chance. I promised not to cause him any problems with *Giselle*. He listened. He knew that nothing I said mattered in the least—because he knew that I had a cocaine problem—and he knew that I knew that he knew. He granted my wish.

Giselle was the first full-length ballet that we had done in ages. Our performance in March caused a major sensation for the audience and critics. The Los Angeles *Times* was still writing about it a year later. Misha seemed to be more careful about his partnering than he had ever been. It was a technically flawless exhibition. I had become a true Romantic heroine, a status that seemed to be enhanced by my drugged state. I was more vulnerable than ever.

Yet this was not the same ballet that I had danced years before. I was incapable of virtuosity. I was incapable of forgiving myself. My spirit had no resiliency. Giselle was as hopeless as I was.

The question was whether or not to fire me. Management must have kicked that one around on an almost daily basis. I could not have been more obvious if I had had a big red "C"—for cocaine—emblazoned on my chest. "Constance," a sympathetic secretary in the administrative offices of ABT, sometimes left written notes in my dressing room, urging me not to give up. She hid them carefully, fearing perhaps that someone might discover she was on my side.

I received another letter from Misha when the company arrived at the Northrup Auditorium in Minneapolis:

April 3, 1983

Dear Gelsey:

Before we can exercise our option to proceed with a contract for the Met season, I must meet with you to discuss your repertory and performance schedule. I have asked Constance to make an appointment for us to meet during the time we are in Detroit.

Yours sincerely,

Mikhail Baryshnikov

Repertory and schedule were the crucial areas of managerial control. My attitude may have been incorrigible, but my name was bankable. The unspoken dilemma was a curse on Misha and the entire company: who would want to dance with a junkie?

In Detroit, later in April, I rehearsed with Misha again and performed *Other Dances*. Offering him a technical correction in front of the other dancers caused a new round of explosions. He seemed to think I was making a fool of him, undermining his authority as artistic director. Before returning to New York, he informed me by telephone that I was a "terrible" person. Charles France informed me that Misha did not want to dance *Giselle* with me again. I was pleading as usual; whatever I said was meaningless, pathetic.

Only weeks later, Misha stood in the wings at the Met when I performed the wedding pas de deux from *The Sleeping Beauty*. I was partnered by another principal, Ross Stretton. Management had not included me in this gala, but I replaced another ballerina who bowed out. I danced like the "abominable snow-woman." The embarrassment was excruciating. After my performance, Misha approached me, saying, "Gels, you should be proud. Really! Vas good for first time!"

His opinions were meaningless to me. At the end of April, George Balanchine died, succumbing to a mysterious, slow-acting virus. His central nervous system had been deteriorating for some years. I wept, but I did not attend the funeral services. Misha did, along with mourners from the dance world. Unlike those who eulogized him, Mr. B preferred not to call himself an artist or a genius. I did not think that he would have appreciated such effusive praise, but maybe I was wrong about him. I was troubled by the outpouring of sentiment, especially from those who had never known him. I felt somehow closer to the man than ever before, but I could not forgive him for all those years of grief.

Several days later, on May 7, 1983, I had another brain seizure, in the cafeteria at the Met. I had been awake for days and ran out of Valium. I was scheduled for a rehearsal. At a cashier's counter, I shrieked and flipped backward into the air, crashing to the floor and splitting open my scalp.

The attack included the usual blackout and convulsions. I woke in the arms of my faithful supporter Constance. I was covered with blood. Two policemen were standing nearby. I learned later that two grams of cocaine had been found in my possession. An ambulance arrived. I was taken out by wheelchair. I had the strange feeling that my life had never happened at all.

I was treated at Roosevelt Hospital by Dr. Howard Goldsweig. Six stitches were required to close my head wound. Management almost succeeded in covering up the affair entirely. The New York *Post* reported only that I had had an accident in the cafeteria. Drugs were not mentioned. I never did find out the details of why the police had not arrested me or filed a full report. Patrick told me I was lucky, that they figured I had enough problems.

Charles France met once with Dr. Cancro, who wanted me to continue dancing. The therapist explained to Charles that I was suffering from a medical problem. Charles explained the corporate point of view of the theatre, that he had a business to run. Several days later, I was back on the boards at the Met, performing *Giselle* with Misha. I had returned to cocaine before leaving the hospital. Another unspoken dilemma was now in the air: would I die on the stage?

The performance of *Giselle* was as extraordinary as the events that preceded it. Misha must have been repulsed by my presence. I am sure that he never danced with a ballerina whose head was held together by six gruesome black stitches. It was not a pretty sight. I felt like a skunk—Misha's nose was bound to catch my scent.

I tried to keep the mood light. I was a penitent, trying to atone for years of folly. In the second act, my partner and I tangled our feet, which appeared to some as if I had kicked him. The review by Clive Barnes appeared in the New York *Post,* Friday, May 13, 1983:

> This is one of ballet's legendary partnerships. Miss Kirkland has had her problems, but here she was dancing with an exquisite, dramatic fever. I came in at the end of her first act, caught her mad scene, and, of course, all of the second act. Both she and Baryshnikov were fantastic . . .
>
> Baryshnikov was like a distraught hero, his mind outdistanced by love, and Miss Kirkland, the divine and fragile Miss Kirkland, gave us a Giselle that we must remember with awe.
>
> Miss Kirkland has a fugitive grace, a sense of style, some kind of comprehension, that in a curious way adds up to a totally personal Giselle. She even suffers with the music.

Though the dance was appreciated, the final curtain call brought down the house. I had been trying to look on the bright side. It could have been worse. Yet Misha was acting like a real pill. Was he smiling or scowling? I felt I had to show my appreciation to him and to the audience. For a fleeting instant, I was my old self again, on the verge of tears. I plucked a rose from a bouquet and held it out for him. He hesitated. When he reached for it, I pulled it away, teasing him.

I just wanted to shake him out of his mood, which seemed to cast an evil spell over the festivities. Under the circumstances, my actions were pathetically inappropriate. He must have thought I was trying to embarrass him. When he reached for the rose again, I playfully snatched it away again. It was as if I had broken a rule that I never knew existed.

Misha turned and stomped off the stage, growling in Russian under his breath. I was shocked. I bowed and placed the rose where he had been standing. I took the rest of my bows alone, completely distraught. When the curtain came down, my friend Dina was the only one who had the nerve to come near me.

When I entered the hallway to the dressing rooms, I heard Misha scream, "She's fired! She's fired!" The place was a madhouse. I retreated to my dressing room, crying aloud, "Oh my God, what have I done now?" Tears were streaming from my eyes. A wave of shivers swept through my body. I was inconsolable, barely aware of those around me. I wanted to crack my face against the mirror.

Dr. Cancro, who had been in the audience, came backstage to see me. He said simply, "Gelsey, good joke . . . wrong person." Later he tried to make me understand the effect that I had on Misha. "Did you ever stop to think that he might be more insecure than you?"

Misha told the press that his sudden disappearance at the curtain call was intended to give me the share of limelight that I so richly deserved. Who was he kidding?

I was not fired. The following month we performed *Giselle* together for the last time. Misha replaced an injured Ross Stretton as my partner, occasioning another critical success. The artistic director decided to keep me in the company but would not dance with me again. The partnership was dead. I suppose it had been for years.

I had begun a cocaine romance with the owner of one of the restaurants near Lincoln Center. Middle-aged and respectable, he had the local police literally eating out of his hand. Classy and popular, the restaurant was a convenient cover. After visiting one day, I ran into Peter Martins on the street. Peter was dressed in white, a fashionable ghost. He asked, "What is the problem Misha has with you? I never had any problem."

What could I say? I avoided even thinking about the question.

On July 4, 1983, Clive Barnes wrote that the box office of American Ballet Theatre was in trouble. He speculated about a possible connection between the financial difficulties and the artistic direction, what he called the "Balanchinization of Ballet Theatre." The critic noted that only "four bankable stars" remained with the company, none of whom were dependable: Misha, Fernando Bujones, Cynthia Gregory, and myself. Mr. Barnes was one of the first to question Misha's leadership:

> Mikhail Baryshnikov, a nice guy with an absolutely brilliant mind, has had control of Ballet Theatre for three years. Baryshnikov was a fantastic choice as the company's artistic director—everyone knew that. But what has he done to justify our faith? Does he really know what Ballet Theatre is all about?

Although one of the managers, Herman Krawitz, was replaced later in the year, Misha was retained and the critic's call for action ignored. Nothing changed. The board of directors apparently did not mind throwing people and money away. I was in no condition to see why I was still on the stage.

During that summer, I was pushed into a ballet with a young dancer named Robert LaFosse. Perhaps someone thought his career would be given a "shot in the arm" by appearing with me. The situation was worse than the pun.

The ballet was Balanchine's *La Sonnambula*. The irony was that I was now perfect for the role of the Sleepwalker. The character was lost and alone, almost entirely devoid of humanity. The action was a haunting study in despair, deeply compatible with the drug mentality.

There were critical raves. Jennifer Dunning reviewed the ballet for the New York *Times*, July 10, 1983:

> Miss Kirkland's Sleepwalker—the mysterious woman who appears from out of her dark tower in the midst of a party, enchants a strange young poet, causes his death and then carries him back into the tower and away with her into the night—had the grandeur of madness and the fine detail of a nightmare, though a beautiful one.
>
> There was a whole expressive vocabulary of bourrées across the stage, driven, racing and shivering, as the Sleepwalker drifts from the Poet's embrace. Her turns looked blown by some unearthly wind. And the almost convulsive gesture of her arms and head when she came flush with his suddenly dead body, her white sleeves hanging like sculptured wings, had a look of terrifying, cataclysmic truth.

Was that performance a revelation of beauty and truth? In retrospect, I think not. It was an illusion without perspective, much like my life. How many nightmares did I have to dance?

Mr. B originally had the Sleepwalker and Poet ascend to a climactic bed-chamber in the tower. Misha had them wind up in a fairy-tale heaven, a spotlight suggesting their skyward journey. Those two final destinations were the familiar poles of modern and Romantic sensibility, love and death stretching from bedroom to oblivion. Either way, the ballet translated into a symbolic act of poetic impotence, or perhaps another triumph of steps over words. All the bourrées in the world could not relieve the boredom for me. Only cocaine could accomplish that trick.

I was insensible enough to dance along with a story that contradicted everything I had ever learned to love. I spent hours in the studio teaching my young partner how to deliver the kiss. Finally he sobbed, "Gelsey, I'm just so afraid you'll give up on me." As wretched as I was, I tried to comfort him.

At the beginning of the autumn rehearsal period, one of the corps members introduced me to a dealer named "Hugh." He was a Vietnam veteran who lived with his wife and young daughter in an Upper East Side apartment. Always well dressed, Hugh looked the part of the responsible family man. He was a yuppie who liked to buy furs for his wife and watch the stock quotations on television. He played the market and the field. At our first meeting, he asked me, "Have you ever had coke up your ass?" So began my sickest relationship to date.

I bought from Hugh each morning, meeting him at his door, carrying on an affair under his wife's nose. When he found out who I was and that I was not represented by a personal manager, he introduced me to one of his customers, "Burt," an accountant who lived in the same building. I told Burt that I wanted only enough money to maintain a steady supply of cocaine. I signed a contract with him for that explicit purpose.

Burt, of course, was a legitimate front. He and his lawyer negotiated my contracts with the ABT management. Burt and Hugh began to plan movie and book deals for me. They later arranged a night in my honor at Studio 54, at that time a popular discothèque and drug den. When I was touring, they sent cocaine to me by Federal Express. They hired an assistant to travel with me and ration the drug, to make sure that I did not miss rehearsals and performances, to keep me under control.

My life—and death—were now planned down to the tiniest detail, an arrangement that was not without surprises. On New Year's Eve of 1984, in Washington, D.C., I had another coke fling with Patrick Bissell, just for old times' sake. In retrospect, I have only compassion for Patrick; because of his gifts, he was pushed within the company and placed under unrelenting pressure. Like me, he learned lessons that no one should have to learn. I do not know how he accomplished his own reformation. That is a story he will have to tell.

At the beginning of the year, just before leaving for a tour, I stayed up for three days, roaming through Manhattan. I was supposed to fly to Boston. I made a midnight visit to a midtown dope dealer, a former boxer and war veteran who struggled to make ends meet as a photographer. He weighed about three hundred pounds and was fondly known as "Big Ben." He lived with his wife and two kids in one of the rankest places on earth, a basement apartment in the Forties near Eighth Avenue. Ben's home looked like a failed bomb shelter. I often used him to supplement my supply, taking advantage of his surprisingly generous nature. On that night of nights, I met a young man outside the dealer's door. Both of us banged away, trying to wake up the occupant, to no avail.

That young man and I would spend the night together. His name was Gregory Lawrence. Tall and wiry, he was a poet of sorts. He had been working for six years as a free-lance reader of books for Twentieth Century-Fox. With a sad smirk on his face, he called himself a "glorified bookie." He also managed a television production office across the street from the dealer's place. We stopped there and at a bar on our way to his apartment in Greenwich Village. When I told him that I was a ballerina, he grinned and said, "Ballet is about as high a cultural expression as basketball, don't you think?"

I laughed. Greg had never seen a ballet and had no idea who I was. I chose not to enlighten him.

We entered an old building and climbed three flights of stairs. His two-room apartment had no furniture whatsoever, only a mattress on the floor, books and papers scattered everywhere, a typewriter in one of the corners. He seemed to be a mad vagabond like me. He had a girlfriend who was away at the time. We sat and did some coke. Each of us had a small supply. Greg was an abuser who occasionally went off the deep end, but he could not have afforded the steady excess of my habit. Between the two of us, we soon blurred the distinction between "abuse" and "addiction."

Over the next few hours, he read me poetry, beautiful words that sliced through my defenses almost instantly, that forced me to look at life from the point of view of the grave. Hearing him recite, I imagined being six feet under, asking myself in hypothetical retrospect, "What was that all about?" Had my life had any meaning at all? Had my career contributed anything to humanity other than idle entertainment? Oh, I was horrified. I wept in his arms and found that tiny grain of hope. Who was this man?

He read from one of his poems:

> They weep, and through their bedlam of tears
>   a blind heart surges;
> they kiss, and through the eye of the needle of love
>   a mind, poisoned and bound, purges . . .

Such was our first night together.

I remember asking if he worried about people stealing his work, admitting that I was something of a thief myself. He said, "People who worry about their ideas being stolen are usually people who have a limited supply." We talked about art and politics, about everything under the sun. Unlike many men that I had known, he did not make me feel ignorant. He was a funny, tender soul, seemingly as discontent in the film industry as I was in the ballet world. I thought I detected a hint of my own past in his face.

In the morning Greg left for work. I slept until he returned that night. He made me coffee and peanut butter sandwiches. The mood had not changed between us even though the effects of the drug had worn off. But I had missed my flight to Boston and had to hurry away to catch a late plane. Our parting kiss was tinged with such sweetness and sorrow, exaggerated by my fantasy, by thinking he might be the solution to my problems. Could the broken pieces of our lives fit together to make one whole? It seemed we would have no chance to find out, though we promised to see each other again.

With a cross-country tour just getting under way, my mysterious disappearance had caused my manager and my dealer some concern, to say nothing of the company. I recall landing in Boston. I had not used any cocaine on the flight, had not even thought about it. I said to myself, "Gelsey, now this is amazing!"

The following day, I resumed my drug habit and performed Tudor's ballet

The Leaves Are Fading. I was as addicted as ever, but I felt something in that ballet I had not felt in years: inspiration. I seemed to be dancing against the drug, even rebelling against its control over me. I was holding a fragile image in my mind, in my heart. Though secretly thrilled, I dared not give it a name, not yet.

A remarkable review by Laura A. Jacobs appeared in the *Boston Phoenix,* February 14, 1984, entitled "Is There an ABT Beyond Baryshnikov?" I did not know quite what to make of it at the time.

> The gap between Baryshnikov and the dancers in his company is not closing as, at our most idealistic, we'd hope it would—if anything, it's widening. Of the ballerinas that performed during the Boston engagement only Gelsey Kirkland danced with equal stature, with the same eye-opening individuality. And with new meaning. Kirkland's an adult now, and the integrity of her dancing, the unquestioning risk, seems no longer a gift but a choice. It's the difference between daring when you have nothing to lose and daring when you have everything. We saw her only in Antony Tudor's silkscreen reverie *The Leaves Are Fading,* yet it was enough . . .
>
> She made this slippery, ephemeral ballet look substantial—dancing on glass, she found a mental foothold. In her pirouettes she seemed always to be coming out of a whorl (a remembered quarrel; a word that stung). And the quicksilver lick she put on the most treacherous combinations had the glint of epiphany. Kirkland can leave you stranded in a dance, can dissolve your complacency—she's speaking Shakespeare's most mercurial syntax while everyone else is crooning Rod McKuen. We'd never think to ask of her what she asks of herself.

Spurred as I was by the promise of a stranger, my dancing was testimony to an internal crisis I could not yet fully comprehend. That performance was the first time I had ever willfully resisted the effects of cocaine, actually sensing something distasteful, swallowing, and tensing all the little muscles in my throat and jaw. Forcing my mind to focus on the dance, I resented the drug almost as much as I resented myself.

I wondered if that last night in New York had been real. Was it another cocaine illusion? Would I ever see Greg again? He called me at the theatre before I left Boston. He had been thinking about me. He wondered where he might write me. I told him, "You inspired me! I'm not kidding! I gave a great performance!"

I was soon in turmoil on the road. I fell back into my lurid routine, but something inside me had changed. I continued to receive favorable notices for my limited repertory. The box office reportedly increased by about twenty-five percent for my performances across the country. Greg called me in each city, and he sent poems. Usually alone in my hotel room, I read them aloud and spilled more tears. His words constantly reminded me of what I had lost. I no longer wanted to die, at least not while I held one of his poems or letters in my hand, not when I heard his voice.

Greg visited for a weekend in Chicago. We stayed in my room for two days, under the influence most of the time. He did not see me dance, but did see the worst side of me. How could he stand me? I told him repeatedly, "I'm a junkie. I'm hopeless. Let's just have a nice time. While it lasts."

We did. Sitting on the bed, watching me stretch and twist my body into pretzel shapes, he joked, "I think I'll just have to kidnap you, Gelsey! We won't do any drugs. I'll hold you down—I'd love to hold you for a month anyway. You probably don't even remember what life was like without blow."

Snapping at him, I said I did remember and had no desire to return to that former life. He thrust his chin forward and said, "Go ahead, hit me, I have a glass jaw!" We fell into each other's arms, laughing easily. But I was secretly afraid he might not be joking. I imagined his putting me into a sack and carrying me off. That was a real jolt. What if he took me away and I still craved the drug? The fact that his tone had not been patronizing disarmed me. As he used cocaine himself and knew its power, I could not say, "But you don't understand."

There were two unspoken alternatives already in my mind: I might have to change in order not to lose him; I might have to lose him in order not to change.

As deranged as he was by the drug, he was not joking. After returning to New York, Greg called friends and doctors he knew in the various cities where I was performing on tour. This was a safety net. In an emergency, these people were to provide support. He also arranged a possible hideout for us through a filmmaker, Deane Rink, whom I met briefly in Los Angeles. My new lover was playing with fire. He realized I might have another seizure or overdose at any time. He also knew I was not yet ready to quit dancing. During a phone conversation, I told him that I had to finish the tour and angrily refused to cancel. But I could not hang up on him.

Meanwhile, my dealer in New York, Hugh, had begun cutting my cocaine with speed, or perhaps he was buying coke that had already been cut and passing it on to me. The amphetamine was cheaper. Mixing it with my coke meant more profits. Receiving my packages on the road, I was completely unaware of the switch, other than a nervous condition that required fifty milligrams of Valium daily to counteract. By the time I returned to New York in April, I was a speed freak, a Valium addict, a coke casualty, and a total wreck. Even my teeth were falling out.

I had some root canal work done by my dentist, a sweetheart of a man who voiced his concern about my health. Under his laughing gas, I imagined him looking into the cave of my mouth, seeing bats fly out from the dark chamber. It was pure hell. I was a child who had turned into an ugly, old hag. Nothing could numb that pain or release the cry in my throat. How could I go on with the New York season?

I spent the next three weeks with Greg, a period of desperation and utter madness. I tried to keep him a secret from my manager, my dealer, and the company. I feared that someone would either do away with Greg or break us apart. After all, he was threatening to steal everybody's favorite meal ticket. He arranged for me to get off speed by buying relatively pure coke from a dealer that he knew. We kept the drug hidden in the wall of what was now "our apartment." The two of us went through two ounces in those three weeks, four thousand dollars' worth of cocaine. It was a miracle that we survived.

During that time, we went to an Easter egg hunt, a party at the home of one of Greg's cohorts. The "eggs" were packages of various drugs. I was so obnoxious that Greg was reluctant to introduce me to his old friends, mostly characters from the film world. Yet his behavior was as erratic as mine. Still, there was something, intuition or wishful thinking, that made me believe he was different from the other men in my life. Sharing the same intensity, we seemed to be deeply in love, but the trust between us was wavering.

When he stayed out all night on one occasion, I became a shrill monster and tried to drive him away permanently. I accused him of manipulating me just like everyone else. He did not flinch, but said with a level voice, "Gelsey, are you so brainwashed that you can't see the difference?"

The word "brainwashed" hit me like a sledgehammer. He sat me down on a mattress and continued, "Don't you realize how conned you are? Where do you think your money goes, Gelsey? No wonder you have friends at Chase Manhattan! Don't you realize that certain people might like you to be a drug addict? As long as they don't have to know about it. As long as they can watch you spill your guts on the stage. As long as you dance in public and die in private. We've both mastered the art of self-destruction! We've both been duped!"

We talked for hours. Unlike me, Greg was a witting victim. He seemed to know the drug trade from the inside out and tried to teach me about the economics and the politics. The more I found out, the more furious I became. He suggested, "Just follow the trail of dirty money after it leaves your hand."

I learned that billions of illicit dollars were laundered annually through the banking system in the United States alone, that drugs were the most profitable commodity in the world. I learned how the usurious credit policies of the International Monetary Fund promoted cash crops—such as marijuana, coca plants, and opium poppies—instead of food crops. I also learned about the CIA's MK-Ultra program and the research sponsored by the Tavistock Institute, that drugs were not only a source of profit, but an instrument for social control.

My mind conjured up images of children starving and bureaucrats collecting pounds of flesh by computer. Greg's more outrageous exaggerations provoked me, which was exactly what he intended. He likened cocaine to systematic euthanasia: "Think of it as mercy killing on a grand scale. Think of it as both an ultimate form of pain relief and a final solution to overpopulation. Even murder can be merciful if you believe you're performing a public service and ridding the world of useless eaters. If you sat on the board of directors of Dope Incorporated, life would combine the risk of a business deal and the challenge of a medical experiment. You'd have limitless possibilities for fulfillment and happiness."

The sinister implications were too much for me. I argued, "No one could be that evil! No one would deliberately do that!"

He looked exasperated. "It's not a conspiracy. It's the way people think. They never seem to see the consequences of their actions. Look at it this way. We've been invaded. Part of our society has been enslaved, and nobody has issued a new Emancipation Proclamation. The war on drugs is just a public relations joke, a good intention buried in corruption. It would cost too much to treat all these addicts, to really educate children, to stop the drugs at the borders, to bomb the plantations. The budget has to be cut, just like your throat. Look at yourself! Gelsey Kirkland! Ballet star! Drug addict! Do you really think you're free? Free to kill yourself, maybe!"

We did more cocaine. Greg decided to tape our conversation, saying we might want to remember it someday. "You may just have to tell your story in order to live with yourself." At that moment, he looked like an ancient rendering I had seen of Alexander the Great, with huge eyes and prominent nose. I talked for almost an hour, recounting my experiences working on *Romeo and Juliet* in 1980 for the Royal Ballet. I came to a shrieking halt after describing how Kenneth MacMillan directed me, how I used my rage to dance a scene. I was enraged all over again.

Greg had not said a word. His smile took me by surprise. "Gelsey, it sounds like you have the same trouble with choreographers that you have with the audience. You expect them to understand you and automatically share your special love for the art, but that could take a lifetime. Sometimes it never happens at all. There was a German conductor, Wilhelm Furtwängler. He was misunderstood and much maligned. He conducted Beethoven better than just about anybody alive, but people called him a Nazi—except for the Jewish musicians he helped escape from Germany during the war. Well, that wise old man believed that great art was the only antidote for madness. He put it something like this. The public makes demands, and the artist is expected to live up to them. But the artist too has demands. And the public expects such demands from the artist, since these are what give him his own dignity."

I was speechless for a moment, averting my eyes. "Yea, well, I can't say anything about dignity."

"Gelsey, there's always a struggle in that kind of exchange. It's easy to let yourself be destroyed, but much more difficult to assert yourself, especially with your sensitivity. You have to fight for dignity. Nobody is ever going to just give it to you. If anything, people will try to beat it out of you. You have to be more clever and more loving than they are—just to survive as an artist."

I screamed, "I've been trying for years! And I'm sick of it! I'm sick! Period!"

He whispered, "If you're sick, then what are the rest of us?"

He wiped tears from the corners of my eyes and started to tell me about a novel he was writing, *Venus on the Skids*. Set in the pornographic netherworld of midtown, the story concerned a teenage runaway, a mute on the streets on Manhattan. Greg explained, "The hero, Locus, is a child prodigy who has a big problem: he was born without a tongue. He looks like a young Harpo Marx and spends most of the book searching for a golden tongue. Locus wants his own voice—sound familiar? We're all looking for a tongue to wag, aren't we? How often do you want to cry out or at least deliver a few lines when you're dancing? Well, anyway, he thinks an artificial device made of gold may do the trick for him."

I could feel an attack of giggles threatening and asked, "Does he ever get his tongue?"

"No. But he meets a brilliant ventriloquist who knows how to read lips and gives him a voice." My laughter erupted as he continued. "You see, when Locus mouths words, the ventriloquist instantly sees what the kid is trying to say and simultaneously throws his own voice, speaking for him. So he can talk as long as the ventriloquist is around. Unfortunately, whenever the kid does talk, he looks like somebody in a badly dubbed foreign film. The two of them have some amazing adventures. Very mythological." Like his hero, Greg swooped around the room, reading passages and miming the action. He finally collapsed in my arms, exhausted, like a balloon that had run out of hot air.

The sun was rising. I would miss another ballet class. I watched him fall asleep. He had lost about twenty pounds during our three-week binge. He looked like a skeleton, a specimen in some laboratory. I kissed his eyelids and wondered what he saw in me. I was killing him, and I knew it. The cocaine would destroy our love. It was that simple.

I was still hooked, but my mind was stirring. I took my anger into the theatre. We stayed up for a three-day nightmare at the end of April. On May 1, 1984, I performed at the Met for what turned out to be the last time. The ballet was *The Leaves Are Fading*. At the very beginning, I forgot the steps, until I thought of my lover in the audience. I made believe that he was my partner and fought against having a seizure on the stage. I hesitated and heard a voice say, "Come on, Gels! You can make it!" It was another close call.

After the performance, I told Greg that I wanted to quit ABT. I was ready to have him kidnap me. We stayed in my dressing room until three in the morning, discussing the pros and cons of my finishing the New York season. He told me, "Sooner or later, you're going to have to stop dancing and stop doing drugs. Otherwise, we have no chance!" No one ever put it to me that way before. But I was still ambivalent.

A couple of days later, I threw a tantrum in the studio. Management had pushed me into dancing *La Sylphide* with Robert LaFosse. As it was, there were really no partners who wanted to work with me in my drugged condition. My attitude put the blame on everyone but me. I was deceived and used, but how else was a dancer on dope to be treated? I resigned in a rage. Subsequently, having second thoughts, I asked Greg to help me compose a letter, a profuse apology, asking the theatre to help me find a way to fulfill my contractual and artistic obligations. It closed with my stated intention to work with ABT "for many seasons to come."

Greg and I went to meet Misha. The letter outraged the artistic director. Wearing one of his luxurious robes, he sat in my dressing room, waving the note in his hand. He yelled at me, "You did not write this, Gelsey! Who wrote this?"

I introduced Greg. Misha ignored him, screaming at me, "Vhut you vant, Gelsey? Just tell me vhut you vant!"

I finally made my decision, screaming back, "I want to do exactly what you want me to do, Misha! I want to resign! I want to quit!"

Charles France entered. Misha asked me to leave the room. They wanted to speak to Greg alone. Misha put it bluntly, "If I ever read my name in print, or if I ever read about my theatre, I vill destroy her! I vill tell story how ve carried her out of cafeteria. Ve found cocaine on her!"

Greg kept his mouth shut. Misha and Charles France then consulted Charles Dillingham, the executive director of Ballet Theatre Foundation. I was told to sign the following agreement, only the first paragraph of which would be released to the press:

May 4, 1984

"Gelsey Kirkland, today, asked to resign from her contract as a principal dancer with American Ballet Theatre. Miss Kirkland indicated that she wishes to pursue other artistic endeavors which would not allow a full time commitment to the Company. The management has accepted Miss Kirkland's resignation with deep regret. We wish her the best of success with her future plans, and would like to acknowledge the extraordinary artistic contribution this great artist has made to American Ballet Theatre."

We the undersigned agree that the above statement shall be the only statement issued to the press by either party and shall be changed in no way whatsoever.

After withdrawing ungracefully from a final gala, the celebration of the Met Centennial, I made plans to skip town with Greg. All the strings had to be cut. We turned to a young lawyer, Lisa Filloramo, who began to break the contract with my personal manager. At a last meeting between my manager and my dealer, Greg secretly taped the conversation. The dealer, who had previously bragged to me about his mob connections, made threats. The manager tried to be conciliatory. Greg humored him with big plans for my future.

The next day, our apartment was broken into while we were out. Our lives seemed to be in some danger, but paranoia made the situation worse than it was. This was a blessing in disguise because we now had to escape. Scared out of our wits, we spent an entire afternoon in a taxi, driving around Manhattan, trying to decide where to go.

We turned to two dear friends of Greg's, Patrick McCormick and Angela Vullo, sober and ambitious filmmakers who provided cash for our journey. They also provided some tapes of Beethoven sonatas and symphonies, understanding our secret strategy for withdrawal.

We planned to travel to a farm in upstate New York, a refuge offered by playwright Lynne Adams. Her sister, actress Brooke Adams, had offered strong encouragement for me to reform. Her parting words to Greg were, "I can see that you and Gelsey are cut from the same cloth."

Those few friends and Greg himself were all the inspiration I needed to try to go straight. We were amazed that anyone still believed in us. When we boarded a train in Grand Central Station, I was actually happy not to have any cocaine in my possession. I carried only Valium, a drug which necessarily required a phased withdrawal in order to avoid the possibility of a seizure. Filled with hope, I nestled my head on Greg's shoulder and fell asleep. I had not even told my mother where I was going or who was traveling with me. The rumors in the ballet world were that I had married a businessman and flown to Bermuda for a honeymoon.

THE MAIDEN FROM AFAR

Where humble shepherds had their dwelling,
A lonely vale, each new-born year,
As larks were winging, buds were swelling,
A lovely maiden would appear.

When spring awoke one day they'd find her,
From whence she came no one could tell.
The stranger left no trace behind her
And vanished when she said farewell.

Exalted by her blessed presence,
All hearts were gladdened, spirits rose.

Yet sensing there some lofty essence
No mortal dared come too close.

She came with gifts of fruits and flowers
From far-off gardens known to none,
Which watered by serener showers,
Had ripened in a happier sun.

With all alike she shared her treasure,
These fruits and flowers from distant lands.
Both young and old received full measure
And none went home with empty hands.

To everyone she gave her greeting,
But when she saw true lovers there
She most delighted in the meeting
And chose for them the flow'r most rare.

After reading me those lines by Friedrich Schiller during our two-hour train ride up the Hudson River, Greg challenged me, "If you can figure out who the Maiden is, then you can figure out almost anything, even why you became addicted. To know her would be to know yourself. What gift do we all possess? If the two of us are true lovers, then what rare flower can we bring into this world?"

That poem perfectly described the process of withdrawal for me. It was the greatest joy, the greatest gift I ever received. Breaking away from cocaine, going cold turkey, turned out to be quite painless—we had left the agony behind in New York. In a sense, our difficult choices had already been made. My only lingering doubt was this: I was afraid to be alone, fearing that I might be tempted to relapse. But Greg never left my side. He never stopped asking for my help, making me know that I had to encourage him to discipline himself, that he would overcome the drugs with me. We were partners in a dance which I now think was the dream of all dances.

We moved into a barn and later a guesthouse on a sixty-acre farm. Lynne, an angel of mercy, kept our refrigerator full and left us to our privacy. She was sometimes curious about the laughter she heard drifting out from our windows. With my lover leading me in a daily routine of intensive study, I recovered my wits as well as my sense of humor. He seemed to know exactly what he was doing. His method, like Schiller's enigmatic Maiden, was that of art itself, but not just any art. We were searching for a special kind of inspiration.

Could we have kicked drugs by listening to rock music? Could we have reclaimed our lives by staring at soap operas? We were careful about our choices, turning mainly to the classics. Approaching each work of art as a mystery, I was reminded of former times in the studio. But with my fellow detective, I now had no qualms about exploring each moment to the hilt.

Greg suggested, "The idea is to use our minds. What other meaning can our lives have? We've cut ourselves off from everyone and everything that was killing us. Let's gather the best ideas that we can find."

Then he tried to incite me, "If you love me, Gelsey, then think for yourself, find yourself in the works of those artists who share your spirit. There must have been some reason you danced all those years! Let's find out what it was!"

We listened to Bach, Haydn, Mozart, Schubert, and Beethoven. I tried to hear the voices in the music, the dramatic dialogue, the intricate poetry of tones. Each piece was a sublime puzzle in which to immerse myself. How had such artists composed? I had to use my mind, not just my ears.

We pored over paintings by Rembrandt, Botticelli, and Leonardo, trying to see from the perspective of those artists who were bold enough to celebrate the beauty of the human form and hold it up to the world. To discover their method of composition, I had to use my mind, not just my eyes.

While I fought against lethargy, Greg read to me from Plato, Augustine, Dante, Shakespeare, Schiller, and so on. I was making friends across the centuries. We dug into the old notebooks of the artists themselves—they were the ones who created their works, who could tell me how and why they worked the way they did.

I went through all of Plato's *Dialogues*. These were the questions I had always wanted to ask, the sort of discourse I had always wanted to fashion. It was as if Socrates had articulated all the impulses I had ever danced. He was the one who told me that the intensity of my will to perfect was neither disease nor madness.

Each morning, Greg and I read newspapers and magazines, everything we could get our hands on. We were not trying to escape from the present. But how could we understand the present without knowing the past, the moments that led us to where we were?

Over the first few weeks, my concentration span increased. My energy and stamina came back. I gained weight, maybe fifteen or twenty pounds, stuffing myself with food. I made up for a lifetime of starvation. I proved that Dr. Cancro was mistaken in one respect: I was not a lousy lover.

After about a month, I was off Valium. The most severe withdrawal symptoms were a half dozen five-minute depressions. I became a cranky child for those short intervals. They passed as soon as I recognized them for what they were, as soon as Greg reminded me that it would take time, perhaps six months, for the last traces of the drug to be cleansed from my system.

After six weeks, I began to work on my body again, slowly, tentatively, joyously. I worked out in the barn and, later, in the kitchen of our new home in Vermont. I had no intention of dancing, but wanted to teach my partner everything I knew about the art. He was a fast learner, having studied pantomime and acting for some years. We had already begun work on this book, but I still did not understand the nature of my addiction. Our social and mental worlds had changed, but where had I gone wrong with my life in the first place?

A critical answer was provided by Helga Zepp LaRouche, German-born founder of the Schiller Institute. Her polemical writings contained a moving study of Schiller. In spite of her extreme point of view, her unyielding radicalism, this woman provided a crucial turning point for me. Her zealous devotion to the classics and her political war against drugs emboldened me to act, yet in my own way. Her scathing criticism of modern art gave me a clue about the relation between imitation and addiction. She wrote in the June 1980 issue of the *Campaigner:*

> If art were merely imitation and both the artist and the audience became whatever they imagined themselves to be, then all lawfulness in art would disappear, and absolutely anyone could simply set down on paper, canvas or score whatever his state of mind happened to be at the time, and that would be art.

Had I not been taught during my early years that the best dancer was the one who offered the best imitation? Had I not become an imitative expert? I was a chameleon. Drugs induced a state of mind that allowed me to change colors in various ways, to believe in ideals and a form of dance which were alien to me. I relinquished all principles and criteria. Not only was I able to look like someone else, I was able to think like someone else.

If imitation were the highest form of flattery, then whom was I trying to flatter? My distorted copy of a ballerina provided a kind of immediate gratification, like the drug itself, but never really satisfied me. My purpose was to please the audience and my choreographers, but what pleased them was as brief as a dream.

Greg and I began to outline my story, focusing on the men in my life, those who had the most influence on me: my father, Mr. B, and Misha. Their images seemed to have been burned into my psyche, but perhaps I never really knew them. I had followed in my father's footsteps, but now I rejected his chosen path, deciding for myself that self-destruction had no place in any art worthy of the name. I had tried to make myself into a Balanchine ballerina, but his genius gave me no room to think. I had almost turned myself into a Russian ballerina for Misha, but lost him somewhere between Leningrad and Hollywood.

One of Shakespeare's dark-lady sonnets made me realize how my misguided love for these men led me to a dead end. The final couplet was most telling:

> But thence I learn, and find the lesson true,
> Drugs poison him that so fell sick of you.

Such realizations brought angry tears and still more questions. As my anger was released, the image of myself clarified, like a photographic negative slowly developing in the palm of my hand.

Where did my obsessive efforts to imitate end and actual originality begin? That which was created by imitation seemed transitory, as fleeting as pleasure itself. But a truly original creation would have to live forever in some sense. That piece of the creative puzzle was emphasized for me by Peter Wyer, a New York City medical doctor and musical theoretician at the Classical Frontiers Foundation, along with his wife, Judy. The task was to create something immortal in my life, to expand the classical repertory, to articulate the dance perfectly. Yet, I secretly wondered if I would ever dance again, vehemently resisting any suggestion of that kind for many months.

Greg and I involved ourselves in the politics of the drug culture. We wrote letters of critical support to the White House, and to Alan García Pérez, the newly elected President of Peru, a courageous man leading the war against drugs and austerity in South America. The letters, whatever their impact may have been, were an indication of my remoralization, a recognition that acts of conscience may have some effect in this world after all.

I began to study science—anatomy, biology, and physics—subjects I found intimately related to my art. I made a lot of mistakes at first, errors of judgment and scholarly blunders, but I took heart from the words of Beethoven:

> You will not find a treatise that is too learned for me; without laying claim to any genuine learning, I yet accustomed myself from childhood onwards to grasp the spirit of the best and wisest in every age. Shame on the artist who does not consider it his duty to achieve at least so much.

In my own field, Beethoven led me to his one-time collaborator, Viganò, who, in turn, introduced me to Noverre. These two ballet masters of the past suggested future projects for me, new directions.

I was providing myself with the education that I never had. My approach was not academic. I was looking for ideas and values that I could use in my life. It was not any particular work of art that helped me overcome drugs, but the continuous process of mobilizing my mental resources, supported by a man who needed to be saved as much as I did. Together we became more aware of the creative process itself, which made our choices more deliberate and impassioned. Our relationship was in the end a marriage of minds as well as hearts. We refused to replace one addiction with another.

Our education has continued for almost two years. In August 1984, Greg and I signed a contract to write this book. The writing has been the final therapeutic stage of my recovery, a labor of constant love. We were sustained in our collaboration by the hope that others might at least recognize, if not avoid, the traps I found waiting for me. Our purpose allowed me to sort out both my priorities and my personal history.

To privately acknowledge the bond between us, we were married on May 13, 1985, in West Dover, Vermont. The ceremony was performed by a local justice of the peace in her rural home. There were no other witnesses to our vows, other than the One, perhaps, who witnesses all of our actions. There is no word strong enough to describe what passes between us, yet our exchange is mediated by words, a language of tenderness and constant provocation. Our voices sometimes blend; we like to finish each other's sentences.

The days have passed in quietude and light. Our hours have been organized around these pages, scribbled longhand and stored in a computer. Our existence has been idyllic. The natural delights of the countryside were exhilarating, diverting, even when our bedroom was invaded by crickets. I rode horses as I had as a child. I watched the seasons change. But I never forgot that I was an urban creature, a woman of the city. My fears about returning have departed. I am no longer daunted even by the prospect of dancing.

It has taken me more than thirty years to grow up, to reach maturity, to leave childhood and adolescence behind. I have been reconciled with my mother and stepfather, but have kept only a few friendships from my past. My stepfather, a real skeptic, was the last to come round, to believe in me. I had hurt him deeply. My mother has finally been relieved of her worries about me. I think she is as proud of our friendship as I am to be her daughter. The rest of my family may take more time. My brother, Marshall, has always sent his affection by telepathy. My sister Johnna has her own life now outside of dance. I still wonder if we shall ever manage to bridge the distance between us, to know the women we have become.

The nature of the change in my life is illustrated by two unrelated anecdotes. On my birthday in 1980, Patrick Bissell called me. He played a nostalgic pop tune over the telephone, a seemingly innocuous injection of rhythm and blues. On my birthday in 1985, a young pianist and composer from Milan, Carlo Levi Minzi, called to sing me an aria. I suppose I have learned the hard way—it is the quality of thought that counts.

London, March 1, 1986. My husband and I have moved back into the thick of things. I am preparing to dance *Romeo and Juliet* with the Royal Ballet. The first week of rehearsals has been a wondrous struggle. My new command of language has given me an advantage and a responsibility in the studio. I am remiss now unless I can explain what I know, how I do what I do. I realize I have become a teacher, but I know I shall always be a student, always asking questions.

Committing myself to paper as well as to the theater, I am ready to fight for my ideas, to turn my tears and laughter into something rare: an honest and unflinching love. I cannot lose. My life has revealed its full worth beyond the stage. I look around me in a moment of supreme joy and confidence, alone, and out there my spirit finds its beautiful partner. There is someone with gentle arms waiting for me in the wings.

I am not afraid of what may come. I have already seen my grave, my place of birth as a ballerina and an artist. Though this season may be my last, the steps continue after the body has been stilled. *The dance goes on forever. So shall I. So shall we.* Let that be my epitaph, my prayer, my final gesture.

PERMISSIONS